THE ROUGH GUIDE TO

Frank
Sinatra

Chris Ingham

Rough Guides online
www.roughguides.com

Credits

The Rough Guide to Frank Sinatra
Editor: Daniel Crewe
Design: Dan May
Proofreading: Ken Bell
Production: Julia Bovis

Rough Guides Reference
Director: Andrew Lockett
Series editor: Mark Ellingham
Editors: Peter Buckley, Duncan Clark, Daniel Crewe, Matthew Milton, Joe Staines

Picture Credits
Albert Fisher: pp.8, 146.
Corbis: pp.1, 11, 13, 19, 24, 27, 28, 32, 35, 39, 42, 47, 50, 55, 59, 63, 65, 69, 76, 79, 82, 89, 95, 101, 105, 109, 116,
120, 123, 128, 137, 141, 167, 254, 277, 296, 319, 328, 337, 341.
Redferns: pp.6, 91, 131, 143, 237, 270, 364.
Judith Miller/Dorling Kindersley/Cooper Owen: p.57.

Front cover photograph: © Redferns
Back cover photographs: © Corbis

Publishing information

This first edition published June 2005 by
Rough Guides Ltd, 80 Strand, London WC2R 0RL
345 Hudson St, 4th Floor, New York 10014, USA
Email: mail@roughguides.co.uk

Distributed by the Penguin Group:
Penguin Books Ltd, 80 Strand, London WC2R 0RL
Penguin Putnam, Inc., 375 Hudson Street, NY 10014, USA
Penguin Group (Australia), 250 Camberwell Road, Camberwell, Victoria 3124, Australia
Penguin Books Canada Ltd, 10 Alcorn Avenue, Toronto, Ontario, Canada M4V 1E4
Penguin Group (New Zealand), Cnr Rosedale and Airborne Roads, Albany, Auckland, New Zealand

Printed in Spain by Graphy Cems

© Chris Ingham, 2005
400 pp; includes index

A catalogue record for this book is available from the British Library

ISBN 1-84353-414-2

1 3 5 7 9 8 6 4 2

CONTENTS

Introduction

Why does Sinatra fascinate us? It starts with the music. It seduces us, pulls us in, involves us and inhabits us, just as it seems to involve and inhabit him. Sinatra's best recordings feature some of the great compositions of the golden era of American popular song in definitive interpretations; from his straightforwardly romantic readings of the 1940s to his deep-grained, layered work of the 1950s and 1960s, Sinatra transforms these pieces from pretty reflections of an era into music of timeless beauty, personal resonance and enduring excitement. If one has any interest in twentieth-century song, Sinatra's work is inescapable.

His allure continues with his screen presence. His film career included movies ranging from the sublime to the abysmal but a handful of his performances may be among the most truthful and affecting in the history of cinema.

But the pull of Sinatra has always been about more than just well-crafted songs and a singer-actor with charisma. It's about Sinatra the phenomenon: the force of nature who loved the world's most beautiful women and kept questionable, powerful company, in both the underworld and the White House, yet whose street-born egoism and individualistic swagger seemed to mark him as an eternal outsider.

There are many Frank Sinatras to consider. From when he first became a star in 1943 until his death in 1998, the different manifestations of the man have created a variety of images. Yet the crooning idol of the "bobbysoxers" seems to bear little resemblance to the consummate actor of *From Here To Eternity*, the stylish, swinging bachelor of *Songs For Swingin' Lovers!*, the leering lush of the Rat Pack years or the faintly bitter tuxedoed monolith of the 1970s and 1980s. With every season there's another Sinatra.

And while there was much to admire, there was much to be wary of. We see in Sinatra love and hate, affection and anger, kindness and cruelty, sensitivity and insensitivity, intense involvement and careless boredom – conflicting qualities that seem sometimes to be fighting for supremacy. And the same contradictory feelings occur in us, often at the same time, when we engage with who Sinatra was and, more, with who this complex, contradictory man was to us.

In the end, it isn't easy to make sense of Sinatra. He doesn't make it easy. But we soon understand that it wasn't easy *being* Sinatra, which is part of the reason we find him so compelling. In some ways, he seemed to live his extraordinary life for all of us – which is just as well, because none of us could have done it.

CHRIS INGHAM, 2005

Acknowledgements

Among the many authors whose wildly contrasting insights and motivations have helped inspire this Rough Guide, acknowledgements are particularly due to Will Friedwald, Charles Granata, Pete Hamill, Donald Clarke, Arnold Shaw, Earl Wilson, J. Randall Taraborrelli, Kitty Kelley, Nancy Sinatra, Tina Sinatra, Robin Douglas-Home, Bill Zehme, Fred Dellar and Mal Peachey, George Jacobs, Michael Freedland, Michael Munn, Daniel O'Brien and Shawn Levy. Also invaluable were the websites www.songsbysinatra.com and www.sinatraarchive.com.

Thanks also to David Peschek, Erik James and Simon Heller at Warner, Debra Geddes at EMI, Peggy Sutton at PPR, Spencer Pollard at Sanctuary, Kim Lyon at Quantum Leap and IMC Vision; and all at Rough Guides, especially editor Daniel Crewe, who has honed and refined tirelessly.

Love and thanks to: Ken Miller, my dear uncle who doesn't know what he started when he began engaging his 12-year-old nephew with pronouncements like "Really, aside from *Swingin' Lovers*, *Nice 'N' Easy* is probably the best of the lot"; his personal book, magazine, video and radio recording archive was invaluable to this project, and for that, among other things, I dedicate it to him. All the other Millers, my mother and father (in the 1970s: "Did you see Sinatra on telly last night? *Teeeerrible!*"), Joe Cushley (CI: "Don't you think you drink a bit too much?" JC: "Don't you think you've got too many Frank Sinatra books?") and Jim Irvin (the idea of Sinatra "setting a lyric free" is his). My beautiful family: Tracy (a *Wee Small Hours* girl, always has been), Polly (has fancied FS since she was ten) and Alex (as *Anchors Aweigh* is cued, "I'm going upstairs"). Last one, promise.

Readers: feel free to address comment, correction and commendation to the author at cjr@ingham78.freeserve.co.uk.

PART ONE

The Life

Little town blues

"Someday, that's gonna be me up there."

FS, AFTER SEEING BING CROSBY IN JERSEY CITY, SUMMER 1935

Anthony Martin "Marty" Sinatra, an illiterate boilermaker, and Natalie Catherine "Dolly" Garavente, a midwife, were an unusual couple. They both lived in Hoboken, New Jersey, and were the offspring of early-twentieth-century Italian immigrants, but **the Sinatras** were originally from Sicily, the rural southernmost tip of the country, while **the Garaventes** hailed from smarter Genoa, in the north. Naturally, Dolly's family refused the couple a wedding, whereupon, equally naturally, the single-minded Dolly did what she pleased. The couple eloped and married in Jersey City in 1913, on Valentine's Day.

Marty and Dolly moved into a flat at 415 Monroe Street, Hoboken; and on December 12, 1915, Dolly gave birth to a son, their only child. It was a traumatic, forceps-assisted birth and the baby nearly died before he was held under a cold tap. He escaped with a substantial scar (visible throughout his life beneath his left ear) and a punctured eardrum, but his injured mother was left unable to bear further children. After mother and baby had recovered, **Francis Albert Sinatra** was eventually baptized in April 1916.

Marty worked variously as a bootleg liquor protector, dock labourer and part-time boxer who fought under the Irish pseudonym Marty O'Brien. Dolly established herself not only as a midwife, who performed illegal abortions, but also as a Hoboken "ward-heeler" (a neighbourhood political boss, for the Democrats), which generated enough influence to get Marty a job in the fire service; and for a while during the Prohibition era, the Sinatras ran a saloon, **Marty O'Brien's**. The family could even afford in 1927 to move to Hoboken's smarter Park Avenue. But young Frank's parents didn't have much time for him, and he was passed from

DOLLY SINATRA: HER WAY

"She scared the shit outta me."
FS TO SHIRLEY MACLAINE

In Hoboken, **Dolly Sinatra** was legendary. A vivacious, larger-than-life woman who spoke her mind, she often used language that according to one mayor "would make a longshoreman blush". Yet she would wash out Frank's mouth with soap for imitating her profane language.

Ambitious for her family and for herself, she became influential through being a political activist and leader of the third ward in Hoboken's ninth district. She could be fiercely judgemental and snobbish, which made many cautious in dealing with her, but she could also be charming, generous and funny, and as her political clout increased she appeared to be genuinely community-minded. She represented immigrants in court, translating for them and arguing their cases.

But Dolly's ruthless approach to life made her a controversial figure. Many young girls and their mothers were grateful for her **illegal abortions**, but many more were appalled. Her activities were against the law of her country and her religion, but Dolly was able to justify them, unblinkingly, as a social service that God understood. On one occasion, after being arrested when

his aunt Mary to his grandmother, Rose, to his aunt Rosalie. He would look back on his childhood as a lonely period.

Frank was an impatient, uninterested student and absented himself from school for long periods; at one point he was able to skip school for a year before his parents noticed. Whether being subjected to ethnic taunts or being bothered by policemen for appearing to wear stolen clothes – he was nicknamed "**Slacksie O'Brien**" because he was so well dressed, and "**Scarface**" because of his birth injuries – he learnt the street-scrapping ways of survival at a young age.

Frank left A.J. Demarest High School in 1931 without graduating and took a paper-bundling job at the *Jersey Observer* with his godfather, Frank Garrick, Marty's closest friend, after whom he was named. When the paper's young sportswriter was killed in an accident, Sinatra, at Dolly's suggestion, went to see Garrick about a promotion. In Garrick's absence, Sinatra apparently made himself too cosy at the deceased's desk for the office's comfort and Garrick, on his return, was forced to speak to

one of her patients was admitted to hospital after an operation went wrong, she continued her work while on probation.

As regards Frank's treatment by his mother, the rough went hand in hand with the smooth. "When I would get out of hand she would give me a rap," he remembered. "Then she'd hug me to her breast." And with a go-getting spirit that at one point led her to consider **running for mayor** – Marty vetoed the idea – she had little time for a growing boy and Frank was often left to fend for himself; but she also spoiled young Frank, giving him his own account at the local clothing store.

Sinatra adored his mother, but, like everyone else, he was wary of her. Even as he became an adult, he would dread having to impart news that he knew she would disapprove of – such as his third and fourth marriages.

But he clearly learnt from her. He inherited her fiery temper, a preoccupation with hygiene and a fantastic obstinacy, particularly when crossed. ("My son is like me," she once said. "You cross him and he never forgets.") And Dolly's political machinations showed him the appeal of **power**. He saw that doing people favours is one way of generating it and that to have it means living by one's own laws.

Sinatra once said of his mother: "She was the force."

the cocky kid, at which point Sinatra let rip with a flood of obscenities and stormed out. He didn't speak to his godfather for nearly 50 years – one of many silent rifts that Sinatra would make a part of his life.

Marty and Dolly became worried that their only son was growing up to be a bum. He quit everything that he started, including book packing (too tedious) and a shipyard job (after a red-hot rivet missed him by inches). A frustrated Marty – in an uncharacteristically assertive moment – suggested that his son leave home to find work. Frank packed and went to New York but was home before long, jobless and restless.

The early performances

Frank had always dabbled with performing. His impersonations of radio celebrities had made kids laugh at junior school and his early singing efforts

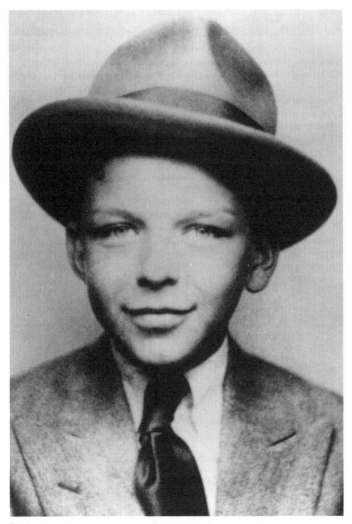

SINATRA AS A BOY – ALREADY SPORTING HIS TRADEMARK HAT

were applauded at high school. This, along with his fascination with the biggest star of the day, **Bing Crosby**, inspired in young Frank a focussed if far-fetched ambition to become a singer. In his late teens, he persuaded his disappointed parents to lend him the money to buy a small public address system, a microphone and some stock musical arrangements, and he began his apprenticeship. Working during the day, he sang at night and at weekends at roadhouses, school dances, nightclubs, meeting houses – anywhere that would have him – often for sandwiches and cigarettes. He wasn't great – he was advised several times to quit – but he looked good, he could be charming and he was surprisingly determined. "I worked on one basic theory," he later said. "Stay active, get as much practice as you can."

Once she had accepted his singing activities, Dolly was helpful in pushing her son forward. She organised a regular paying gig at the local **Union Club** and her hustling led to his first big break in 1935. When a local singing group, The Three Flashes, and local bandleader Harold Arden were approached by the talent scout Edward "Major" Bowes, from the radio programme *Major Bowes And His Original Amateur Hour*, she persuaded the leader of the trio to include Sinatra in the films that promoted the show. Frank appeared as a non-singing waiter in *The Night Club* and as part of a blackface group in *The Big Minstrel Act*.

More significantly, however, he featured on the show in September 1935 as part of **"The Hoboken Four"**, comprising Frank and The Three Flashes. After the group was introduced Sinatra said, "My name is Frank and we're looking for jobs. How about it?" The group sang the Mills Brothers' version of **"Shine"** and received more than 40,000 votes – a record for the programme; they then went on a tour of US theatres with a Bowes variety show. Although Sinatra was now the lead vocalist, he was resented by the group and apparently bullied – mainly, it seems, for attracting more than his fair share of female admirers. He left after three months and returned home.

Back in Hoboken in 1936 and 1937, Sinatra carried on lugging his public-address system around the local gigs for a pittance and singing on local radio for no payment and continued to take himself seriously, even if no one else did. He took a few singing lessons – though this remained the full extent of his formal musical training and he was barely able to read

WITH MAJOR BOWES, FROM LEFT TO RIGHT: FRED TAMBURRO, LARRY EISLER (NOT PART OF THE HOBOKEN FOUR), PATTY PRINCE, FRANK SINATRA AND JIMMY PETRO

music throughout his career; he considered changing his name to Frankie Trent; he kept fit; he studied other singers in clubs; and eventually, in 1938, he got another Dolly-influenced break at a New Jersey roadhouse, **the Rustic Cabin**. The attraction was not the job itself – he was a singing waiter, paid $15 a week – but the radio wire linked to WNEW in New York, which broadcast *The WNEW Dance Parade* every night. "I never stopped," said Sinatra, remembering his roadhouse duties. "But I didn't mind; I was learning."

He was not only learning his musical trade; he was also learning to juggle a complicated private life. He was arrested after a Rustic Cabin performance late in 1938 on a **"morals charge"** after an ex-lover (who had apparently been pregnant but had miscarried) accused him of "breach of promise". The case was dismissed in court in January 1939 – the complainant was found to be married – and within days Sinatra was married to **Nancy Barbato**, his girlfriend of four years. His wedding present to his bride was his first record: a privately made recording of "Our Love".

He moved onto $25 a week at the Rustic Cabin, but with the popularity of big swing bands at its peak, vocalists knew that landing the singer's chair in a band was the way to get ahead. Hearing that the trumpeter **Harry James** had left Benny Goodman to start his own outfit, Sinatra had some pictures taken and made sure that James saw them. But it was apparently James's wife – a singer with Goodman called Louise Tobin – who noticed him one night in the spring of 1939 when he was broadcasting live from the Rustic Cabin. Missing the name, Mr and Mrs James attended the roadhouse the following evening to investigate and heard Sinatra singing "Begin The Beguine". Impressed with the singer's "way of talking a lyric", James offered Sinatra $75 a week to join him on a two-year contract and suggested that he change his name to Frankie Satin. He resisted the change of name, but took the contract.

He was on his way.

Mrs Sinatra 1: Nancy Barbato

"In Nancy I found beauty, warmth and understanding; being with her was my only escape from what seemed to be a grim world."

FS

It was while they were on holiday in **Long Branch** on the New Jersey shore that Nancy, then 17, met Frank, then 19. She was sitting on a porch manicuring her nails when he serenaded her with a ukulele. He later worked for a while in her father's plastering business, but when they went to see Bing Crosby and he told her of his dream to be a singer, she did not discourage him.

Living in **Jersey City** and married to a struggling band singer who was often on the road, in the winter Nancy sent Frank gloves with dollar bills stuffed in the fingers, and lived on fried onion sandwiches. Later, when he was a popular band singer and then an enormous solo star, she answered his fan mail, sewed his trademark floppy bowties and watched him change as fame went to his head. She bore his children Nancy and Frank Jr. and, as her mother had with her father, half-tolerated her husband's frequent indiscretions in the way she thought a good Italian wife should. After all, Frank provided very well for his family and could be affectionate and attentive when he was at home. And he kept coming home.

When they lived in **Hollywood** it was a different matter. Frank's affairs out on the road had previously been anonymous one night stands; now his romances were with stars and the news was all over town. It was humiliating for Nancy, but when she faced difficulties, as she did on New Year's Eve in 1946, she made a fight of it. Nancy had earlier discovered a diamond bracelet in Frank's car, but put it back, assuming that it was a surprise gift for her. When she found the actress **Marilyn Maxwell** wearing it at the Sinatras' New Year party, she threw her out of the house and confronted her husband. With Frank's dalliance with **Lana Turner** making the news that same year, Nancy, as was first related in Tina's memoir, hit back the hardest way she could; she aborted her third pregnancy. Horrified, Sinatra promised to change his ways, and they conceived again. Their third child, Tina, was born in 1948 but by the end of the year Sinatra had left home for good, his affair with **Ava Gardner** all over the papers.

Nancy handled the aftermath of the final betrayal with the dignity of a mother who puts her children first and the loyalty of a woman who loves her man and hopes he will return. Throughout the 1950s she kept her home open to Frank so that the children could see him and refrained from criticizing him in their presence. She took his phone calls when he was at his lowest and for more than twenty years she was his friend, confidante and, between his subsequent marriages, Tina suspects, occasional lover.

"I married one man for life," Nancy told her daughters, "and with my luck, it had to be your father." Frank always called her "sweetheart" and trusted her completely. "She's the only woman who understands me," he told his friends. He never stopped loving her – but he never went back to her.

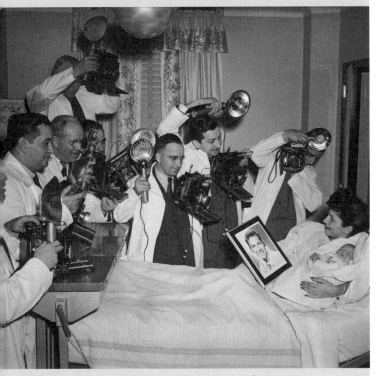

NANCY SINATRA WITH FRANK JR. AFTER HIS BIRTH IN JANUARY 1944

START SPREADING
THE NEWS
1939–48

Start spreading the news

"Working in a band was … a career builder, a seat of learning, a sort of cross-country college that taught you about collaboration, brotherhood and sharing rough times."

FS

The **Harry James Orchestra** had mixed fortunes. Though James had been a star in the Goodman band, he did not have a high profile as a bandleader, and while reviews were good, the size of the audiences was erratic. The band survived on a shoestring and developed a robust attitude, fuelled by humour. (They needed it when their hopes for a big break at the Palomar in Los Angeles in October 1939 were dashed before they even arrived – the ballroom burnt down.) Sinatra would remember the tough days with James fondly, recalling the band's "spirit and enthusiasm".

In addition to his valuable touring experiences with James during this period, Sinatra did his first professional recordings; he was featured on ten Harry James sides for **Brunswick** and **Columbia** (none of which were hits at the time), including "From The Bottom Of My Heart" and "All Or Nothing At All". He also received his first important notices from *Metronome*, which praised his "easy phrasing", though *Billboard* thought "he touches the songs with a little too much pash".

But James valued Sinatra. When in a financial spot and choosing between his male and female singers, he let **Connie Haines** go at a time when "canaries" (female band singers) were still considered a bigger part of a band's appeal than their male counterparts.

Tommy Dorsey

At the end of 1939 the orchestra was still struggling, but for Sinatra life was looking good. Although previously Sinatra had nervously bombed trying to sing in the presence of **Tommy Dorsey**, one of the biggest bandleaders in the country, the virtuoso trombonist had been aware of the singer's development. And when the James and Dorsey bands were appearing in Chicago, Dorsey – having fallen out with his vocalist Jack Leonard – offered Sinatra the singer's chair.

He was so ecstatic that he forgot to enquire about the money, even though Nancy was expecting their first child. The pay was $125 a week but, more importantly to Sinatra, this was a chance to operate at a completely different level of the business. Moreover, upon hearing of Sinatra's opportunity Harry James tore up their contract and wished him luck. When the band bus dropped Sinatra in Buffalo after their last engagement, he panicked as he watched it drive off. He even tried to run after it. But after a few days at home and a couple of train-rides he was in Rockford, Illinois, the new "boy singer" with The Tommy Dorsey Orchestra.

Dorsey, "the Sentimental Gentleman Of Swing", was an inspiration to Sinatra: his presence, musical perfectionism and business acumen were qualities that he would develop himself. (His daughter Nancy later suggested that he learnt compassion from Harry James and from Tommy Dorsey, discipline.) And Dorsey's melodic virtuosity, smooth tone and seamless phrasing were major influences on the evolution of Sinatra's early singing style.

But it was also clear that Sinatra already had something different. **Jo Stafford** of The Pied Pipers, Dorsey's vocal group, hadn't expected much from the underweight 23-year-old who had replaced Jack Leonard. "But before he'd sung four bars we knew," Stafford remembered. "We knew he was going to be a big star." Stafford was impressed that unlike many male singers of the time, he didn't sound much like Bing Crosby: "He didn't sound like anybody else I'd ever heard."

Start spreading the news

At his first New York nightclub appearance with Dorsey, at the Astor Roof in May 1940, Sinatra was a hit with **"Begin The Beguine"**. He had still not been assigned many full features in Dorsey's set, and when the crowd demanded an encore, he sang a few more impromptu numbers, with his improvised backing group gradually dwindling until he was accompanied only by **Joe Bushkin** at the piano. When the pianist eventually got lost, Sinatra found himself singing "Smoke Gets In Your Eyes" to a delighted audience *a cappella*.

But Sinatra was not immediately comfortable with the Dorsey outfit. Accustomed to James's easy charm, his new boss was by comparison a hot-tempered disciplinarian and was not entirely convinced by his new singer; Dorsey even suggested that Sinatra listen more closely to Bing Crosby. And Sinatra didn't feel accepted by the musicians – several of whom, naturally, were friends of Jack Leonard – or by the audience. "For the first five months with Dorsey," he later confessed, "I missed the James band." Eventually he came to realize that, compared with many other bands, Dorsey and his arrangers – the people who fashioned popular songs into the prevailing style of the time, and who for Dorsey included **Axel Stordahl** and **Sy Oliver** – presented singers very well. Even on the earliest of the RCA Victor Sinatra/Dorsey sides, such as "I'll Be Seeing You" and "Fools Rush In", he was given sympathetic settings. Before long, he would often feature as the main attraction of the arrangement, doing more than merely deliver an incidental vocal refrain. The inevitable result was that as Sinatra grew in confidence, he attracted more and more attention.

It was common practice at the time for bands and singers to compete with others' recordings, and one of the first indications that the Dorsey/Sinatra team had potential in the record market came when their recording of the sentimental new **Jimmy Van Heusen** and **Johnny Burke** song "Polka Dots And Moonbeams" reached a higher position in the charts in the spring of 1940 than the version by Glenn Miller that featured the hugely popular singer Ray Eberle. But the watershed moment came in July, when **"I'll Never Smile Again"**, sung in perfectly blended close harmony with The Pied Pipers, reached number one in the Hit Parade – and stayed there for several weeks. Given that it had little to do with "swing" music, this maudlin ballad can be seen in retrospect – as can the subsequent sides that Sinatra led for Dorsey – as heralding the end of the Big Band era and pointing to **the era of the voice**, when singers, and particularly Sinatra, would supplant bandleaders as the kings of entertainment.

"I'll Never Smile Again" was Dorsey/Sinatra's biggest hit and Sinatra mimed it on the big screen when the Dorsey orchestra made a cameo appearance in the Paramount picture *Las Vegas Nights*. In the period until 1942 they also made regular and respectable chart appearances, with singles including "The One I Love Belongs To Somebody Else", "Stardust", "Oh! Look At Me Now", "Dolores", "Everything Happens To Me" and "This Love Of Mine", which Sinatra himself helped to compose.

But perhaps the most important factor in taking Sinatra to new heights of fame across the country was the Dorsey orchestra's regular exposure on the radio. A weekly show on NBC called *Fame And Fortune*, which ran from October 1940 until April 1941 and showcased the orchestra performing songs by amateur songwriters, was listened to by millions.

Sinatra had become Dorsey's most valuable asset. Audiences were showing up at least as much to see the singer as the band, and the audience's **swooning** – a kind of collective sigh of female longing – had begun. Dorsey was amazed. "Remember, he was no matinee idol," he recalled. "He was a skinny kid with big ears. And yet what he did to women was something awful."

And it wasn't only the women who were impressed. The whole country was. In May 1941 Sinatra came **top of the male singer polls** in both *Billboard* and *Down Beat* magazines – displacing Bing Crosby, who had dominated such polls for years.

Going solo

Sinatra couldn't help but notice the fuss he was causing, and it was this that gave him the impetus to make the break and aim for a solo career. He also felt that other bands' boy singers would try to do the same. With reference to **Bob Eberly** in Jimmy Dorsey's band and **Perry Como** with Ted Weems, and to Crosby, Sinatra remembered thinking, "If I don't make a break with this band soon … I'll have to fight all three of them, from Crosby all the way down to the other two, to get a position."

Start spreading the news

CROSBY AND SINATRA MEET FOR THE FIRST TIME IN SEPTEMBER 1943; "THE OLD GROANER" HAD UNWITTINGLY ENCOURAGED "THE VOICE" TO BECOME A SINGER

BREAKING DORSEY'S CONTRACT

*"You can quote Sinatra as saying that he believes it is
wrong for anybody to own a piece of him and collect
on it when that owner is doing nothing for Sinatra."*
FS TO THE NEW YORK HERALD-TRIBUNE, 1943

For the first year of his solo career Sinatra reluctantly went along with
Dorsey's contract, which entitled the bandleader to a third of all Frank's
earnings. It was Bing Crosby who suggested to the younger singer that he
sort out this situation before the big bucks were earned. Sinatra tried not
paying and Dorsey sued. Sinatra then began to give interviews complaining
about the punitive deal and made light-hearted references to it in radio
broadcasts. His press officer, **George Evans**, even organized a picket at an
engagement of Dorsey's comprising Sinatra fans holding up placards with
the words "Dorsey unfair to our boy Frankie". Dorsey was furious, but the
publicity was embarrassing enough for him to enter negotiations.

The myths abound of **underworld involvement** in Sinatra securing his
discharge from Dorsey. One legend has it that a mobster acquaintance of
Sinatra's, Willie Moretti, and his boys, visited Tommy Dorsey and secured

He gave Dorsey a year's notice in September 1941, only twenty months
after he'd joined. But if he was hoping for the same good luck cheer he'd
received from Harry James, he'd reckoned without Dorsey's hard-nosed
business sense and petulance. While he was working out his notice
Dorsey barely spoke to him.

He did sing two numbers in the second film to feature Dorsey, *Ship
Ahoy*, which was being made in Hollywood in December 1941 when
Pearl Harbour was bombed. But when it came to recording his first
solo material in January 1942, while still with the band, he was obliged
at Dorsey's insistence to relocate to a lesser RCA imprint, Bluebird. The
excellent results – four romantic melodies, including **"Night And Day"**
(which edged into the US top 20) and "The Song Is You" (adorned with
Axel Stordahl's lavish strings) – only strengthened Sinatra's resolve to go
solo.

When the time to leave came in September 1942, Dorsey enforced the
letter of **the contract**, which gave him a third of Sinatra's earnings for

a release from the harsh terms by putting a gun to his head. (Moretti apparently bragged about putting a gun down Dorsey's throat and getting Sinatra released for $1.) Another story concerns Dorsey being visited by intimidating characters without Sinatra's knowledge thanks to **Hank Sanicola**, Frank's friend and business manager since 1936.

Dorsey himself contributed to this kind of gangster story, but most accounts of the period lend little credence to them. On balance, it appears more likely that Frank's lawyer Henry Jaffe, who also represented the American Federation of Radio Artists, strongly suggested to Dorsey that it might become difficult for the bandleader to continue his profitable NBC broadcasts if he did not release Sinatra from the contract. Dorsey was apparently unimpressed with that veiled threat but saw the light when **Jules Stein**, the head of MCA talent agency, which was hoping to represent Sinatra, offered a deal that involved lucrative bookings for Dorsey and a $75,000 buyout. MCA paid $50,000 and Frank chipped in the rest.

Dorsey's final words to Sinatra when he eventually let him go: "I hope you fall on your ass."

the rest of the singer's career. How Sinatra eventually extricated himself from this punitive situation has been the subject of much conjecture and rumour, but at this point he went along with it. He had signed with the General Amusement Corporation booking agency, and when Dorsey and RCA let him, he also signed with **Columbia**; and he poached Axel Stordahl, who became his personal arranger, at the rate of $650 a week – five times what Dorsey was paying. He was on the way to being what he always wanted to be: bigger than Crosby.

After the affair with Dorsey progress for Sinatra was slow. With a world at **war**, news of a singer going solo didn't seem to be that important and the press didn't make too much fuss. He was one of many musicians who were drafted, but his punctured eardrum left him categorised as unfit for service. Although ostensibly free to pursue his career, he was prevented from making records by a **musicians' union strike** against the record companies in August 1942, which was a protest against recordings, rather than live broadcasts, being played on the radio. He rehearsed a little, featured a little on a radio series called *Reflections* and mimed "Night And Day" in a cameo in the movie *Reveille With Beverly*.

It was just enough to set a ball in motion. When the manager of New York's **Paramount Theatre**, Bob Weitman, caught Sinatra's act in Newark, New Jersey, he was impressed, and booked him as an "Extra Added Attraction" at the theatre's New Year presentation, which included the movie *Star Spangled Rhythm*, comedians Moke and Poke, a 17-year-old singer called Peggy Lee and the king of swing himself, Benny Goodman. "I still don't know why I did it," remembered Weitman, "but there was something about this kid."

Goodman casually introduced Sinatra, on the opening day, **December 30, 1942**. When he walked onto the stage the audience gave a deafening, sustained, almost hysterical roar of approval. Goodman, caught mid-cue in front of his orchestra, turned around and said: "What the fuck is that?"

Sinatramania had begun. That, the press decided, *was* news.

"Psychologists tried to go into the reasons with all sorts of deep theories. I could have told them why. It was the war years and there was great loneliness, and I was the boy in every corner drug store, the boy who'd gone off drafted to the war. That's all."

FS

Although George Evans had hired a few **bobbysoxers** – so-called because of the white socks they wore – to exaggerate their reaction to Sinatra, he was only replicating what female audiences had been doing since the Dorsey days. Skinny, soulful and singing with a heartfelt commitment to expressing romantic feeling, Sinatra became the lust-object of a generation of teenage girls who barely knew what their feelings were. A downward swoop of melody would have them sighing, a smile would have them squealing, and a caress of the microphone stand (Evans's idea) would literally have them wetting themselves.

Top of the heap

The run at the Paramount – the "Home Of Swoon" – was extended for a month into February 1943, and with *Reveille With Beverly* now giving those from outside New York a glimpse of the star, Evans made sure that the press missed no detail of the Sinatra phenomenon. The queues, the hysteria and the mobbing were lapped up, as were Evans's nicknames – "Swoonatra", "the Sultan Of Swoon" and the one that stuck for many years, **"the Voice"**. Sinatra joined the chart show featuring live performances of the day's hits, *Your Hit Parade*, which was one of the biggest radio events of the week, and soon become its star.

> *"It is a slightly disturbing spectacle to witness the almost synchronised screams that come from the audience as he closes his eyes or moves his body slightly sideways."*

THE NEW YORK HERALD-TRIBUNE, 1943

Records were less important than radio and live shows in the 1940s, but it was a frustration to Sinatra's camp that the musicians' union dispute ground on, preventing any new recording. **Manie Sachs**, the executive who by the spring of 1943 had waited six months for Sinatra to be legally free of Dorsey and RCA, was particularly anxious to exploit the singer's new popularity, and wanted him to launch his Columbia career with a new recording of **"All Or Nothing At All"**. The obvious answer was to re-press and re-package the version recorded with Harry James nearly four years earlier, and this led to a massive hit, which was followed by several more James-era reissues.

A more ingenious solution involved *a cappella* **recordings** featuring only singers who were not eligible for membership of the musicians' union and were free to record during the strike. Thus, from June 1943, Sinatra was accompanied by The Bobby Tucker Singers on nine tunes, including "Close To You" (a new song, published by Sinatra's own company, Barton Songs),

The Life

"I Couldn't Sleep A Wink Last Night" and two from the new Rodgers and Hammerstein musical *Oklahoma!*, ensuring a steady output.

And it wasn't just teenage hysteria. As early as March 1943, Sinatra had triumphed at an engagement at a club for grown-ups from Manhattan, **the Riobamba**. He sang "God Bless America" at the rallies that encouraged US citizens to buy bonds to help fund the US war effort. And he started to appear with symphony orchestras, a controversial move that culminated in an appearance in August at the Hollywood Bowl, which was usually exclusively classical but was suffering severe financial problems at the time. Before attempting "Ol' Man River" he announced "I'm not going to sing it like Paul Robeson, I'm not in his class, yet" – and most onlookers were charmed.

Sinatra – in front of 10,000 people – at the Hollywood Bowl in August 1943

Start spreading the news

While on the West Coast he made the move into **films** and signed with RKO, starring in frothy vehicles *Higher And Higher* and *Step Lively*. It was clear that much of the star's new life was going to be on the West Coast, so in the spring of 1944 he moved the family that he hardly had time to see – wife Nancy, three-year-old daughter Nancy and three-month-old Frank Jr. – to **California**. Still under contract to broadcast *Your Hit Parade* every week from New York, he paid for the studio, orchestra and broadcast feed, so that he could be recorded on the West Coast, putting him out of pocket by $2000 a week but ensuring that his radio exposure could continue.

His next film was for MGM. The studio boss **Louis B. Mayer** had apparently been moved to tears by Sinatra's performance of "Ol' Man River" at a charity concert early in 1944 and bought out his RKO contract. Sinatra's fee per film rose from $25,000 to $130,000 overnight, though for *Anchors Aweigh*, a nautical song-and-dance romp, he had to work for it, eventually learning to hoof quite respectably following hours of rehearsal under the expert and patient tutelage of his co-star, **Gene Kelly**.

When Sinatra returned to the Paramount in October 1944 he caused pandemonium. With a theatre full of fans who wouldn't budge after the first show, and 30,000 more in Times Square waiting to get in, the ensuing unrest on October 11 – the **"Columbus Day Riot"** – took all day for the police to diffuse.

In November 1944 the musicians' union strike was finally called off and Sinatra could properly commence his recording career with Columbia. Over the coming months, Sinatra, mostly in the company of Axel Stordahl, produced dozens of sides and his many hits were a major part in America of the soundtrack to the war and the immediate post-war years. These tunes included "Saturday Night (Is The Loneliest Night Of The Week)", "I Fall In Love Too Easily" (from *Anchors Aweigh*), **"Nancy (With The Laughing Face)"** and lengthy production numbers "Ol' Man River" and "Stormy Weather", released on 12-inch 78s rather than the standard 10-inch records.

When the producer of *Your Hit Parade*, gambling that it was the song and not the singer to whom the public were listening, refused to relocate the show to Los Angeles, or to let Sinatra take a break or have a raise, Frank parted company with the programme, after almost two years. (Sinatra was replaced by the opera singer Lawrence Tibbett and the ratings dropped immediately.) But he still had high profile radio exposure throughout 1945 and 1946 with *The Frank Sinatra Show* (its theme being "Put Your Dreams Away"), which allowed him to broadcast weekly from wherever he happened to be.

On screen, the significant event for him in 1945 was *The House I Live In*, a short, Oscar-winning RKO movie instigated by the Sinatra camp in which the bigotry-hating singer, playing himself, chatted to a group of children about religious and racial tolerance. That same year Sinatra went on a campus lecture tour promoting the same attitudes and in Gary, Indiana, he found himself facing an angry strike, protesting at the integration of black and white children at a local high school. Using the racial language of the street, he told them plainly how wrong he thought they were. With all this progressive liberal activity from the wide-reading Sinatra, it's little wonder that the right-wing press labelled him a "pinko".

> *"Believe me, I know something about the business of racial intolerance. At eleven, I was called a dirty guinea back home in New Jersey. We've all done it. We've all used the words nigger or kike or mick or polack or dago. Cut it out kids. Go back to school."*

FS, TO THE STRIKING STUDENTS OF
FROEBEL HIGH SCHOOL, GARY, INDIANA, NOVEMBER 1945

In 1945 and 1946 Sinatra was at the height of his fame and popularity and he worked incessantly. When performing live in those days, entertainers were expected to do multiple shows, often starting mid-morning and going on into the evening, as new groups moved in and out of the theatre. (It was the reluctance of his early audiences to budge that caused such mayhem on the streets outside the theatre.) In 1946 he was doing 45 shows a week and singing between eighty and a hundred songs a day.

BOBBYSOXERS OUTSIDE THE PARAMOUNT, NEW YORK, IN NOVEMBER 1945.
SONG HITS MAGAZINE OFFERED THEM "ANTI-SWOON" MINTS

He also recorded prolifically, and his records sold well. "Oh What It Seemed To Be" and "Five Minutes More" both stayed at the number one slot for weeks, while "Soliloquy" from Rodgers and Hammerstein's *Carousel* occupied both sides of a 12-inch 78 and displayed his developing abilities as a dramatic singer. His 1945 set of four 78s in a cardboard picture sleeve entitled ***The Voice*** featured eight romantic songs and is recognised as one of the first "themed" albums – a signpost that pointed to the future. His personal appearances satisfied both the teen-squealers

LANA TURNER, WHOSE LIAISON WITH SINATRA WAS FODDER FOR LEE MORTIMER

in the Paramount and the uptown set in the Wedgwood Room of the Waldorf Astoria – and the reviews of *Anchors Aweigh* noted that the crooner could act a little too.

SINATRA AND LEE MORTIMER

"Next time I see you, I'll kill you, you degenerate."
FS TO LEE MORTIMER, CIRO'S RESTAURANT, HOLLYWOOD, APRIL 1947

In the presidential election of 1944, Sinatra campaigned for **Franklin D. Roosevelt**, who was seeking a fourth term (and after whom he apparently named his son). This not only risked alienating the Republican section of his public, but also made him enemies in the right-wing press of William Randolph Hearst, who tried to imply that the singer's liberal politics displayed leanings towards communism.

The *New York Daily Mirror* columnist **Lee Mortimer** was particularly critical of Sinatra, and his fans, calling them "imbecilic, moronic, screemie-meemie autograph kids". And when Sinatra began his indiscreet liaisons with Marilyn Maxwell and Lana Turner, Mortimer let the insinuations fly on a regular basis. Sinatra's intermittent consorting with members of the Mafia was also exposed with gleeful outrage.

Sinatra maintained that the bad feeling started when he judged as unfavourable a song that Mortimer had submitted for consideration. The climax of their feud came in April 1947 when Sinatra verbally and physically attacked the columnist in a Hollywood nightclub. Mortimer sued and Sinatra was forced to make a financial settlement.

When internal **FBI** memos later became available under the Freedom of Information Act, Mortimer's regular smearing of Sinatra was found to be part of a mutual arrangement between the columnist and the bureau in which the two parties exchanged largely uncorroborated information; the FBI filed gossip and Mortimer printed it. Mortimer also received information from the Commissioner of the Federal Bureau of Narcotics, Harry Anslinger, who opposed Sinatra's liberal politics and associations with dangerous dope-smoking musicians.

According to Brad Dexter, when Mortimer died several years later, Sinatra went to the trouble of urinating on his grave, shouting, "I'll bury the bastards, I'll bury them all." He would remain unrepentant. "If he was alive today, I'd knock him down again," he said in 1977. "Oh, he was a fink!"

But while Sinatra's career blossomed, there was something in his character that was gradually making his personal life chaotic. Driven, arrogant and increasingly intolerant of the press and certain aspects of his career, such as hanging around on film sets, he had a fast mouth that would often get him into trouble. In an interview in the 1940s he complained that the "pictures

FRANK AND THE MOB: THE EARLY YEARS

"No business. Just 'hello' and 'goodbye'."
FS TO THE KEFAUVER COMMITTEE INVESTIGATING ORGANISED CRIME, 1951

Although Sinatra downplayed it, evaded it or outright denied it over the years, the indications are that from his earliest days the singer had associations with men who murder, extort drugs, traffic drugs and control prostitution. In later times that association came to include personal friendships and business dealings.

Some tales have been substantiated more than others, but a good proportion of the stories citing a connection between Sinatra and the Mob seem to come in gossipy, **piqued testimony** from former friends (such as Peter Lawford) and minor Mafia figures (such as Joseph "Doc" Stacher). Even the information contained in the 1275 pages on Sinatra in the publicly available FBI files is described by *Crime* magazine columnist J.D. Chandler as "an uneven amalgam of fact, rumor, suspicion, allegation, unvarnished gossip, false leads and trivia". While Sinatra is rarely accused of being a "member" of the Mafia and was never officially indicted for any wrongdoing, the weight of hearsay and circumstantial evidence suggests that the rumours about Sinatra and the Mob should perhaps be taken as substantial but largely unproven.

Sinatra was born into a neighbourhood in New Jersey where gangsters were both heroes and employers. Marty Sinatra worked for a time during the Prohibition era guarding trucks of bootleg alcohol and when Dolly sought help in getting Frank work she turned to **Willie Moretti** (aka Willie Moore), a New Jersey mob boss. After Frank and Nancy were married, Moretti came to look upon the singer paternalistically, hiring him for his various clubs, and he was later heard to claim responsibility for freeing Frank from the punitive contract with Tommy Dorsey. (In a classic expression of the particular sense of Mafioso honour, when Sinatra was dallying with Ava Gardner, Moretti sent him a stern telegram: "I am very much surprised at … what I have been reading in the newspapers between you and your darling wife. Remember, you have a decent wife and children. You should be very happy. Regards to all. Willie Moore.")

In the 1940s Sinatra was friendly with **Joe Fischetti**, brother to the notorious Chicago mobsters Charlie and Rocco Fischetti and a booker for Mob-owned clubs that included the Fontainebleau in Miami, and it was he who invited Frank to Havana in 1947. It turned out to be a "boss of bosses" meeting. When "Lucky" Luciano's Naples apartment was searched in 1949, police apparently found Sinatra's private number and a gold cigarette case with the inscription "To my dear pal Charlie, from his friend Frank". Both the photos and lighter are now missing.

Joseph "Doc" Stacher was also present in Havana and told Kitty Kelley for her sensationally iconoclastic biography *His Way*: "The Italians among us were all very proud of Frank. They always told me they had spent a lot of money helping him in his career ever since he was in Tommy Dorsey's band. Lucky Luciano was very fond of Frank's singing. Frankie flew into Havana with the Fischettis, with whom he was very friendly, but of course, our meeting had nothing to do with hearing him croon… "

Sinatra, for his part, would later be described in a memo by J. Edgar Hoover, the director of the FBI, as having a **"hoodlum complex"** – a wide-eyed, groupie-style regard for gangsters' toughness, wealth and power. Phil Silvers and Sinatra would, according to Phil's ex-wife Jo-Carroll Silvers, "brag about Bugsy [Siegel, the Los Angeles mob boss], what he had done and how many people he had killed." The singer Eddie Fisher remembered Sinatra once saying to him: "I would rather be a Mafia don than President of the United States."

But Sinatra also had genuine reason to be grateful to the Mob. When his career was on the skids, **Skinny D'Amato** in Atlantic City and Moe Dalitz in Las Vegas, and Willie Moretti in New Jersey, all gave him work in their clubs, even if the audiences didn't always fill the places. **Mickey Cohen**, a West Coast boss, even threw an encouraging testimonial dinner for the singer in the Beverly Hills Hotel in the early 1950s.

As well as singing in joints controlled by the Mob – which virtually every entertainer in America was forced to adopt as a career strategy – Sinatra was sometimes linked to Mob-associated **business ventures**. To ensure good publicity he invested $15,000 in a magazine that was owned by Mickey Cohen, *Hollywood Night Life*, though the deal later went sour. This was the first inappropriate business relationship on which Sinatra had to answer questions during private, late-night testimony to the **Kefauver Committee** in 1951.

But Sinatra was evasive: "I asked Hank Sanicola, my manager, to handle it and that was the last I heard of it … I don't know the rest of the story." At other points during the hearing Sinatra was vague and disingenuous about what he knew of the Mafia ("some kind of shakedown operation, I don't know") and about his relationships with mobsters. "Those guys were okay," he said of his early gangster acquaintances. "They never bothered me, or anyone else as far as I know."

He would adopt similar semi-cooperative tactics whenever he later faced impertinent official questioning, though he never resorted to the gangster's giveaway, the Fifth Amendment. This was the favourite response of a later Sinatra associate, the Chicago crime boss **Sam Giancana**.

stink, and most of the people in them do too". After entertaining the troops in 1945 as a straight man for the comedian Phil Silvers, he was heard to describe the United Service Organization personnel as "shoemakers in uniform". His **temper** was unpredictable, as was his behaviour while shooting movies, and his petulant telegrams to columnists who dared to report such behaviour were a public relations disaster. George Evans tried to limit the damage, but the singer's egotism, temper and defiantly indiscreet relationships with starlets and mobsters made him his own worst enemy.

SINATRA LYING IN HIS DRESSING ROOM AT THE PARAMOUNT

Start spreading the news

In 1947 there was more trouble. Sinatra was reported by Lee Mortimer to have been socializing on a two-day visit to Havana with the brothers Rocco and Joe Fischetti and **Charles "Lucky" Luciano**, an exiled Mafia boss. The trip was soon interpreted by the press as a $2 million drop from the Mob to Luciano, with Sinatra as the carrier. That same year his old "morals charge" from 1938 was rehashed for public consumption and the columnist Westbrook Pegler linked Sinatra to an impressive array of gangsters, including Bugsy Siegel, Meyer Lansky and Willie Moretti.

"Just continue to print lies about me, and my temper – not my temperament – will see that you get a belt in your vicious and stupid mouth."

TELEGRAM TO ERSKINE JOHNSON, COLUMNIST
WHO CRITICISED FS'S MOVIE SET BEHAVIOUR, 1946

It was a bizarre duality for the public to interpret. On the one hand Sinatra was a man who could stir a nation's heart with his music and in April 1947 received **the Thomas Jefferson Award** for his fight against intolerance. On the other he could be seen as a womanizing, hot-tempered thug with communist leanings who beat up journalists and hung out with gangsters. Even if people didn't believe it, or didn't want to believe it – some columnists rallied round him and he wrote an open letter of thanks to his fans for the support – the negative publicity made a lasting difference to the public's perception of him.

"You, my fans and friends, rushed to defend me like some vast avenging army … The one thing I can do in return is to live in such a way, both as a performer and a human being, as to merit your confidence, respect and affection."

FS, OPEN LETTER, 1947

As if that wasn't bad enough, there was evidence that Sinatra's artistic standards might be slipping. There were still plenty of good songs that were hits: "Mam'selle" was number one and "Time After Time", from his amiable movie from 1947 *It Happened In Brooklyn,* came close. But then there was also **"The Dum Dot Song"**, a novelty about a guy trying to talk with chewing gum in his mouth. It was a tentative admission that in the post-war years – with the men back from the campaign and in the arms of the former teenage fans – his cuddle-up ballads and the odd swinger might not be enough to keep the public's interest. And things would get much worse before they got better.

Vagabond shoes

1948–52

◀ SINATRA AND AVA GARDNER ON HONEYMOON IN MIAMI IN NOVEMBER 1951

Vagabond shoes

*"Me, I did it. I'm my own worst enemy.
My singing went downhill and I went
downhill with it … It happened because
I paid no attention to how I was singing."*

FS, 1955

Despite returning to the ever-popular *Your Hit Parade* radio show in early 1948 after a break of more than two years, Sinatra was having no substantial hits of his own. In a dry year for all new recordings – thanks to another musicians' strike from January until November – Sinatra still had only moderate showings with stockpiled sides and tracks with a pre-recorded orchestra and overdubbed vocals. Two songs from the Fred Astaire movie *Easter Parade* stalled in the lower reaches of the charts and even his version of "Nature Boy" – in an established *a cappella* style – foundered when compared with Nat "King" Cole's smash hit. Sinatra's two film appearances in 1948 – *The Kissing Bandit* for MGM and *The Miracle Of The Bells* for RKO, his first non-singing role – were roundly panned and flopped at the box office.

At the end of 1948, a year when Sinatra felt rightly that his career was stalling, he confessed to Columbia boss Manie Sachs that he felt **"all washed up"**. Despite Sachs's encouragement and genuine belief in Sinatra's talent, his slip in the *Down Beat* male singer polls to fifth – his lowest since the early 1940s – and the magazine's criticism of his strident attempts at "Some Enchanted Evening" and "Bali Ha'i" from *South Pacific* did nothing for his spirits.

Nor did his financial situation. Although his salaries from recording and from films remained healthy, he was behind with his taxes. He was heard to mutter that he was planning to write a book called *All That I Am I Owe*.

The following year was at least a little better in terms of films. He co-starred in two lively musicals, *Take Me Out To The Ball Game* and *On The Town*, with the genial, relatively uncomplicated Gene Kelly. But the big hits were going to a new generation of pop singers such as **Johnnie Ray** and **Frankie Laine**. While newspapers came up with cruel taunts, such as "Frankie is wonderful… Frankie Laine that is", the critic at *Down Beat* magazine commented on Sinatra's "indecision of phrasing and tone" – and those who listened to *Your Hit Parade* could hear what he meant. Sinatra quit the show in May 1949, complaining about the current state of pop material he was being asked to sing ("decadent … bloodless"), and signed up to do *Light Up Time* instead.

Behind the scenes

But if his career and reputation were suffering, his personal life was even worse. For years a compulsive philanderer, Sinatra had left and returned to the marital home several times. In the late 1940s he was ostensibly a family man – their third child, **Tina**, was born in June 1948 – but he remained unsettled. He was restless enough in the middle of the decade to convince himself that Marilyn Maxwell and Lana Turner were worth throwing it all away for. George Evans would talk him out of the liaisons, knowing that they would be unpopular with the fans who bought into the myth of the romantic crooner Sinatra as a faithful, loving husband and father, and could be a catastrophe for Frank himself.

But there was nothing that Evans could do about **Ava Gardner**. Frank had met her in 1945 when he was new in Hollywood and she was newly married to Mickey Rooney. In the summer of 1947 she turned out as cheerleader (along with Marilyn Maxwell, Virginia Mayo and Shelley Winters) for Sinatra's celebrity softball team, **"The Swooners"**. By 1948 his flirting had become more intense and by 1949 they were lovers. With Sinatra still married and both being on contract at MGM, the gossip columns had a field day and Louis B. Mayer became extremely annoyed, pointing to a "morals clause" in both stars' contracts.

Vagabond shoes

SINATRA AND GARDNER IN NOVEMBER 1951, ON THEIR WEDDING DAY

MRS SINATRA 2: AVA GARDNER

"Sure, it's easy for someone to say give her up,
when they're not in love with her."

FS

A poor, uneducated 19-year-old with a virtually unintelligible southern drawl, **Ava Gardner** was signed to MGM in 1941 purely on her looks. The MGM talent scout George Sidney said of her, "She can't act, she can't talk, but she's a terrific piece of merchandise."

She was taught in the studio how to walk correctly and talk correctly, and appeared in bit parts and small roles throughout the early 1940s. In 1942 she married Mickey Rooney, but the union did not last long. In 1945 she married **Artie Shaw**, who put her on a course of psychotherapy, which left her with low self-esteem and a life-long distrust of analysis.

But from the moment Frank saw Ava's picture on the cover of a magazine in the mid-1940s, he was smitten. On the page she was alluring – her fearless, almond-shaped green eyes, tumbling brown hair, high cheekbones and full, glossy-red mouth epitomized the idea of a temptress – and Sinatra was hopelessly drawn to her when they met. The pair became acquainted during the late 1940s on the Hollywood social scene, flirted and by 1949 were lovers. There was much common ground. They both liked **sex, smoking, drinking, swearing, partying and fast-living**. One of their first dates involved driving out of Palm Springs, having got drunk, and shooting at stores and injuring a passer-by, which led to Frank being arrested in Indio. His publicity team spent money hushing up the incident and then energy dissuading him from seeing Ava again, sensing further trouble.

It was no use. When Nancy filed for divorce and it became clear that Frank and Ava were a couple, the public, the church and Louis B. Mayer all made their disapproval clear. **The press** delighted in trailing them and reporting their tempestuous affair – and there was much to report. Temperamentally, Frank and Ava were combustibly similar: both were restless, arrogant and insecure. The voraciousness of their passion was matched only by the ferocity of their jealousies, and the fights were loud. "It was always great in bed," Ava once famously said. "The quarrelling started on the way to the bidet." Once, when Frank flirted with a waitress, Ava left to spend the evening with her ex-husband Artie Shaw and Frank phoned and pretended to shoot himself.

She lost patience with him for feeling guilty about leaving his family and had no time for his mobster pals, but she believed in him, and when she wasn't arguing with him she encouraged him. An onlooker remembered her speech to the shaken singer in March 1950 before he took the stage at **the Copa** in New York. "Francis Albert Sinatra, you are the greatest goddamned entertainer who ever walked the face of this earth … I love you and I salute you." A reporter remembered hearing her tell a disheartened Sinatra in 1952, "No one with your talent is ever washed up."

As his divorce proceeded the pair drew together, and with the public and press getting used to the idea, they became one of Hollywood's most glamorous couples. They **married** in November 1951, but the sleepless nights and the daily fights continued. It didn't help that Ava aborted a pregnancy before Sinatra was aware that she was pregnant. At one engagement in New York, Ava accused Frank of directing a love song at his old flame Marilyn Maxwell, who was in the audience, and left for California, posting her wedding ring back to him. Frank used the press to woo her back – "Frankie Ready To Surrender; Wants Ava Back, Any Terms" ran one headline – and he did, briefly. But the jealousies, infidelities and petulance continued, with both parties seeming to expect more than the other could give. As the behaviour got crueller, the reconciliations became rarer, and the official end came in October 1953 when MGM announced that Ava was seeking a **divorce**. It was finalised in 1957.

For many years Sinatra's living quarters in California were almost a shrine to his second wife, replete with softly-lit pictures and mementos. Some subsequent partners would complain of him being a "moping bore" and friends would simply observe that he never got over her. But they remained confidantes, friends and sporadic lovers until her death in 1990. Ava, who described Sinatra as both "a scared monster" and "the love of my life", never remarried.

Their tumultuous relationship coincided with and undoubtedly exacerbated the slump in Sinatra's career. The guilt, sleeplessness and emotional trauma caused his voice and appearance to suffer and his susceptibility to belligerence and self-destruction increased. Yet it was Ava who persuaded her friend Joan Cohn to persuade, in turn, her husband Harry, the head of Columbia Pictures, to consider Sinatra for a part in the film *From Here To Eternity*, which transformed his life, and his ongoing passion for Gardner undoubtedly fuelled his ever-deepening feeling for lyrics that were lovelorn. As Nelson Riddle, the arranger who presided over Frank's classic Capitol recordings in the 1950s, declared, "It was Ava who … taught Sinatra how to sing a torch song."

Without Ava, Frank might never have fallen so low. But equally, he would not have risen so high or sung so deep.

Evans foresaw disaster and begged Sinatra to give her up. But he couldn't; he was obsessed. It was the last straw for Evans and by the start of 1950 he was no longer working for Sinatra. On January 27 the long-suffering press agent died of a heart attack. He was 48.

A distraught Sinatra attended **Evans's funeral** in New York and then flew straight to Houston, where he had his first non-theatre engagement in many years, at the Shamrock Hotel. With Ava in attendance ("a major mistake", Sinatra later admitted), the pair were caught together in a restaurant by the press and Sinatra lost his temper. Reports of their liaison became more explicit and harder to smooth over with bland denials. On Valentine's Day, humiliated and heartbroken, Nancy filed for divorce.

Throughout the upheaval in his personal life – the separation from his family and the tempestuous affair with Ava, which together took up most of his emotional energy – Sinatra ground on with his career in the early 1950s. But things wouldn't go his way. In limited demand, he played club engagements that two years previously he would never have considered, and with stress and fatigue taking its toll on his voice, he struggled to impress the public and the critics. At the Copa in April 1950, his voice failed him completely due to a **throat haemorrhage**, and his doctor

SINATRA REHEARSING DURING A VISIT TO LONDON IN JULY 1950

ordered a week's silence. But he was warmly received at **the London Palladium** in July 1950 and by September 1951 he had played his first engagements in Las Vegas. Other performances were scarce, however, and he gladly accepted help in the form of bookings from hoodlums such as Skinny D'Amato in Atlantic City.

In a flush of optimism he attempted to regenerate enthusiasm with a season at the Paramount in early 1952, but with attendances conspicuously moderate, it was hard for commentators not to compare it unfavourably with the Times Square events of eight years earlier. One unflinching headline read: "Gone on Frankie in '42: Gone in '52". An engagement at Chez Paree in Chicago soon afterwards attracted a meagre crowd of 150 in a club that could hold more than 1000.

His recording career also took a nosedive. Manie Sachs left Columbia in 1950 to be replaced by the oboist-turned-pop-producer **Mitch Miller**. Sinatra's musical association with Miller started with the tasteful up-tempo album *Sing And Dance With Frank Sinatra*, arranged by George Siravo. But the album wasn't a hit and part of an ongoing effort to get Sinatra into the charts saw him singing reams of material that rank as his worst run of records.

At first he tried to refuse some of the songs, such as "My Heart Cries For You" and "The Roving Kind", but when he saw them become hits for other Miller-produced singers such as Guy Mitchell, he succumbed to the banalities of "Goodnight Irene" (which was a hit), "Tennessee Newsboy", "Bim Bam Baby" and, most infamously, in the company of the flavour-of-the-week blonde bombshell Dagmar, **"Mama Will Bark"**. Unfortunately, the most significant impact that most of these records had was on Sinatra's self-esteem. "I'm A Fool To Want You" was a heart-rending performance of Ava-inspired passion, but it was an exception. Later he would accuse Miller of nearly ruining his career, but in truth Sinatra always had control of what he recorded; the direness of some of the records he allowed himself to make merely reflected his lack of self-confidence.

Meanwhile, his film career had also dipped. Despite the success of *On The Town*, MGM dropped Sinatra, seemingly because of his fading popularity, the increasing notoriety of his private life and a loose remark about **Louis B. Mayer's mistress**, overheard on a film set and reported back to the boss. A pair of flops for other studios – *Double Dynamite* for RKO and *Meet Danny Wilson* for Universal – did nothing for his reputation. He did in 1950 land his first series on the relatively new medium of television, *The Frank Sinatra Show* (see page 325), but compared with *The Milton Berle Show* against which it was programmed the ratings were mediocre. Slapdash and under-rehearsed by its semi-interested star, it was poorly received, and the five-year contract was cancelled after two seasons.

It is an understatement to say that Sinatra had not always been tactful with the press. Through snarling at photographers, sniping at columnists and indulging in arrogance and belligerence – he claimed that he was attempting to protect his privacy – he had generated substantial bad feeling within the fourth estate. After he had flown into Las Vegas for his divorce in June 1951, he refused to cooperate with waiting journalists, calling them "newspaper bums" and asking why he should give them anything. "I ought to give a cocktail party for the press," he said, "and put a Mickey Finn in every glass." Sinatra's new press agent **Mack Miller** and Ava Gardner begged him to try a conciliatory approach, which resulted in some awkward interviews that were heavy with strained humility. "I won't mind if it pans me," he told the *Cosmopolitan* writer George Frazier in 1952 when he was warned that the upcoming article might be less than complimentary, "just as long as it helps me correct the things I've been doing wrong."

With his profile, prospects and spirits at an all-time low, some friends, such as the songwriter Sammy Cahn, were embarrassed to go to Sinatra's thinly-attended show at the Coconut Grove in Los Angeles, and others, including the song-and-dance maestro Sammy Davis Jr., were uncomfortable even saying hello to the downbeat singer on the streets of New York. When his record company, Columbia, and his booking agency, MCA, dropped him within weeks of each other in the middle of 1952, it was almost official: with no recording contract, no agent and no movie studio, Frank Sinatra was a 36-year-old has-been.

From Here To Eternity

But an ember of self-belief kept Sinatra alert to the opportunity for a comeback. When he read *From Here To Eternity*, the best-selling novel

Vagabond shoes

by James Jones about GIs before Pearl Harbour, he saw himself as the spunky Italian underdog Angelo Maggio and campaigned to be cast in the movie version planned by Harry Cohn at Columbia. So convinced was the singer that this was the right part for the right man at the right time, he even offered to work for no payment – which was a considerable suggestion given that he was living off Ava's earnings and in massive debt to the taxman. Ava got behind Frank and appealed to Cohn's wife Joan, who persuaded her husband to test Sinatra, before pestering Cohn himself with pleading phone calls.

The singer's screen test was good, but so was that of Cohn's preferred choice, **Eli Wallach**; Joan Cohn, however, suggested that Wallach, though brilliant, was not sufficiently "skinny", "pathetic" or "Italian". In the end Wallach, committed to a Broadway play, made himself unavailable – the details of the story are still not agreed upon – and at the end of 1952 Sinatra heard that he had the part. It was news that heralded the beginning of the rest of his life.

A BRAND NEW
START OF IT
1953–61

A brand new start of it

*"I realised I was pushing forty so
one day I decided to get up and go to work."*

FS

With his movie career looking up, though not his finances – he agreed to do *From Here To Eternity* for a paltry $1000 a week – Sinatra's recording opportunities also took a modest turn for the better. Manie Sachs had been unable to secure Sinatra a place at his new record company, RCA Victor, but, not least thanks to June Hutton (Axel Stordahl's wife and a Capitol recording artist), Sinatra was offered a recording deal by **Capitol**. It was non-committal, to say the least: a one-year contract with no advance and with Sinatra having to meet his own recording costs. Still, he felt confident enough to veto the idea of working with Capitol's jazz producer Dave Dexter, and the job fell to the former drummer **Voyle Gilmore**, though in practice Sinatra would produce his recordings himself.

Stordahl conducted Sinatra's first Capitol session, which produced a moderate hit, "I'm Walking Behind You", a ballad in a similar vein to his sides for Columbia. But when Stordahl was lured away to work with Eddie Fisher – one of the hottest singing stars around, who had a number one with the same song – it was a chance for Sinatra to move on. He suggested using Billy May, whose arrangements were as driving and jazzy as his personality, but he was unavailable. The head of Capitol A&R, Alan Livingston, persuaded Sinatra to try the former Dorsey arranger **Nelson Riddle**. He was drafted in to create a pastiche of May's style on "South

Of The Border" and put his own stamp on "I've Got The World On A String".

This was the start of one of the great partnerships in twentieth-century popular music, and, in vocal terms, a new Sinatra: swinging, insouciant and irresistible. Although the initial singles didn't set the charts alight, the first two Capitol 10-inch albums, which each gathered eight tracks from Sinatra's initial Capitol sessions, fared better. ***Songs For Young Lovers*** and ***Swing Easy***, the latter reaching number three, marked a fundamental change in how Sinatra's music was consumed by the public. At Capitol, Sinatra became an album artist; he would still have hit singles, but from the 1950s onwards most of the material that made him interesting came in long-playing form.

Sinatra spent seven weeks filming *From Here To Eternity* in spring 1953 before leaving for an unsuccessful singing tour of **Europe**, where he played to half-empty venues and was booed by an audience in Rome that

SINATRA, OPPOSITE MONTGOMERY CLIFT, AS ANGELO MAGGIO IN
FROM HERE TO ETERNITY – AN OSCAR-WINNING PERFORMANCE

seemed disappointed that Ava wasn't with him. When he returned to the US, however, he found that he had received rave reviews for the film, and with the industry buzz suggesting that Frank was back in a big way, his confidence sky-rocketed.

Unfortunately, the upturn in his professional fortunes did nothing for his second marriage. "When he was down and out, he was sweet," Ava reportedly said. "Now he's successful again, he's become his old arrogant self. We were happy when he was on the skids." Indeed, because both stars were an exhausting blend of cruelty, vulnerability, brashness and sensitivity, Frank and Ava had only been sporadically happy. After a series of public break-ups and reconciliations, in October 1953 **"the Battling Sinatras"** (as the papers had it) announced their separation.

> *"Ava Gardner and Frank Sinatra stated today that having reluctantly exhausted every effort to reconcile their differences, they could find no mutual basis on which to continue their marriage. Both expressed deep regret and respect for each other. Their separation is final and Miss Gardner will seek a divorce."*
>
> MGM PRESS RELEASE, OCTOBER 29, 1953

Although the statement implied that the decision was mutual, it was Ava who had left Frank, and he took it badly. He drank excessively, behaved as if bereaved, let his weight fall and, in a particularly depressed state at the house of his songwriter friend **Jimmy Van Heusen** in November 1953, slashed his wrists. While beginnning a course of psychoanalysis, he attempted a reconciliation at the end of the year in Italy, where Ava was filming *The Barefoot Contessa*. When Sinatra discovered that she was seeing the bullfighter **Luis Miguel Dominguin**, he trashed her room and flew home.

He did, at least, have his revitalised singing and acting career to distract him. When "Young At Heart" hit the charts in March 1954 Frank found

SINATRA THE GAMBLER

Sinatra's association with and part-ownership of **Las Vegas** – in the 1960s he owned a 9 per cent stake in the Sands hotel – is a potent part of his image. One of the most famous stories about Sinatra's approach to gambling was told by the vibraphonist and bandleader Red Norvo. "I've seen him go up to the baccarat table with ten thousand dollars," said Norvo, "sit down, put a bundle on the table, ride it up to thirty thousand, lose it, and walk away with a shrug." But as the comedian Don Rickles said about Sinatra: "He gets up in the morning and God throws money on him." For most of Sinatra's professional life, cash-flow was not an issue.

It should also be remembered that much of Sinatra's gambling was bankrolled by the venue, especially at the Sands. He used house credit to gamble, so if he won, he kept the winnings as a perk of the job, and if he didn't, he didn't have to pay his marker. He did, after all, part-own the place.

So Sinatra's gambling had little to do with gaming; it was all about the way he ran his life, in which impatience and vision led him to make risky decisions and turn his world around. He could have had a comfortable few years with Tommy Dorsey, but he gambled on a solo career, which at the

himself with his first top-five hit in eight years. And at **the Academy Awards** that same month, the winner in the category of Best Supporting Actor, as announced by Mercedes McCambridge, was Frank Sinatra for *From Here to Eternity*. The audience roaring with approval, he bounded on to the stage, where he spoke of being "deeply thrilled and very moved". This was the crowning moment of perhaps the greatest comeback in show business history. He cancelled his psychoanalysis.

Journalists were mostly pleased for him, but if they expected humility, they were wrong. He was soon telling them that "luck is fine and you have to have luck to have the opportunity," before adding "but after that, you've got to have talent and know how to use it". He soon tired of the references to a "comeback" and advised reporters to refer to the "Rise and Fall and Rise Again of Frank Sinatra".

The offers of work came fast. By the end of 1954 Sinatra was able to take out a full-page advert in *Billboard* about his recent and current work, including the completed movies (the thriller **Suddenly** and the romantic drama **Young At Heart**), the film currently shooting (the

time was unknown territory for a singer. He could have carried on making movies for whoever paid him, but he chose to take a risk with his own production company. He could have carried on making records for Capitol, but he gambled on Reprise and pioneered the artist-run record company. The odds of success were in his favour because he wasn't just waiting around for good luck. Things didn't happen to him: *he made things happen*. And of course, sometimes he failed, but he rarely sat around long enough to nurse his bruises.

The biggest gamble of all was trading his family for **Ava Gardner**, and it didn't come off. Permanent losses included his press agent and his sense of where home was. Temporarily, he lost his confidence, his voice, his fans and his will to live – and eventually he lost Ava too. The failure created the energy that he would bring to the rest of his life to fill the void; but his daughter Tina wrote of a man who became racked with almost catatonic depression, full of the pain and regret that he had staved off for years. "I should never have left you," his first wife would hear from her aging ex-husband, "I should never have left home". It was the one bet that he was unable to walk away from with a shrug.

drama *Not As A Stranger*) and his next one (the musical *Guys And Dolls*). He signed it "Busy, busy, busy – Frank." Meanwhile he was named the top male vocalist by the magazines *Billboard*, *Down Beat* and *Metronome*.

But despite this frantic activity and professional acclaim, Sinatra was a tormented man who was startlingly underweight and heartbroken. The songwriter **Jule Styne**, who lived with Sinatra for several months during this period, remembered him never sleeping, always drinking, phoning his first wife for comfort and constantly singing songs of helpless love.

The pain in his voice was recorded in early 1955, when, with Nelson Riddle, Sinatra taped sixteen exquisite readings of some of the saddest love songs ever written. The music was issued as *In The Wee Small Hours* and was the first, and one of the best, in a memorable series of "losers-in-love" albums that Sinatra would record for Capitol. Everyone knew about Frank and Ava and through this album everyone could hear his pain. No one, it seemed, had loved and lost like Frank, and no one had let it be heard so clearly and so beautifully.

But the bittersweet heartache of *In The Wee Small Hours* was only half of Sinatra's image during this period. The Ava saga had hardened him, leaving him less vulnerable in close romantic entanglements and even less guilty than before about taking pleasure where it could be found. Always cocky and restive, with a new toughened heart and soaring career, Sinatra hit the good times with ruthless abandon. He hung out with **Humphrey Bogart's "Rat Pack"**, a group of hard-drinking, fun-loving non-conformists, including Lauren Bacall, Judy Garland and David Niven, who thumbed their noses at authority and at the press. Sinatra's recent acquisition of a percentage of **the Sands hotel** in Las Vegas had him performing regularly there, and also indulging in sprees of drinking, gambling and sex. Some of the women were the great stars and beauties of their day; some were what the columnist Dorothy Kilgallen called the "fluffy little struggling dolls of show business"; and some were simply paid for.

A diluted version of this side of Sinatra manifested itself in the characters that he played in comedy films where he played compulsive (though ultimately reformed) womanizers, such as *The Tender Trap* in 1955 and, in 1963, *Come Blow Your Horn*. It was also apparent in records such as ***Songs for Swingin' Lovers!***, a jaunty, hip album from 1956 full of the joy of love and living and one of his undisputed classics. This heartbroken/hedonistic duality was first established in the mid-1950s and became a vivid part of Sinatra's personal style, which during the following 35 years was sustained and accentuated.

One side of Sinatra that didn't find its way into his art was his propensity for bad-mouthed brawls and **scandals**. There were the ongoing rumours of associations with figures in the underworld, which had dogged him since the episode in Havana in 1947 and which delayed his Nevada state gambling licence approval when he bought into the Sands in 1954. After the Lee Mortimer episode that same year, Frank's fist was felt by a bartender who didn't serve his drink quickly enough, a photographer who got in the way of his car and a reporter who asked the wrong question at the wrong time. A typical incident came in December 1954 when Sinatra attacked Mel Tormé's publicist, Jim Byron, in an ill-tempered misunderstanding following a question about Sinatra's companion, **Judy Garland**.

Slightly stranger, but equally notorious, was the event involving the baseball star **Joe DiMaggio** that became known as **"the Wrong Door**

Raid". Sinatra and DiMaggio not only had in common their status as Italian-American heroes; both had agonies over their respective estranged wives – in DiMaggio's case, **Marilyn Monroe**. He had heard from his private detective that Marilyn was taking drugs and having a lesbian affair. An anguished DiMaggio decided that the way forward was to break in and catch his wife in the act and in November 1954 he persuaded Sinatra to drive him to the West Hollywood apartment block that was suspected to be the location of the alleged tryst. Having met up with private detectives, DiMaggio and others broke into an apartment, but there was no Marilyn and no drugs – just an innocent lady woken from her sleep and shocked to be photographed by strangers while in bed. (Marilyn was apparently in the apartment above with her voice coach.) The lady sued for trespass damages and the peculiar non-story ran and ran, mainly in the scandal rag *Confidential*. Did Sinatra take part in the raid, or did he wait by the car? He stated under oath that he

SINATRA THE FRIEND AND BENEFACTOR

"If you say to Frank, 'I'm having a problem,' it becomes his problem."
BURT LANCASTER

For every story about Sinatra's temper, impatience and revengeful petulance, there is another one about his generosity, compassion and **thoughtfulness**. Some stories made the papers – which was a useful antidote to some of the bad press he received – but many others did not.

In September 1947, for example, when **Phil Silvers** had lost his straight man, Rags Ragland, a fortnight before opening at the Copa and had tried to cancel, only for the club to insist that he perform, Sinatra stopped filming *It Happened In Brooklyn* to join his USO partner, raising Silvers' spirits and contributing to glowing reviews.

When **Sammy Davis Jr.** lost an eye in a car accident in November 1954, Sinatra was there to save him from self-pity and restore his confidence, despite an article in *Confidential* that suggested intimacy between Davis and Ava Gardner.

When **Lee J. Cobb**, an actor who Sinatra knew from their appearance together in *The Miracle Of The Bells* but was not especially close to, nearly died of a heart attack in 1955, Sinatra gave him moral support, paid his bills and housed him during his recuperation. In Cobb's words, "He built an insulated wall around me that shielded me from tension, worry and strain."

When the owner of the Hollywood club the Mocambo, **Charlie Morrison**, died in 1957, leaving his widow virtually penniless, Sinatra stepped in and packed the place for two weeks, and the club grossed $100,000 in a fortnight. When the B-movie horror star **Bela Lugosi** checked into hospital as a drug addict in 1955, Sinatra sent him a gift and a message of support. "It gave me such a boost," said Lugosi, who had never met Sinatra. "He was the only star I heard from."

There are many stories of Sinatra's routine generosity and goodwill, to individuals – strangers and friends – and to institutions. It was a trait

never entered the apartment and, although suspected of perjury, was ultimately found innocent. (During a trial in 1957 investigating the methods of scandal magazines, a witness who claimed that Sinatra was in the raid was mysteriously beaten up.)

that some interpret, however, as an expression of his inability to show conventional care. "Frank doesn't know how to express affection," said Phil Silvers. "He does it with expensive gifts." Others connected his reactions to his need to be in control. "Once his friend, you're a friend for life," wrote **Vincente Minnelli**. "Of course, he [is] prone to *tell* friends how he'll help them rather than *ask* how he can help. But I suppose that's the prerogative of any leader."

According to the book by daughter Nancy, when Frank's mother Dolly visited Rome she had an audience with **Pope Paul VI**, who told her: "Your son is very close to God." When she asked him to explain, he said: "Because he does God's work and he does not talk about it."

F_S

September 22, 1988

Dear Ken,

I've just been informed that you are under the weather and I thought a note might cheer you up...I hope so...get well soon...hope to see you.

Affectionately,

Francis Albert

Frank Sinatra

A second career

A substantial cover story in *Time* magazine in August 1955 described Sinatra as being "well away on a second career that promises to be, if anything, more brilliant than the first", and in the mid-to-late 1950s Sinatra directed his considerable energies to making it so.

One of the busiest actors in Hollywood, he filmed no fewer than five movies in 1955, most of them good (see pages 294–298, 301), and his performance as a heroin addict in **The Man With the Golden Arm** was admired perhaps even more than that in *From Here To Eternity*. (Thereafter he averaged two films a year for nearly a decade.) He had hit singles – "Hey! Jealous Lover" and "Witchcraft" among them – but it was his LPs with Nelson Riddle from 1956 and 1957, *Songs For Swingin' Lovers!*, *Close To You* and **A Swingin' Affair**, that set new artistic standards for popular vocal records.

Sinatra somehow found time for an artistic detour in 1956 to serve as **the conductor** for a specially commissioned orchestral album for Capitol, *Tone Poems In Color* (see pages 166–167). He even indulged in a little nostalgia, rejoining The Tommy Dorsey Orchestra at the Paramount for a week in August 1956. And there was also his new Western, **Johnny Concho**, made by his newly-formed film company, Kent Productions.

"How do you do all these things?" asked George Sidney, the director of *Anchors Aweigh* and *Pal Joey*, one of Sinatra's film successes of 1957. "Very simple." answered Frank. "One thing at a time." He explained his **extreme productivity** another way to Vincente Minnelli, who directed him in the 1958 drama *Some Came Running*. "This is something I can't help," he told him. "I have to go. No one seems able to help me with it, doctors, no one. I have to move." His daughter Tina ventured a poignant analysis many years later. "My father fit the mould of a classic over-achiever," she wrote in her memoir *My Father's Daughter*. "He had his own void inside, the product of his emotionally meagre childhood. As long as he kept moving, kept working, he might outrun his loneliness."

Despite all his production, profile and increasing power in the entertainment business, Sinatra couldn't control the press – and it drove him mad. When the showbiz columnist **Dorothy Kilgallen** wrote a six-part series in 1957 for the *New York Journal* entitled "The Real Frank Sinatra Story", which detailed his recent romances, he sent her a tombstone with her name carved on it and ridiculed her appearance in his live performances – a practice that he continued for years. "Dorothy Kilgallen isn't here tonight," he would announce. "I guess she's out shopping for a new chin."

He attempted a more dignified reprisal that same year when he sued *Look* magazine, who had printed a three-part series by Bill Davidson

A brand new start of it

SINATRA ON STAGE AT THE SANDS IN OCTOBER 1956, WATCHED BY KIM NOVAK
AND COLE PORTER (FOREGROUND) AND JACK BENNY (IN GLASSES)

called **"Talent, Tantrums and Torment"**, which made much of Sinatra's contrasting character traits. "There is a Sinatra who fights for the underdog and a Sinatra who bullies his underlings," wrote Davidson. "There is a cocky Sinatra, a scared Sinatra, a gay Sinatra, a brooding Sinatra. There is Sinatra the devoted family man and Sinatra the libertine."

A libel suit was issued by Sinatra and then dropped on legal advice, but was replaced by an invasion of privacy suit, which he dropped when a similar case involving the conductor Serge Koussevitsky led to a ruling that a public figure cannot sue for invasion of privacy. From this point onwards, Sinatra adopted and maintained a distant, very selective relationship with journalists. He took to ostracizing reporters who wrote anything that he perceived to be critical of his personal conduct, even if they had been largely supportive of him on other occasions, and he continued to snipe at the press during live performances for the rest of his career.

Although Sinatra was musically at an all-time peak and his films did well consistently, he had yet to conquer the small screen. His series for ABC in 1957, *The Frank Sinatra Show*, was ambitious – twenty-one musical shows of an hour and ten half-hour dramas featuring the biggest names in show business as guest stars – but indifferent audience figures and lukewarm reviews meant that it lasted only one season.

Reluctant to be allied with a single arranger, despite the artistic and commercial success of the Nelson Riddle records, Sinatra diversified by employing Gordon Jenkins in 1957 for the ballad set *Where Are You?* and Billy May for the 1958 travel concept album *Come Fly With Me* and the upbeat terpsichorean selection *Come Dance With Me!* in 1959. All were up to the remarkable standard that Sinatra had set on his Capitol long-players, but for many, the highlight of his Capitol years came in 1958 with the heart-rending **Frank Sinatra Sings For Only The Lonely**, a magnificent collection of elegiac Nelson Riddle settings which for both men was a career high.

From Capitol to Reprise

His films in the late 1950s were a varied bunch – war dramas (*Kings Go Forth* and *Never So Few*), a post-war drama (*Some Came Running*), a family comedy (*A Hole In the Head*) and a lavish musical (*Can-Can*) – but none were hits and Sinatra began to get restless. He was even getting bored at Capitol. He was apparently concerned about the onset of **recording technology** and over-production, but essentially he wanted more money and more control of his recording career; he considered his ongoing 5

A brand new start of it

percent royalty rate to be exploitative given the amount of money that he had made for the company. He asked Capitol to give him his own label, but the record company refused, so he did not record for several months in 1959 and 1960 until his release was agreed. Eventually negotiations produced a severance deal that required Sinatra to record four more albums for Capitol before he would be free to join the record company that he had founded himself to fulfil his artistic and entrepreneurial ambitions, **Reprise**.

While Sinatra managed to maintain a relationship with his children, who were being brought up by Nancy in **Holmby Hills**, by being a "Sunday father" as often as he could, his bachelor pad in **Palm Springs** was at the heart of a unique social scene that included film stars, call girls, politicians and mobsters. Sinatra was on the seduction trail almost every night, with professional ladies – according to his valet, **George Jacobs**, in his book *Mr S* – granted the same courtesies and hospitality as anyone. Jacobs would prepare elaborate candlelit dinners and arrange for chauffeur services and payment (if required). If the girls provided pleasant company, they would be recommended to friends.

Marlene Dietrich, Sammy Davis Jr., and Joe and John F. Kennedy were among Sinatra's houseguests, but none, according to Jacobs, received more careful hospitality than **Sam Giancana** – the shrouded part-owner of various clubs and casinos where profits were "skimmed", who was apparently involved in 200 underworld killings. Although Sinatra's attachment to the mobster was assumed at the time to be an ill-judged continuation of his youthful worship of underworld power, Jacobs felt that it showed admiration for the gangster's business acumen. This was something that Sinatra was keen to acquire, particularly in relation to casinos and gambling. Giancana was a man who had gambled in business and won.

He kept his performance adrenalin pumping by embarking in early 1959 on a rare tour, unusually for him with a small jazz group led by the vibraphonist Red Norvo (a recording of which was released by Blue Note in the 1990s). But what he really loved was hanging out with the latest incarnation of **"the Rat Pack"**, whose drink-fuelled pursuit of good times was a Sinatra-led extension of the original Bogart gang – though this time they made more music together and there was more sex. The core of the group comprised Sinatra, **Sammy Davis Jr.** and the boozy crooner **Dean**

THE RAT PACK ACT

*"We ain't figured out ourselves what the
hell we do up here. But it's fun, baby."*
FS ON STAGE AT THE SANDS, JANUARY 1960

Reviewing Dean Martin's guest spot on Sinatra's TV show in December 1957, the *Chicago Sun-Times* wrote, "They performed like a pair of adult delinquents, sharing the same cigarette, leering at girls, breaking up on chatter directed to the Las Vegas fraternity, plugging records, movies, and the places they eat for free, and swigging drinks at a prop bar." After the effervescent all-rounder Sammy Davis Jr. was added to the mix, along with, for a while, Peter Lawford and Joey Bishop, this shambolic shrug of an act was considered **the hippest entertainment of its age**.

The material was thin, consisting of endless **jokes** about "broads" and being drunk. "You're not drunk if you can lay on the floor without holding on," Dean would say, echoing Joe E. Lewis. "These aren't cufflinks, they're curbfeelers." Bishop, a teetotaller, observed with deadpan showbiz disapproval: "You can get high *watching* this show." The lines, though seemingly ad-libbed, were largely scripted, by Bishop – but with aching hiatuses between the throwaway gags, the few recordings available make for painful listening.

The rare filmed evidence – no footage of the nightclub act was released officially – makes more sense, showing the casual but alluring **charisma** of performers who only had to walk around in a tuxedo to create a little magic. Onlookers, digging the unusual slang that was employed and aspiring to the Rat Pack's intoxicating lack of responsibility, felt privileged to be there and part of an exclusive gang of boozy but nicely turned out ne'er-do-wells. By the end of the show, the audience laughed at anything they said.

Sinatra was the obvious "leader" and Martin was the coolest and funniest ("How did all these people get in my room?"). But Davis outdid both for sheer showbiz pizzazz. A black entertainer in a white world, he was set up as a whipping boy and the racial jokes flew fast. But there was a more complex

Martin; satellite members included Shirley MacLaine (a co-star of two contemporary Sinatra movies), the songwriter Jimmy Van Heusen, the laconic comedian **Joey Bishop** and the actor **Peter Lawford** (a louchemeister of limited gifts who was married to JFK's sister Pat). The press had taken to naming the group "the Clan"; Sinatra, disliking any association with the

undercurrent. Given Sinatra and Martin's genuine love and respect for Davis, and his ripostes, the racial aspect of the Rat Pack act not only was a source of easy laughs but also can be seen as a sly satire on the ignorant attitudes that prevailed. The reaction these days, however, may be to recoil, particularly when Davis, agonisingly grateful to be part of the gang, slaps his thighs and stamps his foot with hysterical laughter at every lame joke thrown at him.

A RAT PACK PERFORMANCE DURING THE 1960S: PETER LAWFORD, FRANK SINATRA, DEAN MARTIN, SAMMY DAVIS JR. AND JOEY BISHOP

KKK, attempted to have it known as "the Summit"; but the name that has stuck was the original one: the Rat Pack.

In January 1960 Sinatra – who thought "the Rat Pack" was a "stupid phrase" – combined his professional and personal pleasures for a month in **Las Vegas**. Sinatra, Davis and Martin, and Bishop and Lawford all made

SINATRA, THE MOB AND THE KENNEDY CLAN

"Let's just say that the Kennedys are interested in the lively arts and that Sinatra is the liveliest art of all."
PETER LAWFORD, 1960

The Kennedy family had long-standing links with show business. **Joe Kennedy**, bootlegger-turned-ambassador, had been a business partner of RKO film studios in the 1940s and the actress Gloria Swanson had been his mistress. When Joe's daughter Pat married Peter Lawford in 1954 and moved into the former house of Louis B. Mayer, JFK – always attracted to Hollywood – spent much time socializing in California, got to know Lawford's circle and became particularly friendly with Sinatra. JFK loved hearing the gossip about sex in Tinseltown and was fascinated by Sinatra's swinging lifestyle.

When JFK, a Catholic, was seeking the Democratic nomination for president in 1960, Joe Kennedy approached Sinatra to ask **Sam Giancana** to help swing a primary in anti-Catholic West Virginia. Giancana agreed, as a favour to Sinatra, undoubtedly imagining that a candidate he had helped to secure power would be useful, or at least able to reduce the FBI surveillance that he had to endure. Funds were dispersed, bribes were accepted, and Kennedy won the primary and then the presidency.

Outside the political arena, JFK was introduced to many girls by Sinatra – often his former lovers, including the most glamorous and vulnerable movie star of all, **Marilyn Monroe**, who became his mistress. As in thrall to his

a movie during the day – *Ocean's 11* – did a show at the Sands at night and partied until it was time to show up on set the following morning. Sleep was some way down their list of priorities. The movie wasn't a classic, but that wasn't the point.

Sinatra's charisma, music and lifestyle were as irresistibly glamorous to the Las Vegas punters who packed the Sands as they were to the most powerful people in the country. The royalty of show business, politics and the underworld were often ringside when Sinatra and his chums hit town and it was these sorts of people whom he threw behind the campaign to get **John F. Kennedy** elected to the White House.

Sinatra's energetic political support for the Democrats had been sincere for much of his life: he'd sung and campaigned for Franklin D. Roosevelt in

A brand new start of it

gangster buddies as he was to politicians, Sinatra sometimes introduced the same girls to Sam Giancana, including a 25-year-old starlet, **Judith Campbell**. During one brief period in history, Campbell was probably mistress to both the leader of the Mob in Chicago and the President of the United States.

And at the centre of this tangled web of corruption and power was the skinny crooner from Hoboken.

1944, Harry S. Truman in 1948 and Adlai Stevenson in 1952 and 1956. But Kennedy was different. JFK admired Sinatra for being a charismatic show business personality, talented singer and unmatched ladies man almost as much as Sinatra admired JFK's policies and potential power. Sinatra devoted himself to campaigning for his friend, and inspired his showbiz buddies – renamed **"the Jack Pack"** – to do the same. He used all the methods he could: political and underworld connections, fund-raising concerts and even a campaign song – a specially recorded version of "High Hopes".

But Sinatra had to make certain political compromises during and after the Kennedy campaign that cut deep into his ideals of tolerance and opposition to prejudice. The first came after he hired **Albert Maltz**, who had written *The House I Live In*, to write a screenplay based on *The*

Execution Of Private Slovik, a book by William Bradford Huie about the only soldier to have been killed for desertion since the American Civil War; Maltz had been fined and imprisoned for not cooperating with the notorious, anti-communist House Un-American Activities Committee, and having been blacklisted he had lived since 1951 in Mexico. The Hearst press kicked up a fuss about Sinatra hiring "an unrepentant enemy of the country" and, sensing that JFK's campaign would be threatened by a perception of softness towards communism, Joe Kennedy let Sinatra know that he had to choose between Maltz or JFK. (Sinatra's ex-wife Nancy also let him know that their daughter Tina was suffering communist taunts at school.) With a heavy heart, Sinatra fired the writer, paying him in full ($75,000) for the unwritten screenplay, and the movie was abandoned.

"My conversations with Maltz indicated that he had an affirmative, pro-American approach to the story. But the American public has indicated that it feels the morality of hiring Maltz is the more crucial matter, and I will accept the majority opinion."

FS's STATEMENT ON SETTLING WITH ALBERT MALTZ, 1960

Sinatra's friendship with Sammy Davis Jr. led to another compromise for the Kennedy campaign. Sinatra recognised Davis's brilliance as a performer early in his career, and fought for him to be treated equally in hotels, casinos and nightclubs at a time when it wouldn't have happened naturally. It was a genuine contribution to the fight for racial equality, and as Davis later said, "Frank cared when nobody else did – before it became popular." However, during the close fight for the White House in 1960 between JFK and Richard Nixon, Davis was due to marry the white Swedish actress **Mai Britt**, and the JFK team did not need a high-profile campaigner in a mixed-race marriage; it made sense pragmatically. Once again, Joe Kennedy leaned on Sinatra, and the couple were persuaded to delay their marriage. The wedding took place five days after JFK's victory in November 1960, with Frank as best man.

The White House then barred Davis from either attending or performing at **the inaugural gala for President Kennedy** in Washington in January 1961 – which Sinatra and Peter Lawford were organizing. Frank was furious, and hurt for Davis, but was unable to do anything about it: JFK ducked his calls and a White House aide blamed Robert Kennedy, the Attorney General. But Sinatra remained immensely proud that he had a friend in the White House, and felt partly responsible for him getting there. The singer was later observed listening repeatedly and in disbelief to a recording made of Kennedy's speech at the close of the gala that thanked "a great friend".

"I know we're all indebted to a great friend – Frank Sinatra. Long before he could sing, he used to poll a Democratic precinct back in New Jersey. That precinct has grown to cover a country ... long after he has ceased to sing, he is going to be standing up and speaking for the Democratic party, and I thank him on behalf of all of you tonight."

JOHN F. KENNEDY, INAUGURAL GALA, WASHINGTON D.C., JANUARY 1961

King of the hill

1961–71

King of the hill

1961–71

"I am what I am, and I'm not askin' myself any questions. The time you start talkin' to yourself is when you're unhappy, when you wanna change. I don't wanna change. I'm satisfied with what I am."

FS

In the wake of Kennedy's election victory, Sinatra's star had never been higher. His life appeared to be **one long, successful party**. He was an admired friend of one of the most powerful men in the world and he was the leader of the Rat Pack, who were considered (by those who didn't like rock'n'roll) the hippest entertainers on the planet. And his own business world was expanding: he was the owner of film and publishing companies, he had a deal with United Artists to distribute any movie that he saw fit to make and he had a growing stake in his personal playground, the Sands. And free at last from his Capitol contract, he even had his own record company, Reprise.

Recording intensively, he used different arrangers for each of his first seven Reprise projects and there was a glut of Sinatra records in 1961 and 1962, when Reprise sought to establish itself while his final Capitol albums were being released. Thus Reprise's *Ring-A-Ding Ding!* (arranged by Johnny Mandel), *I Remember Tommy* (Sy Oliver), *Sinatra Swings* (Billy May), *All Alone* (Gordon Jenkins) and *Sinatra And Strings* (Don Costa) vied with Capitol's *Nice 'N' Easy*, *Sinatra's Swingin' Session!!!* (both Nelson Riddle), *Point Of No Return* (Axel Stordahl) and *Look To Your Heart*, the singles collection. Sales were inevitably divided and Reprise chart positions were steady but not spectacular.

Yet while, as a businessman, he was as busy and powerful as ever – it was around this time that he began to be described throughout the media as **"the Chairman Of The Board"**, a name used in *Playboy* in May 1957 – his artistic career was on a plateau. Sinatra took his recording responsibilities very seriously and the records were generally fine and occasionally excellent; but with many remakes not improving on the earlier versions, and faint evidence that Sinatra's voice was not the instrument it once was, it was generally felt that the records for Reprise were probably not as good as his best Capitol albums. The feeling would become stronger as the decade went on.

Moreover, many of the movies that Sinatra appeared in during the early 1960s suggested a man with dormant talent who preferred having fun and making money to thinking about quality. He acquired a small cameo habit and popped his head over the scenery to little effect in *Pepe*, *The Road To Hong Kong* and *The List Of Adrian Messenger*, and **the Rat Pack films** of the period (*Ocean's 11*, *Sergeants 3*, *4 For Texas* and *Robin And The 7 Hoods* – see pages 310-311) oozed complacency. There was, however, an exception – *The Manchurian Candidate*, a chilling movie in 1962 about brainwashing, communism and assassination that was proof that when Sinatra the actor had the material he could still be compelling.

Meanwhile Sinatra's relationship with the Kennedys was beginning to unravel. The Kennedy camp had started to get nervous, even before JFK's victory, of being involved with someone as controversial as Sinatra, however useful he was, and once the presidency was won the White House kept him at a discreet distance. **Jackie Kennedy**, the First Lady, actively disliked Sinatra, and **Robert Kennedy**, who as the newly-appointed Attorney General had set his sights on tackling organized crime, was reportedly irritated by Peter Lawford's requests – allegedly on behalf of Sinatra – to ease up on Giancana. Moreover, he had received a memo from J. Edgar Hoover flagging up Sinatra's alleged ties with organised crime. To Bobby, Frank was a liability.

JFK in Palm Springs

The President, however, remained fascinated by the singer, quizzing his mistress Judith Campbell for gossip about Sinatra's latest exploits and still phoning him occasionally. And although Sinatra was never invited to any official events at the White House, he had been on a Kennedy family weekend trip (without Jackie) to Hyannisport in September 1961. So when it was announced that JFK would be paying **a visit to Palm Springs** in February 1962, Sinatra assumed that he would be his host and prepared by building extra bungalows and a heliport, paying the builders overtime to work around the clock.

Sinatra was crushed when Peter Lawford told him that the President would be staying with Bing Crosby (a Republican). The official line was that the choice was made for security reasons – Crosby's place backed onto a mountain and Sinatra's was open on all four sides – but the move was a clear attempt by the White House to dissociate itself from Sinatra.

However hurtful this was, Sinatra understood that his own image had become somewhat tarnished over the years, and from the middle of 1962 he made considerable efforts to redress the balance. **A tour of Europe** was organized that would benefit underprivileged children, an orphanage was named after him in Tokyo, and he received honours in Nazareth and Paris and mingled with royalty in London. His new public relations officer, Chuck Moses, made sure that everything was covered in the newspapers. Sinatra even gave some amiable interviews, notably to the British journalist Robin Douglas-Home, which led to the book *Sinatra* (see pages 365–366). A celebrated *Playboy* interview that appeared in January 1963 did much to present Sinatra as an articulate, deep-thinking, compassionate liberal. (The still widely-quoted article, thoroughly approved by Frank, was crafted – questions and answers – by the Reprise advertising man Mike Shore, whom Sinatra considered a genius.) But PR couldn't save him from the disaster that was **Cal-Neva**.

> *"I'm not unmindful of man's seeming need for faith. I'm for whatever gets you through the night, be it prayer, tranquillisers or a bottle of Jack Daniel's."*

FS, QUOTED IN PLAYBOY, JANUARY 1963

In the summer of 1961 Sinatra had opened the **Cal-Neva Lodge**, his own hotel, casino and cabaret resort on Lake Tahoe's Crystal Bay. Built on the California-Nevada border, it allowed gambling on the Nevada side of the resort, but the main attraction was the Celebrity Room, which hosted shows by the top stars of the day, including Eddie Fisher, Dean Martin, Victor Borge and Lena Horne. Sinatra enjoyed playing host to the scores of celebrity visitors and took a close interest in all aspects of the business.

But it wasn't long before various incidents made Cal-Neva a hothouse of controversy. An employee was apparently the victim of an attempted murder on the lodge's front steps. A local deputy sheriff who was married to an ex-girlfriend of Sinatra died in a car accident only weeks after he had an argument with Frank in the kitchens; no accusations were made and no charges were brought, but years later there were still rumours.

Cal-Neva attracted the wrong sort of attention. **The FBI** investigated allegations that there was a system in which prostitutes, flown in from San Francisco, could be ordered as easily as room service. Gaming investigators attempting to monitor the takings were offered bribes but reported the incident instead. And although Sam Giancana was forbidden on the premises of any Nevada casino, he frequented the lodge and was reportedly observed by the FBI both playing golf with and dining with Sinatra. Ostensibly, he was visiting his girlfriend Phyllis, one of The McGuire Sisters, who were singing there; but even though Cal-Neva was officially owned by Sinatra, Hank Sanicola and Sanford Waterman, a bookmaker and ex-manager of Meyer Lansky's casinos in Havana, it was believed – certainly by the FBI – to be backed by silent Mob money.

Giancana's presence at Cal-Neva was reported by the FBI to the Nevada Gaming Commission and in autumn 1963 Sinatra had to answer some awkward questions. Starting with a reasonable manner and a line that he saw him but didn't invite him, Sinatra soon became irritated at the issuing of subpoenas and the refusal of the chief gaming commissioner, **Ed Olsen**, to take an informal approach. He lost his temper on the phone, launching a foul-mouthed tirade that was hard to interpret as anything but a threat. Olsen sought to revoke Sinatra's licence as a result of the Giancana incident, the attempted bribery and the intimidation. Intending at first to fight the charges, Sinatra gave in when it became clear that Olsen's office had been listening to his outburst and had a signed witness statement that gave details of a fight at the lodge involving Giancana. In the absence of a defence, his gambling licence was revoked, and this perceived injustice ate at him for years.

Despite his troubles, for Sinatra's company it was another busy year, with several of his own albums appearing: *Sinatra-Basie*, which featured the first meeting between the singer and the legendary band, and *The Concert Sinatra* and *Sinatra's Sinatra* with Nelson Riddle. There was an ambitious multi-album project called **the Reprise Musical Repertory Theatre**, featuring several musical scores (*Kiss Me Kate*, *Finian's Rainbow*, *Guys And Dolls* and *South Pacific*) in the Sinatra contemporary swing style by a selection of friends, including Dean, Sam, Bing, Jo Stafford and close harmony group The Hi-Lo's. Even the jazz bandleader and composer Duke Ellington and Bing Crosby were signed to Reprise.

But the Cal-Neva episode had left Sinatra with much of his capital tied up in a business that he was no longer allowed to run, so in what appeared to be a life-saving deal he sold a majority share of Reprise Records to Warner Brothers. The end of 1963 saw Sinatra dealing with two further crises. The first, **the assassination of President Kennedy** on November 22, was a national catastrophe, which Sinatra took hard on a personal level. Though he'd been marginalized by the Kennedy administration, which had also persecuted his friends, Sinatra couldn't bring himself to blame JFK, whom he had liked and believed in. He locked himself in his room for days to mourn.

The second crisis was **the kidnapping of Frank Sinatra Jr.** on December 8. He had just launched himself as a singer, very much in the mould of his father, and had even appeared with what was left of The Tommy Dorsey Orchestra. Working that month at a lounge in Lake Tahoe, while he was eating a pre-show meal in his room, he answered the door, expecting room service – but found two kidnappers instead. They tied up and blindfolded his companion and bundled Frank Jr. into a car, driving to a house in Los Angeles. By phone, they demanded $240,000 from Frank Sr., who followed the convoluted delivery instructions and deposited personally the brown paper bag containing used notes; but when he went to the designated spot to collect his son, no one was there and he had to return, shaken, to his distraught family empty handed. His son was eventually dumped on the freeway, alive, was spotted by a patrolman on a road only two miles from ex-wife Nancy's house and was delivered back

Sinatra, in the driveway of his ex-wife's home, talks to the press for the first time after the capture of his son's kidnappers to his family 54 hours after he was taken. The kidnappers were arrested the following day and a hugely relieved Frank Sr. threw a three-day party to celebrate. He sent every FBI officer who had worked on the case a gold watch.

At the trial the kidnappers' defence suggested that it was a stunt to gain more publicity for Frank Jr.'s singing career. This claim was thrown out of court and was later admitted by the kidnappers to be fabricated. Nevertheless, the rumour dogged Frank Jr. for years.

If the events of 1963 took their toll on Sinatra, his work rate in 1964 didn't show it. He recorded *Days Of Wine And Roses,* with Nelson Riddle arranging, and, with Quincy Jones and Count Basie, *It Might As Well Be Swing.* And, for the first (and only) time, he directed a film, the anti-war story **None But The Brave**.

However, after 1963, even those close to Sinatra noticed a change in his mood, a shift that daughter Nancy described as "a push closer to the line between scepticism and cynicism". Always mercurial, as he approached the age of fifty his mood swung more than ever. When elated his generosity was unbounded, but when low he could be short-tempered and cruel. Sinatra would sit with an ailing Joe E. Lewis and wipe his mouth as he ate and would send anonymous financial gifts to those whose misfortunes he had read about; but he would also upend a table in a restaurant if he didn't like the look of the waiter and would throw the plate at his valet if his pasta was not *al dente*.

The situation was not helped by **a near-drowning incident** in May 1964. When bathing off the coast of the Hawaiian island where *None But The Brave* was being shot, Sinatra got into difficulties and after more than half an hour he was dragged from the sea unconscious. The actor **Brad Dexter** is usually cited as having made the rescue, though in daughter Nancy's *An American Legend* Dexter goes unmentioned and neighbours and fire lieutenants are given credit. (Dexter fell out with Sinatra in 1966 while producing *The Naked Runner*, and when he made himself and his unfavourable reminiscences available to Kitty Kelley in the mid-1980s, he was excised from "official" Sinatra histories. The near-drowning episode is one of several examples of the Sinatra estate's accounts being at odds with others.)

Then, while in Italy in the summer of 1965 shooting *Von Ryan's Express*, Sinatra hooked up briefly with **Ava Gardner**, who was shooting *The Bible* nearby. Officially separated for more than ten years, the pair would liaise from time to time, though this particular meeting was a break for her from the drunken, violent temper of her co-star and lover at the time, **George C. Scott**. When Frank saw how frightened Ava was, he apparently had to be restrained from exacting revenge, and made do with hiring bodyguards to watch her for the remainder of the shoot. In September 1965, when they had finished filming their respective movies, and after Ava had suffered another bout of Scott's violence in London, she stayed at Frank's house in Palm Springs to recuperate.

Although his house was still full of pictures of Ava, and although he still cared deeply for her, it seemed to be around this time that Frank could allow the torch he carried for Ava to cool a little. He began to see her dependence on alcohol and attraction to dangerous relationships as a weakness, and one that grew less enticing as she got older. Moreover, Frank had recently been drawn to a charming, elfin young actress called **Mia Farrow**.

Half a century

The press made much of the fact that 49-year-old Frank was running around with 19-year-old Mia. Even the broadcasting legend **Walter Cronkite** was moved to ask Sinatra about her during a CBS television profile, *Sinatra*, for his **50th birthday**, despite the producer's assurance that the subject wouldn't be broached. A furious Sinatra later walked off the set – "the great voice raised to a level seldom heard in a concert hall", remembered Cronkite – before returning to complete the interview. But the programme, broadcast in November 1965 and featuring contributions from Dean, Sammy and daughter Nancy (who talked, to Frank's annoyance, about how her father always "having a marvellous time … bothers me") was essentially respectful, and successful.

Though the movies he shot around this time, including *Marriage On The Rocks* and *Assault On A Queen*, were dull, the latter part of 1965 gave rise to fine Sinatra musical output, much of it of a retrospective or nostalgic nature. There was the lovely ***September Of My Years*** album made with Gordon Jenkins, that celebrated maturity and featured the hit "It Was A Very Good Year". There was the TV special ***A Man And His Music***, which won an Emmy. And there was an elaborately packaged double

King of the hill

SINATRA ON TELEVISION WITH WALTER CRONKITE IN NOVEMBER 1965

album with the same name that won the Grammy for album of the year. The programme and the album were unrelated in content, but both were satisfying attempts at a career summation.

The fanfare heralding Sinatra's 50th birthday had re-established him in the public consciousness as a great entertainer who sang saloon songs, love songs and swing songs better than anyone. But there remained for Sinatra – and for other entertainers of his generation – the question of how to approach a music world increasingly oriented towards youth. He'd survived **Elvis Presley**, and despite famously denouncing rock'n'roll as "degenerate" had even duetted with him on a 1960 TV special; but by 1966, as daughter Nancy reached number one with the suggestive boogaloo of "These Boots Were Made For Walkin'", on Reprise, Sinatra's way was starting to look like the old way.

Mrs Sinatra 3: Mia Farrow

"I really like this one. I'm pushing fifty but, what the hell?
Let's say I've got a good five years left. Why don't I enjoy them?"
FS, 1965

Mia Farrow was born into Hollywood royalty: her father was the film director John Farrow and her mother was Maureen O'Sullivan, a star of the 1930s Tarzan movies. By the time she encountered Frank, Mia was the 19-year-old star of the soap opera **Peyton Place**. The show was shot at the same studios (20th Century Fox) as *Von Ryan's Express* and Mia was hanging around the set in a translucent dress when Frank spotted her. The attraction was mutual. He was intrigued by her naïve purity and she was bowled over by his charisma. "I liked him instantly," she said later. "He rings true, he is what he is." When Mia accepted an offer of a weekend at his house in Palm Springs, the romance between the hipster and the hippie began.

She was the opposite of the women who usually attracted him: skinny ("my measurements are 20-20-20"), unimpressed by wealth, interested in mysticism and yoga, and as fresh as a flower. Frank was amused by and protective of her lack of conventional social grace and Mia was in awe of his worldliness and intrigued by his aloofness.

They tried hard not to make the age difference matter. They shared many romantic hours doing crosswords and watching TV in bed. She called him **"Charlie Brown"**, after the *Peanuts* comic strip character, and he called her "My Mia", "Doll Face" or, after her hair was shorn, "My Little Boy". They had rows about his family not inviting her to Sinatra's 50th birthday party and split in early 1966, but were reunited three months later.

Frank's association with Mia had given him a lease of life that was obvious to those who were close to him, but friends and family were divided over the wisdom of a long-term union. After some hesitation and much press speculation, however, the couple married suddenly in Las Vegas in July 1966 during a break in the filming of the movie he was making, *The Naked Runner*. The ceremony took place in the suite of the manager of the Sands, **Jack Entratter**, in front of a select group of friends, and none of Frank's family was present.

Although some detected a mellower Sinatra, there were flashes of his old cruelty. When Mia attended his engagement at the Sands in November 1966, he introduced his new wife to the audience. "Yeah, I sure got married," he went on to say. "I finally found a broad I could cheat on." This was seemingly a joke, sending up an argument that they had earlier had in which she suspected him of being unfaithful, but Mia was understandably humiliated. Ironically, when she was in Europe in the spring of 1967 making the movie *A Dandy In Aspic*, Sinatra convinced himself after seeing a promo shot that she was having an affair with her co-star **Laurence Harvey**. Even though she flew back to assure him otherwise, he flew into a classic Sinatra rage.

Their different outlooks on life would soon take their toll. Mia later wrote of their lack of "understanding in everyday life as well as the major, deeper themes". To adapt Sinatra's 1981 song "I Loved Her", she was Beatles, he was Basie; she was marijuana, he was JD; she was 21, he was 50.

Sinatra had discussed the subject of marriage in an interview for *Life* magazine in 1965. "If I would marry again, it would have to be somebody out of show business or who will get out of show business," he said. "I feel I'm a fairly good provider. All I ask is that my wife look after me and I'll see that she's looked after." He'd already, however, had to compromise that ideal with Mia, who was happy to look after him some of the time but was also determined to have her own career. She had agreed against her better judgement to appear opposite Sinatra in his forthcoming movie *The Detective* ("if I were his leading lady," she had said, "too many people would think he had handed me the role"). But when *Rosemary's Baby*, the film she was working on in autumn 1967, ran over schedule, he insisted that she leave Roman Polanski's picture to fulfil their arrangement and she refused. Sinatra's response was to send his lawyer, Mickey Rudin, to serve her with divorce papers in her trailer – written in her name.

Mia was devastated. A few weeks later she asked Sinatra if she could come back, and she was allowed to spend Christmas with Frank and a group of friends at Palm Springs. But then Sinatra didn't call – and she knew it was over. She agreed to a quick Mexican divorce, but refused to cite Sinatra's "mental cruelty" as the ground, insisting on mere "incompatibility". She also refused a financial settlement, saying that she just wanted to remain friends, which they did. In February 1968 she went to meditate in India with **Maharishi Mahesh Yogi** and The Beatles.

She went on to marry the conductor and pianist André Previn and had a long-term relationship with **Woody Allen**, which ended when she discovered that he had been having an affair with her step-daughter. Sinatra, always supportive from a distance, apparently offered to have Allen's legs broken.

MIA FARROW AS A MYSTERY GUEST ON THE TV SHOW WHAT'S MY LINE IN
NOVEMBER 1966. FRANK IS ON THE PANEL, SECOND FROM THE LEFT

His answer was to explore tentatively modern styles and songs. This was
a commercial tactic that he had employed to some extent throughout his
career, but whereas obviously fashionable tunes such as "Bop! Goes My
Heart" (1949), "Castle Rock" (1951) and "Everybody's Twistin'" (1962)
had been opportunistic singles, contemporary sounds were now creeping
onto the albums. Those produced by Jimmy Bowen, such as *Sinatra '65*
and *That's Life*, dabbled with R&B and country ballads, in the style of
Ray Charles. In early 1966 he had his biggest hit for years with a soft rock
ballad, **"Strangers In The Night"**, but later that year the album of the
same name combined its mushy single, Petula Clark covers and hard
swingers. However, while some of Sinatra's records during this period had
this Jekyll and Hyde side to them, they were popular with the public, and
the high-quality, old-style theme albums such as ***Moonlight Sinatra*** were,
in comparison, ignored.

Spending time with a woman thirty years his junior not only put Frank
closer to what was happening; it also gave him a new gentleness. He
hinted as much in the Cronkite interview. "I've always admired people

who are gentle and have great patience," Sinatra said. "And, apparently, what I've done is aped these people and begun to follow down that kind of line."

But he wasn't following that line in June 1966 at the Polo Lounge of the Beverly Hills Hotel, when a local businessman, **Frederick Weisman**, asked Sinatra's party of ten, which was celebrating Dean Martin's birthday, to keep the noise down. After the incident escalated into violence the complainant ended up in hospital with a fractured skull having been hit on the head with a telephone, according to one account. Weisman recovered after two weeks of treatment but no charges were brought.

After months of speculation, and having been temporarily separated in the spring, in July 1966 Frank and Mia suddenly **married**. Frank Jr., whose relationship with his father had been distant for some years and who even boycotted the family party held for Sinatra's 50th birthday, first heard about the wedding when asked for his reaction by a reporter. That night in his nightclub act he announced: "I'm going to devote exactly five minutes to my father because, as he once confided to me in a moment of weakness, that's exactly how much time he devoted to me."

Sinatra's output at this time was mixed. Another TV special, *A Man And His Music II*, was broadcast in December 1966 and was a little modish – pop star daughter Nancy was a guest – but kept up the standard that was set by the first programme. In 1967 a disastrous mish-mash of an album, *The World We Knew*, was offset by two notable collaborations with legends of popular music – *Francis Albert Sinatra & Antonio Carlos Jobim*, a surprising classic and probably as good a record as he ever made, and, with Duke Ellington, *Francis A. & Edward K.*. He also made another showing at the top of the singles charts with the gooey love song **"Somethin' Stupid"**, a duet with daughter Nancy that struck some as rather inappropriate.

In May 1967 the issue of Sinatra's connection with the Mafia re-emerged when Frank was chosen by **the Italian-American Anti-Defamation League** to lead a campaign against TV programmes such as *The Untouchables* that tended to give their gangster characters Italian names and attitudes. A retired police officer, Ralph Salerno, rehashed all of Sinatra's alleged underworld associations in *The New York Times*, suggesting that he was the last person the Italian-American Anti-Defamation league needed to speak for them.

Endings

Though still a draw like no other in Las Vegas, Sinatra's special relationship with **the Sands** came to an abrupt end in September 1967. As a part-owner and the entertainment legend who had helped to build the place, he had become accustomed to the perk of getting credit in the casino when he asked for it, keeping the winnings if he won but ignoring his marker if he lost. The wealthy eccentric Howard Hughes had taken over and a change of owner had resulted in a change of policy; but no one told Sinatra. When he was entertaining a group of astronauts at the tables after his show, he asked for credit and was refused; and his response was to go on the rampage, railing and cursing at the staff and (with a terrified Mia by his side) driving a golf cart into the lobby and smashing it into a massive plate-glass window. An ensuing fistfight with the executive vice-president of the Sands, **Carl Cohen**, resulted in Sinatra losing two front-tooth caps and walking out of the Sands forever. The next time that he appeared in Vegas, in 1968, he was along the Strip at Caesar's Palace.

With Mia resolutely pursuing her own career against Frank's wishes, his marriage started to disintegrate, and so did he. Sinatra went through a period of **finishing relationships**. Jack Entratter, who had given Mia away at the wedding, was excommunicated after the Carl Cohen incident. Brad Dexter was fired as a film producer for Sinatra Enterprises, one of his several companies, when he wouldn't acquiesce to Frank's scheduling demands on *The Naked Runner*. When Sinatra heard reports of George Jacobs, his faithful valet for 14 years, dancing with Mia, whom he had come upon by accident in a nightclub, he was fired and never spoken to again.

At this point, in 1967, when Mia refused to leave the over-running shoot of *Rosemary's Baby* to join him in *The Detective*, he ended the marriage. But it didn't make him happy. By the middle of 1968 he was depressed and ill. Sweating in his bed with a temperature of 104°, his assistants made pessimistic calls to his family and Frank received visits from his ex-wives, children and parents. "Everyone needs a little loving when they feel bad about themselves," his mother Dolly later said, when he'd recovered from what turned out to be a dose of pneumonia. "He's a little boy, he feels lonely."

In January 1969 Frank's father **Marty** died at the age of 74 in Houston from a ruptured aortic aneurysm. Frank spent many hours with his

King of the hill

father during Marty's final days and soon after his death raised more than $800,000 to found the Martin Anthony Sinatra Medical Education Centre next to the Palm Springs Desert Hospital. He also persuaded his mother to live next to him in Palm Springs in a specially built condo complete with state-of-the-art fittings and a team of domestic staff.

Professionally, Frank had increasingly been trying to find his place in the changing entertainment world, with variable results. In December 1967 his TV special *A Man And His Music + Ella + Jobim* had been a quiet classic with guests Ella Fitzgerald and Antonio Carlos Jobim; but only eleven months later *Francis Albert Sinatra Does His Thing* featured 52-year-old Frank in a Nehru jacket and love beads and cavorting with the psychedelic soul pop group The 5th Dimension. His album *Cycles* that year featured uncomfortable attempts at tunes written by a new generation of songwriters, including Joni Mitchell and Jimmy Webb, and fared only moderately.

But there were also projects in the late 1960s that fitted Sinatra more happily. His last three films – *Tony Rome*, *The Detective* and *Lady In Cement* – had him playing tough crime investigators with a customised swagger and at the end of 1968 he recorded one of his most famous pieces, **"My Way"**. A French pop tune written by the ex-teen star Paul Anka, with magnificently overblown, self-regarding lyrics, it was an enormous hit in 1969 – and in Britain it was in the charts for 120 weeks – and it was responsible for keeping Sinatra and his myth as vivid in the public consciousness as it ever had been.

That vivid image was assisted in the late 1960s and early 1970s by the press coverage of the circles in which Sinatra moved, the contrasting nature of which had never been more pronounced. Forced by subpoena to testify before a state investigation into organized crime, Sinatra claimed in February 1970 not to know anybody involved with Cosa Nostra or the Mafia; and that if he did know them – "I meet all kinds of people" was his regular shrug – he did not know of their involvement in organised crime. And yet in May 1970 he was in London performing in high-profile charity concerts and hobnobbing with **Princess Margaret**, and by July he was campaigning for the election of **Ronald Reagan** as Governor of California and on his way to ingratiating himself again with the most powerful person in the land.

In September 1970 Sinatra got into a fracas at **Caesar's Palace** in an incident that had an identical upshot to the episode at the Sands three

Sinatra's political change

"The older you get, the more conservative you get."
FS to daughter Tina

Sinatra's decision to support the Democrat **Hubert Humphrey** in his battle against Richard Nixon for the White House in 1968 was not a popular one. Humphrey, as Lyndon B. Johnson's Vice-President, was part of the pro-Vietnam circle and many of Sinatra's fellow liberal performers backed Bobby Kennedy (until his assassination in June 1968) or Eugene McCarthy. And although Sinatra raised much money and gave tips on TV presentation, Humphrey's camp must have wondered what Sinatra's endorsement was worth when the old complaints of the singer's underworld associations appeared in Justice Department memos and *Wall Street Journal* articles. "Once you get Sinatra on your side in politics," said the satirist Mort Sahl, "you're out of business." Sure enough, in November 1968, Nixon won.

In the summer of 1970 Frank made the surprise decision to back **Ronald Reagan** – a man whose politics and personal qualities he had previously scorned – in the arch-Republican's bid to be re-elected as Governor of California. The Democratic candidate, Jesse Unruh, had been a follower of Bobby Kennedy and had not been helpful during Humphrey's unsuccessful campaign. Despite Sinatra's protestations that he now backed individuals

years previously. On this occasion, an IRS investigation into the Palace's financial arrangements had made the managers wary of what might have been construed as irregular activity and, once again, Frank was refused credit. An ugly incident ensued which culminated in the casino manager (and ex-partner in Cal-Neva) **Sanford Waterman** pulling a gun on him. The singer stormed out. Later, he told the press that he was through with Vegas. "I have no intentions of going back," he said. "I've suffered enough indignities."

He had suffered indignities elsewhere too. Although the album *My Way* did well in 1969 on the back of the single, other albums during this period fared less well. *A Man Alone* and *Watertown* were bold but unpopular attempts at a modern Sinatra "concept" album (see page 215–217), while the blend of Jobim songs and modern folk pop on *Sinatra And Company* captured no one's imagination. All three albums sold

rather than parties, this was not how the move was interpreted. "They say your hatred of Senator Bob Kennedy was so great," wrote the entertainer and TV talk show host Steve Allen in an open letter to Sinatra, "that you have waited a long time to get revenge." Allen offered Sinatra the forum of his show to explain himself, but Frank ignored it, and instead backed candidates from Democratic and Republican parties for a variety of posts in California and New York.

He later confused his critics further by vocally criticizing **President Nixon** – "He's running this country into the ground, he scares me" – but cultivating a close relationship with the Vice-President, **Spiro Agnew**, who became a regular guest at Frank's home in Palm Springs. Frank often accompanied him on the official plane, Air Force 2. And they found much to complain about together, such as the radical protest generation – "rebellion without a cause", as Sinatra put it – and the amorality of modern American life.

His political about-turn was complete when he supported Nixon's re-election campaign in 1972, and by 1973 he was singing at the White House. And even after Agnew and Nixon had resigned in disgrace, the former for income tax evasion and the latter after Watergate, Sinatra remained loyal to them as friends. "People make mistakes," he said. "Even Presidents make mistakes."

poorly. Meanwhile his appearance in the ribald western *Dirty Dingus Magee* in 1970 was ignored by the public and slammed by critics.

In March 1971, tired and deflated by personal and professional developments, Sinatra announced his retirement from show business. In June he gave his farewell performance at the Los Angeles Music Centre in front of the Reagans, the Agnews, Henry Kissinger, wife Nancy and their children and scores of show business friends. The media appreciated the momentousness of his withdrawal, with a writer in *Life* magazine declaring that the final line of the final show, from "Angel Eyes", was the most stunning moment he had witnessed on stage: "Excuse me while I disappear…"

The same month, several congressmen, including John Tunney and Hubert Humphrey, saw fit to enter fulsome tributes to the retiring entertainer in the official account of the proceedings of Congress,

MARIO PUZO AND THE GODFATHER

"He prostituted his own business making up such a phoney story."
FS ON MARIO PUZO, 1969

That Sinatra's public image was still unsavoury in the late 1960s was partly due to the rumours surrounding Mario Puzo's bestselling Mafia novel **The Godfather**. Turned into a film in 1971, it included a fictional singer of Italian extraction named Johnny Fontane who is assisted in his career by the intervention of the Mob, and specifically Don Corleone, the Godfather. Fontane is chasing a movie role but the producer is not interested in casting him, despite an attempt to persuade him by Corleone's lawyer. The producer wakes up one morning to find himself lying in bed next to the decapitated head of his beloved racehorse. Fontane is cast. When asked how he got the film producer to change his mind, Corleone says that he made him an offer he couldn't refuse.

Puzo admitted that he had based some of the scenario on the usual rumours surrounding Sinatra, the Dorsey contract and the *From Here To Eternity* hearsay. Sinatra felt that in doing so he merely perpetuated the damaging gossip for the sake of cheap sensationalism. Happening upon the author one evening in Chasen's restaurant in Hollywood, Sinatra subjected him to a verbal tirade, the ferocity of which even surprised Sinatra's bodyguard, Jilly Rizzo. Puzo left the restaurant, shocked at the attack, with words from Sinatra ringing in his ears: "Go ahead and choke."

the *Congressional Record*. Tunney wrote that he was a "man of deep feeling, a man who in a thousand silent acts has worked to better the lives of those around him". For Humphrey his talent was "a magical instrument with the power to help the unfortunate and the infirm as well as mark the memorable milestones in the international world of entertainment".

King of the hill

SPORTS FAN SINATRA AT THE FRAZIER–ALI FIGHT AT MADISON SQUARE GARDEN, NEW YORK, IN MARCH 1971, TAKING PHOTOGRAPHS FOR LIFE MAGAZINE

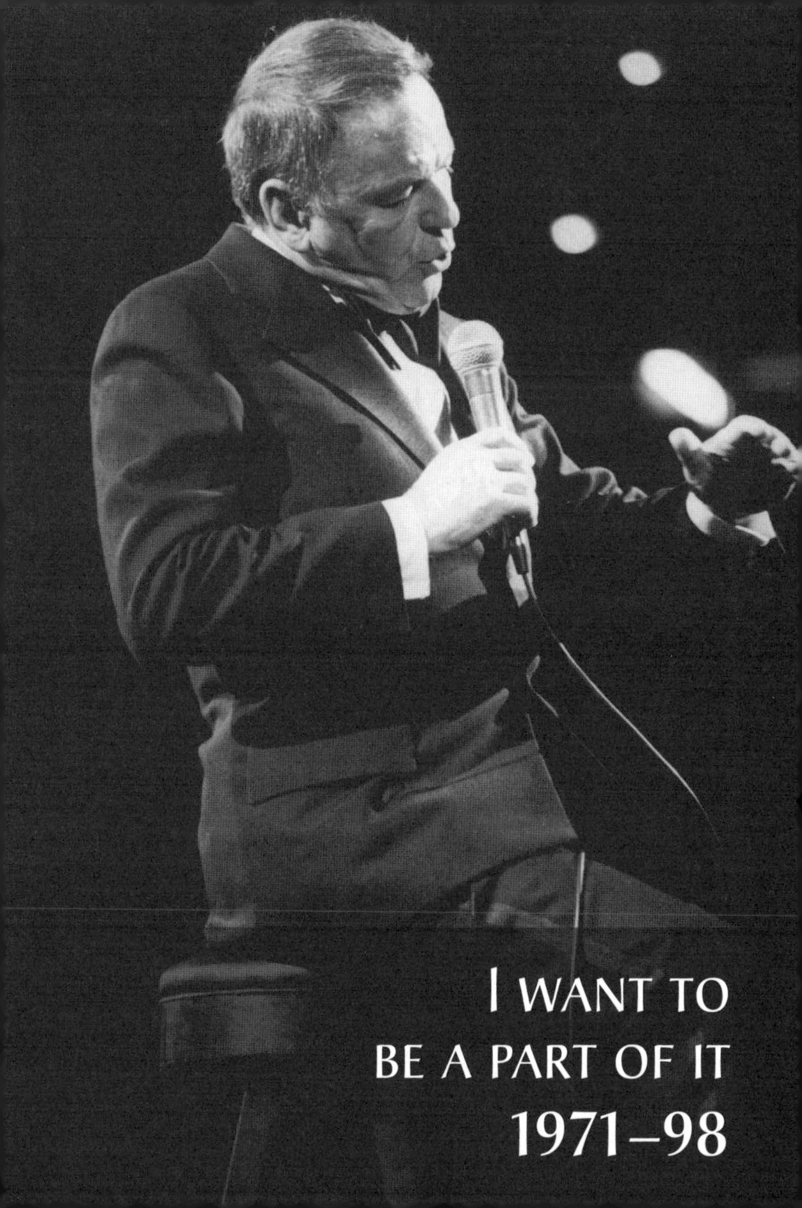

I WANT TO
BE A PART OF IT
1971–98

I want to
be a part of it

*"I don't know how to stop doing things.
I gotta do something."*

FS, 1983

Aside from singing a dozen songs at a fund-raiser for the Italian-American Civil Rights League in November 1971, Sinatra seemed to be taking his retirement seriously. He did a little painting, appeared at some charity golf tournaments and took some long holidays.

But in June 1972 a congressional committee wanted to talk to him on television about his investment in 1962 of $50,000 in Berkshire Downs, a Massachusetts racetrack part-owned by the Mafiosi **Raymond Patriarca** and **Tommy Lucchese**. Amid the usual non-committal responses, he admitted to having met Lucchese a few times, but when he was asked if he knew that Lucchese was a mobster, he went on the offensive. "That's his problem, not mine," he snarled. "Let's dispense with that kind of question."

The committee backed down and some newspapers carried amused reports along the lines of "House Committee Appears Before Sinatra". But that wasn't enough for Frank, who was furious with the public hoopla of the process. He employed the journalist **Pete Hamill** to ghost an essay that appeared in *The New York Times* in July 1972, questioning the validity of an investigation procedure "in which facts are confused with rumor, gossip and innuendo, and where reputations and character can be demolished in front of the largest possible audiences".

SINATRA THE OUTLAW

Aside from the Mafia associations and shady business dealings that dogged his image, Sinatra frequently walked the line that separates common notions of acceptable and non-acceptable. Part of the problem was an inability to deal with being told what to do – by anyone, whether a woman or a policeman. But if he was sometimes provoked, only he was responsible for his reactions.

According to legend, Sinatra was influenced during his fancily-clad Hoboken days by being roughed up by a couple of **policemen**, who were convinced that he had stolen his clothing. "He's a cop hater," observed Humphrey Bogart later. "If he doesn't know who you are and you ask him a question, he thinks you're a cop."

Sinatra once indicated himself why he was so suspicious of authority. "You know what we all thought growing up?" he said to Pete Hamill. "We thought *everybody* was on the take. We *knew* the cops were taking. They were right in front of us. But we thought the priests were on the take, the schoolteachers, the guy in the marriage licence bureau, everybody."

This helps to explain his evasive – or in some cases aggressive – answers when being questioned officially about his **underworld connections**. He refused to recognise the authority of anyone asking him questions about anything.

Sinatra's retirement saw him complete his political *volte-face* from Democrat to Republican. He backed Nixon in the presidential race of 1972, much to the dismay of his daughter Tina, who was actively campaigning for George McGovern. When Nixon won, Sinatra was invited to stage his inaugural ball, just as he had for President Kennedy – but he refused. "He simply doesn't want to be treated as a performer anymore," said his publicist, Jim Mahoney.

Meanwhile, since his marriage to Mia, Frank had enjoyed several affairs, but none had blossomed into anything substantial. Among his conquests was **Lee Remick**, his co-star in *The Detective*, who panicked and broke up with him by leaving a note on his front door. There was also the cultured and beautiful **Edie Goetz**, who was not only the widow of Frank's friend Bill Goetz, a co-founder of 20th Century Fox, but also the daughter of Louis B. Mayer. She enjoyed his attention for a while until he suggested marriage, whereupon she reportedly laughed, "Why Frank, I couldn't possibly marry you, you're nothing but a hoodlum." He left the room and never spoke to her again. In the early 1970s Sinatra dated the actresses Eva Gabor (sister of Zsa Zsa), Hope Lange and future *Dallas* star Victoria Principal.

The only woman to engage his attention for long at this time was **Barbara Marx**. The wife of Zeppo – the good-looking Marx Brother who provided romantic relief in their early movies – she filed for divorce in December 1972, and she and Frank were then regularly seen together, most conspicuously at Nixon's pre-inaugural parties in Washington in January 1973. It was there that an incident involving Barbara took place when Sinatra ran into **Maxine Cheshire**, the society reporter for *The Washington Post* who had asked Frank at an earlier Agnew gathering, "Do you think your alleged associations with the Mafia will prove the same embarrassment to Vice-President Agnew that it was to the Kennedy administration?"

SINATRA WITH BARBARA MARX, THEN HIS FIANCÉE, IN JUNE 1976

Although he sidestepped this question, when, at the Fairfax hotel during the pre-inaugurals, Cheshire had the brazenness to question Barbara about her marital status, Sinatra snapped. "You've been laying down for two dollars all your life," he snarled, depositing a couple of notes in her hand and then insulting her further. Cheshire was outraged; Barbara was proud of him. The Government was perturbed enough by the incident and the ensuing media uproar to consider cancelling Sinatra's White House appearance in front of the Italian Prime Minister, **Giulio Andreotti**. But it went ahead, in April 1973, and Sinatra the performer triumphed. "Once in a while there is a moment when there is magic in the room, when a performer, singer and entertainer is able to capture us all," said Nixon. "Frank Sinatra did that tonight."

Ol' Blue Eyes Is Back

Encouraged by the President and by 30,000 letters from fans urging him to return to work, Sinatra was back in the studio by June, with Gordon Jenkins and Don Costa. Coining a catchphrase, Sinatra called the ensuing album and TV special *Ol' Blue Eyes Is Back*. Some critics were delighted. "We thought we were through writing love letters to Frank Sinatra," confessed the *New York Daily News*, "but here we go again." But for others the product fell short of the hype. "A vocal has-been," thundered *The Toronto Globe*, "ripping off those who care about his music rather than his personality."

His voice on record, separated from the charisma that could shine through only in person, had lost much of its flexibility and control – and he knew it. As regards his vocal instrument he had "let everything go, and it all fell down". Though revitalized by hundreds of live appearances in what might be called the third phase of his career, he released only one more studio album during the 1970s, *Some Nice Things I've Missed* in 1974. It was an admission by omission that his best recording years were long behind him.

Meanwhile, more than three years after Sinatra stormed out of Las Vegas, Sanford Waterman had been sacked from **Caesar's Palace**, leaving the way open for Frank to return, which he did in January and June 1974, playing to capacity crowds. Guests received medallions inscribed "Hail Sinatra. The Noblest Roman Has Returned" and the city of Las Vegas gave him its "Man of the Year" award.

His press remained mixed and Sinatra, as ever, bristled. While most journalists admitted that he still had a singular way with a song, a significant number declared that he was over the hill. He responded during his performances with regular snipes at reporters, and in particular the women. Barbara Walters was ridiculed in his act as "the ugliest broad on television" and he suggested that Rona Barrett was "so ugly, her mother had to tie a pork chop around her neck just to get the dog to play with her". When the German newspapers called him a "super-gangster" he cancelled the tour and ranted on stage in London. "I could have answered and told reporters to 'look to the sins of your fathers'," he spat from the stage of the **Royal Albert Hall**. "I could have mentioned Dachau."

His battle with the fourth estate continued in **Australia** in July when, having been irritated by the tone of the news coverage about his imminent arrival, he laid into the press from the stage of Melbourne's Festival Hall, calling them "bums", "parasites", "fags" and "buck-and-a-half hookers" – an old favourite. The next day the Australian Journalists' Association demanded an apology, and was supported by the Stagehands' Union, the Waiters' Union and the Transport Union. Unable to get his shows set up, or be served, or be transported, Sinatra had to cancel the tour, and merely perform on a TV special. He issued a semi-retraction – "I did not intend any general reflection upon the moral character of the working members of the Australian media" – just to get out of the country.

It wasn't much better at home. At the much-trumpeted televised concert from Madison Square Garden in October 1974, *The Main Event*, he delivered a particularly coarse performance, though typical for the period, and like other live appearances it divided the critics. Rex Reed called him a "bore" and one performance was described in *Women's Wear Daily* as being replete with "self-destructive vulgarity" and "ego-infested arrogance". But Thomas Thompson in the upmarket women's magazine *McCall's* wrote: "He fascinates. He endures. He commits excesses, but he has the talent and the charm to back them up. Frank Sinatra will not go silently into the night, and I, for one, am rather glad."

Thompson clearly spoke for many. Throughout the 1970s, on US and European tours, as well as his regular Las Vegas residencies, crowds

Mrs Sinatra 4: Barbara Marx

"He turns every day into Christmas."
BARBARA SINATRA, 1976

In the early 1970s Barbara was a near neighbour and regular visitor to Frank's complex at Palm Springs, and he admired her amiability, tennis skills and blonde good looks: she had been a model, a Californian beauty queen, a beauty school proprietor and a Las Vegas showgirl. After marrying **Zeppo Marx** in 1959, she settled into a life of Palm Springs racquet clubs, secure in the knowledge that she and the son from her first marriage were well provided for. After falling for Frank – "there's no way to avoid that flirtation, no way" – she divorced Zeppo and became Sinatra's constant companion, serving as cheerful hostess, accompanying him everywhere and tolerating his mood swings.

Unfortunately, **Frank's mother** could not stand her son's new girlfriend. Dolly suspected Barbara to be a gold-digger and was openly hostile to her whenever they were together. Weary of his mother's disapproval and of Barbara's desire for marriage, Frank ended the relationship towards the end of 1974. But they were back together soon after his reported dalliance with Jackie Onassis, and announced in May 1976 that in October they would tie the knot. In a ruse to throw the media off the trail, they married beforehand, in July, at what the guests thought was an engagement party.

No one in Frank's family was happy with the new marriage. Frank Jr. claimed a prior singing engagement on the day of the wedding. Tina and her sister Nancy were hurt when they realized that their father would never now return to their mother, who Frank had been dating again before deciding to marry Barbara.

On the surface the Sinatras were a happy, jet-setting couple with a glittering, respectable social life. Frank never passed up an opportunity to publicly toast the "love of my life, Barbara", and the couple founded the Barbara Sinatra Children's Center, for victims of abuse. But if daughter Tina is to be believed (see pages 374–375), the marriage was a cold union that not only alienated Frank from his children but also plunged him into inert domestic misery.

clamoured to be at his shows and gave him standing ovations every night. Though he often performed on the same bill as other show business legends such as Count Basie, Ella Fitzgerald and Sarah Vaughan, and comedians Milton Berle, Pat Henry and John Denver, Sinatra's set was usually considered the highlight.

I want to be a part of it

His **charitable work** also became conspicuous and his energetic performing served many good causes. Among the bodies to benefit from his fundraising concerts in the mid-1970s were the Muscular Dystrophy Association, the Frank Sinatra Youth Center for Arab and Jewish Children in Israel, the Eisenhower Medical Center in Palm Springs and St Jude Children's Research Center in Memphis, where the Frank Sinatra Child Care Unit was established.

And the honours rolled in. In the coming years there was Israel's Medal of Valor, the Medallion of Citizenship from the city of Chicago and the Cavaliere Ufficiale, the highest award from the Italian government. He was also named the Songwriters of America's **Entertainer of the Century**.

The romance with Barbara Marx ebbed and flowed during the early 1970s and during a separation period Frank had various liaisons, including an evening with JFK's ex-wife, **Jackie Onassis**. She attended a performance of Sinatra's at the Uris Theatre in New York in September 1975, having had dinner with Frank beforehand, and reportedly spent the night in his room at the Waldorf Towers. But if she had briefly conquered her natural antipathy towards him, it soon returned and she subsequently froze him out, refusing his calls and messages. The Sinatra biographer J. Randall Taraborrelli ventures that eventually a previously oblivious Jackie was told by friends about Frank's role in JFK's Hollywood liaisons. "Something happened between the two of them, that I can tell you," Sammy Davis Jr. told Taraborrelli. "But what it was, I got no idea, 'cept it was big."

Frank and Barbara Marx reunited and were married in July 1976; meanwhile Dolly, always feisty and single-minded, had become an obstreperous, argumentative old woman. But she was also loved dearly by Frank and his children and they were devastated when the small private plane carrying her to his engagement at Caesar's Palace in January 1977 crashed into **Mt San Gorgonio**, killing Dolly and her friend, and the pilot and co-pilot.

In an effort to comfort her husband, Barbara suggested that Dolly, who had become increasingly religious, might be pacified in the afterlife if their marriage was recognized by the Catholic Church. This would mean Frank returning to Catholicism and Barbara converting, and the annulment of Frank's marriage to Nancy. (Those to Ava and Mia were not Catholic ceremonies and would therefore be irrelevant to the process.) The annulment was granted in 1978 and Frank and Barbara **remarried** accordingly that same year. This was somehow kept from the press until the following year Frank was spotted receiving communion, prompting the *Los Angeles Herald Examiner* to ask: "Did Frank Make The Vatican An Offer It Couldn't Refuse?"

The issue hurt Frank's children, who already felt marginalized by his new life and were concerned that the move would somehow make them illegitimate. It didn't, but the rift between the Sinatra children and his new wife deepened.

Throughout the 1970s the rumours (and sporadic instances) of his return to the studio led Sinatra connoisseurs to expect and hope for a new album. It eventually came in 1980 in the form of *Trilogy*, an ambitious themed triple album: *Past* (standards, arranged by Billy May), *Present* (pop tunes, mainly with Don Costa) and *Future* (an original song suite composed by Gordon Jenkins). Most reviewers wondered why he hadn't stuck to standards, but sales were healthy and from the *Present* album came **"Theme From *New York, New York*"**. It became another strident Sinatra anthem that lodged in the public's imagination, and from this point onwards he was happily obliged to sing the new theme song at every one of his concerts.

A much better record was his album from 1981, **She Shot Me Down**, an affecting set of deep, dark torch songs that suited his ravaged voice. To some critics it was Sinatra's best album for nearly fifteen years, but the public felt otherwise and it stalled in the lower reaches of the charts, which led Sinatra to lose interest in records for a few years.

Meanwhile he had dipped back into acting by reprising his tough but tortured cop routine for the 1977 TV movie **Contract On Cherry Street** and the 1980 film *The First Deadly Sin,* his final starring role, but what really interested him was winning back the gaming licence he had lost in 1963. Knowing that this would involve his past being raked over, Sinatra gambled that preparation, chutzpah and having the Reagans, among other luminaries, as character references would see him through. With Sam Giancana, Ed Olsen and the Kennedys having died, Judith Campbell not called to testify and the testimony of Phyllis McGuire ignored, Sinatra survived more than five hours of questioning from the Nevada Gaming Commission.

Some old stories were dealt with – the 1947 trip to Havana ("to find sunshine"), Giancana ("I never had anything to do with him business-

I want to be a part of it

Sinatra performs at President Reagan's inaugural gala in January 1981

wise and rarely, *rarely* socially"), and Carl Cohen ("A dislike was formed by two people and there was a scuffle"). And some new stories were dealt with – most notably the backstage photo from **the Westchester Premier Theater** in 1976 where he has his arms around Mafiosi ("I didn't even know their names, let alone their backgrounds").

The performance, televised by CNN, though undoubtedly intended to be a definitive straightening of the record and an attempt to iron out the creases in **the Sinatra myth**, fell short of being entirely candid. But it was good enough for the Nevada Gaming Commission, and he got his licence.

The 1980s and early 1990s were a constant round of sold-out tours, fundraising benefits and official honours, starting with **the inaugural gala for President Reagan** in 1981, which Sinatra produced and directed. He worked as hard in his late sixties and seventies as he ever had, buoyed and rejuvenated every night by the music and the audiences. On stage he was still commanding, charismatic and unshakably confident. But his vocal powers were diminishing, and he was less assured in the studio; the album *LA Is My Lady*, made with Quincy Jones in 1984, disappointed him and most listeners, despite the all-star band and the polished arrangements.

The publication in 1986 of Kitty Kelley's unofficial 500-page biography *His Way* (see pages 367–368) was beyond disappointing: it was traumatic. Kelley related every unsavoury event, rumour and insinuation that had dogged Sinatra's career, and most humiliating of all was her depiction of Dolly performing illegal abortions, an aspect of Sinatra's past that to most people was unfamiliar. Sinatra was livid. His failed legal attempt to stop publication, claiming that only he "owned" the right to his own story, contributed juicy publicity to the book, so he instructed his family and friends not even to acknowledge it with a defence. Naturally, *His Way* was a best seller. His daughter Nancy had just written *Frank Sinatra: My Father* – an updated version, *Frank Sinatra: An American Legend* (see page 368), was published in 1995 – but in keeping silent in the wake of Kelley's book, she wrote later, "We nearly strangled on our pain and anger."

As Sinatra carried on working, many of his friends and contemporaries passed away in the middle of the 1980s, including Grace Kelly, Don Costa, Count Basie, Nelson Riddle and Buddy Rich. In 1987 Dean Martin's son Dino died when he crashed into the same mountain that had taken Dolly Sinatra's life ten years earlier.

The final fling

In an effort to distract their heartbroken friend, Sinatra and Sammy Davis Jr. persuaded Martin to join them for some shows. When the **"Together Again Tour"** was announced in December 1987 the return of the Rat Pack was big news. But the press conference did not bode well. "Is there any way we can call this whole thing off?" asked Martin. He got a laugh, but he wasn't kidding. He struggled to remember words during rehearsals and when the first shows came around in March 1988 it was clear that his heart wasn't in it. He lasted just over a week and then stopped. Liza Minnelli took his place – and the tour, renamed **"The Ultimate Event"**, was a huge success.

In November 1989 Sinatra sang at a televised all-star celebration of Sammy Davis Jr.'s 60 years in show business. Davis had just had throat cancer diagnosed and six months later he died. Ava Gardner had died in January 1990, and Frank dealt with the losses in what had become his customary way: he grieved and then he worked. He toured during the summer with the comedian Don Rickles and in 1991 with Steve Lawrence and Eydie Gormé in what was billed as **"Frank Sinatra's Diamond Jubilee World Tour"**.

It was on this tour that audiences started to see evidence of confusion in Sinatra. Introductions would ramble and words would go astray. Lyrics were present on teleprompters but the cataracts in his eyes didn't make reading them easy.

In 1991 his daughter **Tina** became involved with upholding the Sinatra legacy with the publication of *A Man And His Art*, a book about his private paintings. She also produced the five-hour TV mini-series *Sinatra*, a project that had been years in the preparation and was broadcast in November 1992. Though dismissed by some as a whitewash – her father had approved the script – it was more candid, for example in its portrayal of his friendship with Sam Giancana, than might have been expected.

It was even more surprising – certainly to Frank – when the 77-year-old crooner reached number one in the *Billboard* charts in the autumn of 1993 with his new album ***Duets***. The idea of rock and pop celebrities recording Sinatra standards with the old man himself hit the spot for a new generation of fans who regarded him as a vintage king of cool. ***Duets II*** came a year later, and was almost as popular, and while seasoned Sinatra followers were mostly unimpressed with the records themselves, Frank was delighted. And no one could deny that it was extraordinary for the singer to be back on top after 54 years in the business.

> *"Frank's the chairman of bad attitude.*
> *Rock'n'roll players have been tough,*
> *but this guy is boss. The chairman of boss …*
> *I'm not going to mess with him."*

BONO INTRODUCING FS AT THE GRAMMYS, MARCH 1994

At **the Grammy awards** in March 1994, having been introduced by Bono, who sang "I've Got You Under My Skin" on *Duets*, Sinatra was honoured with the legend award. But for Frank the ceremony was a mild embarrassment: he was not asked to perform, which he complained about, and was cut off mid-speech as he started to blather, apparently by his own press agent. Despite his need for performances and sporadic triumphs, he was starting to realize that the end was near.

A few days after the Grammys, while singing "My Way" in Richmond, Virginia, he collapsed on stage through overheating and dehydration. In April 1994 he told the audience at Radio City Music Hall that "this may well be the last time we will be together", though he fulfilled 40 more concert commitments that year. His **final performance** was on February 25, 1995, at a private party for 1200 invited guests on the last day of the Frank Sinatra Desert Classic golf tournament. *Esquire* magazine judged the 79-year-old to be "clear, tough, on the money" and in "absolute control". His final song: "The Best Is Yet To Come."

At the end of 1995 Dean Martin died, just as Frank hit 80. Barbara produced an odd TV special, ***Sinatra: 80 Years My Way***, featuring rappers and rockers, but Frank wasn't in the mood, and neither were his children, who refused to have anything to do with it. Tina and Nancy also stayed away when Barbara and Frank renewed their vows in July 1996.

SINATRA, WITH WIFE BARBARA, CELEBRATING HIS 80TH BIRTHDAY, IN 1995

In 1997 Sinatra was awarded **the Congressional Gold Medal**, an accolade created in 1787 that had been bestowed on fewer than 400 people. His daughter Nancy, who accepted the award on his behalf, said: "It's more than just an honour from his country, as far as I'm concerned. It's like the country saying, 'Ok, Frank, we know the truth, and we love you.'"

After several months of illness, Frank Sinatra died on **May 14, 1998**, aged 82, in Cedars-Sinai Medical Center with Barbara at his bedside. There was a two-hour Mass at Beverly Hills Good Shepherd Catholic church on May 20, at which Tony Bennett, Gregory Peck and Frank Jr. addressed the 400 invited mourners and the choir sang "Ave Maria". Ex-wives Nancy Sinatra and Mia Farrow attended, as did ex-girlfriends Jill St John and Angie Dickinson. Other guests included Joey Bishop (the last surviving Rat Packer), Jack Nicholson, Faye Dunaway, Tony Curtis, Sophia Loren, Nancy Reagan, Liza Minnelli, Kirk Douglas, Robert Wagner, Don Rickles, Bob Newhart and Tom Selleck. A guard of honour escorted the casket to

NANCY, FRANK JR. AND TINA: THE KIDS

Although Nancy, Frank Jr. and Tina all made their mark, much of their lives has been spent grappling with the towering legacy of Frank Sr. as a musician, a star, a public figure and a father. Whether for reasons of commerce or catharsis, or to straighten the record, each of Sinatra's children has become attached to projects concerning him.

When **Nancy** approached her father for advice in the early 1960s about getting into show business, he simply said: "Don't do what I do." She didn't. Hooking up with country-pop producer and songwriter Lee Hazlewood and capitalizing on her image as a photogenic chick who was tough and trashy, Nancy scored a string of hits in the mid-1960s, including the worldwide smash "These Boots Were Made For Walkin'". She appeared with her father in his 1966 TV special and had a huge hit the same year when they duetted on "Somethin' Stupid". The hits dried up in 1968 but there were TV specials and ten albums before she retired from performing in the early 1970s to raise a family.

In the absence of an autobiography of her father, she published the book *Frank Sinatra: My Father* in 1985; an updated version ten years later, *An American Legend* (see page 368), was a repudiation of criticisms of Sinatra that had emerged. A documentary is in the pipeline.

She attempted to relaunch her career in 1995 at the age of fifty, with a new album and a *Playboy* pictorial, but the real renaissance began in 2004 when Morrissey invited her to London to play at London's *Meltdown* festival, where she was a huge success. The album that followed, *Nancy Sinatra*, featuring collaborations with hip rockers such as Jon Spencer and Sonic Youth, garnered excellent reviews. Her reputation as an influential, inspirational 1960s icon seems secure.

Frank Jr. became a singer too, but unlike his sister, he did exactly what his father had done – even though Frank Sr. had announced "No following in Dad's footsteps" when he was born. He sang quality standards in a swing style, even touring with what was left of The Tommy Dorsey Orchestra in the early 1960s – and he was good. His father, while undoubtedly uncomfortable

the **Desert Memorial Park** in Cathedral City, Palm Springs, where his mother and father were buried.

The **tributes** to Sinatra were fulsome. Martin Scorsese called him "a great Italian-American, a great American, and a great actor" and Johnny Depp described him as "a great, uncompromising hero". Some

with his son's decision, praised the boy's musicianship and technique. "He's better than I was at his age," he judged, when Frank Jr. made his Las Vegas debut. Predictably, despite his obvious abilities, Frank Jr. was never thought to be more than a diluted version of his father, even in his own estimation: he once described himself as the "Volkswagen in the Sinatra garage".

Frank Jr. never reached the same commercial heights as his sister. But he was given a TV special in 1969, with his father and Nancy guesting, recorded four albums, and branched out into acting. Mostly, however, he sang with a big band. He vacillated between embracing the Sinatra connection (he worked with Nelson Riddle and Billy May) and fighting it (he recorded country and western music in the early 1970s), until 1988, when his father asked him to be his conductor. Their relationship became prickly, with Frank Jr. occasionally being humiliated in concert (his tempos were corrected, he was introduced unkindly), but he remained loyal and displayed no rancour. Father and son even sang on "My Kind Of Town" together on *Duets II* in 1994, and in 1996 Frank Jr. produced an excellent Sinatra reminiscence album, *As I Remember It*. Since his father's death in 1998, Frank Jr. has succumbed to the inevitable: a series of well-received shows featuring members of Frank Sr.'s touring orchestra, including Bill Miller, entitled *Sinatra Sings Sinatra*.

Tina, the youngest child, had no ambition to perform. Indeed, sister Nancy had to cover for her at the last minute on her father's TV show in 1957 when she was overcome by nerves. She was still "in a coma" with fright in 1968 when *The Sinatra Family Wish You A Merry Christmas* album was recorded. In 1991 she oversaw the publication of a book of her father's paintings, *A Man And His Art*. She became an independent film producer responsible for, among other projects, the 1992 TV movie *Sinatra* – which took up six years of her life – and the 2004 remake of *The Manchurian Candidate*.

Although she was the child who had the dimmest recollection of her father – he left before she was two years old – the significance of her emotional dealings with him was revealed in *My Father's Daughter* (see pages 374–375), her searing memoir published in 2000.

of the comments from politicians were a little more cryptic. "I think every American," said **President Clinton**, "would have to smile and say he really did do it his way." The feelings of many pop fans had already been summed up by the author David Hajdu: "To hell with the calendar. The day Frank Sinatra dies, the twentieth century is over."

Sinatra's will, made in 1991, was expected to cause quarrels among the disparate members of his family, but he had inserted a clause that disinherited anyone who contested it. The friction came later when his children, who retain the rights to his Reprise recordings, fought off Barbara and her son Bobby to keep that part of Sinatra's musical legacy in the singer's bloodline. Barbara, for her part, was reported to be unhappy when **Sheffield Enterprises**, the corporation run by Sinatra's children with the right to his name and image, was behind "officially" endorsed products including pasta, champagne, hats and singing plates. Tina's book *My Father's Daughter* suggested that the bitterness and suspicion with which the Sinatra children continue to regard their father's fourth wife is even deeper than the press suggest.

Public interest in Sinatra, so high throughout his career, has barely waned after his death. The exploits of the Rat Pack are regarded as examples of vintage misbehaviour by a new generation of "lads". Sinatra's way with a song continues to inspire everyone from the impersonators in karaoke bars to aspirant pop stars such as **Robbie Williams**, Westlife and Michael Bublé, who crib his style. Books published after his death that couldn't have been written while he was alive and that produced further revelations – most notably by his daughter Tina and George Jacobs – were best sellers.

When Tina was asked at the opening of Radio City Music Hall's multimedia tribute show to her father in 2003 why she thought interest in Sinatra had endured, she said: "He's a part of our culture. It isn't that he's reinvented, it's that the generations have passed him on."

The Inner Circle

**A select group of friends and
lovers who made a difference**

*"When it was good, it was so good,
you had to be there … but when it was bad
between you and Frank, it was piss-poor bad."*

DEAN MARTIN, TO J. RANDALL TARABORRELLI

HUMPHREY BOGART (1899-1957) AND LAUREN BACALL (1924-)

"They tell me you have a voice that makes girls faint," said Humphrey Bogart when first introduced to Sinatra in the mid-1940s. "Make me faint."

Sinatra adored the sophisticated, self-contained Bogart, and observers at the time thought that he even attempted to model himself on the hard-drinking but well-read actor who could not tolerate being told what to do. Sinatra certainly based his wry, tough investigator in the mid-1960s movies *Tony Rome* and *Lady In Cement* on Bogart's performances in films such as *The Maltese Falcon* and *The Big Sleep*.

In the mid-1950s the Bogarts ran an open house in **Holmby Hills** and Sinatra would often drop in for drinks and laughs. "I don't know what it is about this joint; it seems to be some kind of home for him," said Bogart. "It's as though he doesn't have a home of his own. We seem to be parent symbols or something." He thought that Frank was not emotionally an adult and couldn't settle down.

But Bogart did like Sinatra, and smiled at his rough edges. "He's kind of a Don Quixote, tilting at windmills, fighting people who don't want to fight," he said. He also joked about Sinatra's romantic life, once telling a reporter that his notion of heaven was a place with a lot of women and no newspapermen. "He doesn't realize it," Bogart said, "but he'd be better off if it were the other way round."

Sinatra was distressed when Bogart had throat cancer diagnosed in 1956 and visited him frequently. As **Lauren Bacall**, the actor's wife, noted, "He cheered Bogie up when he was with him – made him laugh – kept the ring-a-ding act in high gear for him." When Bogart died in January 1957 a devastated Sinatra had Sammy Davis Jr. cover his show at the Copa and the good cheer stopped for a while.

> *"He's a hell of a guy. He tries to live his own life.*
> *I like his style."*
>
> HUMPHREY BOGART

As Bogart deteriorated, Bacall became more dependent on Sinatra to keep her afloat. The pair became close and were seen stepping out soon after Bogart died. After a period of uncertainty, with Sinatra as mercurial as ever – "adoring one day," Bacall remembered, "remote the next" – in March 1958 Frank asked her to marry him, and she accepted. When the engagement made the papers a few weeks later, against Sinatra's wishes – it had been leaked by a mutual friend, the literary agent **Irving "Swifty" Lazar** – Sinatra ended the relationship. Some say that he panicked when he saw the reporters around his house; others suggest that he was warned away by his mother and by his first wife, Nancy. (George Jacobs remembers Sinatra complaining about Bacall's unwillingness to perform oral sex.)

Bacall was heartbroken by the brutal end of the affair and the ensuing years of silent treatment from Sinatra. She poured out her hurt in her autobiography **By Myself**, published in 1978. Sinatra considered the book unfair. "There's another side to it, but I'm not going to give it," he commented. "Some things should rest." Later still, he told daughter Tina,

"I wanted to take care of her, and it got out of hand. It should never have happened."

SAMMY CAHN (1913-1993)

No lyricist had more work recorded by Sinatra than Sammy Cahn. Between "I Could Make You Care" in 1940 with Tommy Dorsey and "Guess I'll Hang My Tears Out To Dry" in 1993 for *Duets*, Sinatra recorded around sixty of his works. These included some of the singer's most famous songs, such as **"Time After Time"**, written with **Jule Styne**; **"I Should Care"**, written with **Axel Stordahl**; and "The Tender Trap", "All The Way" and **"Come Fly With Me"**, written with **Jimmy Van Heusen**. In addition, Sinatra used specially commissioned lyrics from Cahn for private parties, such as the cabaret at the Sinatras' New Year's Eve bashes in the 1940s; tributes, such as the version of "Nancy" rewritten for Mrs Reagan in the 1980s; and political promotion, such as the version of "High Hopes" for JFK in 1960.

Along with Jule Styne, Cahn supported Sinatra's early solo career; he attended his opening show in 1943 at the Riobamba and was an identified member of Frank's 1940s coterie, **the Varsity**, which included Hank Sanicola, Manie Sachs, the businessman Ben Barton and a couple of boxers. Following Styne and Cahn's work on the 1944 movie *Step Lively*, Sinatra held out for the writing team to join him in the MGM musical ***Anchors Aweigh***, against the producer's wishes and much to the amazement of Cahn himself. "It was one of the truly, truly memorable moments in my life," Cahn told the author Michael Freedland. This, he said, was when he came "to the decision that Frank Sinatra was one of the great people in the world".

Cahn went on to receive regular commissions from the Voice, and won **Oscars** for "All The Way" and "High Hopes" and Emmys for "Three Coins In A Fountain" and "Love And Marriage". He was a satellite member of Sinatra's **Rat Pack**, often on hand to play the piano, but like most who were close to Frank, was also on the receiving end of his unpredictable behaviour. "He has hurt me more than once, Frank Sinatra," Cahn once said. The singer and the lyricist drifted apart during the 1970s; Sinatra was looking for new sources of material and Cahn disapproved of Sinatra's friendship with **Spiro Agnew**. He was not invited to Frank and Barbara's wedding in 1976, but agreed to write special lyrics for "Teach Me Tonight" on the *L.A. Is My Lady* album from 1984.

An old-style song craftsman, Cahn, who died in 1993, latterly recognized that there might not be a place for him in the modern music industry, where artists largely write their own material. "If Sinatra were one of those new people in the business," he noted, acknowledging how much he owed the singer, "I doubt if there would be a Sammy Cahn."

SAMMY DAVIS JR. (1925-1990)

When he was in the army in the early 1940s, Sammy Davis Jr. attended the recording of Sinatra's radio programme *The Old Gold Show*; and in 1947, when Davis appeared in vaudeville dancing act **the Will Mastin Trio** on the same bill as Sinatra, the singer remembered him. From then on Sinatra went out of his way to promote Davis by booking the trio, also featuring his father and uncle, on other bills, and encouraged him to develop his singing. It was after an engagement at the Copa in 1952, when the trio opened for Sinatra, that Davis was signed to Decca.

Soon afterwards, he was involved in a car accident in which he was injured and lost an eye, and Sinatra spent a great deal of time with him, using his sense of humour to breathe life back into the depressed entertainer. (Frank sent both him and Jilly Rizzo, who had lost the opposite eye, half a pair of binoculars, with a note saying, "You two should get together.") Davis once recalled of Sinatra's approach to his welfare, "That kind of sensitivity is rare, rare."

Sinatra made Davis part of his circle, sang his praises and took a successful (and at the time unusual) stand when in places that were segregated. And Davis appreciated Sinatra's approach to **integration**, not to say his musical talent and personal power, to the point of idolatry. "I wanted to be like him so bad," he said. But he also saw Sinatra's flip-side – and in 1959 he made the mistake of mentioning this in an infamous radio interview. "Talent is not an excuse for bad manners," he said. Sinatra heard this and immediately cut him out of the film *Never So Few* – and out of his life. After a few months, and much grovelling apologizing from Davis, they made up, before shooting *Ocean's 11*.

SINATRA THE LEADER

In the spoof film *This Is Spinal Tap*, a limo driver tries to engage the rock band with a joke about Sammy Davis Jr.'s biography being called *Yes I Can!*; he thinks it should have been called *Yes I Can If Frank Sinatra Says It's Okay*. This piece of satire points towards the truth.

The portrayal of Sinatra as the man who called the shots is pervasive. And it wasn't just because he owned the record company, or the film production company – it was because he was perceived somehow as a leader of men, who set the tone and started the action. This was clear when Norman Fell looked out of his hotel room window during the shooting of *Ocean's 11* and saw Davis, Martin and Lawford all running somewhere fast. When asked where they were going, Sammy shouted, "Frank's *up!*" In the company he kept, once he was awake, the day began.

He was a man for whom others wanted to do their best partly from fear of his wrath, partly out of respect for his standards and partly because he inspired them to do so simply by his presence. "You feel an *impact* even if he doesn't do or say anything," said the singer Steve Lawrence, who toured with Sinatra in the 1990s. The film director Stanley Kramer, who had a difficult time accommodating Sinatra when on set, said, "When Sinatra walks in, tension walks in beside him."

But this charisma and aura of power, when carried without grace, could manifest itself simply as **bullying**. It was this side of Sinatra's authority that even Sammy Davis Jr. felt moved to criticize. After he was forgiven for the infamous radio interview, he would not only refer to Sinatra obsequiously onstage as "the Leader"; he would also jump whenever Frank called, whether for dinner at Puccini's or drinks at Jilly's. This did not please Sammy's second wife.

Professionally, it was often **Sinatra's way** or nothing. When shooting a film, his impatience with the process and unwillingness to do more than a single take if he could avoid it made for an uptight set; no one wanted to be the one to annoy him. He could be better in the recording studio, where he was often prepared to sing and sing until it was right. But no engineer would have wanted to inform him of a technical fault that was nothing to do with the music.

During performances by **the Rat Pack** many of the jokes about Davis were based on his colour and religion; but this did not mean that Sinatra had deserted the cause of racial equality. When Frank agreed to be best man

Sinatra and Dorsey before their reunion at the Paramount in August 1956

at the controversial mixed race wedding between Davis and the Swedish actress **Mai Britt** in 1960, Sammy recognised the significance of the gesture. "It was not a minor thing to do for Frank to be my best man," he said.

The pair remained friends during the 1960s, but in the 1970s Davis walked on a wilder side than Sinatra, dabbling with **Satanism and pornography**. It was his cocaine use, in particular, that estranged him from Sinatra, who was against drugs, until Frank called a reconciliation dinner and made him promise to quit. He did. They were reunited on the boards in 1988 on **the "Together Again Tour"** and Sinatra opened the televised celebration of Davis's sixty years in show business in 1989. The following May the man whom Frank called "Smokey", because he always had a cigarette on the go, died from throat cancer. "He was a class act," said Sinatra, "and I will miss him forever."

TOMMY DORSEY (1905-1956)

While he was in Tommy Dorsey's band Sinatra came to regard the trombonist, who exuded discipline and musical wisdom, as a father figure. But Sinatra also recognised Dorsey's loneliness and often kept him company at the card table into the night, only to be woken by **"the Old Man"** (as the 40-year-old bandleader was called by the musicians) a few hours later for a game of golf. Once this relationship had been established, Sinatra found himself serving as a go-between, conveying the band members' issues to their leader.

But when Sinatra's solo ambitions became clear, Dorsey, "the Sentimental Gentleman Of Swing", was hurt, and he froze him out during his latter months in the band. After the singer went solo in 1942 and **contract negotiations** ensued, the relationship between the pair deteriorated further. There were occasional reunions, including a radio show in 1945 ("I knew you'd come crawling back to me," Dorsey joked on air) and a week together at the Paramount just before Dorsey died in his sleep in 1956. But for some reason Sinatra refused to participate in a TV tribute to his old boss soon afterwards. Perhaps he had read what Dorsey had said about him: "He's the most fascinating man in the world, but don't stick your hand in the cage." Or perhaps he overheard what Dorsey told his band at the Paramount: "I showed him all his shit. Everything he does, he got from me."

Sinatra later showed mixed feelings towards Dorsey. On the one hand, one of the first Reprise releases, *I Remember Tommy*, saluted Dorsey, and as Sinatra got older, he would affectionately reminisce, unprompted and at length, about the Dorsey days. But he would occasionally remonstrate with the ghost of his former boss for laughs, stamping on the stage, pointing downwards and saying, "You hear me Tommy, I'm talkin' to you!"

GEORGE EVANS (1901–1950)

A public relations whiz with the patience of a saint, it was George Evans who spotted a girl in the audience swooning and moaning while Sinatra did his thing in 1943 and then hired a dozen teenagers to do the same at the Paramount – thereby creating **the bobbysox phenomenon**. He invented all the catchphrases of the era, including **"the Voice"**, and as well as playing up Sinatra's image as a loving family man, he lectured him in private on his misbehaviour, of which he disapproved for personal and professional reasons. One of the few people around Sinatra who would stand up to him, he encouraged Frank to return to Nancy on several occasions, and broke up several extra-marital romances before they went on too long. He kept as much detail from the press as he could, often by being blunt. "Okay, we know what a son of a bitch he is," he told the reporters, "but here's what you're going to print."

Knowing that Sinatra would need to counter the simmering bad press, he encouraged him to display a social conscience in the 1945 film *The House I Live In* and played up Sinatra's role as a priest in *The Miracle Of The Bells* in 1948. His son Phil remembered that he regarded Frank "as a sort of son and a creation of his as well". But the pair reached an impasse when Evans refused to fire his assistant **Jack Keller** after Sinatra thought that he had mishandled the famous drunken drive with Ava Gardner (see page 40), and with Frank refusing to stop seeing her. With Ava encouraging Frank to free himself from Evans's influence, he had to choose between his press agent and his lover. Evans left Sinatra's employ at the end of 1949.

Speaking to the show business writer **Earl Wilson** soon afterwards, Evans predicted that Sinatra was finished. "A year from now, you won't hear anything about him," he said. "Professionally, he'll be dead … The public knows about the trouble with Nancy now, and the other dames, and it doesn't like him anymore."

Evans was heard rueing Sinatra's choices and defending his creation the night before he died of a heart attack in 1950, at the age of 48. When Sinatra found out he flew to New York to attend the funeral, distraught.

SAM GIANCANA (1908-1975)

Sinatra socialized with mobsters for years, and was grateful to the Mafia, mostly for giving him work when no one else would; but his relationship with Sam Giancana, the Chicago crime boss in the ever-present **hat and sunglasses**, went beyond the courtesy extended to an occasional employer. The mobster stayed at Sinatra's home in Palm Springs and was treated as an esteemed guest. Giancana was attracted to the highlife and the women of Sinatra's world, and was the subject of disapproval in the underworld when he stepped out with **Phyllis McGuire** of The McGuire Sisters.

That Sinatra was close to **the Kennedys** also contributed to the friendship, as Giancana thought that he could get close to political power. It is implied in the book by his brother and nephew, *Double Cross*, that he told Sinatra to introduce John F. Kennedy to enticing women so that the he could wiretap the liaisons and leave the Kennedys open to blackmail. (In the book Sinatra is not described by name on this matter, but one figure is "a fellow Kennedy carouser … close to Peter Lawford …[who] owes the outfit".) These women included Sinatra's former girlfriend **Judith Campbell**, who became JFK's mistress and then Giancana's.

Having helped Sinatra and the Kennedys with the primary in **West Virginia** in 1960 Giancana expected them to return the favour. He expected the FBI surveillance to ease up, but after Robert Kennedy became Attorney General it intensified. Giancana assumed that Sinatra would have a word on his behalf, but his relationship with the increasingly wary Kennedys waned after the election, and according to some sources Sinatra promised Giancana favours with no intention of delivering. Giancana felt betrayed. FBI wiretaps indicate his increasing frustration with Sinatra.

His plans for payback involved "inviting" Sinatra and the Rat Pack to perform at his club, the **Villa Venice** gambling joint in Chicago, for no

GIANCANA HANDCUFFED TO A CHAIR AFTER BEING ARRESTED IN APRIL 1957

payment. Sinatra, Martin and Davis performed there in November 1962 and Giancana made a financial killing. When Sinatra was asked by FBI agents why he had agreed to donate his services for nothing, he said that he was doing a favour for Leo Olsen, the man recorded as being the owner of the club.

After **the Cal-Neva incident** in the summer of 1963, the relationship between Giancana and Sinatra cooled. Although they were allegedly business partners in the lodge, Sinatra found associating with the mobster increasingly uncomfortable; this was, according to some, because of his suspicions concerning the death of Marilyn Monroe. Moreover, **Ava Gardner** hated Sinatra's mobster pals, Giancana in particular, and warned Sinatra that he would end up dead if he continued to hang around them. According to *Sinatra: The Untold Story* by Michael Munn, he had already received a death threat from the Mafia in the form of a skinned goat's head.

Giancana, for his part, was furious with Sinatra for blowing his top with the Nevada Gaming Commissioner, **Ed Olsen**, and jeopardizing their investment. He was further offended when Frank Sr. turned down his offer of help in finding the kidnapped Frank Jr. in December 1963. Munn claims that Sinatra subsequently colluded with the Government to help to bring Giancana down. There was certainly little reported contact between the mobster and the singer from 1964 onwards, and Giancana was jailed for a year in 1965 for contempt of court. When released in 1966, he no longer commanded the underworld respect he once had, and he went in exile to Mexico. When deported in 1974, he returned to Chicago, and in 1975, just before he was due to give evidence on complicity between the CIA and the Mafia in attempts to assassinate Fidel Castro, he was gunned down in his home.

PETER LAWFORD (1923-1984)

Peter Lawford was a handsome, London-born actor who had known Sinatra since the singer arrived in Hollywood in 1945 and became friendly with him in 1947 when they both starred in *It Happened In Brooklyn*. The friendship came to an abrupt end in 1953 when it was reported, shortly after Ava announced the Sinatras' separation, that

Lawford had been seen stepping out with her. After Lawford received a furious, threatening phone call from Sinatra the pair didn't speak for five years.

The reconciliation came after Lawford married **John F. Kennedy's sister Pat**. At a Hollywood dinner party at the house of Gary Cooper and his wife in the late 1950s she had a quiet word with Sinatra, intimating that JFK and Sinatra could establish a mutually beneficial relationship if Peter and Frank became friends again.

They did, becoming pals and business buddies; the Lawfords even gave their daughter Victoria the middle name Frances. And it was brother-in-Lawford, as Sinatra sometimes called him, who located the script that was developed into the film *Ocean's 11*, so when the Rat Pack first convened in 1960 Lawford was one of the gang, despite his limited talents.

It was Lawford who introduced Sinatra and JFK to each other's worlds. In 1983 he told Kitty Kelley, "I was Frank's pimp and Frank was Jack's. It sounds terrible now, but then it was really a lot of fun." Lawford and Sinatra campaigned for JFK together and between them organized the entertainment at **President Kennedy's inaugural ball**, but Sinatra's relationship with Lawford soured alongside his relationship with the Kennedys.

As the conveyer of the bad news that JFK would be staying at Bing Crosby's house on his visit in 1962 to Palm Springs, Lawford was cut dead, as was Sinatra's wont. It is also said that an already irritated Sinatra was appalled by Lawford's proximity to the death of **Marilyn Monroe** and the aftermath, and outraged by Lawford's suggestion that Sinatra should be interviewed by the FBI after she died about his relationship with her. Lawford was banned from Sinatra's circle and written out of the Rat Pack movies *4 For Texas* and *Robin And The 7 Hoods*.

Although the full story remains a mystery, it is accepted that Lawford was involved with Bobby and John F. Kennedy's relationship with Monroe and with her final hours. It appears that the incident left Lawford in a state of guilt from which he never quite recovered. His post-Sinatra career was characterized by ill-health, which was exacerbated by alcohol and drug addiction, and of his former circle only Sammy Davis Jr. remained close; they made a pair of films together in the late 1960s. Lawford died in 1984, at the age of 61. Sinatra made no comment.

DEAN MARTIN (1917–1995)

Though both of Italian extraction, Martin and Sinatra couldn't have been more different temperamentally. Dean was of the impassive **Abruzzese** variety from Tuscany and Frank was a zealous Sicilian. As Martin summarized: "Frank takes things seriously, I don't."

It was in the 1940s that Sinatra first encountered Martin, the handsome straight-man in a double act with **Jerry Lewis**. His reported review: "The Dago's lousy, the little Jew is great." They became firm friends after

REHEARSING AT DAVIS'S HOUSE IN MARCH 1988 BEFORE THE RAT PACK REUNION TOUR; MARTIN WALKED OUT AFTER ONLY A WEEK

The Inner Circle

Sinatra cast him in *Some Came Running* following Dean's informal pitch at a party. They shared a love of late-night drinking, though Martin would sometimes make excuses to avoid another night on the tiles ("I got a girl in my room"), preferring to watch TV, turn in and get up early to play golf.

While on stage with **the Rat Pack**, an act that took its cue from the laconic act of Martin's and its famously fake drunkenness, it was almost as if Dean allowed Frank to act like the leader because he couldn't be bothered to argue about it. Although Martin often came over as cooler and funnier than Sinatra, he never approached Frank's depth, energy or passion as a performer; Martin, for all his casual gifts as a musician and comedian, just didn't seem to care about being *great*.

While Sinatra seemed to fall out periodically with most of his circle, for years he and Martin remained best friends. "Frank and I are brothers, right?" Dean once explained. "We cut the top of our thumbs and became blood brothers. He wanted to cut the wrist. I said, 'What, are you *crazy*? No, *here's* good enough.'" Martin also put the longevity of their friendship down to its light footing; it never became too heavy. "I don't discuss his girl with Frank or who he's going to marry," Martin once said, explaining how Sinatra and he got on. "All I discuss are movies."

Yet Martin did still enter Sinatra's bad books, when he walked out on the Rat Pack reunion tour in 1988. Still shaken by **the loss of his son** in a plane crash in 1987, the 70-year-old Martin felt uneasy around Sinatra. "There was something cold about Frank, you know?" he told J. Randall Taraborrelli. "I didn't want to be around him. I felt he thought I was a putz." Unwilling and unable to match Sinatra's determined defiance of age, and humiliated when told off by Frank for flicking a lit cigarette into the audience, he gave up after a week. Martin remembered Sinatra kissing him on the cheek and telling him, "Get the fuck out of here, you bum, go home."

He went home and refused Sinatra's calls for a couple of weeks, as he did periodically. But they would occasionally still dine together. "We shoot the shit, you know," Martin said in 1994, "Two old guys. Frank wants to talk over old times. Only problem is, I can't remember the old times." When he died in 1995, Sinatra, then 80, broke down while he was getting ready for the funeral and did not attend.

BILL MILLER (1915–   )

The pianist Bill Miller was, perhaps more than any arranger or musician, Sinatra's musical partner. A veteran of the group from the Thirties led by vibraphonist **Red Norvo** and singer Mildred Bailey, and of the 1940s combo of saxophonist Charlie Barnet, he was playing piano in the lounge of the Desert Inn, Las Vegas, in 1951 when Sinatra was the feature in the main performance area, the Painted Desert Room. The singer was having trouble holding on to pianists at the time, due to irascibility and a shortage of money, so when **Jimmy Van Heusen** heard Miller playing "great chords and everything" he reported the news. Miller joined Sinatra in the Painted Desert Room and thereafter for the vast majority of the singer's recordings for Capitol and Reprise during the next 40 years.

He also appeared in most live shows, during which Sinatra invariably introduced Miller either as **"Suntan Charlie"**, drawing attention to his paleness of visage, or as his "right arm". It was Miller, occasionally Sinatra's musical director and conductor, who rehearsed him before sessions, teaching him tunes, setting the key signature for particular songs and setting tempos. Comparing the piano and voice treatment of "One For My Baby" in 1954 (in the film *Young At Heart*) with that recorded 39 years later (for *Duets*) shows how they matured together.

In 1969 Miller's house in Los Angeles was hit by a landslide, and the pianist lost his wife; Sinatra paid the hospital bills, set him up in a new apartment and bought him a new set of clothes. The album recorded at that time, *My Way*, was the only Sinatra record not to feature Miller until the album *Trilogy* in 1979, by which time Miller and Sinatra had fallen out. "What happened was we had been like bucking heads for a little while, six months or a year," Miller told Will Friedwald. "I think I was there too long, and so I took him for granted and he took me for granted." They had made it up by the mid-1980s and Bill was back as Sinatra's pianist until Frank sang his final notes in public in February 1995. Outliving his boss, Miller played at Sinatra's funeral in 1998 and was talked into contributing to Robbie Williams's album from 2001, *Swing While You're Winning*, duplicating his celebrated **"One For My Baby"** piano part.

MITCH MILLER (1911–   )

A successful record producer who as a respected oboist had appeared on Charlie Parker's album *Bird With Strings*, Mitch Miller had an unflinching sense of low-brow commercial appeal, and in the drive to make records efficiently he established as standard practice, among other things, the taping of individual elements, and particularly vocals, separately, as opposed to recording everything simultaneously or "live". He took over from **Manie Sachs** as head of A&R at **Columbia** in 1950, when Sinatra was in debt to the company and not selling records. Miller's initial strategy was to have Sinatra record more upbeat rhythm tunes – hence the Dixie-style "American Beauty Rose" and the worthy album *Sing And Dance With Frank Sinatra*. But these didn't quite do the trick.

Sinatra saw that Miller was producing big hits with rather gimmicky records for **Frankie Laine** ("Mule Train") and **Rosemary Clooney** ("Come On-A My House") and that other Miller-produced singers, such as Guy Mitchell, were having hits with material that Miller had offered Sinatra but which the singer dismissed as "crap". Vulnerable both professionally and personally, he occasionally allowed Miller to record him on songs with barking dogs and washboards and in a variety of banal musical settings, such as "One Finger Melody", with its childish piano part, and "Come Back To Sorrento", with its inflated breast-beating. That some of the records were hits, such as "Goodnight Irene" in 1950, didn't make him feel better about it.

The pair worked together in sporadic sessions for more than two years, with Miller bullishly trying to forge hits and Sinatra feeling powerless and growing increasingly resentful. Although reports of Sinatra's disgruntlement had reached the pages of *Billboard* even by November 1951, the paper magazine referring to a "long-smouldering feud", it was when Sinatra was reborn at **Capitol** and free from Miller that he could really blame Miller for everything that had gone wrong in his world. "Before Mr Miller's advent on the scene," he told the press in the mid-1950s, "I had a successful recording career, which went into decline." Miller's response: "His career went down the drain because of his emotional turmoil over **Ava Gardner**. I had nothing to do with him losing his movie contract, losing his television show, losing his voice. He should look to himself as the cause of his own failures and stop trying to blame others."

In the late 1950s Sinatra even suggested that the substandard material he was "forced" to record was part of a payola scam, but the claim has not been substantiated. And as Miller pointed out, "His contract gave him total control over all his material. He didn't have to record anything he didn't want to." Miller appeared to bear no malice and when he was introduced to Sinatra years later at the Sands he was happy to bury the hatchet. But Sinatra wasn't, and told him to "fuck off".

JULIET PROWSE (1936-1996)

Sinatra met Juliet Prowse, a beautiful dancer born in South Africa, in 1959 on the set of the film *Can-Can* and she and the movie gained a certain reputation after the film offended **President Khrushchev**. The day after visiting the set and seeing a sequence in which knickerbockers were displayed, he complained that the dance was "immoral" and announced that "a person's face is more beautiful than his backside".

Sinatra arranged for Prowse to appear in his TV specials, telling the press, "The kid's got it. She's the sexiest dancer I've ever seen." But the pair conducted their romance in private, and even the bust-ups seemed dignified. While admitting that she had feelings for Frank, she coolly told a reporter, "I go my way and he goes his. I have my life to lead and I'm not going to sit around. If I want to go out with someone else, I go out. No strings." One of the men she was rumoured to have gone out with was **Elvis Presley**, with whom she appeared in the movie *G.I. Blues* in 1960, though she turned down the chance of a second film with him.

During one of their separations, Sinatra found himself missing her, and in 1962 he proposed. Sinatra said, when **the engagement** was announced, "Juliet has been my one romance. I'm 46 now. It's time to settle down." But when it became clear that Prowse wasn't going to put her career on hold to play house for Sinatra – however sweetly he sang "It's so nice to have a Prowse around the house" – the engagement was called off, after 43 days, the press release citing a "conflict of career interest".

Prowse, who died in 1996, told a reporter: "Frank wanted me just to be his wife, to travel with him, to be with him constantly … I would have married Frank, but I've always been a bit difficult for him." On stage, Dean

"JULIET HAS BEEN MY ONE ROMANCE," FRANK SAID WHEN THEY BECAME ENGAGED

Martin's line was, "Frank and Julie broke up, Julie wanted Frank to give up his career, but he wouldn't."

Some press reports were sympathetic to the 46-year-old Frank's plight as an ageing playboy. The columnist Sidney Skolsky wrote, "On any night, when the laughs get sleepy, and there's no more booze, and there are no more hours, Dean goes home to his wife, Lawford goes home to his, Sammy to his. But Frank just goes home."

BUDDY RICH (1917–1987)

"I want you to meet another pain in the ass." This is how Sinatra remembered **Tommy Dorsey** introducing him to the virtuoso drummer Buddy Rich. He and Frank were close for a while, but the relationship soon became volatile. When roommates on tour, Rich would complain about Sinatra's bedtime habits – reading until the early hours and clipping his toenails. Although he admired the singer's work, Rich was irritated at Sinatra's growing celebrity and would sometimes play behind his ballad performances with deliberate insensitivity, overemphasizing the beat or pushing the tempo. The drummer would prime fans to ask for Sinatra's autograph and then have them loudly announce that for "three more of these, I can trade them for one of Bob Eberly's!"

At the Hotel Astor in New York in August 1940 the ill-feeling developed into a fist-fight, and the result was that Sinatra was suspended by Dorsey. A few days later Rich was beaten up in the street by two thugs, and he was convinced that they were Hoboken hoodlums whom Sinatra had hired. However, the pair lasted another eighteen months together with Dorsey, and in 1943, when Rich mentioned to Sinatra that he was thinking about starting his own band, the new solo star immediately offered to put up the money.

Their professional lives rarely crossed during the Forties, Fifties and Sixties. But Rich was seen ringside at Sinatra's *Main Event* concert in 1974 and the pair appeared together on the same bill at several concerts in the mid-1980s, including the televised *Concert For The Americas* in 1981, when Sinatra used Rich's band for his own set but retained his own touring drummer, Irv Cottler. The relationship became so significant that Sinatra overcame his tendency to avoid funerals when Rich died in 1987.

NELSON RIDDLE (1921–1985)

When Sinatra arrived at Capitol in 1953 he wanted Axel Stordahl again, or failing that, Billy May; but the Capitol A&R director **Alan Livingston** wanted Frank to try Nelson Riddle, who had just started making his name as the arranger for Nat "King" Cole. Though Sinatra would later say he aspired to the excellence of the Cole/Riddle tracks, others remember an initial wariness towards the new man. Sinatra liked the swinging **"I've Got The World On A String"**, but was also cautious about Riddle's advanced ballad writing. "Whew, we gotta be careful with him," he told Bill Miller. But the pianist recounted that he was excited by how well Sinatra's sound blended with Riddle's modern harmonies.

The Riddle-Sinatra partnership worked so well that Riddle went on to arrange Sinatra's first six **Capitol** albums and the large majority of his singles. He went on the road with the singer, enjoyed the high profile financially and personally, and settled into the role; for a few years the pair were musically inseparable. Riddle recalled: "He said I was the best secretary he ever had … I took the notes of what we discussed and that's what he got."

But in 1957 Sinatra decided to try new sounds and hired Gordon Jenkins for the album *Where Are You?* and Billy May, the following year, for the album *Come Fly With Me*. Although this was apparently not intended as a slight, that was how Riddle took it, even though most arrangers flitted from one musician to another. And as with all arrangers who were being paid for piecework – and during the mid-1950s Riddle also arranged for Nat "King" Cole and Billy Eckstine – he already considered himself to be undervalued, and his sensitive, pessimistic nature meant that he never felt the same way about Sinatra again.

Although he was employed during the next three years for four more of Sinatra's Capitol albums, Riddle was barely used during Sinatra's first three years at Reprise. He was eventually hired for five albums between 1963 and 1967, a couple of which, **The Concert Sinatra** and **Moonlight Sinatra**, were excellent. But for the next ten years, with Sinatra's arranger of choice being Don Costa, his commissions for Riddle were meagre. The one album that he was called to work on, in 1977 – a collection of songs with girls' names in the titles, called **Here's To The Ladies** – was canned after Sinatra recorded only five of the ten arrangements that Riddle had prepared (see page 351).

RIDDLE, WHO ARRANGED MOST OF SINATRA'S GREAT CAPITOL ERA TUNES

By the time *Trilogy* was mooted in 1979, Riddle's resentment was such that he turned down the offer of arranging the album of the triple set called *The Past*. His son Chris remembers him wanting to do all three albums or nothing at all; in the end, his only contribution was the beautiful arrangement of **"Something"** on *The Present*. In what was widely regarded as retaliation, Sinatra, when he was supposed to host a testimonial dinner for Riddle, managed to double-book himself. When the event was rearranged he failed to turn up, and Riddle was devastated.

Riddle, who was not even approached in 1984 for *L.A. Is My Lady*, told the author Robert Windeler that he was hurt by his exile. "But I think I was dimly aware that nothing is forever," he said. There was a reconciliation of sorts at a dinner in January 1985 that celebrated Ronald Reagan's re-election; Sinatra apparently spent much of the evening with Riddle, making plans for albums of old tunes that he had never recorded. When Riddle died later that year at the age of 64, there was an unfinished chart for Sinatra left on his piano.

JILLY RIZZO (1917–1992)

Sinatra initially knew the short, square-built man with the glass eye as the proprietor of **"Jilly's"**, a favourite New York restaurant of his that served Chinese food and had live music. (The restaurant was name-checked in Sinatra's single "Me And My Shadow" from 1962 and its exterior is briefly seen in *The Manchurian Candidate*.) Sinatra was taken with his toughness and his coarse "dese, dems and dose" mode of speech, which sounded like lines from *Guys And Dolls* spiced up with expletives. His wife Honey sported blue hair, so Frank called her "Blue Jew"; Jilly called Frank "the Boss".

When **Hank Sanicola** quit as Sinatra's business partner in 1962, Rizzo became Frank's ever-present companion-assistant-bodyguard, even moving to California, where Sinatra helped him to open "Jilly's West". Rizzo was nearly always on hand to help Sinatra do what he had to do – whether this was walking down the street unbothered or just relaxing. Sinatra liked him to throw ice cubes in the air and try to catch them. "Frank says, 'Hey Jilly, throw the ice cubes!' So I do it," Rizzo said. "He gets a kick out of it. Anything I can do to take the tension off the guy."

Sometimes he would head an entourage of equally burly associates. "How's it feel to be Frank's tractor?" quipped the comedian Don Rickles, when Sinatra's gang arrived during a performance. "Yeah, Jilly keeps walking in front of Frank clearing the way." Unquestioningly loyal to Sinatra, Rizzo and his assistants became known as a little over-enthusiastic in their physical protection of Sinatra's dignity. Even the comedians Shecky Greene and Jackie Mason claimed, in Kitty Kelley's *His Way*, to have been attacked in the mid-1960s after making disparaging remarks about Sinatra.

An insurance salesman even sued Sinatra for assault in 1973 after he allegedly allowed Rizzo and another assistant to beat him up following an incident in a restaurant. The outcome favoured Sinatra, but **damages of $100,000** were awarded against Rizzo, who denied at the trial that he was Frank's bodyguard. "Sinatra don't need no protection," he said. "He's man enough to stand up and defend himself in his own way like any man should." But it sometimes seemed that the older Sinatra was hiring someone to do the brawling that the younger Sinatra would have done himself, though he once intimated that what he called his "Dago secret service" was partly to protect the public and his press from the fallout of his temper.

Despite his hard-man role and image, Rizzo was loved by **the Sinatras** and he was accepted as one of the family. In her book *My Father's Daughter* Tina called Jilly "the brother my father never had" and he was even instrumental in helping Frank and Barbara to bury the hatchet after a falling out in the mid-1980s. But the dynamic that later developed between Frank and Barbara left little room for Rizzo, and eventually he graciously absented himself. After Barbara sensed that her ageing, increasingly melancholy husband was missing something at the beginning of the 1990s, Rizzo accepted her offer of joining Frank again for some carefree boys' nights out. Tina noticed that there was an improvement in Frank's spirits.

When Rizzo was killed in a car crash in 1992, the day before he was due to spend his 75th birthday with Sinatra, Barbara ensured that there was a doctor on hand when Frank heard the news, anticipating his devastation.

MANIE SACHS (1901–1958)

Manie Sachs was the man who helped Sinatra to decide that he should start a solo career. As head of **Columbia** A&R in the early 1940s, he let the singer know that he would be interested if Sinatra left Dorsey. Thereafter, Sachs was closely involved with Sinatra's professional and personal life: it was Sachs who throughout the 1940s would assist Sinatra in picking appropriate material to record, thereby helping to shape the character of Sinatra's classic repertoire from the period and his feeling, that would remain with him, for the great standard song. (When, however, Sinatra and the Columbia producer George Avakian mooted the idea of making a record with Duke Ellington in 1947, Sachs wasn't interested, considering Ellington to be artistically important but commercially marginal.)

It was also Sachs who suggested that Sinatra use **George Evans** as his press officer, and this was perhaps the most important factor in Sinatra's early solo success. Both became embroiled in Sinatra's tumultuous private life; Sachs was Frank Jr.'s godfather in 1944, and when Frank Sr. left the marital home in 1950, it was at Sachs's suite at the Hampshire House hotel in New York that he and **Ava Gardner** began living together. It was also there that Frank, while on the phone to Ava, faked a suicide attempt to frighten her by firing two shots into his mattress; Sachs helped to swap the mattresses before the police arrived. With his protégé at his lowest point, he also helped to arrange Frank and Ava's nuptials, and when they were married, at Sachs's brother's house, it was Manie who gave the bride away. Always protective of Sinatra's welfare, he took Ava quietly aside and ask her "to look after him … help him get back his self-confidence".

By this time Sachs's ability to help Sinatra's career was limited, having moved record companies, first to Capitol and then to RCA, leaving Sinatra at the mercy of the new head of Columbia A&R, **Mitch Miller**. Within two years the label had dropped Sinatra, and though his old mentor was willing to sign him to RCA, the company had no interest in him. Sachs told Sinatra that he was better off with a company who wanted him.

The pair remained close friends for twenty years. Sinatra described Sachs as a "father confessor", and admired his charm and erudition – he spoke four languages. When Sachs was ill with leukaemia in 1958 Sinatra shut down production of the film *Kings Go Forth*, at his own expense, to be with him. "When I holler for help," said Sinatra after he died that year, "he ain't gonna be there any more. There's a little bit of Manie in everything good that has ever happened to me."

HANK SANICOLA (d. 1979)

Sinatra once called Hank Sanicola one of "the five most important people in my life". He added, "I couldn't have made it without him. Without his encouragement, I very easily might have tossed in the sponge."

An **ex-boxer** and former song-plugger, showing off publishers' new tunes to singers and producers in the days before demo tapes, the burly Sanicola was first associated with a young Frank in the mid-1930s, becoming his sidekick and bodyguard, occasional rehearsal pianist and personal assistant in the Dorsey days, and his manager and loyal right-hand man in his solo years. He was there to accompany Frank through most things, including the Ava affair. "Ava loved Frank, but not the way he loved her," Sanicola said during the mid-1950s. "He needs a great deal of love. He wants it 24 hours a day. He must have people around. Frank is that kind of guy." Though Ava left, Hank hung around.

Sanicola was credited as joint composer on several of the songs on which Sinatra also got a credit, "This Love Of Mine" and "Mistletoe And Holly" among them. He helped to pick Sinatra's songs – he didn't like "Witchcraft", but did like "Nice 'N' Easy" – and was credited as producing the film *Johnny Concho*. Sinatra and Sanicola became business partners in various ventures, including **the Cal-Neva Lodge** and the Barton Corporation, a song publishing company.

For all his experience on the streets, Sanicola often adopted the voice of reason with the hot-headed Sinatra. He tried to talk him out of his stubbornness in hiring the black-listed scriptwriter Albert Maltz, though to little avail. Cal-Neva, however, was the real problem. With an investigation in the early 1960s into an alleged prostitution ring and **Sam Giancana** showing his face around the resort during the same period, Sanicola got nervous. In the summer of 1962 he asked to be bought out of the resort, whereupon Sinatra apparently told him: "Out of Cal-Neva, out of everything." Sanicola agreed, accepting five of Sinatra's publishing companies as payment for his stake. In a car at the time of this verbal exchange, Sinatra dropped Sanicola in the desert and the two men, friends and partners for more than 25 years, never spoke again.

After Sanicola died in 1979, Sinatra was spotted being driven by Jimmy Van Heusen in a car that circled the church while the funeral took place.

JULE STYNE (1905–1994)

The London-born composer Jule Styne was effusively supportive when Sinatra made his society debut at the Riobamba in New York in 1943; and after he and **Sammy Cahn** had written the tunes for Sinatra's first few films, Frank put himself on the line for them when it came to his 1945 MGM debut, ***Anchors Aweigh***, threatening not to act in the picture if his songwriters of choice were not hired – and they were. The Styne/Cahn team wrote several Sinatra classics of the 1940s ("Time After Time", "I Fall In Love Too Easily") as well as special material for the private cabaret held at Frank and Nancy's house each New Year's Eve during this period.

In 1953, with Frank in the depths of despair over Ava, Jule (pronounced "Julie") found that his belongings had been moved into Sinatra's apartment – by Frank himself, who was desperate for companionship. "I was flattered, of course," said Styne. While keeping Sinatra company, he witnessed his pain and misery close-up; Sinatra would talk to a picture of Ava, rip it up, and then frantically try to put it back together, calling his first wife, Nancy, for comfort.

Suddenly, after eight months, in a note from Sinatra, Styne was asked to leave. He thought that he'd upset the singer by allowing the Styne/Cahn song "Three Coins In A Fountain" to be published by a company other than Sinatra's Barton Corporation; but Frank didn't seem unhappy with Cahn. It turned out that Styne had been less than discreet when it came to discussing what Sinatra was like to live with. This had found its way back to him, and Sinatra perceived it as the worst disloyalty possible.

He didn't speak to Styne for several years. And by the time that Styne figured out what he'd done, the Cahn/Van Heusen team had been established as Sinatra's house songwriters for half a decade.

Styne went on, however, to compose the hit show ***Gypsy*** with Stephen Sondheim, from which Sinatra recorded "All I Need Is The Girl", and, with

STYNE (LEFT) AND CAHN AT A GATHERING OF COMPOSERS IN JUNE 1988

Robert Merrill, *Funny Girl* – whose big song "People" was criticized by Sinatra for being rambling. But on the televised Sinatra tribute in 1979, *The First 40 Years*, it was Styne who presented him with The American Society of Composers, Authors and Publishers' "Pied Piper" award, which was awarded for Sinatra's "significant contribution to words and music". Dean Martin introduced Jule to Frank by saying: "Your pal … I think. You only hit him once." Styne, who died in 1994, described Sinatra as the man "mainly responsible for my career".

LANA TURNER (1921-1995)

"Keep Betty Grable, Lamour and Turner," sang Sinatra in "Nancy (With The Laughing Face)" in 1945; and the following year, having been entranced by her performance as the lusty femme fatale Cora Smith in *The Postman Always Rings Twice*, he was ready to keep the platinum blonde Lana Turner to himself. Although observers such as MGM star Esther Williams characterized the ensuing affair as mere sexual infatuation, Frank informed Nancy and George Evans that this was the real thing and packed his bags.

He moved into a new bachelor pad in Hollywood, but Turner – "Sweater Girl", as she was known at the time – was unimpressed with it and they reconvened at **the Beverly Hills Hotel**. Within weeks, however, Sinatra's passion had cooled. When he performed at the Hollywood nightclub Slapsie Maxie's in October 1946 with Phil Silvers, Nancy was there, at Jule Styne's table, and the result was a heart-warming public reconciliation, in which Sinatra, overcome while singing a song called **"Going Home"**, was led by Silvers to Styne's table, where husband and wife embraced. It was a brilliant stunt (with George Evans's signature all over it) and duly made the following day's papers.

Along with the rest of the country, Turner found out through reading a newspaper. Her maid overheard her making furious phone calls and she apparently pestered Sinatra's home for a while, until the family changed phone numbers. Close reference to the Sinatra affair was reportedly present in the original draft of Turner's biography in 1982, *The Lady, The Legend, The Truth* – but was removed. She died in 1995.

SINATRA THE LOVER

In one show at the Sands, Sinatra was singing **"What Is This Thing Called Love"** when Dean Martin interrupted by quipping, "Frank, if you don't know, we're all dead." On another occasion Martin announced, "When Sinatra dies they're giving his zipper to the Smithsonian."

Even when he was a nobody, Sinatra was, by all accounts, mad about **sex** and **romance**; when he hit Hollywood in the mid-1940s, he made a list of the starlets he wanted to get to know, and he got to know them all. After his marriage to Ava Gardner he spent the next couple of decades dating and sleeping with the most glamorous women in the world.

To men, Sinatra was one of the world's greatest lovers. He was the guy living the life they could never live, bedding the women they could never bed: **Kim, Lauren, Marilyn, Marilyn, Juliet, Angie, Marlene, Jill, Eva, Judy, Lana** – and those were only the ones they'd heard of. But Sinatra wasn't one to brag, and even tried to deny it. "I can honestly say to you, slaves of the press," he said at a journalists' lunch in 1965, "that if I had as many love affairs as you have given me credit for, I would now be speaking to you from a jar at the Harvard Medical School." And his wooing could certainly be tender. "I loved them all," he told the writer Pete Hamill, "I really did." Hardly any of them had anything bad to say about him. Marlene Dietrich: "He is the Mercedes-Benz of men." Judith Campbell: "He knows how to make you feel a like a complete woman." Occasional lover Marilyn Monroe, to valet George Jacobs: "Nobody compares to him, and I should know."

His behaviour during his forties, after Ava and before Mia, has been described as the longest **mid-life crisis** in history, and yet he claimed not to have gained any wisdom from his experience of swinging. "I'm supposed to have a Ph.D. on the subject of women, but the truth is I've flunked more often than not," he said. "I'm very fond of women, I admire them. But like all men, I don't understand them."

As always, however, there is a darker aspect to Sinatra's unquenchable ardour – the infidelities, the abortions and the distraught ex-lovers that are perhaps the occupational hazards of being a Lothario. "The one I've really loved, Frank Sinatra, you've done me wrong," read a note cited by Kitty Kelley written by the actress **Shirley Van Dyke**, who Sinatra had dated and then distanced himself from, before her attempted suicide in 1957. "You're so big and I'm so small."

Dean Martin once said on the stage of the Sands, "Everyone hates a smart-ass, Frank." Sinatra replied, grinning, "Yeah, but everybody loves a lover."

JIMMY VAN HEUSEN (1913-1990)

Born **Chester Babcock** – the name of Bob Hope's character in the film from 1962 *The Road To Hong Kong* – the composer Jimmy Van Heusen (pronounced "Van Hughes-n") renamed himself at the age of 15 after the famous brand of shirt. An ex-World War II test pilot, he became one of America's premier songwriters, and pursued a debauched bachelor lifestyle that Sinatra was drawn into after the Ava affair. A friend since the mid-1940s – he wrote **"Nancy (With The Laughing Face)"** – he was often there for Frank during the ill-fated romance. It was in Van Heusen's apartment block that Sinatra decided to slit his wrists in a fit of anguish in November 1953; Jimmy got Frank to the hospital and paid the desk clerk for his discretion. Thereafter, as Sinatra's valet George Jacobs observed, Van Heusen took it upon himself to ensure that Sinatra had as good a time as possible.

An inveterate ladies man, the moon-faced Van Heusen populated his house – Rattlesnake Ranch, overlooking Palm Springs – with an endless supply of **prostitutes, starlets and air hostesses**, and Sinatra did his best to keep up with it all. Sometimes he would join Van Heusen for the bacchanals at the ranch; on other occasions he would emulate the songwriter's approach through private pursuits at his own home. When on tour, brothel connoisseur Van Heusen would often accompany Sinatra, simply to round up the girls for the usual tour party or to start his own.

But there were also disagreements. On one occasion in 1961, Sinatra, in a rage over the portrayal of gangsters as Italians in the TV series *The Untouchables*, destroyed an original painting by Norman Rockwell in Van Heusen's apartment; when challenged by a girlfriend as to why he put up with such nonsense, Van Heusen told her, "I'm a whore for my music." There was another brief spat during **JFK's visit to Palm Springs** in 1962, when Van Heusen allowed his house to be used by the secret service while Kennedy stayed with neighbour Bing Crosby. Sinatra took this as a personal betrayal and, as Billy May recounted to Charles Granata, he let loose at Van Heusen when he was recording his song "The Boys' Night Out". "Tell you what, Chester," Sinatra said. "Why don't you get Jack Kennedy to record this fucking song and then see how many records it sells?"

SINATRA AND VAN HEUSEN REHEARSING IN WASHINGTON DC
FOR JOHN F. KENNEDY'S INAUGURAL GALA IN JANUARY 1961

Sinatra and Van Heusen remained friends for decades, even as both playboys settled down, though Sinatra's family regarded Van Heusen as a bad influence during the wilder years. Nevertheless, Jimmy attended **Frank and Barbara's wedding** in 1976 and the following year was a pallbearer at Dolly's funeral. He died in 1990.

The Music

The recording career

A comprehensive guide to Sinatra's entire recorded output, covering the big band years, the Columbia solo years and the classic albums on Capitol and Reprise

"You know, I adore making records. I'd rather do that than almost anything else."

FS, 1961

THE HOBOKEN RECORDINGS: 1935–39

There are a couple of surviving recordings of radio broadcasts of The Hoboken Four on *Major Bowes And His Original Amateur Hour* in September 1935, with Sinatra making recognisable solo interjections; the best known and most easily found is "Shine", which is available on a CD with Nancy Sinatra's book *An American Legend*. But Sinatra's first solo studio recording was "Our Love", an arrangement of a melody based on Tchaikovsky's *Romeo And Juliet*, made at the end of a March 1939 recording session led by the New Jersey saxophonist Frank Mane. Not available on CD, it can be heard online at www.songsbysinatra.com. Presented on a 78rpm disc as a wedding gift to Nancy, it demonstrates the beginning of a distinctive smooth, relaxed style.

THE APPLICATION FROM "FRANK SINATRA AND THE 3 FLASHES", WHO ALSO WENT
BY THE NAME OF THE HOBOKEN FOUR, FOR MAJOR BOWES AND HIS ORIGINAL
AMATEUR HOUR, ON WHICH THEY FEATURED IN SEPTEMBER 1935

THE HARRY JAMES RECORDINGS: 1939

Arranged by Andy Gibson and Jack Mathias; recorded July–November 1939; * radio broadcasts

AVAILABLE ON HARRY JAMES/FRANK SINATRA: THE COMPLETE RECORDINGS (COLUMBIA /LEGACY)

The Harry James Orchestra, dominated by the startling bluster of the leader's trumpet, had formed not long before the recording, and give the impression of a new group experimenting: they get growly like Duke Ellington on **"Melancholy Mood"**, hum and chant like Tommy Dorsey on **"It's Funny To Everyone But Me"** and swing sweetly in the smoochy generic style of the period on **"Here Comes The Night"**. They seem to be looking for their style, with Sinatra, their boy singer, very much part of the search.

JAMES ON SINATRA: *"He was always thinking of the lyrics. The melody was secondary … The feeling he has for words is just beautiful."*

SINATRA ON JAMES: *"A dear friend and a great teacher … a real nice guy with real know-how as a musician."*

In July 1939, in his inaugural session with the orchestra, Sinatra recorded **"From The Bottom Of My Heart"**. The song was a commercial original by James and the arranger Andy Gibson in which Sinatra was given a chorus and a half. The arrangement appears to be more of a singer's showcase than the many swing band sides of the era that were heavily instrumental and gave vocalists only a single chorus.

Most of Sinatra's numbers were new songs; indeed, four are co-written by Jack Lawrence, the most famous of which is **"All Or Nothing At All"**. But Walter Donaldson's **"My Buddy"**, from the early 1920s, given a jaunty swing treatment here, represents Sinatra's first recorded "standard" – an established popular song of timeless appeal. Other songs include a vocal version of

James's signature tune "Ciribiribin", a turn-of-the-century Italian aria recast as a rhythm number, and "On A Little Street In Singapore", faintly seedy exotica in which Sinatra sounds wide-eyed with wonder.

Sinatra is marvellous here, bringing a gentle panache to everything he sings. If compared with his later work his tone as **a young crooner** is light, but the pitching is good and the phrasing is already smooth. There

CROSBY VS SINATRA

Bing Crosby was, along with **Louis Armstrong**, one of the fathers of jazz-influenced singing. Broadly in the mould of crooners such as **Rudy Vallee** and **Russ Columbo** but with the rhythmic panache of a jazzman, in the 1930s "the Old Groaner", as he was sometimes affectionately known, was the biggest singing star in America; and the young Sinatra, like the rest of the country, was charmed by his many radio appearances and his apparently ultra-relaxed way with a song. When, as a nineteen-year-old, Frank saw Crosby in person – and the brouhaha that seemed to accompany being a music star – he knew that he had to be a singer.

In his early years he made particular efforts *not* to sound like him – "every kid on the block was boo-boo-booing like Crosby," he said – with the result that there were as many differences between them as there were similarities. Although Sinatra soon achieved Crosby's warmth of tone – especially on his **Columbia** recordings of the 1940s – he rarely matched Bing's relaxed style. This is clear if his 1941 recording of **"You Lucky People You"** is compared with Crosby's performance of the song on the soundtrack to the film *Road To Zanzibar*. Where Sinatra makes relatively heavy weather of Jimmy Van Heusen's elaborate little melody – pulling away from the beat to make sense of the phrasing – Crosby breezes through the line with insouciant swing *and* makes perfect sense. Sinatra would learn later to relax on rhythmic lines, but even then his swing remained edgier than Crosby's. "I believed, because of [Crosby's] leisurely manner of working, that if he could do it, I could do it," Sinatra said in the mid-1950s. "The funny switch is that I've never been able to do it. It's just a trick he has, a wonderful relaxed feeling about performing."

Nelson Riddle had a slightly different take on the differences between the rhythms of the two men. "Sinatra digs into a song and tries to get *into* it," he noted. "Crosby has a calculated nonchalance – he tosses off a tune." This made for terrific rhythmic bounce and cheerful irony, but when contrasted with the vulnerability and poignancy that the volatile Sinatra could achieve is also evidence of commitment to the material: he does more than just sing the songs. Already there's a sense of the young Sinatra teasing out a bit more beauty and meaning than there might be on the page, caressing the melody and elevating the text.

The Columbia/Legacy release gathers together all ten of the commercial James/Sinatra sides and several radio broadcasts. The highlight of

with a song, there could be a certain emotional distance in Crosby's work, as there apparently was in his life. Crosby was the original cool singer; Sinatra was the opposite of cool – as a man and an artist. And Crosby recognised the difference himself. "He creates a mood, which very few people are able to do," Bing once said of Frank. "I don't think I create a mood when I sing."

The two men had different voices, too, and different approaches to them. Crosby rarely ventured from his smooth baritone range to indulge in bravura finishes or extremity of tone. Sinatra not only learnt to make more than Crosby of the expressive "grain" in his voice, but would also, at various times in his career, venture to extremes, bringing startling drama to the music, as he did with the high F of **"All Or Nothing At All"** in 1939 and the low E of **"Ol' Man River"** in 1963. "Sinatra's voice is more 'live' and vibrant and fraught with shadows and colouring than Crosby's voice," Riddle observed.

Sinatra was always quick to pay tribute to Crosby, saying in the 1940s, "Bing was my first singing idol, and still is." The Old Groaner, meanwhile, acknowledged the rise of the Voice with the oft-quoted quip: "Frank Sinatra is the kind of singer who comes along once in a lifetime – but why did it have to be *my* lifetime?" He even sent an open letter of advice to the young crooner that was published in *Motion Picture-Hollywood Magazine* in December 1943. "Keep riding that skyrocket you're on, Frankie! I'm all for you," it said. "Yes, when I heard the whispers about you and me being bitter rivals, I just smiled."

Though entirely different temperamentally and for much of their careers politically, the two singers remained friendly throughout their lives, with Sinatra even signing the old man to his **Reprise** label in 1962, casting him in the Reprise Musical Repertory Theatre projects and the movie *Robin And The 7 Hoods*. Their professional encounters, mostly on radio and then TV, were never less than amiable, and their **"Well, Did You Evah"** duet in the movie *High Society* was a magical glimpse of the singers' respective performance styles.

these bonus tracks is a vocal chorus of **"Stardust"**. Given its stark accompaniment and unintegrated positioning, it sounds as if it's been tacked on the front of an existing arrangement, but Sinatra sounds splendidly relaxed and in control, making the legendarily intricate melody seem easy. A couple of delightfully casual variations on the composition underline the 23-year-old's growing confidence.

THE TOMMY DORSEY RECORDINGS: 1940–42

Arranged by Axel Stordahl, Sy Oliver, Fred Stulce, Heinie Beau; recorded February 1940–September 1942; * previously unreleased

AVAILABLE ON 5-CD SET THE SONG IS YOU (BMG/RCA/BLUEBIRD)

With the exception of Crosby, the popular music idols of the day came from the swing big bands, which were divided into two broad categories: **"hot" bands** (such as those of Benny Goodman and Artie Shaw), which emphasised jazz instrumentalists and hard swing, and **"sweet" bands** (Kay Kyser, Guy Lombardo), which emphasized written as opposed to improvised melodies through featured vocalists, and played gentler sounds for dancing. Dorsey's orchestra, like others, straddled the styles. His players (Bunny Berigan on trumpet, Bud Freeman on saxophone and the drummer Dave Tough among them) kept the jazz fans happy, while vocalist **Jack Leonard** and ballads featuring Dorsey on trombone ensured a wide commercial appeal. The Dorsey orchestra was voted *Down Beat* magazine's number one sweet band in 1939.

Though **personnel changes** were commonplace in the swing orchestras, with an estimated 250 musicians in and out of Tommy Dorsey's band between 1934 and 1946, there were particularly significant developments for the orchestra in late 1939 and early 1940. Not only did it have a new boy singer, but it also had recruited the hip close-harmony group **The Pied Pipers**, featuring Jo Stafford. Bunny Berigan returned to the fold after a failed period as a bandleader and bassist Sid Weiss, trumpeter Chuck Peterson and powerhouse drummer Buddy Rich were imported from the recently disbanded Artie Shaw outfit. Also important was Dorsey's hiring of Jimmy Lunceford's arranger **Sy Oliver**; it was his light-swinging jazzy charts that persuaded Rich to join and influenced Sinatra's developing sense of rhythm.

This music from Dorsey and Sinatra – spread here over five CDs – wasn't meant to be consumed in one sitting, for the boy singer features were just one part of the variety of attractions (not gathered on Sinatra/Dorsey collections) that formed the show that was Tommy Dorsey and his orchestra. The songwriter Sammy Cahn described his experience of the act's performance at the Paramount Theatre in New York: "Dorsey would be playing his theme song, 'Getting Sentimental Over You'. When the pit went up, he went into 'Marie', and he would stop the show with that. Then he would introduce Connie Haines. Big hit. Then he'd introduce The Pied Pipers. Big hit. Jo Stafford with The Pied Pipers. Big hit. Then he'd introduce Ziggy Ellman on the trumpet. Big hit. Then he would introduce Buddy Rich, who would really shatter the theatre. When all this was finished, out came a thin, frail human being … and he just topped the whole show."

Sinatra would top the show with his romantic ballads. With Dorsey an established name with an established approach, Sinatra, for most of his tenure with the band and even when he became a major attraction, had little choice but to fill the shoes of Jack Leonard, who had left in 1939, and to be part of a successful formula, which went like this: an intro setting a gentle foxtrot tempo, a chorus or so of Dorsey's (sometimes muted) trombone playing the melody, a brief interlude often incorporating a key-change, a chorus of an earnest, sweet-voiced young man singing about love, and a livelier chorus or so featuring solos and ensembles, all squeezed into three minutes. It's all as smooth as silk, with the whole band phrasing in Dorsey's legato style; and before long the boy singer was too.

Of the 87 sides that Sinatra recorded with Dorsey, relatively few became standards. Many of the songs were current plugs – that is, modern songs published by Dorsey – or pop and movie tunes that other publishers were promoting to whoever would do them. There were also several **Bing Crosby** film tunes: "Too Romantic" from *Road To Singapore*, "April Played The Fiddle" and "I Haven't The Time To Play The Millionaire" from *If I Had My Way*, and "It's Always You" and "You Lucky People You" from *Road To Zanzibar*, the latter being unusual in featuring a singer in both

The Influence of Dorsey and Heifetz

One of the most noted aspects of Sinatra's singing is his seamless, legato phrasing – his way of flowing one musical line into another – which allows the song and story to follow a graceful arc of sound. Sinatra was always clear about where he learnt to do this. "The thing that influenced me most was the way Tommy played his trombone," he said. "He would take a musical phrase and play it all the way through, seemingly without breathing, for eight, ten, maybe sixteen bars." Some commentators have put this down to Dorsey practising circular breathing, an arcane technique whereby breath is stored in the cheeks and exhaled through the mouth while further breath is drawn in through the nose, and ludicrously attributed the same skill to Sinatra. For a brass player it's hard, but for a singer it is physically impossible. The truth was more prosaic: Dorsey snuck little breaths through the corner of his mouth – what Sinatra called a "pinhole". Sinatra taught himself a similar technique.

Sinatra took Dorsey's legato style yet further by studying other instrumentalists, such as the classical violinist **Jascha Heifetz**, whose smooth bowing technique, producing what Sinatra called a "sustained quality", fascinated him. "[The sound] never broke," he remembered. "There was never a feeling of it stopping." He also developed extraordinary **breath control**, by regular running and by swimming under water, which allowed him to continue with a musical phrase between stanzas where other singers may have paused for breath. He displayed this smooth, unexpected conjoining of lines, often after a note that was long-held, throughout his career. There are examples in **"I Fall In Love Too Easily"** from 1945 ("...love to ever last/My heart should be...) and **"Ol' Man River"** from 1963 ("...lands in jail/I gets weary...").

Though Sinatra would later imply that this fusion of separate lines was an attempt to generate the flow of meaning that the text suggested, his initial impulse was musical, and his initial influence was Dorsey. "Even without lyrics, Tommy made it sound so musical," said Sinatra, "you never lost the thread of the message."

an opening chorus and a reprise. But they don't challenge Bing's versions very much. Sinatra is fulsome with a light touch and never less than exemplary, moving in some places and swinging in others, but it's all very *efficient*: heard together in one go, these sides have an air of prescribed routine about them.

The Tommy Dorsey recordings

There are a few diversions, however, to break the homogeneity. A group within a group called **The Sentimentalists**, featuring Sinatra and The Pied Pipers in close harmony, plus rhythm and a muted Dorsey, had a crack at the seriously slow **"I'll Never Smile Again"**, and it was a huge hit; this dreamy format was duly revisited on "Whispering", "Stardust" and "There Are Such Things". Another Sinatra-plus-Pipers novelty was comic call-and-response between singer and group on "The One I Love (Belongs To Somebody Else)" and "Dolores", with Sinatra as the straight man.

A more expansive manifestation of this playful device had been established in 1937 by the Dorsey orchestra's hit **"Marie"**, with Jack Leonard singing it straight and the entire band singing hip musical interpolations: "Living in a great big way ... Mama!" Sinatra is heard delivering this number on the bonus CD of radio broadcasts, and had his own similar songs, arranged by **Sy Oliver**, "East Of The Sun" and "Blue Skies". The latter, pulling at his straight-man chains, had him bending notes and stretching phrases: no wonder Dorsey was heard to mutter to his singer occasionally, "Get on the beat, kid!"

Sinatra has duets with **Connie Haines** on three numbers: "Snootie Little Cutie", "You Might Have Belonged To Another" and one of his Dorsey-era highlights, **"Oh! Look At Me Now"**, which allows the musical banter to take on a more personal nature. But the large majority of the Dorsey/ Sinatra sides are romantic ballads, some of which Sinatra would revisit and update at Capitol (including four Matt Dennis/Tom Adair songs) and Reprise (largely on *I Remember Tommy*). Given that the songs that he would reinterpret were often carried off more successfully later in his career, it may be that the obscure nuggets are the most interesting part of this set. There are enough minor Van Heusens, Yip Harburgs and Irving Berlins to keep vintage song buffs amused for weeks.

Also here is the singer's four-side solo session of January 1942 with **Axel Stordahl**, recorded while Sinatra was still in the Dorsey band for RCA Bluebird and the first time the singer was heard with strings. Dorsey added strings to his band not long afterwards and the final few Sinatra/ Dorsey sessions (including the final song that Sinatra broadcast with the band – "The Song Is You", on September 3, 1942) point towards the singer's classic Columbia style.

Some listeners who come to Sinatra via a more vibrant period of his artistic career may find his Dorsey-era output relatively plain and stuck in its time. While it's true that this music is unlikely to stir the soul like *Only The Lonely* or quicken the pulse like *Live At The Sands*, there is a great deal of fascinating, frivolous pop to delve into here. For those who want more than the RCA 5-CD box, there are further rare radio broadcasts that are notably different to the commercial recordings on the 20-track compilation *Young Blue Eyes: Birth Of The Crooner* (BMG); everyone else may be content with the 12-track sampler of this *The Song Is You* set called *I'll Be Seeing You* (BMG), or the budget 23-track compilation *There Are Such Things* (ASV).

THE COLUMBIA RECORDINGS: 1943–52

> *"For me, it began at Columbia. Having the opportunity to immerse myself in the talents of people like Alec Wilder, Axel Stordahl, Nat "King" Cole, Johnny Mercer, Rodgers and Hammerstein, the Gershwins, Jerome Kern and so many others was a rare opportunity and a treasured gift."*
>
> FS, 1992

Arranged by Axel Stordahl, Heinie Beau, Sy Oliver, Percy Faith, Ray Conniff, George Siravo, Norman Leydon, Jeff Alexander, Sid Cooper; recorded June 1943–September 1952

AVAILABLE ON 12-CD SET THE COLUMBIA YEARS: THE COMPLETE RECORDINGS (COLUMBIA/LEGACY) WITH HIGHLIGHTS ON THE 4-CD SET BEST OF THE COLUMBIA YEARS (COLUMBIA/LEGACY).

Sinatra's period at Columbia is sometimes characterised as a nine-year warm up for his classic period at Capitol. To some listeners, his tunes from the 1940s, compared with the timeless music that he made in the 1950s or 1960s, sound like old-fashioned music that evokes a distant era. Sinatra, this argument continues, may be soft and smooth and clear, but he is not yet the vivid vocalist that he would become; and the arrangements, while exemplary in themselves, are time-tied products of their age and therefore interesting only as a musical adjunct to the Swoonatra phenomenon and when compared with his later work.

While that may be true to a point, there's an innocent perfection in much of the Columbia output that is hard to deny. Sinatra's singing is at its easiest and sweetest, and Axel Stordahl's arrangements are faultless and often stirring examples of how a romantic pop song should be scored. The songs are among the best compositions in **the Great American Songbook** and some – "She's Funny That Way", "You Go To My Head", "I've Got A Crush On You" – became enduring standards simply because they were recorded by Sinatra. And although Sinatra recorded many of them again for Capitol and Reprise, it could be argued that some of his interpretations when older and wiser didn't improve in all ways on his 1940s readings, but merely provided alternatives.

The Voice's solo career started alongside **The Bobby Tucker Singers**, who helped to start it by fashioning an ingenious *a cappella* solution to the 1943 musicians' strike. The results, like "Close To You" and "People Will Say We're In Love", are delightfully homely. Thereafter, the vast majority of Sinatra's Columbia output was swoonsome and romantic, sung with depth and subtlety and scored by **Axel Stordahl** with artful lushness. Adorned with strings, harps, celestas and the occasional choir, a baritone sings variously of Nancy, Stella, Mam'selle, his melancholy baby, and how she's funny that way, how day by day he's falling more and more in love with her and how she goes to his head. He implores her to embrace

him, to watch over him. He admits he falls in love too easily, sometimes has to hang his tears out to dry and is inclined to dream, dream, dream. Sometimes, several of these mushy masterpieces would be gathered on an "album" of four 78rpm discs, examples being *The Voice Of Frank Sinatra* or *Frankly Sentimental* (later released as 10″ albums), but mostly they appeared as a steady stream of

The Music

THE ORIGINAL COLUMBIA ALBUMS

The Voice of Frank Sinatra

YOU GO TO MY HEAD/SOMEONE TO WATCH OVER ME/THESE FOOLISH THINGS/WHY SHOULDN'T I?/I DON'T KNOW WHY/TRY A LITTLE TENDERNESS/A GHOST OF A CHANCE/PARADISE

Arranged by Axel Stordahl; recorded July 30 and December 7, 1945; released March 1946 on 78 and June 1948 on 10"

Songs By Sinatra, Volume 1

I'M SORRY I MADE YOU CRY/HOW DEEP IS THE OCEAN/OVER THE RAINBOW/SHE'S FUNNY THAT WAY/EMBRACEABLE YOU/ALL THE THINGS YOU ARE/THAT OLD BLACK MAGIC/I CONCENTRATE ON YOU

Arranged by Axel Stordahl; recorded December 19, 1944-January 10, 1947; released April 1947 on 78 and January 1950 on 10"

Frankly Sentimental

BODY AND SOUL/LAURA/FOOLS RUSH IN/SPRING IS HERE/ONE FOR MY BABY (AND ONE MORE FOR THE ROAD)/GUESS I'LL HANG MY TEARS OUT TO DRY/WHEN YOU AWAKE/IT NEVER ENTERED MY MIND

Arranged by Axel Stordahl; recorded July 30, 1946-November 10, 1947; released June 1949 on 78 and July 1949 on 10"

Dedicated To You

THE MUSIC STOPPED/THE MOON WAS YELLOW/I LOVE YOU/STRANGE MUSIC/WHERE OR WHEN/NONE BUT THE LONELY HEART/ALWAYS/WHY WAS I BORN?

Arranged by Axel Stordahl; recorded January 29, 1945-December 27, 1947; released June 1950 on 78 and 10"

Sing And Dance With Frank Sinatra

LOVER/IT'S ONLY A PAPER MOON/MY BLUE HEAVEN/IT ALL DEPENDS ON YOU/YOU DO SOMETHING TO ME/SHOULD I/THE CONTINENTAL/WHEN YOU'RE SMILING

Arranged by George Siravo; recorded July 10, 1949, April 14, 1950 and April 24, 1950; released October 1950 on 78 and 10"

The Columbia recordings

78rpm singles (thirteen double-sided discs in 1945, seventeen in 1946, nineteen in 1947), many of which made the *Billboard* top 10.

Between these came occasional rhythm pieces arranged by **George Siravo**, such as "Saturday Night" (number two in 1944) and "Five Minutes More" (number one in 1946); and more pumped-up, highfalutin material, such as Jerome Kern's "Ol' Man River" and Kurt Weill's "Lost In The Stars", designed to show that there was more to the Voice than tunes to make the bobbysoxers sigh.

By 1947 it was clear that the old romantic tunes weren't hitting the spot, or the charts, quite as they had in the war years, and there were concerted efforts by Sinatra and Columbia to find a fresh musical approach. Sinatra was paired with **Dinah Shore** ("My Romance"), the gospel vocal group **The Charioteers** ("Jesus Is A Rock In The Weary Land"), **Doris Day** ("Let's Take An Old Fashioned Walk") and even his old partners **The Pied Pipers**, on a novelty piece that boded ill, **"The Dum Dot Song"**. He attempted to hook himself onto prevailing trends with the hopefully hip "Bop! Goes My Heart" ("Foodley-dee-bop, what you do to me") and the blatant commercial jive of "The Hucklebuck" ("Yah Dad! Right Now!") – the latter doing the trick, but the former not. But while his record sales waned he didn't entirely abandon **the ballads**, and the years between 1947 and 1949 saw deep readings of "Autumn In New York", "I'm Glad There Is You", "Laura" and "Body And Soul" (with gorgeous trumpet obbligatos by Bobby Hackett), among others.

In the simplified versions of events that describe Sinatra rising to artistic glory during the Capitol period, there are three commonly propagated myths concerning the latter part of Sinatra's Columbia tenure. **The first myth:** *Sinatra was forced to record nothing but schlock novelties when Mitch Miller took over as his producer in 1950.* But Sinatra had been happy to record schlock novelties before Miller arrived; indeed, he had a top 10 hit with the silly jump-jive of **"Chattanoogie Shoe Shine Boy"** early in 1950. Moreover, although the shamelessly commercial Miller did oversee "Castle Rock" and "Mama Will Bark" and "Bim Bam Baby" – all classics of vulgar market-chasing dreck – he was also responsible for the tremendous album *Sing And Dance With Frank Sinatra*, the terrific **"Birth Of The Blues"** and the lovely "Azure-Te". Finally, no one forced Sinatra to do anything; he always had the final say on what was recorded, and his occasional taste-free pursuit of the charts was a career-long strategy and by no means exclusive to this period.

The second myth concerning the latter part of Sinatra's Columbia tenure: *He had no hits.* True, he had more misses than hits, but **"Goodnight Irene"**, a folksy song by Huddie "Leadbelly" Ledbetter, reached number eight. (When a DJ enthusiastically mentioned to Sinatra that "you oughta do a lot of songs like that", he replied, "Don't hold your breath.") "Castle Rock" peaked at the same spot, while "Mama Will Bark", "Bim Bam Baby" and "Birth Of The Blues" all made the top twenty.

The third myth: *Sinatra's singing wasn't very good.* Yes, there was a mixed response to Sinatra in the press during a low point of their build-'em-up-knock-'em-down cycle. Yes, he's undoubtedly in transition, between the silky-smooth crooner of the 1940s and the edgy supremacy of his Capitol voice; and perhaps he is less than fully confident in 1949 on "Some Enchanted Evening". And yes, in 1950 he suffered from haemorrhaged vocal cords. But his powerful, sensitive singing on **"April In Paris"**, **"I'm A Fool To Want You"** and **"My Girl"**, to name only three examples, belies the idea that his singing was poor. Even if neither Sinatra nor the public believed in him as a singer during this period, the proof is in the listening. He is persuasive, compelling and occasionally outstanding, up until, and on, the final tune of his final Columbia session in May 1952, the poignant ballad that in retrospect sounds like a pointed plea to a company about to drop him, **"Why Try To Change Me Now"**.

The Columbia period is represented by a sprawling discography and disparate releases then and now. Genuine enthusiasts and scholars of Sinatra should track down *The Complete Columbia Recordings* (Columbia/Legacy, 1993), a stunning 285-track, 12-CD set that brought everything together for the first time. Of the selective compilations, the official one is *The Best Of The Columbia Years 1943-1952* (Columbia/Legacy, 1995), a 97-track, 4-CD reduction of the *Complete* set, beautifully packaged and annotated, and concentrating on the high-quality tracks. As all the Columbia recordings are now more than fifty years old, there are public domain collections, of which *All Or Nothing At All* (Properbox), a 102-track, 4-CD set, is one of the best; covering the periods with James, Dorsey and Columbia, and including rarities and radio broadcasts, it mops up some nice surprises that the Columbia *Best Of* misses, including the cowboy ditty "When The Sun Goes Down" and the playful duet with Pearl Bailey "A Little Learnin' Is A Dangerous Thing". Recent single-disc issues include the excellent repackage of Sinatra's 1950 album *Sing And*

Dance With Frank Sinatra with extra George Siravo arrangements as *Swing And Dance With Frank Sinatra* (Columbia/Legacy, 1996) and his 1946 album *The Voice Of Frank Sinatra* (Columbia/Legacy, 2003) with extra tracks, which are mostly alternative takes of other romantic classics. Two good compilations, *Sinatra Sings Gershwin* and *Sinatra Sings Porter* (both Columbia/Legacy, 2003), attempt to ensnare the casual purchaser with the perennially appealing concept of a single composer's songbook, and the collector with rare recordings of TV and radio performances.

THE CAPITOL YEARS: 1953–61

"I knew Frank would pick his songs and that he knew what he wanted to do."

ALAN LIVINGSTON, VICE-PRESIDENT OF CAPITOL, TO WILL FRIEDWALD

When the Capitol executive **Alan Livingston** announced at the company's convention in 1953 that he had just signed Frank Sinatra, there was a collective groan. It was understandable. Sinatra was regarded by most of the entertainment industry as a loser whose time had passed. Yet even Livingston, who believed in Sinatra's talent, could not have foreseen the achievement of the Capitol period.

Sinatra was just hitting his stride as a storyteller and mood-setter, and on the road he had honed a new rhythmic verve, melodic audacity and attacking assertiveness. In 1953, when he cut **"South Of The Border"** and **"I've Got The World On A String"** on an early session, he was still a year away from his career-changing comeback (the Oscar for *From Here To Eternity*), but both performances brim with jazzy confidence. The faultless intonation of the 1940s had perhaps slipped a little but there was a wider expressive range and a meticulous attention to emotional detail that the increasingly revealing recording quality, made possible by technological innovations with magnetic tape, captured beautifully.

THE INFLUENCE OF BILLIE HOLIDAY AND MABEL MERCER

In September 1939 a young Frank was photographed near the front of the stage of Chicago's **Off-Beat** club watching Billie Holiday, the languid jazz song stylist whose horn-like paraphrasing of a melody and rhythmic audacity demonstrated musical and emotional possibilities that most singers couldn't get close to. Although a much smoother singer than Holiday, Sinatra can be heard in the mid-1940s adopting a similar approach. His version, for example, from 1945 of **"You Go To My Head"** – a ballad that Holiday recorded in 1938 – hangs back luxuriously from the beat and even duplicates her four-note variation on the third reprise of the title line. Sinatra's **"All Of Me"** – both the 1947 version with Siravo and that from 1954 with Riddle – utilises Holiday's "eyes that *cry*" deviation from the written tune, where she sings the ninth note on the chord instead of the tonic – a sophisticated melodic move.

Sinatra was rumoured to have had **a brief affair** with Holiday in the early 1940s and even to have attempted some drug running as she lay in hospital dying during the late 1950s; if this is true, it indicates the narcotic-despising Sinatra's regard for her. His tribute to her was certainly fulsome. "With a few exceptions, every major pop singer in the US during her generation has been touched in some way by her genius," he said. "It is Billie Holiday whom I first heard in 52nd Street clubs in the early Thirties, who was, and remains, the greatest single musical influence on me." (When asked what Sinatra may have learnt from her, Billie shrugged. "Bending those notes," she said. "That's all I helped Frankie with.")

On another occasion, however, Sinatra said, "Everything I know, I learnt from Mabel Mercer." The British-born queen of cabaret, known for her regal manner, rarefied repertoire and crisp enunciation, Mercer had been well-known in the supper clubs of Paris during the 1930s among the cultural émigrés, including **Ernest Hemingway**, **Cole Porter** and **the Prince Of Wales**, before moving to America when the war started. Songwriters such as Cole Porter and **Alec Wilder** and singers including Sinatra, Billie Holiday and **Tony Bennett** made a point of seeing her in the 1940s during her long New York tenures at clubs such as The Blue Angel and Spivy's.

Mercer, who often resorted to an almost *sprachspiel* or *parlando* style of delivery often on little-known, song connoisseur's material, is an acquired taste. "People say, 'Why, she can't sing for toffee,'" she once admitted. "I know that – I'm telling a story." Her impact on Sinatra's feel for a lyric and for the narrative at the heart of a song, and his clarity of diction, is audible throughout his music.

The Capitol years

The Capitol producers appointed by Livingston were **Voyle Gilmore** and, from *Only The Lonely* onwards, **Dave Cavanaugh**, but by all accounts Sinatra was his own producer, deciding when to push for a better take and when to move on, and having control over album concept and the selection and the order of the songs. Sinatra would even make suggestions to the arrangers about the shape and tone of the musical settings, in meetings before recordings. He exploited brilliantly the possibilities of the relatively new long-player format by programming the great songs of the 1930s and 1940s in albums with a consistent mood or theme, whether romantic, lonely, upbeat or relaxed.

And on top of this, with his faithful 1940s arranger Axel Stordahl out of the picture after the initial session – he took a job with the singer Eddie Fisher – Sinatra hooked up with the relatively unknown **Nelson Riddle**. Although Gordon Jenkins and Billy May, other arrangers for Sinatra during this period, brought new colours to Sinatra's musical palette at Capitol, it was his legendarily fertile partnership with Riddle that was central to the breezy swinging and the poetic despair that epitomized the **"New Sinatra"** sound.

In 1961 it all ended in tears. But along the way came imperishable, timeless long-playing classics that represented the height of pre-rock pop music – and the peak of Frank Sinatra as a musical artist.

Songs For Young Lovers

THE GIRL NEXT DOOR/THEY CAN'T TAKE THAT AWAY FROM ME/VIOLETS FOR YOUR FURS/ LITTLE GIRL BLUE/LIKE SOMEONE IN LOVE/A FOGGY DAY/ I GET A KICK OUT OF YOU/MY FUNNY VALENTINE

Arranged by Nelson Riddle and George Siravo; recorded November 5-6, 1953; released January 1954

ORIGINALLY AN 8-TRACK, 10″ ALBUM, THE CURRENT CD FORMAT COMPRISES SONGS FOR YOUNG LOVERS AND SWING EASY. THE 22-CD BOX SET THE CAPITOL YEARS FEATURES THE ALBUM WITH FOUR ADDITIONAL TRACKS (SOMEONE TO WATCH OVER ME/MY ONE AND ONLY LOVE/ IT WORRIES ME/I CAN READ BETWEEN THE LINES), WHICH FORMED THE 1960 12″ LP.

This is Sinatra's debut album for Capitol – and his sweetest. Beautifully light and airy, it's all polite romance in mild climates and is comforting and uplifting in turns. Scored delightfully for a small chamber orchestra

of four strings and two reeds, along with rhythm and tinkling celesta evoking raindrops and dappled sunlight, the album's faintly old-fashioned air makes it an almost uniquely quaint item in Sinatra's Capitol canon. Although the sleeve credits Nelson Riddle as the sole arranger, the collection is based almost entirely on the charts of **George Siravo**, as used by Sinatra in his club act during the early 1950s.

But in retrospect it's obvious that the cute swing figures played on guitar on "They Can't Take That Away From Me" and on guitar and clarinet on **"I Get A Kick Out Of You"**, which were judged "too square" by Sinatra's pianist Bill Miller, aren't Riddle's style at all. Neither is the jaunty rhythm guitar on "My Funny Valentine", but the Debussy-like interlude on Riddle's one original arrangement on this album, **"Like Someone In Love"**, certainly is.

While Sinatra is recognisable as the singer who only months earlier had sung "Why Try To Change Me Now" at his final Columbia session, he is now a stronger, fresher, more mature singer. Confident and warm, his superbly judged blend of passion and breeziness was never more persuasive. Highlights include the picture-a-scene ebb and flow of the verse of **"Violets For Your Furs"**, the much-admired breath control of **"My Funny Valentine"** and his echoes of the word "shining" on **"A Foggy Day"**: has the excitement at seeing the sun come out ever been more vividly conveyed? A transitional record, but a charming one.

Swing Easy

JEEPERS CREEPERS/TAKING A CHANCE ON LOVE/WRAP YOUR TROUBLES IN DREAMS/ I'M GONNA SIT RIGHT DOWN AND WRITE MYSELF A LETTER/GET HAPPY/ALL OF ME/SUNDAY/ JUST ONE OF THOSE THINGS

Arranged by Nelson Riddle and Heinie Beau; recorded April 7 and April 19, 1954; released August 1954

The Capitol years

ORIGINALLY AN 8-TRACK, 10″ ALBUM,
THE CURRENT CD FORMAT COUPLES
SWING EASY WITH SONGS FOR YOUNG
LOVERS. THE 22-CD BOX SET THE CAPITOL
YEARS FEATURES THE ALBUM WITH FOUR
ADDITIONAL TRACKS (LEAN BABY/I LOVE
YOU/ HOW COULD YOU DO A THING LIKE
THAT TO ME/WHY SHOULD I CRY OVER
YOU) WHICH FORMS THE 1960 12″ LP.

This is the long-playing rebirth of Sinatra as **a hipster**. Wanting the world to know that he's sitting on a rainbow, he oozes rhythmic élan and melodic daring and is at the peak of his presumptuousness. It's not quite a masterpiece, but it's close: the Sinatra/Riddle partnership has only a small way to go before its summit.

The core sound of the album is a small swing group that's bursting with neat invention and Riddle's blossoming signature sound. The witty intro riffs sound like paraphrases of familiar material used elsewhere; indeed, the fluttering clarinet figure of **"I'm Gonna Sit Right Down"** was itself a reprise of the brassy introduction to "Why Should I Cry Over You". And Riddle's reharmonizations (his harmonic choices, rather than the composer's, on the giddy descending sequence in "I'm Gonna Sit Right Down") and advanced harmonic colours (the bold dissonances in "Sunday"), while pleasing in themselves, in retrospect sound like dry runs for what's to come.

But perhaps what leaves *Swing Easy* just short of the Capitol pantheon of all-time classics is the repertoire. Like *Songs For Young Lovers*, it is largely selected from the previous generation of standards, further establishing Sinatra's dedication, in the golden age of arranging, to what is considered **the golden age of song writing**, the period between the end of World War I and the advent of rock'n'roll. And yet however perfected they are here, "Jeepers Creepers", "I'm Gonna Sit Right Down And Write Myself A Letter", "Sunday" and "Wrap Your Troubles In Dreams" (its downward spiralling bridge notwithstanding) are little more than vintage novelties and rarely featured in Sinatra's later live sets. Of the other songs, Cole Porter's "Just One Of Those Things" is terrific, though probably not quite as good as Sinatra's alone-at-the-piano version in the film *Young At Heart*, and "Taking A Chance On Love" is a medium-grade Vernon Duke tune with wearing triple rhymes. Only **"Get Happy"**, with its bubbling trombone pedal point – staying put while the harmonic and melodic interest is created elsewhere – and the multi-gear **"All Of Me"**, with its thrilling coda syncopations, are unassailable Sinatra/Riddle classics.

Still, other jazz-pop singers of the time – or of any time – would make records as good as this only in their dreams.

In The Wee Small Hours

IN THE WEE SMALL HOURS OF THE MORNING/MOOD INDIGO/GLAD TO BE UNHAPPY/I GET ALONG WITHOUT YOU VERY WELL/DEEP IN A DREAM/I SEE YOUR FACE BEFORE ME/CAN'T WE BE FRIENDS/WHEN YOUR LOVER HAS GONE/WHAT IS THIS THING CALLED LOVE/LAST NIGHT WHEN WE WERE YOUNG/I'LL BE AROUND/ILL WIND/IT NEVER ENTERED MY MIND/DANCING ON THE CEILING/I'LL NEVER BE THE SAME/THIS LOVE OF MINE

Arranged by Nelson Riddle; recorded March 1, 1954, and February 8–March 4, 1955; released April 1955

SINATRA'S FIRST 12" LP, THIS WAS ALSO ORIGINALLY ISSUED AS TWO 10" LPs.

A freshly cuckolded singer and a modern-romantic arranger getting into his stride buff sixteen lovelorn, beautifully crafted songs from the Thirties and Forties into a plaintive art-song hue, to create an album that is emotional (but not hysterical) and hugely moving. The muted tones and warm mono recording settle around the listener like an enveloping fog, transporting the imagination to a comforting place where bittersweet regret is expressed with warmth and wisdom.

Featuring masterpiece after miniature masterpiece, the compositions are perfectly chosen for their literary and musical excellence. As raw material, Duke Ellington's **"Mood Indigo"**, Cole Porter's **"What Is This Thing Called Love"** and Harold Arlen's **"Last Night When We Were Young"** and **"Ill Wind"** are among the best of their genre: jazz-informed songs written during the golden age of American popular song. Add to that material the dramatic interpretative work of a singer and arranger who are perfectly matched and the effect is mesmerizing.

The dynamic of the record ranges from the stark acoustic guitar chords at the opening of "**Can't We Be Friends**" to the cataclysmic climax of **"Last Night When We Were Young"**. But the album mostly languishes in a hushed netherworld of subdued strings, whispering woodwind and chiming celesta, with Sinatra delivering his deepest and best ballad performances yet. He is simply magnificent. The faint technical imperfections that crept into his mature singing, from the Capitol period onwards – a little sand in his tone, occasional tuning that was not right on the note – not only fail to distract from the performance; they also add a devastating humanness to his delivery. When emotional damage is expressed so eloquently and elegantly, it produces more than a record: it's catharsis, an entire environment for the broken-hearted and art as communal healing.

Songs For Swingin' Lovers!

YOU MAKE ME FEEL SO YOUNG/IT HAPPENED IN MONTEREY/YOU'RE GETTING TO BE A HABIT WITH ME/YOU BROUGHT A NEW KIND OF LOVE TO ME/TOO MARVELLOUS FOR WORDS/OLD DEVIL MOON/PENNIES FROM HEAVEN/LOVE IS HERE TO STAY/I'VE GOT YOU UNDER MY SKIN/I THOUGHT ABOUT YOU/WE'LL BE TOGETHER AGAIN/MAKIN' WHOOPEE/ SWINGIN' DOWN THE LANE/ANYTHING GOES/HOW ABOUT YOU?

Arranged by Nelson Riddle; recorded January 9-16, 1956; released March 1956

A timeless vocal record of the hybrid genre of swing-pop that's loaded with jazz feeling, the second Sinatra/Riddle masterwork is the absolute antithesis of the wound-licking melancholy of *In The Wee Small Hours*. Showing the arranger and the singer to be masters at conveying either end of a mood swing, *Songs For Swingin' Lovers!* is a strutting, insouciant celebration of living and loving. The songs are an average of twenty years old, with

fine old Broadway and Hollywood tunes (the title song of Cole Porter's

SINATRA THE CONDUCTOR

"Listen, I don't know the first thing about conducting,
but I know this music and I love it, and if you'll work with me,
I think we can get it down"
FS TO SESSION ORCHESTRA, DECEMBER 1945, AS REMEMBERED BY COMPOSER ALEC WILDER

Frank Sinatra Conducts Alec Wilder (Columbia, 1946)

Frank Sinatra Conducts Tone Poems Of Color (Capitol, 1956)

Peggy Lee: The Man I Love (Capitol, 1957)

Dean Martin: Sleep Warm (Capitol, 1959)

Frank Sinatra Conducts Music From Pictures And Plays (Reprise, 1962)

Sylvia Syms: Syms By Sinatra (Reprise, 1982)

What's New (Reprise, 1983)

Alec Wilder arranged some of Sinatra's 1943 *a cappella* sides with The Bobby Tucker Singers and in 1945 Sinatra recorded the Wilder tune "Just An Old Stone House", whose tortuous modulations put it well away from the mainstream. Around the same time, Sinatra heard and enjoyed some of Wilder's classical work and, with the encouragement of the oboist **Mitch Miller** (a friend of Wilder and future *bête noire* of Sinatra), he persuaded the Columbia boss Manie Sachs to let him take the baton for a recording of Wilder's work. Contemporary and oblique, the product didn't find a large audience but was a cult favourite among some modern-minded musicians.

Wilder also got a couple of cuts when Sinatra repeated the experience ten years later at Capitol for *Tone Poems Of Color*, a specially commissioned series of pieces based on Norman Sickel's poetry, featuring the archetypal work of Gordon Jenkins in his first encounter with Sinatra, untypical offerings from Nelson Riddle and Billy May, and further contributions from Elmer Bernstein, Victor Young and André Previn.

Sinatra felt capable enough to conduct Riddle's charts for Peggy Lee's Capitol debut *The Man I Love* in 1957 and Pete King's charts for Dean Martin's *Sleep Warm* in 1959, and he conceived and produced both albums. Sinatra also once mentioned that he was going to ask Nelson Riddle to write a guitar concerto for him to conduct but the nearest this came to fruition was when Riddle arranged the ultra-rare *Frank Sinatra Conducts Music From Pictures And Plays*, an early release on Reprise.

In Gordon Jenkins's fanciful *The Future* suite on *Trilogy* in 1980, it becomes evident through the libretto that the semi-fictional character of "Francis", above all the things he could do in the future, wants to conduct an orchestra. And soon afterwards he did, on *Syms By Sinatra*, for the cabaret singer Sylvia Syms, whom he had known since the early 1940s, the arrangements being Don Costa's last work; and on *What's New*, an album of ballads by his favoured lead trumpeter of the time, Charles Turner.

Sinatra took his baton-wielding very seriously and the musicians who were there agree that he was physically expressive and competent, at the very least. Even Miller, who had reason to remember Sinatra in an unfavourable light, admitted that the musically untrained singer "had a feel for music ... he didn't get in the way". Peggy Lee recalled that Frank's conducting was "marvellously sensitive, as one would expect".

SINATRA CONDUCTING IN 1956, WITH NELSON RIDDLE ON HIS LEFT

Anything Goes) and crafted cornball ("Pennies From Heaven", "Makin' Whoopee") rubbing shoulders with Tin Pan Alley fripperies ("It Happened In Monterey") and superior, relatively modern pieces (Jimmy Van Heusen's "I Thought About You"). They're all turned into hip standards for a new generation of lovers of adult pop, and thereafter, for everyone.

RIDDLE ON SINATRA: *"The man himself somehow draws everything out of you … He'd never give out compliments either … He expects your best, just that."*

SINATRA ON RIDDLE: *"Nelson is the greatest arranger in the world, a very clever musician … If I say, 'Make like Puccini,' Nelson will make exactly the same little note, and that eighth bar will be Puccini all right, and the roof will lift off."*

TO ROBIN DOUGLAS-HOME, 1961

Swing Easy pointed the way, but *Songs For Swingin' Lovers!* shows the Sinatra/Riddle synergy reaching a pinnacle. Many of the elements of the classic Riddle style had been heard before this album, but it was here that they came together for the first time: **the "heartbeat" tempos** laid down by Alvin Stoller (drums) and Joe Comfort (bass), George Roberts's bass trombone, Harry "Sweets" Edison's wittily improvised asides on muted trumpet, the rhythmic chink of Bill Miller's celesta, and what Sinatra called "sustaining" strings. Riddle would employ his new signature style with many vocalists, but it was with Sinatra that his work sounded its most vital. The two men seemed to inspire the best in each other.

Songs For Swingin' Lovers is an almost perfect example of Sinatra/Riddle magic. The highlights are many (the astonishing **"I've Got You Under My Skin"** [see pages 247–249] among them) but it's the unification of all the musical elements in an intoxicatingly upbeat mood that makes it so irresistible. It's rhythmic and exciting, smooth and sophisticated – and the most satisfying swing set of Sinatra's career.

Close To You

CLOSE TO YOU/P. S. I LOVE YOU/LOVE LOCKED OUT/EVERYTHING HAPPENS TO ME/IT'S EASY TO REMEMBER/DON'T LIKE GOODBYES/WITH EVERY BREATH I TAKE/BLAME IT ON MY YOUTH/IT COULD HAPPEN TO YOU/I'VE HAD MY MOMENTS/I COULDN'T SLEEP A WINK LAST NIGHT/THE END OF A LOVE AFFAIR

Arranged by Nelson Riddle; recorded March 8, April 4, April 5 and November 1, 1956; released January 1957

Similar to *Songs For Young Lovers* in its old-style charm, though darker, and similar to *In The Wee Small Hours* in its intimacy, though less intense, *Close To You* is a delightful, intriguing set of love ballads. Alongside **the remakes** ("Everything Happens To Me" from 1941 during the Dorsey days, and "Close To You" from 1943) there are some **surprises**, which are as obscure as some of those in Mabel Mercer's repertoire. Walter Donaldson's "I've

Had My Moments" (musically a close cousin of Gershwin's "A Foggy Day") is from a forgotten 1935 movie *Hollywood Party*, "Love Locked Out" is a lesser-known Ray Noble song and the glorious "Don't Like Goodbyes" is rescued from Harold Arlen's unsuccessful musical from 1954, *House Of Flowers*.

Scoring the album for only a rhythm section, a solo instrumental voice and the Hollywood String Quartet, led by Sinatra's favourite violinist, **Felix Slatkin**, Riddle worked hard with the self-imposed limitations of the instrumentation to create subtle contrapuntal movement and harmonic tension along with some lovely call-and-response effects, especially in the title track. Although the effect is one of warmth and intimacy – and Sinatra is tender and convincing throughout – in places there's also a gentle restlessness which, while not quite as dramatic as *In The Wee Small Hours*, has a faintly unsettling allure. The unconventional colours of the harmonies in the introduction to "I Couldn't Sleep A Wink Last Night" and the whole of "Don't Like Goodbyes" hint at the impressionistic glories to come in *Only The Lonely*.

An album of great refinement, *Close To You* did quite well at the time of release, despite some sniffy reviews, but it's slightly experimental nature leaves it somewhat undervalued when compared with other Capitol LPs and over the years the title has drifted in and out of the catalogue.

A Swingin' Affair!

NIGHT AND DAY/I WISH I WERE IN LOVE AGAIN/I GOT PLENTY O' NUTTIN'/I GUESS I'LL HAVE TO CHANGE MY PLAN/NICE WORK IF YOU CAN GET IT/STARS FELL ON ALABAMA/ NO ONE EVER TELLS YOU/I WON'T DANCE/THE LONESOME ROAD/AT LONG LAST LOVE/ YOU'D BE SO NICE TO COME HOME TO/I GOT IT BAD AND THAT AIN'T GOOD/FROM THIS MOMENT ON/IF I HAD YOU/OH! LOOK AT ME NOW

Arranged by Nelson Riddle; recorded April 19–November 28, 1956; released May 1957

A Swingin' Affair! is very much a sequel to *Songs For Swingin' Lovers!* – and some fans claim that it is better. Certainly, there's a canny, intoxicating blend of **formula** ("Night And Day" reprises the framework of "I've Got You Under My Skin") and **envelope-pushing** (Riddle's playful variations on the "I Got Plenty Of Nuttin'" motif are audacious). And Juan Tizol's valve trombone brings an exotic Ellingtonian flavour to proceedings. If anything, this album swings and swaggers more than the earlier record.

A further argument for *Affair*'s superiority concerns the quality of composition. Delightful as the buffed-up B-songs were on *Swingin' Lovers*, the raw material just can't hold a candle to much of the repertoire here, which includes four Cole Porters, two Gershwins, a Richard Rodgers, a Kern and an Ellington. Even a lesser-known piece such as Carroll Coates's bluesy **"No One Ever Tells You"** is a gem. Only "The Lonesome Road", with its faintly hokey "weary totin' such a load" lyric, seems out of place.

But occasionally there is the sense of a hand being overplayed and a pressured schedule on the part of both arranger and singer. A few of Riddle's arrangements escalate into routine brashness ("You'd Be So Nice To Come Home To", "I Won't Dance"), and Sinatra, full of pizzazz but sounding vocally tired in places, doesn't pull off everything he tries. He makes some **questionable choices** during "Night And Day", hitting obvious wrong notes on the second "*you* are the one", and in "I Got It Bad And That Ain't Good" his attempts at bluesy phrasing just end up flat.

If that seems to be nit-picking, it's only because these men had recently set such exemplary standards. It's not that *A Swingin' Affair* isn't good; it's terrific. But it's a shade less masterly, perhaps, than the previous three albums.

Where Are You?

WHERE ARE YOU?/THE NIGHT WE CALLED IT A DAY/I COVER THE WATERFRONT/MAYBE YOU'LL BE THERE/LAURA/LONELY TOWN/AUTUMN LEAVES/I'M A FOOL TO WANT YOU/I THINK OF YOU/WHERE IS THE ONE?/THERE'S NO YOU/BABY, WON'T YOU PLEASE COME HOME

Arranged by Gordon Jenkins; recorded April 10, April 29 and May 1, 1957; released September 1957

Where Are You? marked two milestones for the Capitol-era Sinatra. It was his first **stereo record** (though the album wasn't issued in stereo until 1959), made when the format was gradually becoming the norm; even fifty years later, a lusher, more beautifully balanced recording could hardly be imagined, and the full graininess of 41-year-old Sinatra's baritone has never been more vibrant. Also, it was his first Capitol album recorded without Nelson Riddle. After his association in the 1940s with Axel Stordahl, Sinatra was unwilling to be linked with just one man, however fruitful the collaborations with Riddle were, and this torch-song collection with **Gordon Jenkins** was the first of two projects in 1957 with different arrangers.

The Music

The appreciation of the record depends on the listener's response to the Sinatra/Jenkins combination. All the tempos are crawling: the arranger's startling high notes for the strings and three mournful French horns are to the fore and the mood is doggedly downbeat and melodramatic. And in places the pair match each other perfectly in their musical temperaments, with Jenkins's pensive overstatement encouraging the singer, always on the cusp, to tip from a seductive melancholy into an unappealing self-pity. The overall result is a sound that is aching and inconsolable, a tad corny and, on occasion, a little overwrought.

JENKINS ON SINATRA: *"During recording sessions with Sinatra, a magic takes place between Frank and myself. It's as close as you're gonna get without opposite sexes."*

TO RADIO PRESENTER WINK MARTINDALE

SINATRA ON JENKINS: *"[He] was one man that I felt I could almost leave alone – just let him work by himself. I think he was probably the most sensitive man about orchestrations."*

TO RADIO PRESENTER SID MARK

Taken one track at a time, *Where Are You?* is astoundingly emotional and rewarding, even if as a forty-minute album it is heavy going. **"Lonely Town"** is delivered here with full-blooded, heart-stopping romanticism. (Puzzlingly, Sinatra did not further explore Leonard Bernstein's grander works – he avoided the *West Side Story* arias altogether.) And the difference between the recordings from the 1940s of "The Night We Called It A Day", "There's No You" and "Laura" and their remakes here is the difference between boyhood and manhood, and all it might imply about optimism, lightness and callowness being replaced by pessimism, heaviness and wisdom.

Unsurprisingly, perhaps, the unfettered anguish of Sinatra and Jenkins makes more sense as one gets older.

Come Fly With Me

COME FLY WITH ME/AROUND THE WORLD/ISLE OF CAPRI/MOONLIGHT IN VERMONT/
AUTUMN IN NEW YORK/ON THE ROAD TO MANDALAY/LET'S GET AWAY FROM IT ALL/
APRIL IN PARIS/LONDON BY NIGHT/BRAZIL/BLUE HAWAII/IT'S NICE TO GO TRAV'LING

Arranged by Billy May; recorded October 1, 3 and 8, 1957; released January 1958

More than four years after it was mooted, Sinatra and May eventually got together on a multi-mood travelogue "concept" album, with unpredictable results. There is the unsurprising **brassy swing** ("Let's Get Away From It All", "It's Nice To Go Trav'ling", "Brazil") and tongue-in-cheek **exotica** ("Isle Of Capri", "On The Road To Mandalay"), but the album is by no means the party of slurping saxophones that might have been expected from a recently reborn swinger and a high-spirited celebrity arranger with his own bag of musical signatures.

MAY ON SINATRA: *"He knows what to look for. He can look around the band and he can pretty much tell if it's a happy band or there's some bullshit going on."*

TO CHARLES GRANATA

SINATRA ON MAY: *"Recording with Billy May is like having a cold shower, or a cold bucket of water thrown in your face … he'll stop [the orchestra] and he'll say, 'Hey cats, this bar sixteen. You gotta oompah-de-da-da-ch-Ow. OK? Let's go then…' And the band will GO! Billy is driving."*

TO ROBIN DOUGLAS-HOME

Sinatra's quote about working with May says much about the brash immediacy of his work, but doesn't convey the subtlety of which he was capable; and on *Come Fly With Me* May is revealed as perhaps the most

brilliant and versatile arranger of all of Sinatra's collaborators. May's control of dynamics and orchestral colour, for example on **"Come Fly With Me"**, is at least on a par with Nelson Riddle's, and if anything has more wit. (Riddle famously had to ape May's style on his initial Sinatra sessions, and on his inaugural Sinatra album May occasionally seems to return the compliment.) And May's writing for strings on the ballads **"Moonlight In Vermont"** and **"Autumn In New York"** (curiously but effectively programmed consecutively) is as sweepingly lush as anything conjured by Gordon Jenkins. Sinatra, in better voice than on *A Swingin' Affair*, responds accordingly. Whether the setting is majestic ("April In Paris"), cornball ("Blue Hawaii") or comic ("Isle Of Capri"), he's po-faced or light-hearted as required, and provides the passionate but casual sound of the good-humoured, urbane jetsetter on the cover.

The album is also notable for the promotion of the work of Sinatra's in-house writers **Jimmy Van Heusen** and **Sammy Cahn**. Until now their oeuvre had been confined to single releases and film songs (such as "The Tender Trap", "Love And Marriage" and the Oscar-winning "All The Way") but here they contributed the opening and closing cuts. It was not the last time that they would make their mark on a major Sinatra product.

Frank Sinatra Sings For Only The Lonely

ONLY THE LONELY/ANGEL EYES/WHAT'S NEW/IT'S A LONESOME OLD TOWN/WILLOW WEEP FOR ME/GOODBYE/BLUES IN THE NIGHT/GUESS I'LL HANG MY TEARS OUT TO DRY/ EBB TIDE/SPRING IS HERE/GONE WITH THE WIND/ONE FOR MY BABY

Arranged by Nelson Riddle; recorded May 29, June 24 and June 25, 1958; released September 1958

The Capitol years

This is not only the peak of the Sinatra/Riddle collaboration (as nominated by both men) but also – if artistic focus, technical excellence, bold and sensitive imagination, and penetrating, soulful performance are any criteria – one of the great works of twentieth-century popular art. This album goes way beyond what might be expected of a torch-song collection. Featuring the largest ensemble of musicians that Riddle

had ever worked with (including a full woodwind section and rows of strings), it has the emotional sweep and dark grandeur of a jazz-tinged symphony with shades of **Chopin**, **Rachmaninov**, **Ravel**, **Debussy**, **Ellington** and **Vaughan Williams** (one of Sinatra's favourites). It is heavy, spacious, rich and stark, emotionally draining, entirely absorbing and utterly magnificent.

The material ranged from what Sinatra liked to call **"saloon songs"** (pieces of bluesy misery that he sang in bars in films, such as "One For My Baby" and "Angel Eyes"), to **classy standards** of the 1940s ("Gone With The Wind", "What's New", "Spring Is Here") and also included a superb Cahn/Van Heusen title track and a recent pop tune ("Ebb Tide"). All are elevated, beautified and extended – they are about five minutes each – into luscious elegies whose musical colours swirl and hover like the weather in winter; the songs are no longer mere words and music, but more like dark tone poems.

Riddle attributed the gloomy hues of his extraordinary work here to his personal circumstances at the time. In the three-month period before the sessions began, he lost both his daughter and his mother. "If I can attach events like that to music," he said, "perhaps *Only The Lonely* was the result." Riddle was not, however, the conductor for his masterpiece: the initial session was considered unsuccessful, after which he went on tour with Nat "King" Cole, leaving violinist **Felix Slatkin** to take up the baton. To some participants (including Felix's wife Eleanor, a cellist) this only enhanced the hypnotic ebb and flow of the performances. "He turned every phrase to fit Frank," she told Charles Granata. "You have to

FESTIVE FRANK

Christmas Songs By Sinatra

WHITE CHRISTMAS/JINGLE BELLS/SILENT NIGHT/ADESTE FIDELES/O LITTLE TOWN
OF BETHLEHEM/IT CAME UPON A MIDNIGHT CLEAR/HAVE YOURSELF A MERRY
LITTLE CHRISTMAS/SANTA CLAUS IS COMIN' TO TOWN

Columbia; arranged by Axel Stordahl; released June 1948

A Jolly Christmas From Frank Sinatra

JINGLE BELLS/THE CHRISTMAS SONG/MISTLETOE AND HOLLY/I'LL BE HOME FOR
CHRISTMAS/THE CHRISTMAS WALTZ/HAVE YOURSELF A MERRY LITTLE CHRISTMAS/
THE FIRST NOEL/HARK! THE HERALD ANGELS SING/O LITTLE TOWN OF BETHLEHEM/
ADESTE FIDELES/IT CAME UPON A MIDNIGHT CLEAR/SILENT NIGHT

With The Ralph Brewster
Singers

Capitol; arranged by Gordon
Jenkins; released September
1957

The Sinatra Family
Wish You A Merry
Christmas

I WOULDN'T TRADE CHRISTMAS
[THE FAMILY]/IT'S SUCH A LOVELY
TIME OF YEAR [NANCY]/SOME
CHILDREN SEE HIM [FAMILY]/O
BAMBINO (ONE COLD AND
BLESSED WINTER) [TINA AND
NANCY]/THE BELLS OF CHRISTMAS

(GREENSLEEVES) [THE FAMILY]/WHATEVER HAPPENED TO CHRISTMAS* [FRANK
SINATRA]/SANTA CLAUS IS COMIN' TO TOWN [TINA/NANCY]/THE CHRISTMAS WALTZ
[FRANK SINATRA]/THE TWELVE DAYS OF CHRISTMAS [THE FAMILY]

With The Jimmy Joyce Singers

Reprise; arranged by Nelson Riddle and Don Costa*; released
September 1968

The Christmas Collection

I'VE GOT MY LOVE TO KEEP ME WARM/THE CHRISTMAS WALTZ/SANTA CLAUS IS
COMING TO TOWN/THE LITTLE DRUMMER BOY/WE WISH YOU THE MERRIEST
[WITH BING CROSBY]/ HAVE YOURSELF A MERRY LITTLE CHRISTMAS/GO TELL IT TO
THE MOUNTAIN/THE CHRISTMAS SONG [WITH BING CROSBY]/I HEARD THE BELLS
ON CHRISTMAS DAY/I WOULDN'T TRADE CHRISTMAS [THE FAMILY]/CHRISTMAS
MEMORIES/THE TWELVE DAYS OF CHRISTMAS [THE FAMILY]/THE BELLS OF
CHRISTMAS [THE FAMILY]/AN OLD FASHIONED CHRISTMAS/A BABY JUST LIKE YOU/
WHATEVER HAPPENED TO CHRISTMAS/WHITE CHRISTMAS [WITH BING CROSBY]

Reprise; arranged by Nelson Riddle and Don Costa; released October
2004

There was one Christmas album for each record company in each decade.
The record for Columbia, *Christmas Songs By Sinatra*, was his third
"album" and featured eight tracks that took the cuddle-up Forties style that
he had developed with Axel Stordahl and added festive seasoning. The Capitol
set, *A Jolly Christmas From Frank Sinatra*, surprisingly given to Gordon
Jenkins rather than Nelson Riddle, shrewdly used the word "Jolly" in the title,
lest anyone thought their idea of a Christmas record was anything like the
recently released, shatteringly depressing *Where Are You?* It's half-jolly, with
side one (as was) devoted to modern Christmas ditties (including "Mistletoe
And Holly", penned by Sinatra and Sanicola) and side two featuring mournful
carols. *The Sinatra Family Wish You A Merry Christmas* – one of Sinatra
and Riddle's final pieces of work together – was recorded at the time when
Frank and his brood were starting to appear together on TV shows and in
Vegas. Sammy Cahn wrote special lyrics, Frank sang two solos on Jimmy
Webb's regretful "Whatever Happened To Christmas" and the Sinatras made
a perfectly amiable holiday family, although non-performer Tina was petrified.
Originally released on Reprise, the album is currently available on the Sinatra
family label, Artanis. The tracks involving Frank Sr. are also on the recently
compiled *Christmas Collection*, along with some rare Bing'n'Frank duets
from their 1957 Christmas TV special and some singles from the Reprise era.
The highlight is a previously unreleased, extraordinarily moving version of
"Silent Night", featuring Sinatra croaking his way through the carol in 1991,
conducted by Frank Jr., amid overdubbed strings arranged by Johnny Mandel
in 2004; the album contains a DVD documentary about its conception.

be a conductor to do that – that the others couldn't do." (It has also been suggested that Sinatra arranged for the sessions to be done when Riddle – a notoriously unclear conductor – was out of town.)

Sinatra, for his part, is at his strongest and truest. The sleeve note by Cahn and Van Heusen rings true when it refers to "the Frank Sinatra that we know and have known (and hardly know)" being revealed in these dignified but devastatingly open performances. "A Sinatra singing a hymn of loneliness could very well be the real Sinatra," they continue. Indeed, Sinatra is so real, and so right for these songs, that his singing career can almost be seen in two halves; that which gently led to the summit of *Only The Lonely* and that which gently led away. The gradients are not steep, but they're unmistakable.

Come Dance With Me!

COME DANCE WITH ME/SOMETHING'S GOTTA GIVE/JUST IN TIME/DANCING IN THE DARK/ TOO CLOSE FOR COMFORT/I COULD HAVE DANCED ALL NIGHT/SATURDAY NIGHT/DAY IN, DAY OUT/CHEEK TO CHEEK/BAUBLES, BANGLES AND BEADS/THE SONG IS YOU/THE LAST DANCE

Arranged by Billy May; recorded December 9, 22 and 23, 1958; released January 1959

How times changed. On **"Saturday Night"** in 1944, the first real rhythm tune of his solo career, Frank didn't mind Sunday nights at all because his friends would come to "call"; fifteen years later, in Sinatra's ring-a-ding 1950s, they come to "ball".

Swing had moved on too. In the hands of **Billy May** on *Come Dance With Me!* – a strong set of terpsichorean songs – it's tough and jokey, relentlessly energetic but full of musical detail. Out go the heartbeat and sustaining strings of Riddle's swing sides and in come brisk tempos and extrovert brass. Sinatra responds with some marvellous freewheeling vocalizing that is in places almost reckless, and is increasingly replete with his customized groovy insertions ("Basie boots" instead of a second "dancing boots", "aw, let's tear it up" instead of the final "something's gotta give", and "koo koo" all over the place). It was a habit that Sinatra had from live shows that would soon wear thin when it crept into the studio takes.

Aside from the custom of opening and closing with Cahn/Van Heusen numbers, which are a little second rate here, Sinatra rarely used modern works for his Capitol albums. But on *Come Dance With Me* he plunders **contemporary Broadway** for "Too Close For Comfort" from Sammy Davis Jr.'s showcase musical *Mr Wonderful* and recasts waltzes from recent shows *My Fair Lady* and *Kismet* ("I Could Have Danced All Night" and "Baubles, Bangles And Beads") as unforgiving 4/4 swingers.

It's solid, exciting stuff, and won four Grammys, but compared with the generous 15- and 16-trackers of a few years previously, or the 54 minutes of *Only The Lonely*, the twelve cuts here, amounting to half an hour, feel a little perfunctory. However, it was his last decent swing set on Capitol.

No One Cares

WHEN NO ONE CARES/A COTTAGE FOR SALE/STORMY WEATHER/WHERE DO YOU GO?/I DON'T STAND A GHOST OF A CHANCE WITH YOU/HERE'S THAT RAINY DAY/I CAN'T GET STARTED/WHY TRY TO CHANGE ME NOW?/JUST FRIENDS/I'LL NEVER SMILE AGAIN/NONE BUT THE LONELY HEART/THE ONE I LOVE BELONGS TO SOMEBODY ELSE

Arranged by Gordon Jenkins; recorded March 24, 25 and 26, and May 14, 1959; released July 1959

"THE ONE I LOVE BELONGS TO SOMEBODY ELSE" WAS RECORDED AT THE SAME SESSIONS AS THE REMAINDER OF NO ONE CARES BUT WAS OMITTED FROM THE ORIGINAL RELEASE BECAUSE OF THE LENGTH OF THE RECORD. IT WAS REINSTATED AS PART OF NO ONE CARES IN 1998.

Everything noted about the previous downbeat and melodramatic Sinatra/Jenkins album **Where Are You?** applies to *No One Cares*; and there's something about the Sinatra/Jenkins suicide sets that is less palatable than the similar work with Riddle. Is it that Jenkins's relatively simple, jazz-free approach fails to transform Sinatra's suffering from a bleating wallow into glorious tragedy? And is Sinatra too caught up in that wallowing to notice?

Sinatra's loyal pianist **Bill Miller**, who found Jenkins's writing "dull and boring", gives us a clue. "There's a certain squareness about Frank; I say that affectionately," he told Will Friedwald. "He has an old-fashioned side and Gordon Jenkins represents that. As a singer, he doesn't hear the harmonies the way we would. He hears those high singing strings – that was Gordon's gimmick."

"First I decide on the mood for an album and perhaps pick a title. Or sometimes it might be that I had that title and then picked the mood to fit it … Then I get a short list of maybe sixty possible songs and out of these I pick twelve to record. Next comes the pacing of the album, which is vitally important … Once we choose the songs that will be in a particular album, I'll sit with Bill Miller, my pianist, and find the proper key. Then I will meet with the orchestrator … Usually we wind up doing it the way the arranger feels it should be done, because he understands more than I do about it."

FS ON CONCEPT ALBUMS, TO ROBIN DOUGLAS-HOME, 1961

Sometimes, those high singing strings are quite stunning, as in the instrumental break of "Just Friends", but mostly, *No One Cares* is plain dreary. Not that it's all the fault of Jenkins, who does what he does rather well: the problem is that the songs are unwisely chosen. Cahn and Van Heusen's cramped "When No One Cares" never gets off the ground,

SOUNDTRACK SINATRA

Sinatra In Hollywood

Reprise; various arrangers; released April 2002

Of all the movie musicals that Sinatra made, only a handful of official soundtrack albums – *High Society*, *Pal Joey*, *Can-Can* and *Robin And The 7 Hoods* – were released at the time. This 6-CD set not only makes the original soundtrack releases redundant as far as Sinatra collectors are concerned; it also fills a substantial hole in the Sinatra recordings archive. Of the 160 tracks in the set, only 10 percent have been issued in any audio form or have been heard without dialogue and sound effects. A collection that gathered all Sinatra's musical film recordings (including clean studio recordings of the songs from *Meet Danny Wilson* and *Young At Heart*) would be enough for most fans; with additional rarities, too, it's **a Sinatraphile's dream**.

The many highlights include the surprisingly sweet Nacio Herb Brown songs from the otherwise appalling *The Kissing Bandit*; audio snippets that include a hilariously badly scripted promo interview with the gossip columnist Louella Parsons and touching Oscar acceptance speeches for *The House I Live In* and *From Here To Eternity*; twenty minutes of recordings made in 1955 for a scrapped animated version of *Finian's Rainbow*, including Sinatra improvising a blues scat (pretty well) with Louis Armstrong and duetting beautifully with Ella Fitzgerald on "Necessity"; and five minutes of outtakes of Frank, Dean and Sam goofing the recording of "Don't Be A Do Badder".

Handsomely packaged, meticulously researched and annotated with scholarly rigour, this careful package makes the Sinatra enthusiast think about other possibilities for the sumptuous archive-in-a-box. *The Complete "Songs By Sinatra" Radio Recordings*? *Sinatra on TV 1950-1960*? *The Reprise Outtakes and Studio Chat*? We patiently wait.

Willard Robison's "A Cottage For Sale" is mawkish tosh unworthy of the singer, and a similarly tedious song consisting of a triple rhyme before the mention of the title by Cy Coleman and Joseph A. McCarthy, "Why Try To Change Me Now" (a remake of the final pointed Columbia side in 1952), is not much better. And Tchaikovsky's "None But The Lonely Heart" indicates that Sinatra should have left his lumbering classical aspirations back in the 1940s.

By any other standards, parts of *No One Cares* ("Here's That Rainy Day", "Just Friends") are very good indeed. But by the standards set by Sinatra elsewhere on Capitol, it's a sluggish miscue.

Nice 'N' Easy

NICE 'N' EASY/THAT OLD FEELING/HOW DEEP IS THE OCEAN/I'VE GOT A CRUSH ON YOU/
YOU GO TO MY HEAD/FOOLS RUSH IN/NEVERTHELESS/SHE'S FUNNY THAT WAY/TRY A
LITTLE TENDERNESS/EMBRACEABLE YOU/MAM'SELLE/DREAM

Arranged by Nelson Riddle; recorded March 1, 2 and 3, and April 13, 1960; released July 1960

An exquisite updating of blue-chip romantic standards previously recorded by Sinatra in the 1940s, this low-key, wistful and freshly harmonized work is a fascinating study of how far Sinatra and his approach to love songs had come since the floppy bowtie years. His phrasing is looser and loucher; he hangs way back, barroom style, on "That Old Feeling", and his delivery of the line "and I find you spinning *ro-o-ound* in my brain" in **"You Go To My Head"** is heavy with languid lust. Riddle's orchestrations are full of hip little touches (the sax lick on the intro to "Nevertheless", Plas Johnson's tenor solo on "That Old Feeling") and old-fashioned tricks such as Felix Slatkin's violin obbligatos on "Mam'selle". The absence of pretty celesta allows Riddle's jazzy, modernistic sensuality to distinguish itself for the first time on a romantic Sinatra set, yet the steady tempos mean that the music doesn't become too dense and artsy. It's effortless and wonderful.

The album was originally themed around Hoagy Carmichael's "The Nearness Of You", but that song and concept was dumped when the contemporary "Nice 'N' Easy" found favour with Sinatra and was used as a single to trail the album.

Sinatra's Swingin' Session!!!

WHEN YOU'RE SMILING/BLUE MOON/S'POSIN'/IT ALL DEPENDS ON YOU/IT'S ONLY A PAPER MOON/MY BLUE HEAVEN/SHOULD I/SEPTEMBER IN THE RAIN/ALWAYS/I CAN'T BELIEVE THAT YOU'RE IN LOVE WITH ME/I CONCENTRATE ON YOU/YOU DO SOMETHING TO ME

Arranged by Nelson Riddle; recorded August 22, 23 and 31, and September 1, 1960; released January 1961

It was around the time of the sessions for this record that Sinatra was attempting to negotiate with Capitol to leave for his own record label. His impatience to get away is audible here. He apparently called for tempo increases without even hearing run-throughs, and several of these cuts ("Should I", "My Blue Heaven", "You Do Something To Me") are so speedy that they almost get away from him and the band. Elsewhere  on a set of mostly stale standards, the majority revamping the tracks of his 1950 Columbia album *Sing And Dance With Frank Sinatra*, he's in experimental mood, which doesn't always work – his slipshod moves on "I Concentrate On You" are baffling. Capitol knew they had, at best, routine Sinatra product, but by then they had virtually lost him and they hyped it for all they were worth. Dig those insecure exclamation marks!!!

Come Swing With Me

DAY BY DAY/SENTIMENTAL JOURNEY*/ALMOST LIKE BEING IN LOVE/FIVE MINUTES MORE/ AMERICAN BEAUTY ROSE/YES INDEED/ON THE SUNNY SIDE OF THE STREET/DON'T TAKE YOUR LOVE FROM ME*/THAT OLD BLACK MAGIC*/LOVER*/PAPER DOLL/I'VE HEARD THAT SONG BEFORE

Arranged by Billy May and Heinie Beau*; recorded March 20-22, 1961; released July 1961

After withdrawing his labour from Capitol's studios until negotiations to release him were complete, Sinatra returned after seven months to fulfil his contractual obligations. Continuing the policy of his latter albums in re-examining chestnuts from the past, he is at least in marginally better form than on *Swingin' Session*, but when he chooses to sing creaking old dross like "Five Minutes More", "American Beauty Rose" and the appalling faux gospel of **"Yes Indeed"** (almost the worst ten minutes in Sinatra's recorded history), it hardly matters. Billy May's tiring trick of getting two trumpet sections to indulge in ping-pong call-and-response across the left and right of the stereo recording is no compensation for another half-hearted, half-length showing from Sinatra, who has one foot out of the door.

Point Of No Return

WHEN THE WORLD WAS YOUNG/I'LL REMEMBER APRIL*/SEPTEMBER SONG/A MILLION DREAMS AGO/I'LL SEE YOU AGAIN/THERE WILL NEVER BE ANOTHER YOU/SOMEWHERE ALONG THE WAY/IT'S A BLUE WORLD*/THESE FOOLISH THINGS (REMIND ME OF YOU)/AS TIME GOES BY/I'LL BE SEEING YOU/MEMORIES OF YOU

Arranged by Axel Stordahl and Heinie Beau*; recorded September 11–12, 1961; released March 1962

The circumstances did not bode well for a Capitol swansong of any substance. Sinatra was already three recording projects into Reprise and wanted nothing to do with returning to his old bosses. Various tales abound concerning threats of lawsuits and emotional appeals from Axel Stordahl's wife to let the arranger enjoy one last fling with Sinatra. (Stordahl was already ill with the cancer that would kill him only two years later.) Sinatra turned up, bristly and late – he had apparently still not forgiven Stordahl for joining Eddie Fisher eight years previously – and taped all twelve tunes in a pair of two-hour sessions of **almost entirely single takes**.

Amazingly, unlike his last two Capitol records, *Point Of No Return* sounded far from a knock-off. It was a carefully performed and programmed album, a deliberate goodbye (to Capitol, perhaps, or to Axel) stretched to the length of an LP. All the songs – a winning blend of the famous and obscure – are concerned with parting and bittersweet recollection. Unable, therefore, to express his displeasure or indifference through a slapdash vocal behind a rollicking swing chart, as he does in *Sinatra's Swinging Session!!!*, he has to commit wholeheartedly to the recording. After all, if you sing Noel Coward's **"I'll See You Again"** and Eubie Blake's **"Memories Of You"** apathetically, you're not singing them at all. Sinatra's proud compulsion to get under the skin of a ballad just wouldn't allow that kind of slippage.

But as good as Sinatra is, the revelation of the album is the work of **Axel Stordahl**. If anything, he's better than he ever was, raising his game to meet the needs of Capitol-era Sinatra with vivid picture painting, in the strings at the top of "When The World Was Young", and modern harmonic colours, in the Riddle-like range and density of "I'll See You Again". Expert and exemplary throughout, if Stordahl sensed that this was indeed the point of no return, he excelled himself with a fitting and fine farewell.

The Complete Capitol Singles Collection

LEAN BABY/I'M WALKING BEHIND YOU/I'VE GOT THE WORLD ON A STRING/MY ONE AND ONLY LOVE/ANYTIME, ANYWHERE/FROM HERE TO ETERNITY/I LOVE YOU/SOUTH OF THE BORDER/TAKE A CHANCE/YOUNG AT HEART/DON'T WORRY 'BOUT ME/I COULD HAVE TOLD YOU/RAIN (FALLING FROM THE SKIES)/THREE COINS IN THE FOUNTAIN/THE GAL THAT GOT AWAY/HALF AS LOVELY (TWICE AS TRUE)/IT WORRIES ME/WHEN I STOP LOVING YOU/WHITE CHRISTMAS/CHRISTMAS WALTZ/SOMEONE TO WATCH OVER ME/YOU, MY LOVE/MELODY OF LOVE/I'M GONNA LIVE TILL I DIE/WHY SHOULD I CRY OVER YOU?/DON'T CHANGE YOUR MIND ABOUT ME/TWO HEARTS, TWO KISSES (MAKE ONE LOVE)/FROM THE BOTTOM TO THE TOP/IF I HAD THREE WISHES/LEARNIN' THE BLUES/NOT AS A STRANGER/

The Music

HOW COULD YOU DO A THING LIKE THAT TO ME?/SAME OLD SATURDAY NIGHT/FAIRY
TALE/LOVE AND MARRIAGE/IMPATIENT YEARS/(LOVE IS) THE TENDER TRAP/WEEP THEY
WILL/YOU'LL GET YOURS/FLOWERS MEAN FORGIVENESS/HOW LITTLE WE KNOW/FIVE
HUNDRED GUYS/JOHNNY CONCHO THEME (WAIT FOR ME)/YOU'RE SENSATIONAL/WELL
DID YOU EVAH?/MIND IF I MAKE LOVE TO YOU?/WHO WANTS TO BE A MILLIONAIRE?/
YOU FORGOT ALL THE WORDS (WHILE I STILL REMEMBER THE TUNE)/HEY! JEALOUS
LOVER/YOUR LOVE FOR ME/CAN I STEAL A LITTLE LOVE?/SO LONG, MY LOVE/CRAZY LOVE/
SOMETHING WONDERFUL HAPPENS IN SUMMER/YOU'RE CHEATIN' YOURSELF (IF YOU'RE
CHEATIN' ON ME)/ALL THE WAY/CHICAGO/WITCHCRAFT/TELL HER YOU LOVE HER/THE
CHRISTMAS WALTZ/MISTLETOE AND HOLLY/NOTHING IN COMMON/HOW ARE YA' FIXED
FOR LOVE?/SAME OLD SONG AND DANCE/MONIQUE/MR. SUCCESS/SLEEP WARM/NO ONE
EVER TELLS YOU/TO LOVE AND BE LOVED/TIME AFTER TIME/FRENCH FOREIGN LEGION/
ALL MY TOMORROWS/HIGH HOPES/THEY CAME TO CORDURA/TALK TO ME/RIVER, STAY
'WAY FROM MY DOOR/IT'S OVER, IT'S OVER, IT'S OVER/THIS WAS MY LOVE/NICE 'N' EASY/
YOU'LL ALWAYS BE THE ONE I LOVE/OL' MACDONALD/MY BLUE HEAVEN/SENTIMENTAL
BABY/SENTIMENTAL JOURNEY/AMERICAN BEAUTY ROSE/THE MOON WAS YELLOW/I'VE
HEARD THAT SONG BEFORE/FIVE MINUTES MORE/I'LL REMEMBER APRIL/I LOVE PARIS/
HIDDEN PERSUASION/YA BETTER STOP/THE SEA SONG/LOOK TO YOUR HEART/I BELIEVE/
LOVE LOOKS SO WELL ON YOU

Arranged by Nelson Riddle, Gordon Jenkins, Billy May, Felix Slatkin and Skip
Martin; released August 1996

While Sinatra was creating his themed masterwork albums at Capitol, he
recorded around **eighty further tracks**, most of which were released on
around forty singles between the mid-1950s and the early 1960s. Aside
from "No One Ever Tells You" (an album track on *Swingin' Affair*), "Nice
'N' Easy" (the title track of the album from 1960) and a couple of titles
culled from albums after he'd left the label, the songs for Sinatra's Capitol

singles were not taken from albums.
Most of his single recordings were
slung together at the time on the
piecemeal albums *This Is Sinatra!*
(1956), *This Is Sinatra Vol 2* (1958),
Look To Your Heart (1959), *All The
Way* (1961) and *Sinatra Sings … Of
Love And Things!* (1963); but the best
way to get a feel for Sinatra's impulse
for success on the jukebox and radio
is this chronologically sequenced 96-
track, 4-CD set.

The Capitol years

While he would often look to the classics of the Great American Songbook's previous generation to dictate the content of his albums, on his singles he would dabble with fashion, promote the latest songs, publish them himself and be damned. This was nothing less than a continuation of the hit-chasing attitude that Mitch Miller displayed at Columbia, about which Sinatra was so disparaging. It's true that Sinatra's singles for Capitol didn't reach the dim-witted depths of commercialism of those at Columbia, but sometimes – as in the risible "doo-wop" sides with The Nuggets, **"Two Hearts Two Kisses (Make One Love)"** and **"From The Bottom To The Top"** – they weren't far off. Sinatra even recorded the quasi-rock "Five Hundred Guys" and "You're Cheatin' Yourself", the latter written by **Dick Manning**, who had penned the notorious "Mama Will Bark", Sinatra's nadir at Columbia.

There are, of course, several examples here of Sinatra's attempts at commercialism that might be as good as anything he did, including "The Gal That Got Away", "The Tender Trap", "How Little We Know", "I've Got The World On A String", "Young At Heart", "Learnin' The Blues", "Witchcraft" and "Nice 'N' Easy". There are also several examples of semi-novelty tracks that became hits and entered the public's consciousness as Sinatra's songs – but for which discerning fans are unlikely to have much affection. These include the glib "Love And Marriage", the swaggering blunder "Mr Success", the optimistic kids' song "High Hopes" and the astonishing I-can-sing-anything arrogance of "Ol' Macdonald".

Elsewhere, the standard of what he chose to acquire from writers and to sing in single format was erratic to say the least, and few releases made any impact on the charts. Songs such as "Anytime, Anywhere", "I Love You", "Half As Lovely, Twice As True" and "When I Stop Loving You" are songs by hacks that are forgettable and uninspired. "Melody Of Love" is turn-of-the-century corn, and, as their titles suggest, "Don't Change Your Mind About Me", "Fairy Tale", "Flowers Mean Forgiveness" and "If I Had Three Wishes" are mid-Fifties corn. They amount to Sinatra the none-too-canny businessman shrugging and saying, "I dunno, maybe they'll buy this." They didn't.

But this collection also has some pleasant surprises. Most are courtesy of **Jimmy Van Heusen**, and in this company they sound like the work of a composing giant. "I Could Have Told You", with lyrics by Carl Sigman, is one of his sweetest melodies. "The Impatient Years" was the touching B-side of "Love And Marriage" and is a much more appealing song. "You'll Get Yours", a hip swing song of romantic revenge, is a minor Sinatra classic, though it only just scraped into the US top seventy. Two film songs with **Sammy Cahn** – "To Love And Be Loved" from *Some Came Running* and "All My Tomorrows" from *A Hole In The Head* – are genuinely emotive.

The Complete Capitol Singles should not be mistaken for some sort of "Best Of Capitol Sinatra". It is a good-value, well-annotated adjunct to the albums and a fascinating insight into both the duality of his Capitol output – albums and singles being completely different – and the variety, with some laughs, some horrors and some classics.

THE REPRISE YEARS: 1961–91

"A newer, happier, emancipated Sinatra …
untrammelled, unfettered, unconfined."

REPRISE ADVERT FOR COME SWING WITH ME, 1961

If Sinatra had certain powers at Capitol, at Reprise he was *really* in charge. Committing to three album releases of his own per year, he recorded for his own company with massive energy and artistic spirit. But he couldn't keep it up, when he was also pre-occupied with Cal-Neva, JFK, Frank Jr.'s kidnap, the shows, the films and changes in the music business – highlighted by **The Beatles** – that meant that he was no longer sure of his place in the world. As the decade wore on, he wore himself out. The songs kept coming, and he had some amazing successes while also taking some musical risks, but he was taking less interest in what he sang, and it showed. And his voice at the end of the 1960s was in the worst shape of his career. It was a wise move in 1971 to choose rest and temporary retirement.

After his return to show business in 1973 the records were less interesting than the rousing live shows and the TV specials. But at least he was still doing it. And even on the later recordings there was still a spark, here and there, of magic in the air.

Ring-A-Ding Ding!

RING-A-DING DING/LET'S FALL IN LOVE/BE CAREFUL, IT'S MY HEART*/A FOGGY DAY/A FINE
ROMANCE/IN THE STILL OF THE NIGHT/THE COFFEE SONG/WHEN I TAKE MY SUGAR TO
TEA/LET'S FACE THE MUSIC AND DANCE/YOU'D BE SO EASY TO LOVE/YOU AND THE NIGHT
AND THE MUSIC/I'VE GOT MY LOVE TO KEEP ME WARM**

Arranged by Johnny Mandel (with Skip Martin* and Dick Reynolds**);
recorded December 19-21, 1960; released March 1961

Sinatra was free from Capitol at last
– and **Johnny Mandel's** chiming,
effervescent intro on the opener
sounds like a celebratory fanfare of
independence. Thereafter, *Ring-A-
Ding Ding!* is a snappy but rowdy-
dowdy debut for the new label. Hired
after Sinatra heard his work for Vic
Damone's live act, Mandel – with
the help of Skip Martin and Dick
Reynolds, who were drafted in when
he was behind schedule – creates

charts that are consistently engaging and memorable. Although they
are broadly in the established styles of Riddle (the heartbeat of "A Foggy
Day") and May (the fun-filled exotica of "The Coffee Song"), they're
also full of fresh, snazzy ideas, such as the tension-building rhythms
of "In The Still Of The Night" and the bridge-verse-chorus design of
"Let's Fall In Love". Painstakingly organized and beautifully played
throughout, it's as tight as a drum – the sax section is fantastic – but
there's looseness too; Bill Miller gets to tinkle more freewheeling piano
than usual while Don Fagerquist's muted trumpet obbligatos, along
with the occasional interjection by Bud Shank on alto sax and Frank
Rosolino on trombone, give the musical icing a twist of modernism.

The songs are all by **the big hitters** – two Cole Porters, two Berlins, an
Arlen, a Kern, a Gershwin, an Arthur Schwartz/Howard Dietz – with
the exception of "The Coffee Song", "When I Take My Sugar To Tea"
and the Cahn/Van Heusen title track (hijacked in the 1980s to serve
as the television theme tune for Little and Large). The theme of good
living, drinking and dancing is a little less obvious than in most Sinatra

albums though "In The Still Of The Night", "Let's Face The Music And Dance" and "You And The Night And The Music" always seem to belong together by virtue of their complexity and humid atmosphere (and length of title). Sinatra, though not always quite at ease, as the widely heard out-takes demonstrate, still produces much that is good, and *Ring-A-Ding Ding!* is an album that, whenever returned to, delivers on many levels.

Sinatra Swings/ Swing Along With Me

FALLING IN LOVE WITH LOVE/THE CURSE OF AN ACHING HEART/DON'T CRY JOE/PLEASE DON'T TALK ABOUT ME WHEN I'M GONE/LOVE WALKED IN/GRANADA/I NEVER KNEW/ DON'T BE THAT WAY/MOONLIGHT ON THE GANGES/IT'S A WONDERFUL WORLD/HAVE YOU MET MISS JONES/YOU'RE NOBODY 'TIL SOMEBODY LOVES YOU

Arranged by Billy May; recorded May 18, 19 and 23, 1961; released July 1961

Originally called *Swing Along With Me*, Capitol forced Reprise to rename the album *Sinatra Swings* lest it be confused in the marketplace with their *Come Swing With Me*. As that might suggest, compared with the freshly minted swing of *Ring-A-Ding Ding!* this is typical Sinatra and May, and very much a continuation of their final few Capitol titles together. Frankly, it's a dull day at the office – old songs given a stroll through by a couple of pros.

But there are bright spots. "Granada" features May at his over-the-top, music-as-travelogue best with Sinatra pulling out a bravura performance to match; "Moonlight On The Ganges" is transformed into something genuinely exotic; Sinatra casually makes a lovely job of Benny Goodman's "Don't Be That Way"; and it's good to hear him nail the tune that eluded him on the *Ring-A-Ding Ding!* sessions, the tricky **"Have You Met Jones?"**. But the album feels a little flat-footed and in places, such as in

"Don't Cry Joe", Sinatra sounds positively ragged. Only 45 years old – but having already packed in 90 years of living – and still pushing himself as hard as ever, his pipes begin to show the wear and tear that he would try to fight off from this moment onwards.

I Remember Tommy...

I'M GETTING SENTIMENTAL OVER YOU/IMAGINATION/THERE ARE SUCH THINGS/EAST OF THE SUN (AND WEST OF THE MOON)/WITHOUT A SONG/I'LL BE SEEING YOU/TAKE ME/IT'S ALWAYS YOU/POLKA DOTS AND MOONBEAMS/IT STARTED ALL OVER AGAIN/THE ONE I LOVE BELONGS TO SOMEBODY ELSE/REPRISE: I'M GETTING SENTIMENTAL OVER YOU

Arranged by Sy Oliver; recorded May 1–4, 1961; released October 1961

Sinatra's relationship with his former employer had not always been an easy one, but four years after Tommy Dorsey's death he still felt sentimental enough about him to pay tribute by reworking the trombonist's old repertoire in one of the earliest Reprise releases. Remakes had worked elsewhere in Sinatra's post-1940s career, and especially in the brilliant Sinatra/Riddle interpretations of tunes such as "Oh! Look At Me Now"

and "How About You", but *I Remember Tommy* is hit and miss. Sinatra considered the quality of his vocals on the initial sessions in March 1961, which were scored in the style of Dorsey by his former rhythm arranger Sy Oliver, to compare unfavourably with his super-smooth 1940s work and called for more strings to conceal this.

Of the recordings in 1961, neither the big ballads (such as "Take Me") nor the intimate ones (such as "There Are Such Things") really convince. The songs are naïve products of their time and sound uncomfortable in the been-there-drank-that voice of the mature Sinatra. But the swingers, such as "Without A Song", work better and the vocal duet with Oliver (who does a hip paraphrasing of The Pied Pipers' original response part) on **"The One I Love Belongs To Somebody Else"** is outstanding.

I Remember Tommy may not be essential Sinatra, but neither is it the pointless exercise that some commentators consider it.

Sinatra & Strings

I HADN'T ANYONE TILL YOU/NIGHT AND DAY/MISTY/STARDUST/COME RAIN OR COME SHINE/IT MIGHT AS WELL BE SPRING/PRISONER OF LOVE/THAT'S ALL/ALL OR NOTHING AT ALL/YESTERDAYS

Arranged by Don Costa; recorded November 20-22, 1961; released February 1962

A lush ballad album somewhere in tone between *Only The Lonely* and *Point Of No Return*, Sinatra & Strings has a special **Don Costa** sensual shimmer and high drama all of its own, and is one of Sinatra's great albums on Reprise. And at last, this is a Reprise record featuring Sinatra's vocals in their best grown-up state; warm, taut, soaring and with barely a false moment throughout. The heart-stopping **"Come Rain Or Come Shine"** is worth the price of the album on its own, the grand, cinematic colours of old favourites "Night And Day" and "All Or Nothing At All" are intoxicating and Russ Columbo's proto-croon tune from 1931, "Prisoner Of Love", under Costa and Sinatra becomes magnificent and quite above its station.

In "Yesterdays" Sinatra alludes in a few of his vocal melismas to Billie Holiday while Costa makes like **Tchaikovsky** at his most romantic, and the result is extraordinary. "Stardust" is rendered to draw attention to its exquisite verse, omitting the equally exquisite chorus entirely (and apparently irritating the composer, Hoagy Carmichael).

The Sinatra/Costa pairing was later undervalued, because of work that was much less interesting, but *Sinatra And Strings* is the work of an old master and a rising star who were at the top of their game. "*Sinatra And Strings* was, and always will be," Costa said, "the hallmark of my existence."

Sinatra And Swingin' Brass

GOODY GOODY/THEY CAN'T TAKE THAT AWAY FROM ME/AT LONG LAST LOVE/I'M
BEGINNING TO SEE THE LIGHT/DON'CHA GO 'WAY MAD/I GET A KICK OUT OF YOU/
TANGERINE/LOVE IS JUST AROUND THE CORNER/AIN'T SHE SWEET/SERENADE IN BLUE/I
LOVE YOU/PICK YOURSELF UP

Arranged by Neal Hefti; recorded April 10-11, 1962; released July 1962

There's nothing wrong with *Sinatra
And Swingin' Brass*. It cooks along
perfectly well with the former arranger
for Woody Herman and Count Basie,
Neal Hefti, then a general Reprise
producer/arranger, producing burly
work that is unremarkable. The tunes
are a diverting mix of swing-era songs
("Serenade In Blue", "I'm Beginning
To See The Light", "Don'Cha Go
'Way Mad") and reasonable remakes
(notably "I Get A Kick Out Of You");
but with Sinatra in only middling voice, and proving once again that
his spontaneous reworking of a melody was never as reliable or secure
as overt jazz singers such as **Ella Fitzgerald** or **Mel Tormé**, this set is
relatively overlooked in his canon, and probably deservedly so.

Sinatra Sings Great Songs
From Great Britain

THE VERY THOUGHT OF YOU/WE'LL GATHER LILACS IN THE SPRING/IF I HAD YOU/NOW
IS THE HOUR/THE GYPSY/ROSES OF PICARDY/A NIGHTINGALE SANG IN BERKELEY
SQUARE/A GARDEN IN THE RAIN/LONDON BY NIGHT/WE'LL MEET AGAIN/I'LL FOLLOW
MY SECRET HEART

Arranged by Robert Farnon; recorded June 12-14, 1962; released November
1962 in the UK, 1993 in the US

This is a fascinating curiosity in Sinatra's discography – his only studio
album recorded outside the US, and the only set ostensibly devoted

to the output of a single country. **Robert Farnon**, a respected British arranger and composer, described as the "greatest living string writer in the world" by André Previn, provides opulent, effusive settings; but the sessions came on the back of a gruelling world tour for Sinatra, and his pipes weren't always up to the intimate exposure or bravura displays that the scores required of him. He's by no means bad, but when you know how good he could have been – the superb *Sinatra And Strings* was recorded only months earlier – the difference is clear.

But even if he had repeated the form of *Only The Lonely*, most listeners would still not be convinced that the Chairman Of The Board is sincere when singing about gathering lilacs in leafy lanes; Sinatra was not born to sing the fey work of **Ivor Novello**, **Noel Coward** and their ilk (though he had already made a fairly powerful job of Coward's straight-backed "I'll See You Again" on *Point Of No Return*). The most successful tracks are less culturally specific (Jimmy Campbell/Reg Connelly's "If I Had You", Ray Noble's "The Very Thought Of You") but Farnon's work is faultless and inspiring throughout.

However, Sinatra was disappointed with the results, and by Winston Churchill's decision not to provide a picture for the sleeve. The record remained unreleased in the US until 1993.

All Alone

ALL ALONE/THE GIRL NEXT DOOR/ARE YOU LONESOME TONIGHT/CHARMAINE/WHAT'LL I DO/WHEN I LOST YOU/OH, HOW I MISS YOU/TONIGHT/INDISCREET/REMEMBER/ TOGETHER/THE SONG IS ENDED

Arranged by Gordon Jenkins; recorded January 15-17, 1962; released October 1962

Once again Frank and Gordon get together for a musical moan, this time in old-fashioned three-quarter time. Originally called *Come Waltz*

With Me, until the hopeless Cahn/ Van Heusen title track was dropped (though it reappeared on the CD release), the album contains five tracks by **Irving Berlin**, including "When I Lost You", composed after his wife died. This sets the tone: as ever with Sinatra/Jenkins material, occasionally it's moving and lovely, but the album as a whole is too much of a dirge, leaving the listener wishing that the pair would pull themselves

together. If we buy the idea – and we should – that as a singer Sinatra was a great actor, on *All Alone* he's a bit of a ham. And it seems that the Sinatra estate agree: it was passed over for the US 20-bit remastering schedule in 1998 and remains out of print in the US and in the UK.

Sinatra-Basie

PENNIES FROM HEAVEN/PLEASE BE KIND/(LOVE IS) THE TENDER TRAP/LOOKING AT THE WORLD THRU ROSE COLOURED GLASSES/MY KIND OF GIRL/I ONLY HAVE EYES FOR YOU/ NICE WORK IF YOU CAN GET IT/LEARNIN' THE BLUES/I'M GONNA SIT RIGHT DOWN AND WRITE MYSELF A LETTER/I WON'T DANCE

Arranged by Neal Hefti; recorded October 2-3, 1962; released January 1963

This swing album from Hefti was as distinguished as *Sinatra And Swingin' Brass* was not, and when the tracks are this good, there can be no complaints about the running time of 33 minutes. While writing, Hefti was taking into account the style of Basie's orchestra, which he himself had created on albums such as *The Atomic Mr Basie* in the 1950s. Stately tempos, spacious four-beat swing, infectious riffs, crescendos, sudden stops and explosions were all placed on *Sinatra-Basie* to perfection. Of the ten tracks, seven are Basie's aerated strolls, with only "Looking At The World Thru Rose Coloured Glasses", "Nice Work If You Can Get It" and "I'm Gonna Sit Right Down And Write Myself A Letter" breaking into a trot. There is even some extended jazz soloing: tenor sax player Frank Foster is in and out of the apparently casually organized "I'm Gonna Sit Right Down And Write

Myself A Letter" and gets a half-chorus of "Pennies From Heaven" and three-fifths of "Rose Coloured Glasses".

Sinatra, perfecting once again the balance of rhythmic relaxation and alertness, has a great time, and you can hear why; this is an ear-to-ear grin of a record. Try to listen with a straight face if you can through drummer Sonny Payne's percussive responses to each line of Leslie Bricusse's "**My Kind Of Girl**" (the only contemporary tune of the set) or the moment in "**Please Be Kind**" when Sinatra drops out unexpectedly and lets the band stoke things a little.

Half an hour of pure joy, *Sinatra-Basie* was a big hit for Reprise and is worth the whole of *Swingin' Session!!!*, *Come Swing With Me*, *Sinatra Swings* and *Swingin' Brass* put together. But, according to Will Friedwald, Hefti did not enjoy the experience of writing to order – interestingly, his name is conspicuously absent from the LP and CD releases – and he decided not to work with Sinatra, or indeed any other vocalist, again.

The Concert Sinatra

I HAVE DREAMED/MY HEART STOOD STILL/LOST IN THE STARS/OL' MAN RIVER/YOU'LL NEVER WALK ALONE/BEWITCHED/THIS NEARLY WAS MINE/SOLILOQUY

Arranged by Nelson Riddle; recorded February 18–21, 1963; released May 1963

With *The Concert Sinatra*, Frank was thinking big. The songs – six of the eight being **Richard Rodgers** compositions, and five of those with lyrics by **Oscar Hammerstein II** – had big ideas about **the meaning of life**. "Ol' Man River" is Kern and Hammerstein's remarkable portrait of toil and oppression, insignificant next to an indifferent force of nature and the passage of time. Kurt Weill and Maxwell Anderson's "Lost In The Stars" similarly contemplates existence as a godless meander while Rodgers and Hammerstein's "You'll Never Walk Alone" suggests that while there is hope there is spiritual companionship. "Soliloquy" mulls on the meaning of prospective fatherhood while "This Nearly Was Mine" is sung by a character denied "one partner in paradise". "I Have Dreamed" is a giddy reverie of anticipated sensual pleasure while "Bewitched" is deep in the middle of it.

Such elevated material required elevated treatment: a 73-piece symphony orchestra and, nearly five years after *Only The Lonely* (*Swingin' Session* doesn't count), the return of the orch-pop tone poet himself, **Nelson Riddle**. His scoring throughout is stirring, full of swirling strings and piping flutes, and replete with his impressionistic polytones that are reminiscent of Ravel. Sinatra is majestic; full-voiced and solemn, he sings with care and presence and hits unprecedented heights of emotional intensity.

Whether the album is a success – the "new achievement of artistic purity and control", as claimed by the sleeve annotator Lawrence D. Stewart – depends on how much the listener can tolerate the Rodgers/Hammerstein song-as-life-lesson and the bravura epic endings. Unsurprisingly, *The Concert Sinatra* is not to be approached coolly. It takes a heightened dedication to the listening experience to get beyond the bombast into the beauty. But once that commitment is made, the beauty – and perhaps even the divinity – is there to behold.

Sinatra's Sinatra

I'VE GOT YOU UNDER MY SKIN/IN THE WEE SMALL HOURS OF THE MORNING/THE SECOND TIME AROUND/NANCY/WITCHCRAFT/ YOUNG AT HEART/ALL THE WAY/HOW LITTLE WE KNOW/POCKETFUL OF MIRACLES/ OH, WHAT IT SEEMED TO BE/CALL ME IRRESPONSIBLE/PUT YOUR DREAMS AWAY

Arranged by Nelson Riddle; recorded November 22, 1961, January 21, 1963, and April 29–April 30, 1963; released August 1963

The Music

REPRISE MUSICAL REPERTORY THEATRE

Finian's Rainbow/Kiss Me Kate/
South Pacific/Guys And Dolls

Various arrangers; recorded February 19, 1963, and July 10-25, 1963;
released December 1963 as original albums and September 2000 as a
box set

In his commercial and artistic optimism of the early Reprise years, Sinatra showcased his label's roster of artists on swinging recordings of near-complete scores from four revered Broadway shows that had emerged in the late 1940s. He even produced the sessions himself. The veteran Hollywood conductor **Morris Stoloff** was the baton man and the arrangements were farmed out to some usual suspects (Riddle and May) and some lesser-used men, such as Skip Martin, Marty Paich, Nathan Van Cleave, Bill Loose, Jerry Fielding, George Rhodes and Herb Spencer, most of whom would not work for Sinatra at any other time. Recorded quickly and released simultaneously in 1963, the four albums featuring the re-imagined scores are certainly the flamboyant, eventful alternatives to "original cast recordings" that Sinatra intended, though the avoidance of "casting" — some characters' songs are

Part of Sinatra's severance agreement from Capitol required him initially to avoid anything he'd recorded there, and his first five albums for Reprise contained no such songs (though subsequent albums featured a handful). But *Sinatra's Sinatra*, which was partly selected by **Frank Jr.**, while not quite a greatest hits album, was a concerted effort to divert a floating listener from the dozens of Capitol and Columbia titles clogging the racks, by remaking some classic Capitol-era Sinatra tunes with Nelson Riddle.

covered by more than one singer – means that the albums work better as a showcase for songs than as a narrative-led souvenir. The listener is dazzled by the melodic richness of Rodgers/Hammerstein's **South Pacific**, the whimsical wit of Yip Harburg/Burton Lane's **Finian's Rainbow** and the remarkable invention of Frank Loesser's **Guys And Dolls** (even without "My Time Of Day", an assault course of a tune that no one fancied). In this company, Cole Porter's **Kiss Me Kate**, by far the flattest of the four records, sounds like forced, uninspired, old-fashioned work by a composer past his best.

Sinatra doesn't feature himself more than would be appropriate but shows fine form in his occasional solos. Highlights are "When I'm Not Near The Girl I Love", "Old Devil Moon", the roaring **Billy May** treatment of "Luck Be A Lady" and "I've Never Been In Love Before". The **Sinatra/Crosby/Martin** trios on *Guys And Dolls* ("The Oldest Established (Permanent Floating Crap Game In New York)" and "Fugue For Tinhorns") are excellent and **Sammy Davis Jr.'s** routines ("Necessity", "That Great Come-And-Get-It Day" and "Sit Down, You're Rocking The Boat" among them) are so wired with rhythm, they seem to elevate the project to a different level of hipness. The listener might wonder, however, what a square tenor like Clark Dennis is doing there, or take issue with Debbie Reynolds's over-sung Adelaide songs on *Guys And Dolls*. But generally Sinatra's gang (including Rosemary Clooney, The McGuire Sisters, The Hi-Lo's, Jo Stafford and Dinah Shore), wanting to do their best for the boss, give good value.

It wasn't long after these albums came out that, unfortunately, Reprise was forced to face up to financial reality and drop most of the artists, as well as any ideas about developing similar projects.

On those terms, it's not bad. The new **"Nancy"** features a gorgeous fresh score by Riddle and contemporary film stars (Hepburn and Taylor) to replace Grable, Lamour and Turner. And it's good to hear the light swing of "In The Wee Small Hours", and the tweaked but essentially familiar Riddle charts for "I've Got You Under My Skin" and "Witchcraft", in sparkling stereo. Some might find the mature sound of mid-1960s Sinatra incongruous on ingenuous 1940s material such as "Oh! What It Seemed To Be" and "Put Your Dreams Away", but others might be quietly moved.

Frank Sinatra Sings Days Of Wine And Roses, Moon River And Other Academy Award Winners

DAYS OF WINE AND ROSES/MOON RIVER/THE WAY YOU LOOK TONIGHT/THREE COINS IN THE FOUNTAIN/IN THE COOL, COOL, COOL OF THE EVENING/SECRET LOVE/SWINGING ON A STAR/IT MIGHT AS WELL BE SPRING/THE CONTINENTAL/LOVE IS A MANY SPLENDORED THING/ALL THE WAY

Arranged by Nelson Riddle; recorded January 27-28, 1964; released March 1964

Medium-grade Sinatra/Riddle, at best. The dreary "concept" merely exists to hoist a Sinatra record onto the bandwagon of the fashionable arranger and composer **Henry Mancini**, whose name-checked songs in the title were among the most popular of the period. In an early example of what would become a distressing trend on his albums, Sinatra attempts to modishly follow where others led and ends up sounding clueless; it's glaringly obvious that he has no real feeling for the songs "Days Of Wine And Roses" or "Moon River", over-swaggering the former and under-pitching the latter. Elsewhere, "Three Coins In A Fountain" was hokum the first time round; he was right in 1955 when he described "Love Is A Many Splendored Thing" as "worthless"; and "In The Cool, Cool, Cool, Of The Evening" and "Swinging On A Star" barely dent Crosby's originals. Only the relaxed and still-fresh "The Continental" gets anything going.

Sinatra is unlikely to have prepared very hard for the sessions, having just been hammered by the Nevada Gaming Commission and with JFK's assassination and Frank Jr.'s kidnapping occurring only weeks beforehand; and it shows. The album is like a musical sleepwalk through a confidence crisis.

It Might As Well Be Swing

FLY ME TO THE MOON/I WISH YOU LOVE/I BELIEVE IN YOU/MORE/I CAN'T STOP LOVING YOU/HELLO, DOLLY!/I WANNA BE AROUND/THE BEST IS YET TO COME/THE GOOD LIFE/ WIVES AND LOVERS

Arranged by Quincy Jones; recorded June 9-12, 1964; released July 1964

The second leg with Count Basie works out as around half a good record. "Fly Me To The Moon", "I Wish You Love", "I Believe In You", "More" and "The Best Is Yet To Come" pump along in the customary style of Sinatra and Basie, with a fresh twist courtesy of the arranger, **Quincy Jones**. As on the first record, Sinatra revels in the 4/4 swing of Freddie Green (guitar), Buddy Catlett (bass) and Sonny Payne (drums) and rhythmically he sits right with them. No wonder he had them as his house band as often as he could during the next few years.

But there's a continuation of the slip in artistic confidence that is detectable on the previous album, with Sinatra chasing the hits of other stars with mixed results. "The Good Life" and "I Wanna Be Around" are slightly futile retreads of middling **Tony Bennett** songs. Louis Armstrong's return to the charts with Jerry Herman's high-kicking "Hello, Dolly!" is saluted in Sinatra's ho-hum cover. He had already nodded to the explosion in popularity that **Ray Charles** enjoyed in the late 1950s and early 1960s with "Come Rain Or Come Shine" on *Sinatra And Strings*, but his attempt at Sinatrafying the 12/8 country R&B hit "I Can't Stop Loving You" lacks grace when compared with Charles's version. The most successful cover (shockingly condescending lyrics notwithstanding) takes on Jack Jones's "Wives And Lovers", a Burt Bacharach/Hal David waltz recast in prowling 4/4 swing.

There are some classics here, but listening to *It Might As Well Be Swing* also means facing the powerful whiff of second-hand roses.

September Of My Years

THE SEPTEMBER OF MY YEARS/HOW OLD AM I?/DON'T WAIT TOO LONG/IT GETS LONELY
EARLY/THIS IS ALL I ASK/LAST NIGHT WHEN WE WERE YOUNG/THE MAN IN THE LOOKING
GLASS/IT WAS A VERY GOOD YEAR/WHEN THE WIND WAS GREEN/HELLO, YOUNG LOVERS/
I SEE IT NOW/ONCE UPON A TIME/SEPTEMBER SONG

Arranged by Gordon Jenkins; recorded April 13, 14 and 22, and May 27,
1965; released August 1965

Here is the album that Sinatra
and Jenkins were made to make: a
sumptuous celebration of growing
older that represents the peak of
their work together. As one may
have come to expect with this pair,
this elegiac collection teeters on the
verge of maudlin – the strings sob
and wail like never before and there
are sunsets and leaves turning brown
galore – but for once, the ruminative,
self-absorbed mood holds the listener
throughout. *September Of My Years* is compelling because it feels heartfelt
and personal and, unlike *No One Cares* or *All Alone*, it has more to say
than "poor me". It's the sound of **two old sages** looking back with a heart-
tugging blend of wise acceptance and rueful longing. "Neither one of us,"
Jenkins said, "could have made that album at any other time of our lives."

The record is dominated by the towering **"It Was A Very Good Year"**
but the quality of composition is high throughout, and untypical of
Sinatra's previous albums. With the exception of the beautiful remakes
of "Last Night When We Were Young", "Hello, Young Lovers" and
"September Song", all the songs are from the previous ten years and some
are by relatively unknown writers. **Sunny Skylar** contributes "Don't Wait
Too Long", a song that seems to have been written with Frank and Mia
in mind ("You are the summer and I am the autumn"); "I See It Now"
by **Alec Wilder** is an affecting piece of reminiscence with the formal
melodic clarity of his famous "I'll Be Around"; and "Once Upon A Time"
is a beautiful, rarely heard **Charles Strouse/Lee Adams** song from the
1962 musical *All American*.

The title piece is a triumph from **Sammy Cahn** and **Jimmy Van Heusen**, written for Sinatra's "wand'ring ways" and unimaginable sung by anyone else; thankfully, it's rarely attempted. Who else could convey the soft sigh and the gentle smile of approaching dotage with such believable depth? Jenkins himself composed "How Old Am I?" and "This Is All I Ask", which eulogizes the comfort found in love, pretty girls, children's games, rainbows and stars, and music.

It was only two years on from his previous near-masterwork, *The Concert Sinatra*, but given the five preceding album releases, *September Of My Years* was the welcome return of Sinatra the musical artist.

A Man And His Music

PUT YOUR DREAMS AWAY/ALL OR NOTHING AT ALL/I'LL NEVER SMILE AGAIN/THERE ARE SUCH THINGS/I'LL BE SEEING YOU/THE ONE I LOVE BELONGS TO SOMEBODY ELSE/POLKA DOTS AND MOONBEAMS/NIGHT AND DAY/OH, WHAT IT SEEMED TO BE/ SOLILOQUY/NANCY/THE HOUSE I LIVE IN/FROM HERE TO ETERNITY (DIALOGUE EXTRACT FROM FILM)/COME FLY WITH ME/HOW LITTLE WE KNOW/LEARNIN' THE BLUES/IN THE WEE SMALL HOURS OF THE MORNING/YOUNG AT HEART/WITCHCRAFT/ALL THE WAY/LOVE AND MARRIAGE/I'VE GOT YOU UNDER MY SKIN/RING-A-DING DING/THE SECOND TIME AROUND/THE SUMMIT COMEDY ROUTINE/THE OLDEST ESTABLISHED (PERMANENT FLOATING CRAP GAME IN NEW YORK)/LUCK BE A LADY/CALL ME IRRESPONSIBLE/FLY ME TO THE MOON/SOFTLY, AS I LEAVE YOU/MY KIND OF TOWN/THE SEPTEMBER OF MY YEARS

Arranged by Nelson Riddle, Gordon Jenkins, Billy May, Sy Oliver, Count Basie, Ernie Freeman, Johnny Mandel and Don Costa; released November 1965

Part of Sinatra's 50th birthday shenanigans, *A Man And His Music* contains many career highlights that are available on earlier Reprise issues; but also included on this value-for-money 100-minute double package are a *From Here To Eternity* dialogue excerpt, a recording of **"the Summit"** – Frank's preferred term for the Rat Pack – live in Las Vegas, and Sinatra

REPRISE SINGLES COMPILATIONS

Softly, As I Leave You

EMILY/HERE'S TO THE LOSERS++/DEAR HEART/COME BLOW YOUR HORN/LOVE ISN'T JUST FOR THE YOUNG++/I CAN'T BELIEVE I'M LOSING YOU*/PASS ME BY+/SOFTLY, AS I LEAVE YOU**/THEN SUDDENLY LOVE**AVAILABLE**/TALK TO ME BABY*/THE LOOK OF LOVE

Arranged by Nelson Riddle, Don Costa*, Ernie Freeman**, Billy May+ and Marty Paich++; released November 1964

Sinatra '65

TELL HER (YOU LOVE HER EACH DAY)**/ANYTIME AT ALL**/MAIN THEME FROM *THE CARDINAL* (STAY WITH ME)*/I LIKE TO LEAD WHEN I DANCE/YOU BROUGHT A NEW KIND OF LOVE TO ME/MY KIND OF TOWN/WHEN SOMEBODY LOVES YOU**/SOMEWHERE IN YOUR HEART**/I'VE NEVER BEEN IN LOVE BEFORE/WHEN I'M NOT NEAR THE GIRL I LOVE/LUCK BE A LADY+

Arranged by Nelson Riddle, Don Costa*, Ernie Freeman** and Billy May+; released May 1965

My Kind Of Broadway

EV'RYBODY HAS THE RIGHT TO BE WRONG!/GOLDEN MOMENT/LUCK BE A LADY***/LOST IN THE STARS/HELLO, DOLLY!**/I'LL ONLY MISS HER WHEN I THINK OF HER++/THEY CAN'T TAKE THAT AWAY FROM ME*/YESTERDAYS/NICE WORK IF YOU CAN GET IT */HAVE YOU MET MISS JONES***/WITHOUT A SONG+

Arranged by Nelson Riddle, Neal Hefti*, Quincy Jones**, Billy May***, Sy Oliver+ and Torrie Zito++; released November 1965

indulging in some pithy, colourful patter between songs. The result is an entertaining collection that gives a better idea than many subsequent

As on Capitol, Sinatra kept his Reprise singles, usually produced by **Jimmy Bowen**, and film songs largely separate from his serious albums, usually produced by **Sonny Burke**, and mopped some of them up later on compilations such as these. Sinatra's commercial attempts to reach the charts in the 1960s have not worn well overall. Attempts at soft-rock such as "Softly As I Leave You" and Burt Bacharach's "The Look Of Love" at least had the virtue of a nice tune, but "Anytime At All" and "Tell Her (You Love Her Each Day)" are crude attempts to put R&B into the Sinatra sound – and unfortunately they did well enough for him not to be discouraged, as *That's Life* demonstrated. Also containing Reprise Musical Repertory Theatre tracks, film themes and previously released album cuts, these albums are pretty unsatisfactory. It's no surprise to find that they have mostly languished, out of print, since their release; *Softly, As I Leave You* is currently deleted in the US and UK, *My Kind Of Broadway* is absent from the US catalogue and *Sinatra '65* has never been issued on CD at all.

Greatest Hits

STRANGERS IN THE NIGHT/SUMMER WIND/IT WAS A VERY GOOD YEAR/FORGET DOMANI/SOMETHIN' STUPID – WITH NANCY SINATRA/THAT'S LIFE/TELL HER (YOU LOVE HER EACH DAY)/THE WORLD WE KNEW (OVER AND OVER)/WHEN SOMEBODY LOVES YOU/THIS TOWN/SOFTLY, AS I LEAVE YOU

Released 1968

Greatest Hits, Vol 2

MY WAY/A MAN ALONE/CYCLES/BEIN' GREEN/LOVE'S BEEN GOOD TO ME/I'M NOT AFRAID/GOIN' OUT OF MY HEAD/SOMETHING/WHAT'S NOW IS NOW/STAR!/THE SEPTEMBER OF MY YEARS

Released 1972

Not the "greatest" by a long shot. This is simply the commercial highlights and lowlights of Sinatra between 1964 and 1969.

"best of" collections of what was great about Sinatra before it all got a bit vulgar.

Moonlight Sinatra

MOONLIGHT BECOME YOU/MOON SONG/MOONLIGHT SERENADE/REACHING FOR THE MOON/I WISHED ON THE MOON/OH, YOU CRAZY MOON/THE MOON GOT IN MY EYES/MOONLIGHT MOOD/MOON LOVE/THE MOON WAS YELLOW (AND THE NIGHT WAS YOUNG)

Arranged by Nelson Riddle; recorded November 29-30, 1965; released March 1966

An undervalued gem, *Moonlight Sinatra* was overshadowed by the 50th birthday fuss of the previous releases and the commercial success of the subsequent ones. Although it's an apparently obvious punning concept, it's a venerable, almost regal set of lunar tunes given such care in performance and arrangement that the music continues to unfold to the listener many spins later. These comfortingly old-fashioned, mostly obscure songs – largely introduced two or three decades earlier by **Bing Crosby** and **Glenn Miller** – are gently elevated by some artful treatments and heartfelt singing.

Sinatra and Riddle sound at home and inspired throughout the album, particular highlights being the Brazilian-flavoured remake of **"The Moon Was Yellow"** and the aching performance of Irving Berlin's beautiful **"Reaching For The Moon"**. And ignoring the notorious rhyming of moon and June, the various roles that the moon takes on in song are diverting: it is a flatterer ("Moonlight Becomes You"), a magical symbol ("I Wished On The Moon") and, several times, a not entirely reliable enhancer of romance ("Oh, You Crazy Moon", "The Moon Got In My Eyes", "The Moon Is Yellow", "Moon Love"). This is fine Sinatra/Riddle fare, and a song-buff's dream.

Strangers In The Night

STRANGERS IN THE NIGHT*/SUMMER WIND/ALL OR NOTHING AT ALL/CALL ME/YOU'RE DRIVING ME CRAZY/ON A CLEAR DAY (YOU CAN SEE FOREVER)/MY BABY JUST CARES FOR ME/DOWNTOWN/YES SIR, THAT'S MY BABY/THE MOST BEAUTIFUL GIRL IN THE WORLD

Arranged by Nelson Riddle and Ernie Freeman*; recorded April 11, May 11 and May 16, 1966; released May 1966

This final collaboration with **Nelson Riddle**, prefixed ignominiously by the arrangement of the hit title track by **Ernie Freeman**, had the subtitle *Sings For Moderns*, but it's a very odd way to pursue the youth market. There is ungroovy, pervading and distracting electric organ; Tony Hatch's "Downtown", which requires Sinatra to boogaloo like a fool; and no fewer than three musty **Walter Donaldson** numbers from more than

thirty years previously ("Yes Sir That's My Baby", "My Baby Just Cares For Me", "You're Driving Me Crazy") that are given an ultra-cavalier, swaggering Vegas treatment. And there are the extreme, uncomfortable tempos – "On A Clear Day" drags just a few beats per minute above not moving at all and Rodgers and Hart's sweet waltz "The Most Beautiful Girl In The World" bongos itself into a kind of frenzy. Only "Summer Wind" approaches vintage Sinatra/Riddle.

Strangers In The Night is the first album since Sinatra's final Capitol releases on which he sounds as if he has better things to do than make a decent record. He's sloppy and coarse, and on **"Downtown"** he is downright peculiar, sneering his way through a song he clearly despises. Despite the occasional bright spots, it's an ignoble, disrespectful mess of an album, and it seems to have been produced with cynicism. Needless to say, on the back of the mushy soft-rock hit that was the title track it outsold considerably the vastly superior *Moonlight Sinatra*.

LIVE SINATRA

Live In Australia

PERDIDO (INSTRUMENTAL)/BETWEEN THE DEVIL AND THE DEEP BLUE SEA (INSTRUMENTAL)/I COULD HAVE DANCED ALL NIGHT/JUST ONE OF THOSE THINGS/I GET A KICK OUT OF YOU/AT LONG LAST LOVE/WILLOW WEEP FOR ME/I'VE GOT YOU UNDER MY SKIN/MOONLIGHT IN VERMONT/THE LADY IS A TRAMP/SINATRA SPEAKS/ANGEL EYES/COME FLY WITH ME/ALL THE WAY/DANCING IN THE DARK/ONE FOR MY BABY/ALL OF ME/ON THE ROAD TO MANDALAY/NIGHT AND DAY

With The Red Norvo Quintet

Blue Note; recorded March 31–April 1, 1959; released April 1997

Sinatra and Sextet Live In Paris

INTRODUCTION BY CHARLES AZNAVOUR/GOODY GOODY/IMAGINATION/AT LONG LAST LOVE/MOONLIGHT IN VERMONT/WITHOUT A SONG/DAY IN DAY OUT/I'VE GOT YOU UNDER MY SKIN/I GET A KICK OUT OF YOU/THE SECOND TIME AROUND/TOO MARVELLOUS FOR WORDS/MY FUNNY VALENTINE/IN THE STILL OF THE NIGHT/APRIL IN PARIS/YOU'RE NOBODY 'TIL SOMEBODY LOVES YOU/THEY CAN'T TAKE THAT AWAY FROM ME/CHICAGO/NIGHT AND DAY/I COULD HAVE DANCED ALL NIGHT/ONE FOR MY BABY/A FOGGY DAY/OL' MAN RIVER/THE LADY IS A TRAMP/I LOVE PARIS/NANCY/ COME FLY WITH ME

With the Bill Miller Sextet

Reprise; recorded June 5, 1962; released August 1994

Sinatra At The Sands

COME FLY WITH ME/I'VE GOT A CRUSH ON YOU/I'VE GOT YOU UNDER MY SKIN/THE SHADOW OF YOUR SMILE/STREET OF DREAMS/ONE FOR MY BABY/FLY ME TO THE MOON/ONE O'CLOCK JUMP (BASIE INSTRUMENTAL)/"THE TEA BREAK" (MONOLOGUE)/YOU MAKE ME FEEL SO YOUNG/ALL OF ME (BASIE INSTRUMENTAL)/SEPTEMBER OF MY YEARS/GET ME TO THE CHURCH ON TIME/IT WAS A VERY GOOD YEAR/DON'T WORRY 'BOUT ME/MAKIN' WHOOPEE! (BASIE INSTRUMENTAL)/WHERE OR WHEN/ANGEL EYES/MY KIND OF TOWN/"A FEW LAST WORDS" (MONOLOGUE)/MY KIND OF TOWN (REPRISE)

With Count Basie And His Orchestra

Reprise; arranged by Quincy Jones; recorded January 26–February 1, 1965; released August 1966

The Main Event

OVERTURE: IT WAS A VERY GOOD YEAR-ALL THE WAY-MY KIND OF TOWN/THE LADY IS A TRAMP/I GET A KICK OUT OF YOU/LET ME TRY AGAIN/AUTUMN IN NEW YORK/ I'VE GOT YOU UNDER MY SKIN/BAD, BAD LEROY BROWN/ANGEL EYES/YOU ARE THE SUNSHINE OF MY LIFE/THE HOUSE I LIVE IN/MY KIND OF TOWN/MY WAY

Featuring Woody Herman & The Young Thundering Herd

Reprise; recorded October 2-13, 1974; released October 1974

Sinatra 80th: Live In Concert

YOU ARE THE SUNSHINE OF MY LIFE/WHAT NOW MY LOVE/MY HEART STOOD STILL/ WHAT'S NEW/FOR ONCE IN MY LIFE/IF/IN THE STILL OF THE NIGHT/SOLILOQUY/ MAYBE THIS TIME/WHERE OR WHEN/YOU WILL BE MY MUSIC/STRANGERS IN THE NIGHT/ANGEL EYES/NEW YORK, NEW YORK/MY WAY (WITH LUCIANO PAVAROTTI)

Capitol; recorded October 24, 1987, and December 1-4, 1988; released November 1995

This list comprises the officially sanctioned live recordings, but they are essential glimpses into the musical vibrancy that Sinatra generated in front of an audience. *Live In Australia* and *Live In Paris* are particularly valuable in that they capture Sinatra at the peak of his performing power and grooving with a small group, a setting he rarely used in the studio. His energy pulls you in so close that you become part of the freewheeling experience, willing him on to another peak of excitement. He rarely disappoints.

Sinatra At The Sands is the only live album that was officially released during his performing career, and it's a classic. If tingles down the back are a measurement, the Sinatra/Basie/Jones "I've Got You Under My Skin" might be the most exhilarating version ever recorded; although the Riddle version, upon which this was based, is impeccable, this goes further, with Sinatra and the band conjuring a thrilling balance of musicality and raw excitement.

The Main Event, conducted by Bill Miller, came nine years later, when Sinatra's voice was fading, and works better on DVD (Warner Music Vision). The same would probably go for *Sinatra 80th: Live In Concert* if it were on DVD, *Live In Japan* from 1985 being the nearest equivalent. This series of performances from the 1980s ranges from the oddly chosen ("If", "What Now My Love") to the precious ("In The Still Of The Night", "Soliloquy").

That's Life

THAT'S LIFE/I WILL WAIT FOR YOU/SOMEWHERE MY LOVE/SAND AND SEA/WHAT NOW MY LOVE/WINCHESTER CATHEDRAL/GIVE HER LOVE/TELL HER (YOU LOVE HER EACH DAY)/THE IMPOSSIBLE DREAM/YOU'RE GONNA HEAR FROM ME

Arranged by Ernie Freeman; recorded October 18, November 17 and November 18, 1966; released November 1966

Having enjoyed landing a major hit with "Strangers In The Night" – even if he disliked the song itself – Sinatra looked for another one and found "That's Life", a rocker with backing vocals in the style of **Ray Charles and The Raelettes**. Some discerning Sinatra listeners shudder at the crude material and the gruff over-singing, reportedly done in a seething mood after the producer **Jimmy Bowen** had dared to ask for one more take, but it did the trick and took Sinatra back into the charts. The album that soon followed inevitably took a similarly unsubtle approach to a range of uninteresting contemporary material under the arranger **Ernie Freeman**, the singles specialist's only promotion to full-length album status. While some of it is bizarre and fascinating (Frank getting groovy with Gilbert Becaud's "Sea And Sand") or so bad it's funny ("The Impossible Dream"), it's mostly a rotten experience. Only Dory and André Previn's "You're Gonna Hear From Me" was really worth singing, but even that is unclear from this ungainly performance.

Francis Albert Sinatra & Antonio Carlos Jobim

THE GIRL FROM IPANEMA/DINDI/CHANGE PARTNERS/QUIET NIGHTS OF QUIET STARS/ MEDITATION/IF YOU NEVER COME TO ME/HOW INSENSITIVE/I CONCENTRATE ON YOU/ BAUBLES, BANGLES AND BEADS/ONCE I LOVED

The Reprise years

Arranged by Claus Ogerman; recorded January 30–February 1, 1967; released March 1967

Sinatra came to **the bossa nova boom** relatively late. The bewitching melodies of the Brazilian composer Antonio Carlos Jobim and the sensual slow-motion samba rhythms of the bossa nova had been common adult pop currency since **Stan Getz** and **João and Astrud Gilberto** had popularized them in 1962 and 1963. But when Sinatra eventually engaged with this entrancing Brazilian pop music, it made his other efforts to find a foothold

in "Beatleland" (as he had it) look foolish. In the closest he ever came to recording a songbook album by a single composer – Sinatra felt that there were insufficient good English lyrics then to make it an all-Jobim set – seven of Jobim's elegant compositions feature alongside three perfectly chosen and adapted standards, by Berlin, Porter and Adams/Strouse. It's a masterpiece.

In by far the gentlest singing of his career, Sinatra's strong and tender voice is a wonder, warmly weaving through the Brazilian's graceful, economic tunes respectfully, as if to acknowledge the greatness of this new generation of standards. Sinatra said of his vocalizing, the sensual polar opposite approach of his bluesy snarling on "That's Life", that he hadn't sung "this soft since I had laryngitis". He's so persuasive, so seductive, that the question must be asked: why didn't he sing like this more often?

Retaining the key figures from Jobim's delicate Verve recordings, the arranger **Claus Ogerman** and the drummer **Dom Um Romao**, *Francis Albert Sinatra & Antonio Carlos Jobim* is even more minimalist; Sinatra kept urging Ogerman to remove elements of the arrangement until the air played a part.

But the magic ingredient was Jobim, picking at his acoustic guitar and murmuring his **Portuguese counterpoint** on four of the tracks, less a duet partner than a wise appendage. Jobim described Sinatra as "Mount Everest for a songwriter" while Frank rated "Tone", as he called him, "one of the most talented musicians I have ever met". The album that they made surpassed the praise that they gave each other.

The World We Knew

THE WORLD WE KNEW (OVER AND OVER)/SOMETHIN' STUPID* (WITH NANCY SINATRA)/
THIS IS MY LOVE**/BORN FREE**/DON'T SLEEP IN THE SUBWAY/THIS TOWN*/THIS IS MY
SONG/YOU ARE THERE**/DRINKING AGAIN+/SOME ENCHANTED EVENING++

Arranged by Ernie Freeman, Billy Strange*, Gordon Jenkins**, Claus
Ogerman+ and H. B. Barnum++; recorded January 31–July 24, 1967;
released August 1967

A thin collection of other people's hits, tawdry singles and nonsense; H. B. Barnum's big band's "Some Enchanted Evening" is so horribly tasteless that it must be a joke. Although similar to *That's Life* in its indication of Sinatra's sporadic lack of interest in quality control, *The World We Knew* does at least have a few decent cuts. Lee Hazelwood's "This Town" is terrific, over-the-top soundtrack jazz-rock that Sinatra eats up with relish while "You Are There" is a haunting Gordon Jenkins arrangement of the theme from Sidney J. Furie's film *The Naked Runner*. But the highlight is the boozy ballad **"Drinkin' Again"**, the lyrics a variation by Johnny Mercer on his ultimate saloon song "One For My Baby", which inspires Sinatra to reach something approaching his barroom best.

Francis A. & Edward K.

FOLLOW ME/SUNNY/ALL I NEED IS THE GIRL/INDIAN SUMMER/I LIKE THE SUNRISE/
YELLOW DAYS/POOR BUTTERFLY/COME BACK TO ME

Arranged by Billy May; recorded December 11–12, 1967; released January 1968

"There's some disastrous shit in there," Billy May told Will Friedwald, "but some of it is awful good."

The Sinatra/Ellington project was long awaited, not least by Sinatra himself. When it came, the record – eight long, languorous tracks in all

– was short on excitement and tunes, and it captures Sinatra with a cold and Ellington's indifferent orchestra sounding half asleep in places. With neither Ellington nor his recently deceased long-time musical partner **Billy Strayhorn** having anything to do with the arrangements, and the presence of only one Ducal composition ("I Like The Sunrise"), *Francis A. & Edward K.* was generally considered a disappointment.

Yet **Billy May**, hired for his imitative skills, fashions grandeur and a patient stateliness, and space for Ellington's charismatic players to breathe, and here and there everyone rises to the occasion. On Stephen Sondheim/Jule Styne's "All I Need Is The Girl" from the musical *Gypsy*, Sinatra delivers the sort of unforced swing singing that you may have thought he'd given up; and there is glorious Johnny Hodges alto saxophone on "Indian Summer" and on the lovely "Yellow Days", which also features a stunning approximation by May of Ellington's ensemble textures. It's no classic, but *Francis A. & Edward K.* is an intriguing record that retains a mysterious pull.

Cycles

RAIN IN MY HEART/BOTH SIDES NOW/LITTLE GREEN APPLES/PRETTY COLORS/CYCLES/WANDERING/BY THE TIME I GET TO PHOENIX/MOODY RIVER/MY WAY OF LIFE/GENTLE ON MY MIND

Arranged by Don Costa; recorded November 12-14, 1968; released November 1968

When fifty-something Frank does his best at soft rock and country-folk, amid modish electric pick bass, acoustic guitars and tinkling harpsichord, with what he presumably considered to be the best of the day's young songwriters, the result is embarrassing but sweet, like an ageing relative trying to dance in platform shoes. Joni Mitchell's "Both Sides Now" (at a rock tempo that makes a nonsense of her sophisticated-naïve text), Pat

Boone's country twaddle hit "Moody River" and Glen Campbell's "Gentle On My Mind" are the cuts that are the least convincing; but Sinatra manages to make something touching of Gayle Caldwell's **"Wandering"**, the folk-psychedelia of **"Pretty Colors"** and the superior pop of Jimmy Webb's **"By The Time I Get To Phoenix"**. Even Burt Kaempfert's overblown "My Way Of Life" and Teddy Randazzo's outrageously camp "Rain In My Heart" deliver a frisson of kitschy excitement.

But that is based on the idea that anything from the past can be given ironic artistic justification and reinvented as retro-cool; really, it's all highly inappropriate and in excruciating taste. Are those soft-centred pop arrangements by the same man who so masterfully scored *Sinatra And Strings* seven years earlier? On *Cycles* Frank and Don sound like the oldest swingers in town.

My Way

WATCH WHAT HAPPENS/DIDN'T WE/HALLELUJAH, I LOVE HER SO/YESTERDAY/ALL MY TOMORROWS/MY WAY/A DAY IN THE LIFE OF A FOOL/FOR ONCE IN MY LIFE/IF YOU GO AWAY/MRS. ROBINSON

Arranged by Don Costa; recorded February 18–24, 1969; released March 1969

This is more like it. Sinatra and Costa are close to what they do best on Luis Bonfa's **"Day In The Life Of A Fool"**, Paul McCartney's **"Yesterday"** and Cahn and Van Heusen's tender, ten-year-old **"All My Tomorrows"** theme from the film *A Hole In The Head*. Of the swingers, Ray Charles's

"Hallelujah, I Love Her So" and Paul Simon's "Mrs Robinson", re-styled to incorporate meaningless Sinatra-isms, try a touch too hard, but Michel Legrand's "Watch What Happens" hits the spot. Even the soft rock of Jimmy Webb's "Didn't We" and Jacques Brel/Rod McKuen's "If You Go Away" glow with sincerity and sensitivity. The album is dominated, of course, by the inflated title track, but nothing is perfect.

A Man Alone

A MAN ALONE/NIGHT/I'VE BEEN TO TOWN/FROM PROMISE TO PROMISE/THE SINGLE MAN/THE BEAUTIFUL STRANGERS/LONESOME CITIES/LOVE'S BEEN GOOD TO ME/EMPTY IS/OUT BEYOND THE WINDOW/SOME TRAVELING MUSIC/A MAN ALONE (REPRISE)

Arranged by Don Costa; recorded March 19-21, 1969; released August 1969

It could be said that by any clear-sighted standards this collection of folk-pop songs and poetic vignettes, specially composed for Sinatra by the self-celebrating poet and songwriter **Rod McKuen**, is a maudlin travesty. Richly scored in the straight-faced strings of **Don Costa** are glum songs about glorious aloneness (despite a trail of "beautiful strangers") and morose little poems about being let down by the paperboy.

But there's a genuine sadness and diffidence about *A Man Alone* – from the portrait on the sleeve to the beautiful murmuring throughout – that captures an essential truth about Sinatra. Previous images that he created are reinforced: the sad but satisfied Lothario of "It Was A Very Good Year" is recalled in "Love's Been Good To Me" while *Only The Lonely* – the album that Cahn and Van Heusen suggested revealed the real Sinatra – is alluded to not only in the title but also in the "One For My Baby" piano lick of "Lonesome Cities". And in "Empty Is", when Sinatra sings "Empty is … me" he's devastatingly believable. It may be the most enlightening moment in his entire recording career.

A Man Alone may not be very good art, but it's *great* Sinatra.

Watertown

WATERTOWN/GOODBYE (SHE QUIETLY SAYS)/FOR A WHILE/MICHAEL & PETER/I WOULD BE
IN LOVE (ANYWAY)/ELIZABETH/WHAT A FUNNY GIRL (YOU USED TO BE)/WHAT'S NOW IS
NOW/SHE SAYS/THE TRAIN

Arranged by Joe Scott and Charles Callelo; vocal recorded August 25-27
and October 31, 1969; released March 1970

A bold soft-rock concept album composed for Sinatra by The Four Seasons' writers, **Bob Gaudio** and **Jake Holmes**, *Watertown* is a record unlike any other that Sinatra made. On top of an elliptical running order – the songs appear to be programmed out of narrative sequence, alluding to a mid-west family break-up – there's a grimy, down-home quality to it that can pull the listener in. Not an initially attractive or conspicuously musical album, its compositions are mostly flat and dour, and the arrangements a blend of the obvious and odd; and Sinatra sounds much older than he was. Unusually, the vocals were recorded separately from the orchestra, apparently because Frank had not learnt the tunes well enough.

But he adored the songs and gets into the lyrics, bringing vivid life to the story of **a small-town everyman** left behind. A few spins take the listener beyond the rickety pitching and fatigued tone of voice, and deep into the mood, moved by the material. "Michael & Peter" is a heartbreaking letter to the estranged wife about the children growing up, "What A Funny Girl (You Use To Be)" is a warm, heavy-hearted reminiscence and "She Says" is a stunning, spaced-out poem-song that suggests she might be coming home. (She isn't.)

When the album was released it was a commercial flop, selling only 30,000 copies; and with Sinatra losing confidence in his voice and heading towards temporary retirement, a planned TV show based on the album was scrapped. *Watertown* remains an embarrassment in Sinatra's catalogue; it was the last album to be issued on poor sounding CD and no cuts were used on the 4-CD set *The Reprise Collection*. It's hard not to wonder how good it would have been if he was showing the same form as on *A Man Alone*, but there is rewarding, even majestic, Sinatra here for those who care to listen.

Sinatra & Company

DRINKING WATER (AQUA DE BEBER)/SOMEONE TO LIGHT UP MY LIFE/TRISTE/DON'T EVER GO AWAY (POR CAUSA DE VOCE)/THIS HAPPY MADNESS (ESTRADA BRANCA)/WAVE/ONE NOTE SAMBA (SAMBA DE UMA NOTA SO)/I WILL DRINK THE WINE*/CLOSE TO YOU*/SUNRISE IN THE MORNING*/BEIN' GREEN*/MY SWEET LADY*/LEAVING ON A JET PLANE*/LADY DAY*

Arranged by Eumir Deodato and Don Costa*; recorded February 11-13, October 31 and November 7, 1969, and October 26-29, 1970; released March 1971

An album of two halves. Side one of the original LP contained seven tracks intended for a follow-up album to *Francis Albert Sinatra & Antonio Carlos Jobim* and, while good, these tracks never quite approach the magic of the original collaboration. The charts by **Eumir Deodato** are not bad but don't quite capture the delicacy of those by Claus Ogerman. Sinatra is all right but in rougher voice than he was on the album in 1967 and the occasionally uncertain pitching on a more demanding set of Jobim songs frequently breaks the spell.

Side two is a return to the soft-rock style of *Cycles* and is mostly hopeless. Sinatra sounds wrong singing saccharine pop ("Close To You", My Sweet Lady") or with an up-tempo rock beat; he lurches through "Sunrise In The Morning" and "Leaving On A Jet Plane" like a three-wheeled wagon. "I Will Drink The Wine" is a not altogether likeable piece of post-"My Way" self-mythology ("I'll give you back your flowers/I will take the land") but **"Bein' Green"** is a charming I-am-what-I-am song, originally sung by Kermit from *Sesame Street*.

But the disheartening, pervading feature of *Sinatra & Company* is that he just doesn't sound very good any more. It was time for a rest.

Ol' Blue Eyes Is Back

YOU WILL BE MY MUSIC/YOU'RE SO RIGHT (FOR WHAT'S WRONG IN MY LIFE)/WINNERS*/
NOBODY WINS/SEND IN THE CLOWNS/DREAM AWAY*/LET ME TRY AGAIN*/THERE USED
TO BE A BALLPARK/NOAH

Arranged by Gordon Jenkins and Don Costa*; recorded June 4, 5 and 21,
and August 20, 1973; released September 1973

Sinatra's records of the late 1960s may have been hit and miss in places, but he was at least still experimenting. For his comeback recording, however, he plumped for a return to Don Costa's lush orch-pop style (as heard on most of *My Way*), which was adopted by **Gordon Jenkins** on his Costa-produced arrangements. The inflated ballads ("You Will Be My Music", "You're So Right", "Let Me Try Again") are vacuous spectacles but convey some sense of what could be stirring about 1970s Sinatra, especially when seen in person. The acoustic waltz "Dream Away" is as sweet as "Cycles" and although Stephen Sondheim's overexposed **"Send In The Clowns"** has some substance to chew on, Sinatra would make a better job of it later when he was accompanied by Bill Miller on the piano.

Kris Kristofferson's "Nobody Wins", however, is the dullest thing Sinatra ever sang. Also regrettable is his penchant for whimsical songs by **Joe Raposo**, the resident composer for *Sesame Street*; and the excruciating "Noah", a tortuous peace-and-harmony epic, has Sinatra entreating us to "walk with the lion/soar with the eagle". "There Used To Be A Ballpark", which suggests that Sinatra's retirement turned him into a rambling, sentimental old crazy, and the complaint in "You Will Be My Music" of "noise, not melody" suggest an anti-modern irascibility that's not entirely becoming.

Vocally, Sinatra is in better shape than on *Watertown* and *Sinatra & Company*, but, overall, both of those are better records than *Ol' Blue Eyes is Back*.

Some Nice Things I've Missed

YOU TURNED MY WORLD AROUND/SWEET CAROLINE/THE SUMMER KNOWS*/I'M GONNA
MAKE IT ALL THE WAY/TIE A YELLOW RIBBON ROUND THE OLE OAK TREE/SATISFY ME ONE
MORE TIME/IF*/YOU ARE THE SUNSHINE OF MY LIFE/WHAT ARE YOU DOING THE REST OF
YOUR LIFE?/BAD, BAD LEROY BROWN

Arranged by Don Costa and Gordon Jenkins*; recorded December 10, 1973,
and May 7, 8 and 21, 1974; released July 1974

A ragbag of contemporary songs given the Sinatra-Costa treatment that just sounds wrong. On the up side, there are no songs by Raposo. On the down side, there are awful swing charts for the Tony Orlando and Dawn hit "Tie A Yellow Ribbon Round The Ole Oak Tree", Neil Diamond's "Sweet Caroline" and Stevie Wonder's "You Are The Sunshine Of My Life", and silly versions of Jim Croce's "Bad, Bad Leroy Brown" and Floyd Huddleston's "Satisfy Me One More Time" (like "Mack The Knife" but with more sex). Sinatra and Costa turn what was already variable material into a new class of dross – grotesque caricatures that make this era of Sinatra an easy target for impersonators. Bert Kaempfert's "You Turned My World Around", an octave-spanning effort at the big ballad, and the two Michel Legrand songs ("The Summer Knows", "What Are You Doing The Rest Of Your Life?") are about the best of it. But they're not enough to save *Some Nice Things I've Missed* from driving Sinatra's recording career into a dead end.

"One thing they're certainly not writing these days is good lyrics. I know that because I'm more conscious of the words in songs than I am of the melody."

FS

Trilogy

Released March 1980

The Past: Collectibles of the Early Years

THE SONG IS YOU/BUT NOT FOR ME/I HAD THE CRAZIEST DREAM/IT HAD TO BE YOU/LET'S FACE THE MUSIC AND DANCE/STREET OF DREAMS/MY SHINING HOUR/ALL OF YOU/MORE THAN YOU KNOW/THEY ALL LAUGHED

Arranged by Billy May; recorded July 17–September 19, 1979

The Present: Some Very Good Years

YOU AND ME (WE WANTED IT ALL)/JUST THE WAY YOU ARE/SOMETHING*/MACARTHUR PARK/(THEME FROM) "NEW YORK, NEW YORK"/SUMMER ME, WINTER ME/SONG SUNG BLUE/FOR THE GOOD TIMES (WITH EILEEN FARRELL)/LOVE ME TENDER/THAT'S WHAT GOD LOOKS LIKE TO ME

Arranged by Don Costa and Nelson Riddle*; recorded August 20–December 3, 1979

The Future: Reflections on the Future in Three Tenses

WHAT TIME DOES THE NEXT MIRACLE LEAVE?/WORLD WAR NONE!/THE FUTURE/THE FUTURE (CONTINUED): "I'VE BEEN THERE!"/THE FUTURE (CONCLUSION): "SONG WITHOUT WORDS"/FINALE: BEFORE THE MUSIC ENDS

Composed and arranged by Gordon Jenkins; recorded December 17–18, 1979

When Sinatra returned to recording after six years of wowing live audiences, he wanted to make sure that it was with something momentous – and *Trilogy* certainly is. *The Past* (standards), *The Present* (pop tunes) and *The Future* (a specially written suite) form a vast, luxuriously packaged, portentously annotated triple album that features **a cast of thousands**.

Unfortunately, it's not good. The magic may have been there on stage, but even for listeners whose expectations of Sinatra's singing on record had fallen since the mid-1960s much of *Trilogy* is difficult to listen to. It's not helped by **the unattractive sound quality**; it's insensitively processed with washy reverb and brutal post-recording compression, creating a punchy sound but narrower dynamic range – but the real problem is the music.

Sinatra's generally ragged vocalizing is an unconvincing centrepiece but he's not much helped by the orchestrations. Billy May's swing charts on *The Past* rarely rise above the ordinary, even if his writing for strings has a certain panache. On *The Present* – a particularly ill-chosen selection of rock-era songs – Don Costa had little to work with, but swing versions of Billy Joel's "Just The Way You Are" and Neil Diamond's "Song Sung Blue" still plumb new depths. On the first two records only Sinatra's new high-kicking anthem "New York, New York" and Nelson Riddle's magnificent arrangement of George Harrison's "Something" get off the ground.

Gordon Jenkins's much derided *The Future* has Sinatra bantering with a celestial choir and musing on the hopes, wishes and memory of some mythological "Francis" (Choir: "Francis Albert Sinatra!"). It's daft, but features his best singing on the album – as well as a decent song in "I've Been There", in the style of *September Of My Years.* And, unlike the rest of *Trilogy*, is at least enjoyable as a glorious folly.

She Shot Me Down

GOOD THING GOING*/HEY LOOK, NO CRYING/THANKS FOR THE MEMORY/A LONG NIGHT/BANG BANG (MY BABY SHOT ME DOWN)/MONDAY MORNING QUARTERBACK/ SOUTH TO A WARMER PLACE/I LOVED HER/THE GAL THAT GOT AWAY-IT NEVER ENTERED MY MIND (MEDLEY)**

Arranged by Gordon Jenkins, Don Costa*, Nelson Riddle**; recorded April 8–September 10, 1981; released November 1981

Sixty-five years old and back with soaring strings and heartbreaking torch songs, Sinatra made what is undoubtedly the best record of his final 25 years, which proved that despite his ravaged voice, he still had the power to take a text and be convincing.

His weary old voice sounds soaked in disappointment and Jack Daniels, barely functions in places, and generally sounds magnificently

incongruous against the luxury of his accompaniment; but anyone who understands Billie Holiday's album *Lady In Satin* or Tom Waits singing Bernstein's "Somewhere" on *Blue Valentine* – famous examples of **the rough-with-the-lush** – will get *She Shot Me Down*, Sinatra's best record as an actor.

But it's not just texture here: it's substance too, with Sinatra having some unusual material to grapple with. The gentle regret in his soft-rock treatment of "Good Thing Going" by **Stephen Sondheim** makes the listener wish the singer had taken on more of the composer's singular oeuvre. The same goes for that of **Alec Wilder**, who gets two posthumous cuts here, the dramatic "A Long Night" and "South To A Warmer Place". Gordon Jenkins's touching catalogue song of incompatibilities "I Loved Her" wouldn't have been out of place on *September Of My Years* and even "Bang Bang", the 1966 hit that Sonny wrote for Cher, is draped in the musical colours of a *film noir* and elevated to an art song. The only remake on the album is Nelson Riddle's treatment of Arlen/Gershwin's "The Gal That Got Away", famously introduced by Judy Garland in *A Star Is Born* in 1954; on this occasion it sandwiches Rodgers and Hart's "It Never Entered My Mind", with a hard-swing reprise of Garland's hysterical classic bringing the album to its climax.

"A complete saloon album …
tear jerkers and cry-in-your-beer kind of things."

FS ON SHE SHOT ME DOWN

L. A. Is My Lady

L. A. IS MY LADY++/THE BEST OF EVERYTHING*/HOW DO YOU KEEP THE MUSIC PLAYING?*/TEACH ME TONIGHT**/IT'S ALL RIGHT WITH ME/AFTER YOU'VE GONE+/MACK THE KNIFE+/UNTIL THE REAL THING COMES ALONG/STORMY WEATHER/IF I SHOULD LOSE YOU/A HUNDRED YEARS FROM TODAY

Arranged by Sam Nestico, Joe Parnello*, Torrie Zito**, Frank Foster+ and Dave Mathews & Quincy Jones & Jerry Hey & Torrie Zito++; recorded April 13, 16 and 17, 1984; released August 1984

THE ORIGINAL 1984 LP VOCAL TRACK OF "MACK THE KNIFE" IS REPLACED ON THE CD BY A VOCAL RECORDED IN 1986.

The combination of **Quincy Jones's elephantine band** (weighed down further by "guest stars" George Benson, The Brecker Brothers and Lionel Hampton) powering out unattractive contemporary big band swing, and a singer who only occasionally sounds like he knows what he's doing, makes *L.A. Is My Lady* disheartening to listen to. Sinatra had previously *led* on his records, but here he sounds like he's only just hanging on. There are a couple of bright moments – the final minute, in the high-kicking "New York, New York" style, of the otherwise dire disco title track, the special lyrics to the second chorus of "Teach Me Tonight" – but elsewhere Sinatra tries to keep up with Quincy Jones's antiseptic orchestra like a tired old dog.

Sinatra fans are accustomed to his diminished voice during this period, but when his celebrated phrasing is off too – as it is on the majority of this album – there isn't much reason to keep listening. The exception is **"Mack The Knife"**, which on the CD release features a vocal recorded in 1986, two years after the rest of the sessions. Having taken during his mid-1980s live show to newly adapted lyrics (see pages 275–276), Sinatra honed the delivery and grafted the joyful results onto the original track, leaving the rest of the album at the starting gate.

SINATRA COMPILATIONS

LOW-COST SINATRA

I'll Be Seeing You
BMG/RCA/Bluebird; released 1994

Twelve of Dorsey and Sinatra's smoothest tunes.

The Best Of The Columbia Years
Columbia/Legacy; released 1995

An excellent 97-track, 4-CD round-up of the swoonsome 1940s, and a careful selection from the years of decline. Available as a luxurious long box package, or in a cheaper cardboard sleeve.

The Best Of The Capitol Years
Capitol; released 1990

A well-chosen 3-CD set of the vintage years. Good sound and a few rare alternative takes, but the packaging is ready for smartening up.

The Reprise Collection
Reprise; released 1990

A good 4-CD set, demonstrating that Sinatra's period at Reprise was at least as interesting as his Capitol years.

My Way: The Best Of Frank Sinatra
Reprise; released 1997

The commercial compilation from the Reprise Years, available as a 24-track single CD or a much better 46-track double, puzzlingly retailing at about the same price.

The Platinum Collection
Capitol; released 2004

Budget, 46-track, 3-CD selection from the Capitol years. Cheap packaging but fantastic music.

COMPLETE STUDIO SINATRA

The Song Is You
BMG/RCA/Bluebird; released 1994

120 tracks including all studio recordings and a CD of radio broadcasts spread over 5 CDs from the Dorsey/Sinatra years, with a 100-page booklet.

The Complete Columbia Recordings 1943-1952
Columbia/Legacy; released 1992

285 tracks spread over 12 CDs, and a 140-page booklet. An astonishing collection, with much of it rarely heard, let alone compiled, since its 78rpm release.

The Capitol Years
Capitol; released 1998

A box containing 22 CD versions of the original albums, as re-released on vinyl in the mid-1980s rather than the CD versions which were released with bonus tracks in the early 1990s. This comprises sixteen Capitol "concept" albums, five albums that gathered up singles and film songs and *The Rare Sinatra*, an 18-track album of rarities and unreleased material. There is substantial crossover with *The Complete Capitol Singles*, but some tracks are unavailable elsewhere. Disappointing album-by-album sleeve notes, but handsomely packaged.

The Complete Capitol Singles
Capitol; released 1996

96 tracks spread over 4 CDs, and a booklet with 50 pages of excellent annotation by Will Friedwald. Substantial crossover with *The Capitol Years*, but still some tracks unavailable elsewhere.

The Complete Reprise Studio Recordings
Reprise; released 1995

452 songs spread over 20 CDs, programmed in chronological order covering sessions from 1960 until 1986. Known in Sinatraphile circles as "The Suitcase" after its original limited edition packaging, this collection is monumental.

Capitol postscript

Duets

THE LADY IS A TRAMP (WITH LUTHER VANDROSS)/WHAT NOW MY LOVE (WITH ARETHA FRANKLIN)/I'VE GOT A CRUSH ON YOU (WITH BARBRA STREISAND)/SUMMER WIND (WITH JULIO IGLESIAS/COME RAIN OR SHINE (WITH GLORIA ESTEFAN/THEME FROM *NEW YORK NEW YORK* (WITH TONY BENNETT)/THEY CAN'T TAKE THAT AWAY FROM ME (WITH NATALIE COLE)/YOU MAKE ME FEEL SO YOUNG (WITH CHARLES AZNAVOUR)/GUESS I'LL HANG MY TEARS OUT TO DRY-IN THE WEE SMALL HOURS OF THE MORNING (WITH CARLY SIMON)/I'VE GOT THE WORLD ON A STRING (WITH LIZA MINNELLI)/WITCHCRAFT (WITH ANITA BAKER)/I'VE GOT YOU UNDER MY SKIN (WITH BONO)/ALL THE WAY-ONE FOR MY BABY (WITH KENNY G)

Arranged by Patrick Williams, Quincy Jones, Neal Hefti, Billy Byers and Nelson Riddle; recorded July 1, 7 and 9, 1993 by Sinatra and July–August 1993 by guests; released November 1993

Duets II

FOR ONCE IN MY LIFE (WITH GLADYS KNIGHT AND STEVIE WONDER)/COME FLY WITH ME (WITH LUIS MIGUEL)/BEWITCHED (WITH PATTI LABELLE)/THE BEST IS YET TO COME (WITH JON SECADA)/MOONLIGHT IN VERMONT (WITH LINDA RONSTADT/FLY ME TO THE MOON (WITH ANTONIO CARLOS JOBIM)/LUCK BE A LADY (WITH CHRISSIE HYNDE)/A FOGGY DAY (WITH WILLIE NELSON)/WHERE OR WHEN (WITH STEVE LAWRENCE AND EYDIE GORME)/EMBRACEABLE YOU (WITH LENA HORNE)/MACK THE KNIFE (WITH JIMMY BUFFETT)/HOW DO YOU KEEP THE MUSIC PLAYING?-MY FUNNY VALENTINE (WITH LORRIE MORGAN)/MY KIND OF TOWN (WITH FRANK SINATRA JR.) THE HOUSE I LIVE IN (WITH NEIL DIAMOND)

Arranged by Don Costa, Billy May, Patrick Williams, Quincy Jones, Johnny Mandel, Billy Byers, Nelson Riddle and Frank Foster; recorded July 1 and 9, October 12 and 14, December 1993 and April 1994 by Sinatra and 1993-94 by guests; released October 1994

The intentions of the producer, **Phil Ramone**, were good. After all, in 1993, at the age of 77, Sinatra was still performing live; so why not get him back in the studio to sing with a bunch of the younger generation (and a few of the older), who could show what Ol' Blue Eyes meant to them? Sinatra took a little convincing, but after it was made clear that it would be done with as little pain as possible – Sinatra could record first, with the duettists adding their contributions later – he rolled up to Capitol Studios for the first time in more than thirty years.

It went badly. He hated the vocal booth they'd made for him; he wanted to take up his usual position in the middle of the band. But during his next visit, he asked Ramone why he was doing this; and Phil replied, as he told Charles Granata, "It's the legacy of *you*. I want my children and grandchildren to know who Sinatra is at this most important moment." Sinatra took to the podium in the midst of the musicians and nailed nine tracks in one session. The arranger Patrick Williams, who witnessed it, remembered saying at the time: "The courage of this guy is just incredible!" The duettists phoned in their parts and the **Duets** album put Sinatra back on the top of the charts in his 56th year as a professional singer. A year later, **Duets II**, with a different set of guests, enjoyed similar commercial success.

It's a great story – but a shame about the albums. With Sinatra not hearing what his guests were doing and unable to respond to them, there's no chemistry – musical or personal – and a lot of distracting editing: just when you might be getting into Sinatra, an anonymous pop star or a caricature of a diva barges in and spoils it. That on "Come Fly With Me" Luis Miguel sings that "weather-wise it's such a koo-koo day" just as he learnt it from the *Live At The Sands* album is just one of many irritating details. As interruption follows inappropriate interruption, it's hard not to wonder: how did all these people get in Frank's room?

The canon

Fifty great Sinatra songs, including his artistic and commercial successes, selected from the 1800 recordings he made between 1939 and 1993 – and the stories behind them

1. All Or Nothing At All

Written by Jack Lawrence and Arthur Altman; arranged by Andy Gibson; recorded August 31, 1939, in New York; available on Harry James and Frank Sinatra's *The Complete Recordings* (Columbia/Legacy)

A dramatic, long-form song, structured around 64 bars rather than the more usual 32, and broadly in the style of the brooding exotica of Cole Porter, "All Or Nothing At All" was a generic ballad that was not composed for Sinatra but has remained associated with him. Cut at his third recording session led by **Harry James**, in August 1939, it was first available in summer 1940 and received minimal attention, but was famously re-released to launch Sinatra's solo career during the recording ban of 1943 and became a massive seller.

As a record, it remains rather of its time. The arrangement favours bold legato lines in Harry James's signature trumpet style, and Sinatra's singing, though clearly competent, adopts a slightly stiff operetta manner, complete with a bravura high F at the end. But there are hints of the subtlety to come, especially in details such as the pianissimo second "no" five bars before the end of his first chorus.

Sinatra was fond of the song and never underestimated the significance it played in his career; he opened his 1971 "farewell" concert with it, saying that he "might as well begin at the beginning". Although he avoided it during his Capitol period, he had several attempts later at a remake; some were successful (such as the prowling swinger in 1966 with Nelson Riddle on *Strangers in The Night*), but a disco version with Joe Beck in 1977 was not. Lyricist **Jack Lawrence** lived through them all and maintained a preference for the James version. "It's interesting to listen to that young voice, the way he attacked that song and what he did with the breath control," he told Will Friedwald. "Later as he went along he learned a lot more and added a lot more interpretation … but I still prefer to listen to that young voice singing that song."

2. I'll Never Smile Again

Written by Ruth Lowe; arranged by Fred Stulce; recorded May 23, 1940, in New York; available on *The Song is You* (RCA Victor/BMG)

Written by the Canadian songwriter **Ruth Lowe** apparently after the early death of her husband – though this may have been said to create good publicity – "I'll Never Smile Again" was tackled by Sinatra after he had recorded twenty sides with **Tommy Dorsey** in the first part of 1940. Sinatra recalled a silent "eeriness" descending on the orchestra when the piece was first aired at a rehearsal and Dorsey's pianist **Joe Bushkin** remembers an early version of the slow mournful piece being "kinda empty" until Sinatra spotted a celesta in the studio and suggested Bushkin "just fill it in". After the tune had been adapted by saxophonist and arranger **Fred Stulce** to feature Sinatra leading dense but languid harmonies from Dorsey's vocal group The Pied Pipers, the recording was eventually nailed on the second attempt, in May 1940. Although the track, with its mournful, harmony-heavy sound, was the least typical of Sinatra's work with Dorsey, it spent twelve weeks at number one in the summer of 1940 and was their biggest hit together.

The song was Sinatra's first recorded feature with Dorsey's vocal group and it worked superbly well. "Most solo singers don't work too well in a group," **Jo Stafford** commented, "but Frank never stopped working at it." A sparse recording, its emotional pull derives from Sinatra and The Pied Pipers phrasing and breathing as a single legato entity, and from his deep but restrained feeling for the lyric. This was at odds with the prevailing swing band style, but points towards the romantic longing in Sinatra's solo output during the war years.

Despite being a big hit, the song was performed infrequently in radio broadcasts; the band avoided it because it featured so little of the musicians, and also, as Stafford recalled, "You really had to mind your 'p's and 'q's keeping it in tune." Sinatra recorded it in a solo version with **Gordon Jenkins** in 1959 on *No One Cares* – which overplays the song's flavour of melodrama, to its detriment – but wisely revived the Stulce/Bushkin arrangement for the retrospective album *A Man And His Music*.

3. Oh! Look At Me Now

Written by Joe Bushkin and John DeVries; arranged by Sy Oliver; recorded January 6, 1941, in New York; available on *The Song is You* (RCA Victor/ BMG)

Although he became known while working with Dorsey for his romantic ballads, Sinatra was sometimes given the opportunity to sing over the bouncing swing charts of Sy Oliver, and this was a crucial influence on his developing sense of rhythm. The arranger said that he generally encouraged Sinatra to let himself be taken along by the beat and not to try to push it.

On "Oh! Look At Me Now", written by Joe Bushkin, Sinatra not only swings – which he does very sweetly – but also trades teasing lines with girl singer Connie Haines. There was little chemistry between the pair in real life, but they make a cute musical couple here, with Connie and the particularly hip-sounding Pied Pipers admiring Frank's romantic confidence extravagantly before he proudly declares at the climax: "Jack, I'm ready!"

The song was one of eight Top 10 hits that Sinatra had in 1941; it reached number two in March but was denied the top spot by "Amapola (Pretty Little Poppy)" – which was recorded by Tommy Dorsey's brother, Jimmy. Sinatra returned to the song in 1955 for the twentieth-anniversary tribute to Tommy Dorsey and the following year he recorded a version arranged by Nelson Riddle for *A Swingin' Affair*.

4. **This Love Of Mine**

Written by Hank Sanicola, Frank Sinatra and Sol Parker; arranged by Axel Stordahl; recorded May 28, 1941, in New York; available on *The Song is You* (RCA Victor/BMG)

For a significant part of his tenure with Dorsey, Sinatra was compelled to sing "current plugs"; but certain other songs helped him to establish a signature of his own. On "This Love Of Mine" Sinatra was even credited as one of the composers; and it appears that he did indeed make a contribution, though it was not an area of talent that he developed. Matt Dennis and Tom Adair – writers of several Dorsey/Sinatra songs – also contributed to the composition, but were not credited.

For all the compositional attention the song received, and even though it's been covered by several jazz artists and was a favourite of the saxophonist Ronnie Scott, it's curiously old-fashioned and harmonically it's flat-footed. But Sinatra's gently fulsome delivery reveals a maturing balladeer with a growing instinct for expressing passion through understatement. His 1955 reading of the song on *In The Wee Small Hours*, following the affair with Ava Gardner, may be more emotionally resonant, but Nelson Riddle's arrangement there gives the song undeserved sophistication. This recording – a time-trapped arrangement by **Axel Stordahl**, with a 25-year-old Frank over-reaching and triumphing – is majestic early Sinatra.

5. **Night And Day**

Written by Cole Porter; arranged by Axel Stordahl; recorded January 19, 1942, in Hollywood; available on *The Song is You* (RCA Victor/BMG)

A classic of romantic hyperbole from the 1931 Broadway musical *The Gay Divorcee*, "Night And Day" is the highlight of the first Sinatra/Stordahl solo session that was made while Frank was still a featured vocalist with Tommy Dorsey. He made another recording of it eight months later, for the soundtrack of *Reveille with Beverly*, and four more recordings between 1947 and 1977, and it was "Night And Day" that he opened with at the Riobamba in 1943; but it was at this session in January 1942 that Sinatra first sang with Stordahl's strings and discovered the sound and style that would spur him on towards a solo career and that would characterize much of his output for the coming decade.

Light in texture but deep in feeling, the drummerless rhythm section keeps a gentle two-beat pulse while a harp plays arpeggios. Stordahl's violins and cello, meanwhile, dance around Sinatra's phrases, complementing and amplifying, sometimes remaining entirely still and occasionally coming together in glorious, sweeping synchronization. Sinatra's vocal is full of distinguishing detail: the care with which he puts air between "and" and "day", contrasting with the smooth arc of his phrasing elsewhere; the hint of a roar in the "traffic's boom", followed by a subtle diminuendo into his "lonely room"; the static "inside of me" that becomes the gorgeously ascending "way down inside of me" on the reprise of the bridge; and the accepting, minimal "torment won't be through" that becomes the anguished, circuitous "torment won't ever be through".

The song reached only number seventeen on the *Billboard* chart. But the whole piece transmits the aching, vulnerable longing that would soon cause such mayhem among the bobbysoxers on his future recordings, and also conveys the refined musicality that would keep mature popular music fans, and musicians, listening for decades to come.

6. Nancy (With The Laughing Face)

Written by Phil Silvers and Jimmy Van Heusen; arranged by Axel Stordahl; recorded August 22, 1945, in Hollywood; available on *The Best Of The Columbia Years* (Columbia/Legacy)

At a party in the spring of 1944 at the house of Johnny Burke – Bing Crosby's favourite lyricist at the time – the comedian **Phil Silvers** cracked a joke that had Burke's wife Bessie in fits of laughter. Silvers coined the phrase "Bessie with the laughing face", which **Jimmy Van Heusen** thought was a good song title. Burke was having a day off so Silvers wrote the lyric to Van Heusen's music himself, in twenty minutes, changing "Bessie" to "Nancy" to mark the fourth birthday of **Sinatra's daughter**.

Aired on the radio in April 1944, in July it was released as a **V-Disc**, a wartime recording specifically for the US military services overseas. It wasn't given further thought until Sinatra's **United Services Organizations tour** of Europe in June 1945, when it was requested by servicemen who had become attached to the song, as an expression of their own longing for home and family. It was a hit when it was recorded commercially in August 1945 and became one of Sinatra's signature songs.

The later recording features Sinatra and Stordahl at their peak. The arrangement is warm and playful, with shifting lyrical moods reflected discreetly in the musical colours and shapes, from the pizzicato strings of "mission bells ringing" to the wistful, sighing hiatus as we "hear her say hello". Stordahl's introduction and interlude are miniature masterworks, giving an impressionistic quality to the chart – a picture-painting attitude towards orchestration that the Sinatra producer Voyle Gilmore, evoking the title of Delius's impressionistic tone poem, called his "first rustle of spring approach". Sinatra hits a tender tone and stays there, but his conversational phrasing gives his performance the rhythmic ebb and flow of a proud father's speech.

The lyrics are not without irony. Sinatra exhorts the listener to "keep Betty Grable, Lamour and Turner", and in the summer of 1945 he was months away from the affair with **Lana Turner** that threatened his family's stability. A layer of subtext was added again when he sang a specially adapted **"Nancy (With The Reagan Face)"** to the First Lady at Ronald Reagan's inaugural gala in January 1981. Rumours connecting the singer with his friend Mrs Reagan began to circulate extremely quickly.

7. **Soliloquy**

Written by Richard Rodgers and Oscar Hammerstein; arranged by Axel Stordahl; recorded May 28, 1946, in Hollywood; available on *All Or Nothing At All* (Properbox)

In order to flesh out the character of Billy Bigelow, the difficult central figure of their 1945 musical *Carousel*, Richard Rodgers and Oscar Hammerstein hit on the idea of a musical soliloquy in which the feckless fairground barker ruminates at some length on prospective fatherhood and parental responsibility. Hammerstein spent two weeks writing the text, Rodgers spent two hours setting it to music and the result was a masterpiece.

By 1946 Sinatra was *the* romantic pop voice of his generation, but he was also an aspiring concert singer; his recorded repertoire contained adapted classics such as the heaving, dramatic "Ol' Man River", and the substantial, multi-mooded "Soliloquy" provided perfect material for an expansion of his range. Recorded over two sessions in April and May 1946, Sinatra and Stordahl completed two versions of the eight-minute piece. The first was released as a V-Disc, the second as the better-known Columbia issue, and each took up both sides of a 12-inch 78.

Sinatra returned to the song in grander, more masculine style in 1963 on *The Concert Sinatra* and still gave it his best live shot in the early 1990s, but in 1946, at thirty years old and close to the age of the character, he brings an authentically callow, wide-eyed pride to the reading. The switch of mood as he gets carried away with boastful plans for his son before realising his child might be a girl is played delicately and believably. And **the big ending**, when the "bum with no money" vows to "make it or steal it or take it, or die" is impressive bravura.

Slightly cleaned up for the sensibilities of record buyers in 1946 – the "skinny-lipped virgin" becomes the "skinny-lipped wench", the "fat-bottomed bully" becomes "flat-footed" – the song was convincing enough for Sinatra to be first choice for the mooted film version of *Carousel* in the mid-1950s.

8. Sweet Lorraine

Written by Mitchell Parish and Cliff Burwell; arranged by Sy Oliver; recorded December 15, 1946, in New York; available on *The Best Of The Columbia Years* (Columbia/Legacy)

This rare but scintillating occurrence of Sinatra recording with a small jazz group makes most listeners wish that he had done so more often. The occasion was a gathering in December 1946 of *Metronome* magazine's annual poll winners, who were billed as **The Metronome All Stars** and under the arranger Sy Oliver, a pal of Frank's from his Dorsey days. Though Sinatra, as much by his own insistence as the evidence, was never a jazz singer, being named as best singer in a jazz-oriented magazine reflected how much his work was respected by the jazz community, which was known for its occasional narrow-mindedness. And in the company of jazz heavyweights (including Coleman Hawkins on tenor sax, Johnny Hodges on alto, Charlie Shavers on trumpet, Nat "King" Cole on piano and Buddy Rich on drums), Sinatra sounds more than at home: he sounds like he's running the show.

Though it was Cole's own vocal version of "Sweet Lorraine" from 1941 that was well known, the singer-pianist is confined here to crisp, cascading piano licks while Sinatra conjures his most potent swing singing to date. He'd featured the occasional rhythm arrangement in among the ballads during his solo career – the most notable being "Saturday Night Is The Loneliest Night Of The Week" in 1944 – but this was different. His timing reflects Cole's version from the early 1940s, but, as if being the non-jazz musician means that he's got something to prove, he goes further, pushing some phrases, pulling others and showing a degree of rhythmic liberty-taking that for Sinatra was unprecedented.

Although this was an exhilarating indicator of the turn his singing style would take, he didn't return to "Sweet Lorraine" until the aborted *Here's To The Ladies* album in the late 1970s.

9. The Night We Called It A Day

Written by Matt Dennis and Tom Adair; arranged by Axel Stordahl; recorded October 26, 1947, in New York; available on *The Best Of The Columbia Years* (Columbia/Legacy)

"A hell of a week," remembered **Matt Dennis**, then a New York singer and piano player, of the first seven days that he spent writing songs with the part-time poet **Tom Adair** in the early 1940s. During this period they wrote "Will You Still Be Mine", "Let's Get Away From It All" and "Everything Happens To Me", the final two of which were recorded by Sinatra and The Tommy Dorsey Orchestra in 1941, along with their composition from another week, "Violets For Your Furs".

Dennis arranged another new piece for Dorsey, Sinatra and The Pied Pipers in 1941, "The Night We Called It A Day", a sombre piece in which the end of a relationship is reflected in the sounds and sights of night-time. With Sinatra gradually extricating himself from the band, the song was sidelined, but he chose to record it at his first solo session of January 1942, and the composer was delighted. Dennis was known to be particularly pleased that a delayed resolution that he had devised was used by **Axel Stordahl** – probably the moment in the bridge at the end of the line "Soft in the *dark*". He was no less impressed with the singer. "I think his renditions of my songs are just fantastic," he told Will Friedwald. "He knew my style, and sang them the way I'd sing them. How could there be anyone to make me sound better?"

"I'd like to see popular music brought into grammar and high schools as part of the education, if the proper people were teaching it ... explain[ing] the inner intricacies of making a hit song, and a good song. And a poor song."

FS, 1948

The canon

Sinatra is certainly sweet and clear on the 1942 version, and his Columbia recording from **1947** is even better – but it was unreleased at the time and undiscovered until 1993. It contains the same discreet arrangement of strings, woodwind and harp and a distinctive, off-beat pedal point in the bridge; but Sinatra is recorded more successfully and, a discernibly deeper singer, is better equipped to get under the skin of the lyrics. It could be argued that he was even more qualified, emotionally, for the heart-rending version of 1957 with Gordon Jenkins on *Where Are You?*, but Dennis considered Stordahl's delicate work exemplary. "I was thrilled when Ax made that arrangement; it is gorgeous," he said. "The definitive arrangement of that song."

SINATRA IN THE LATE 1940S IN THE COLUMBIA STUDIOS IN NEW YORK

10. My Blue Heaven

Written by George Whiting and Walter Donaldson; arranged by George Siravo; recorded April 24, 1950, in New York; available on *Swing And Dance With Frank Sinatra* (Columbia/Legacy)

"**George Siravo** is one of the untapped arrangers, I feel," Sinatra said in an interview in 1949. "He's a very fresh-style guy." Siravo had been ghosting rhythm charts for Axel Stordahl for a few years by then, but in early 1950 he got the chance to arrange an entire Sinatra album, *Sing And Dance With Frank Sinatra*, and was responsible for eight swing charts, which are full of brightness and bounce.

But when it came to recording, Sinatra was under the emotional strain of a collapsed marriage, and in the middle of a long engagement at the Copa where he famously lost his voice; and his pipes were in poor shape. Producer **Mitch Miller** remembers shutting off the microphone without telling Sinatra and recording only the band; and as it was against musician union rules to record different parts of the music separately, he and Sinatra overdubbed the vocals later in secret midnight sessions with the studio door locked.

The results were terrific. *Sing And Dance With Frank Sinatra* was full of pep and can be heard as the embryonic stages of the Sinatra swing style that would flower at Capitol a few years later. All the tracks have something to applaud, but the chart of the George Whiting/Walter Donaldson warhorse from 1927 "My Blue Heaven", with which Sinatra also spent seven weeks in the British charts in 1961, is particularly relaxed, with Sinatra's rhythmic approach evoking **Bing Crosby** and **Louis Armstrong**. He even sings his second "nest that nestles where the roses bloom" as if an excited Dixieland trumpet break, and then turns the line "Just Molly and me" into a suggestive "mmm … Molly!"

"We've got a lot of jazz things that I'd like you to watch for," said Sinatra to a DJ in September 1950 of the *Sing And Dance* sides. "They're bright and have good jump tempos, both to listen to as a vocal *and* to dance to." He was right; those "jazz things" were swinging down the lane to *Swingin' Lovers*.

11. I'm A Fool To Want You

Written by Jack Wolf, Joel Herron and Frank Sinatra; arranged by Axel
Stordahl; recorded March 27, 1951, in New York; available on *The Best Of
The Columbia Years* (Columbia/Legacy)

In his lean period during the late 1940s and early 1950s, one of Sinatra's
strategies for having a hit record was to record big, semi-classical, breast-
beating ballads such as "Luna Rossa" and "Come Back To Sorrento".
Similar material was doing the trick for Mario Lanza and even **Frankie
Laine**, but it didn't work for Sinatra, commercially or artistically. The
composer Joel Herron had already adapted "Andantino" from Brahms's
third symphony for a song that Sinatra recorded in 1950 called "Take
My Love", and when he was asked to write something similar, he came
up with a haunting minor melody. The lyricist Jack Wolf penned the
tormented lyrics of "I'm A Fool To Want You" in response to the music's
innate melodrama and the pair credited Sinatra as a co-writer when they
heard his recording and realised that he had changed some of the lyrics.

 Recorded in the middle of his tortuous period with **Ava Gardner**, the
legend has it that Sinatra ran from the studio in tears upon completing it.
His performance certainly wrings value from the material and – proving
that it wasn't all dust in the throat in the early 1950s – is among his best
displays of bravura: it's controlled, passionate and moving. Even the
weeping solo violin and the camp swell of **The Ray Charles Singers** don't
make it kitsch. It's too real.

12. Birth of The Blues

Written by Buddy DeSylva, Lou Brown and Ray Henderson; arranged by
Heinie Beau; recorded June 3, 1952, in Hollywood; available on *The Best Of
The Columbia Years* (Columbia/Legacy)

Hokey in its mythology but irresistibly attractive, "Birth Of The Blues" was
written for a mid-1920s version of the Broadway review *George White's
Scandals*, but by the early 1950s Bing Crosby, Louis Armstrong and a host
of others had jazzed it up to the sky.

CONTEMPORARIES AND WANNABES

Though Sinatra's stature as a twentieth-century legend means that he appears to tower over the world of entertainment, throughout his career there were always worthy contenders who operated in the same field. In the 1940s, he left most of his contemporaries who sang in bands, like **Bob Eberly**, behind, though **Dick Haymes**, Sinatra's replacement in the Dorsey band, was a serene-voiced balladeer who carved a creditable solo career and for a while was considered a serious rival for Sinatra and Bing Crosby. Another singer, emerging from the Ted Weems band, was **Perry Como,** whose style was so relaxed that even the ultra-cool Crosby commented that Como was "the man who invented casual." Haymes, Como and **Dean Martin**, who began to have hits in the late 1940s, all modelled their vocal approach on Crosby. Stylistically, in the 1940s Sinatra was on his own.

In the early 1950s Sinatra's ballad style was somewhat overshadowed by the popularity of **Nat "King" Cole**, and by pop singers with more extrovert vocal personalities, such as the emotive "Nabob Of Sob" **Johnnie Ray** and the whip-cracking "crooner with steel tonsils", **Frankie Laine**. By the time that Sinatra had established his 1950s Capitol persona, however, others followed where he led; everyone wanted to be a "swingin' lover". His influence made itself evident on records by Cole, Crosby, **Sammy Davis Jr.** and a new generation of swingers such as **Buddy Greco**, **Vic Damone**, and – most overtly, between his rock'n'roll and neo-folk incarnations – **Bobby Darin**.

In one of his final sessions for Columbia and on the brink of being unemployed, Sinatra summoned the energy to deliver a vigorous, hard-swinging vocal on top of one of the most swaggering charts he'd ever been given. The man responsible was **Heinie Beau**, a sax player who doubled quietly as an arranger and later helped out when the named arrangers were overstretched, as Billy May was on *Come Swing With Me* and Axel Stordahl was on *Point Of No Return*. The brassy fanfares and bump'n'grind groove anticipate the vulgar high kicks of "That's Life" and even "New York, New York" by decades.

The difference is that here Sinatra is magnificent and full-throated – and not as harsh as he had to be later in order to project this kind of music. "Birth of the Blues" was even a top twenty hit (and was a record of the year in *Metronome* magazine's review of 1952). But three months on, Columbia let Sinatra go. What were they thinking?

Another Italian-American singer, eleven years Sinatra's junior, who sang good songs that Sinatra admired, was **Tony Bennett**. "The best singer in the business," Frank said of Bennett in the early 1960s. "He excites me when I watch him – he moves me." He was also impressed in the same period by **Jack Jones**: "He has a distinction, an all-round quality ... he sings jazz pretty good too." Sinatra always liked **Ella Fitzgerald** and had good words to say about **Jo Stafford**, **Peggy Lee** and **Rosemary Clooney**. Of the extravagant jazz singer **Sarah Vaughan** he said in 1965, "Sassy is so good now that when I listen to her I want to cut my wrists with a dull razor."

A generation later, the allure of Sinatra attracts not only jazz musicians but also pop stars, who repackage it to enchant a new audience. The pianist and singer **Harry Connick Jr.** successfully updated Sinatra's swing sound for the 1990s with his own songs and arrangements. **Robbie Williams**, formerly a pop idol in Take That, overdubbed a duet of "It Was A Very Good Year" and devoted his 2001 album *Swing While You're Winning* to material from the Rat Pack era, as did the Irish boy band **Westlife** with their 2004 offering *Allow Us To Be Frank*. Vancouver-born singer **Michael Bublé** has blandly imitated Sinatra's every musical move with enormous commercial success.

13. I've Got The World On A String

Written by Harold Arlen and Ted Koehler; arranged by Nelson Riddle; recorded April 30, 1953, in KHJ Studios, Hollywood; available on *This Is Sinatra!* (Capitol)

At Sinatra's second Capitol recording session in April 1953, 31-year-old **Nelson Riddle**, known for his excellent work at Capitol with Nat "King" Cole, Billy Eckstine and Mel Tormé, was hired as the conductor and arranger. With Sinatra's first choice, Billy May, unavailable, Riddle had to duplicate May's distinctive style on "South Of The Border" and "I Love You", just as Heinie Beau had for "Lean Baby" earlier that month; but he had a freer hand with "I've Got The World On A String", Harold Arlen and Ted Koehler's song written twenty years previously for Ivie

Anderson and Duke Ellington to perform at the Cotton Club in Harlem. Riddle fashioned a joyous chart to which Sinatra responded with all the optimism and verve that he was feeling after shooting had finished on *From Here To Eternity*.

Riddle heralds Sinatra's new dawn with a gleaming brass fanfare that settles into glowing, tempo-free chords from the saxophones as Frank nonchalantly announces that not only does he have the world on a string, he's also got the string around his finger; and off he struts on an irresistible two-beat swing with everything before him, everything to live for. Riddle cranks up the momentum by hitting a four-to-the-bar groove in the bridge, the reprise of which sends an already ecstatic Sinatra into recklessness as he slides one-footed down "If I should ever let it go" and keeps his balance. The final eight bars and coda hit top gear, through a pumping back beat and a singer who hardly seems to know what to do with the excitement ("Man, this is the life … hey now!"). No wonder Sinatra so frequently opened his live sets with this song.

Unwise as it might be to interpret the lyric in biographical terms, it's hard to ignore that the man who is singing that he'd "be a silly so-and-so" if he "should ever let it go" had only just emerged from feeling suicidal; or that the man who sings that "life is a beautiful thing" as long as he is holding the string is on the verge of the self-made golden years of his career. Although Sinatra had already been steering his music that way with the jumping charts by **George Siravo** he'd been performing on club dates during 1952, to the wider world this vivacious, confident music announced in no uncertain terms that Sinatra was back, and ready to swing.

14. My Funny Valentine

Written by Richard Rodgers and Lorenz Hart; arranged by George Siravo (with Nelson Riddle); recorded November 5, 1953, in KHJ Studios, Hollywood; available on *Songs For Young Lovers* (Capitol)

The lyrics to the cabaret tune "My Funny Valentine" – so perennial that one jaded New York nightclub owner apparently inserted a clause into his singers' contracts forbidding its performance – have always been a tricky proposition. A love song from the 1938 Rodgers/Hart musical ***Babes***

In Arms, it's full of barbed insults, and it's seen by some as a disguised reference to male homosexuality. Written as it was by the gay, self-loathing **Lorenz Hart**, that interpretation may have some credibility, but it's unlikely that when Sinatra stepped up to record the song for his first Capitol album he thought it was anything but a classic, quirky love song.

With a lovely, calmly swinging George Siravo chart that skips into waltz time in the second bridge, this "My Funny Valentine" is relaxed and lightly rhythmic, on the cusp of his mature swinging style and yet with a hint of young Sinatra about it. But two moments are extraordinary. The first comes as he exits the bridge and sits on the ninth note of a minor chord on the word "…don't", the kind of jazzy decision that **Billie Holiday** might have made and that musicians much admire. The second is the one-breath phrasing of the second long high D on "stay" that seamlessly leads to "… each day is…". He'd made this kind of phrasing a signature of his work many years previously, but this example is particularly inspirational.

15. Young At Heart

Written by Johnny Richards and Carolyn Leigh; arranged by Nelson Riddle; recorded December 9, 1953, in KHJ Studios, Hollywood; available on *This Is Sinatra!* (Capitol)

In 1953 Carolyn Leigh, who went on to write the words to Sinatra classics such as "Witchcraft" and "The Best Is Yet To Come", was still an aspirant, sending her lyrics off to publishers hopefully. "Young At Heart" arrived at Sunbeam Music and landed with **Tommy Valando**, who assigned it to one of Stan Kenton's jazz arrangers, Johnny Richards. Valando was unhappy with the way it turned out, despite several re-writes, and dumped it on a pile of papers on his desk; but it was found by his brother Artie, who was intrigued. He pitched the song to Sinatra, who was cool at first, but was drawn in after hearing it several times and requested a special recording session for it. The result – despite Tommy's continuing objections – was Sinatra's biggest hit since 1947.

The song is very unusual. There are tricky intervals, quadruple rhymes, lots of syllables and not much space; it's clear why Tommy Valando didn't think the music and words worked together and why Sinatra took some convincing – and, apparently, 27 takes to nail the recording. But the results are charming: a delightful piece of homespun sophistication, made elegant and perfect by singer and arranger. Riddle's strings sing and sigh Viennese-style but in the upper colours of the chord – what Quincy Jones would call putting the "electricity above Frank" – as in the work of **Ravel** or **Debussy**. Sinatra is tender, gently wise and entirely believable.

The song's gracefulness was slightly tarnished when it was tacked on to the movie opportunistically titled *Young At Heart*, in which Sinatra and Doris Day co-starred in 1954, a remake of *Four Daughters*. The film's not that bad, but the song – heard only over the titles and closing credits – is nothing to do with it.

16. Last Night When We Were Young

Written by Harold Arlen and Yip Harburg; arranged by Nelson Riddle; recorded March 1, 1954, in KHJ Studios, Hollywood; available on *In The Wee Small Hours* (Capitol)

"Last Night When We Were Young" is one of the great songs of its era, with an advanced, subtle harmonic sequence; an unusual melody with arcane chromatic movement and octave leaps; and an elevated lyric that concerns time growing cold and an entire season depending on "a look, a kiss". **Harold Arlen** and **Yip Harburg**, who later wrote "Over The Rainbow" together, wrote it for a film in 1935, *Metropolitan*, but it was eventually cut from the movie and used only instrumentally to accompany the credits.

Twenty years later, Sinatra made this extraordinary song his own with a remarkable performance of such contrasting dynamics, attention to detail and emotional range that the listener seems to hear the entire gamut of musical expression of regret and longing. **Nelson Riddle** remembered that recording the song was particularly difficult. "I learned a lot from Frank about conducting for a vocalist," he told the New York DJ Jonathan Schwartz, "but I was still very much in the learning process then. He was extremely patient with me and we went through it thirty times. Not all my fault, but at least half. And in those days, he had voice to burn, obviously."

By far the most dramatic piece on *In The Wee Small Hours*, and recorded a year before the rest of the album, "Last Night When We Were Young" betrays its operetta origins with its climax in the final line, though the dark colours and ebb and flow of what comes beforehand anticipate the intimate majesty and mystery of *Only The Lonely*.

Sinatra would re-examine the piece quite respectably in 1965 with Gordon Jenkins on *September Of My Years*, but his more complex and graceful reading with Riddle is the definitive treatment. It is said that the operatic baritone **Lawrence Tibbett**, who was featuring the song in all its gut-busting splendour in his concert performances, listened to this recording and muttered: "Oh, I see."

17. Just One Of Those Things

Written by Cole Porter; arranged by Nelson Riddle; recorded April 7, 1954, in KHJ Studios, Hollywood; available on *Swing Easy* (Capitol)

Cole Porter wrote "Just One Of Those Things" for the 1935 musical *Jubilee*, but at the time it was overshadowed by another song from the show, "Begin The Beguine". Supposedly Porter spent eight hours perfecting "Just One Of Those Things" and remained stuck for a three-syllable adjective to describe the "wings" upon which the singer imagines he has just flown to the moon. Describing his dilemma at a party, an architect suggested, without hesitation, **"gossamer"**, and a timeless phrase was born. (The sheet music, incidentally, suggests singing the first two notes of the chorus, "It was…", an octave lower than anyone bothers to sing them.)

Sinatra had only just taken another unassuming twenty-year-old Porter song and swung it – **"I Get A Kick Out Of You"** from 1934, on *Songs For Young Lovers* – and he carried on doing this for the next few albums, making the approach one of the traits of his Capitol period; the label later made a compilation called *Frank Sinatra Sings The Select Cole Porter*. His first chorus on the 1954 take of "Just One Of Those Things" is delivered quite straight over a half-time swing feel before a semi-tone key change and another chorus mostly in the more propulsive 4/4 swing, in which hip liberties are taken with melody, phrasing and lyric. This version would form the template for his live performances of the song for the next decade.

Though this deliciously restrained version is one of the subtlest Sinatra/Riddle re-imaginings of Porter, the seeds of Sinatra's later increasingly audacious variations are already present, in the extended "ffff" on "fabulous flights", more goodbyes than are strictly called for, and the downward swoop on "moon". All this **Sinatrification** (see pages 359–360) transformed the songs forever – to Porter's irritation.

18. Mood Indigo

Written by Duke Ellington, Irving Mills and Barney Bigard; arranged by Nelson Riddle; recorded February 16, 1955, in KHJ Studios, Hollywood; available on *In The Wee Small Hours* (Capitol)

Duke Ellington's first big hit, his extraordinarily haunting **"Dreamy Blues"**, which premiered on a radio broadcast in 1930, had two sixteen-bar themes: a long-tone tune written for three horns in Ellington's distinctive upside down voicing (muted trombone on highest note, muted trumpet in the middle, clarinet low) and a looping melody based on clarinettist Barney Bigard's improvisation on similar chords. The whole piece was soon given lyrics and became "Mood Indigo".

Arrangers adored Ellington's music, and Riddle was no exception. He makes a direct allusion to the famous **Ducal textures** at the top of the chart before allowing the strings to usher in his own mood indigo, depicted by polytonal flutes, the impressionistic descending string figure after "down to my shoes" and the jazzy double-time piano passage before the second theme. Sinatra plays straight man to all this business until the reprise of the first theme, when he reaches for his own emotional peak, before "no-no-no-ing" back down to his shoes.

19. Learnin' The Blues

Written by Dolores Silvers; arranged by Nelson Riddle; recorded March 23, 1955, in KHJ Studios, Hollywood; available on *The Complete Capitol Singles Collection* (Capitol)

This jaunty acceptance of love-induced misery has very little to do with blues music – other than a moaning blue note as the title is sung – but everything to do with Sinatra in the mid-1950s. The singles that he released on Capitol during this period were an incongruous mix of swingers ("Why Should I Cry Over You"), corny ballads ("You, My Love") and awkward attempts to jump on the R&B bandwagon ("Two Hearts, Two Kisses") – and they all flopped. Luckily, "Learnin' The Blues", his big hit of the period, reprised the relaxed swing style of **"I've Got The World On A String"** from 1953 and **"The Gal That Got Away"** from 1954.

It was Sinatra's only **US number one** in the 1950s – most of his well known songs, including "My Way" and "Theme from *New York, New York*", did not go to the top of the charts – but its success probably led to the (refined) pursuance of the style on records such as *Songs For Swingin' Lovers!*, for which we should all be thankful. *Two Hearts, Two Kisses: The Album* doesn't bear contemplation.

The song itself had already been a hit in Philadelphia for the local singer Joe Valino when Frank's business partners Frank Military and Ben Barton visited the writer **Dolores "Vicki" Silvers** to secure the song's copyright before Sinatra sang it. Sinatra recalled that of all the semi-professional songs he heard at the time, "Learnin' The Blues" was the only one that had any "professionality". Although the song was eventually recorded by Ella Fitzgerald, Louis Armstrong and Rosemary Clooney – and recently the British chanteuse **Katie Melua** – the mysterious Ms Silvers appears not to have written another one.

20. I've Got You Under My Skin

Written by Cole Porter; arranged by Nelson Riddle; recorded January 12, 1956, in KHJ Studios, Hollywood; available on *Songs for Swingin' Lovers!* (Capitol)

A 56-bar masterpiece of slow-burn minimalism by Cole Porter, with almost imperceptible modulations and gentle, rolling intensity as the words of desire begin to tumble, "I've Got You Under My Skin" was sung originally as a leisurely beguine by Virginia Bruce to James Stewart in the 1936 movie *Born To Dance*. The roaring Sinatra/Riddle treatment of Porter's song of romantic infection not only represents the peak of what the singer and arranger achieved together, but also may be the pinnacle of any jazz-derived popular music.

Riddle takes the sense of intensifying passion in the song and applies his *Bolero*-**inspired** theory of achieving effective crescendos by "gradually adding orchestral weight until the desired peak". This technique is used in various Sinatra/Riddle sides, including "Night And Day" and "Witchcraft"; but "I've Got You Under My Skin" is the apotheosis of the style that Basie arranger Neal Hefti said was as "if you went to Vegas and won five jackpots in a row".

The Music

"Frank seems to have co-invented a style of big band accompaniment that just took off like some big rocket. I could see it on his face, on stage, when the band started to blow on 'I've Got You Under My Skin'. He knew we were going to a place where man had never gone before."

Jimmy Webb

"I'VE GOT YOU UNDER MY SKIN": RIDDLE'S SEXY ARRANGEMENT

Intro and A section: A heartbeat tempo – Riddle said that "the rhythm of sex is the heartbeat" – and half-time swing feel. The syncopated chink of the celesta dances with an upward syncopated lick in the bass clarinet; a downward chromatic lick in the trombones. The music is relaxed, confident and unhurried – as is the vocal. This is the first part of a template for the Riddle-Sinatra style.

A section, bar nine: The addition of sustaining strings, playing long-held chords to give the hint of the symphony that Sinatra always wanted, rather than pure swing. Muted trumpets respond to the vocal line with a polytonal lick, an unexpected, sophisticated adjunct: the olive in the martini.

A¹ section: An almost imperceptible low pedal in trombone, full of sensual portent.

B section: An insistent riff from the saxophones, in gradual crescendo, threatens to overwhelm, but is replaced midway through by a calming sweep of string chords. The vocal is more rhythmically assertive.

Instrumental interlude: A twelve-bar pedal-point crescendo, featuring a capricious, fidgeting trombone figure and rising strings, which increases the tension before an explosive ascending triplet figure in the brass heralding…

Instrumental repeated A¹ section: …a feverish, passionate, climactic trombone solo, over a roaring big band powering out a 4/4 swing with a firm, steady backbeat.

Repeated B Section: The instrumental is calmer at first but there's a rise in intensity to meet the singer's ardour on "Do-o-on't you know…", and then a dead stop for a bar. A return to the decorum of the intro before the shimmering aftershock of a final string chord.

Riddle had an explanation for this enthusiasm, explaining that "music to me is sex – it's all tied up somehow". He continued: "I usually try to avoid scoring a song with a climax at the end. Better to build about two-thirds of the way through, and then fade to a surprise ending. More subtle."

The chart was written quickly to Sinatra's specifications, though bass trombonist George Roberts suggested that Riddle listen to Stan Kenton's **"23 Degrees North, 82 Degrees South"** as inspiration for the off-centre trombone interlude. And when the orchestra ran through it the first time, they were so impressed that they applauded Riddle for his work. With Sinatra pushing for take after take, **Milt Bernhart** blew his brains out on the trombone solo almost a dozen times before the engineers decided that he needed to be closer to the microphone. Sinatra found him a box to stand on, whereupon Bernhart carried on for a dozen takes more. The result: a Sinatra classic that he performed at almost every concert for the next 39 years.

21. Don't Like Goodbyes

Written by Harold Arlen and Truman Capote; arranged by Nelson Riddle; recorded March 8, 1956, in Capitol Studio A, Hollywood; available on *Close To You* (Capitol)

Of almost twenty Harold Arlen titles that Sinatra recorded over the years, a good proportion were genuine career highlights, such as "One For My Baby", "I've Got The World On A String" and "Last Night When We Were Young". Less famous, but no less impressive, was Sinatra's reading of "Don't Like Goodbyes". The song was originally sung by Pearl Bailey in the 1954 musical *House Of Flowers*, which was written by **Harold Arlen** in New York and **Truman Capote** in Paris, largely over the phone.

On their string quartet album *Close To You*, Sinatra and Riddle chose "Don't Like Goodbyes" for their most outré exploration of what was already for them an experimental style. Riddle's quartet writing makes fabulous use within his twentieth-century harmonies of woody colour tones in the strings, and of silence between the notes; and the effect is breathtakingly beautiful. Sinatra is formal and faultless; he makes much more of the upward sliding melisma on "by-yes" and "si-ighs" than Bailey, and retains barely a trace of her blue inflections, though he pronounces "you're" in the bridge as a patois "yer".

The song was recorded at one of Sinatra's first sessions at **the Capitol Tower studio**, where the engineers took months to re-create the sound of the rooms at KHJ. But the new surroundings did not prevent Sinatra and Riddle from creating controlled emotion that is passionate but also graceful and modest.

22. No One Ever Tells You

Written by Carroll Coates and Hub Atwood; arranged by Nelson Riddle; recorded April 9, 1956, in Capitol Studio A, Hollywood; available on *A Swingin' Affair!* (Capitol)

The songwriter Carroll Coates, with his friend the Hollywood arranger Hub Atwood, was responsible for the bluesy song that he wanted to push even though, he recounted to Will Friedwald, he thought it was "nothing very original or brilliant". It was actually an inspired ditty that bemoans not being warned about the trials of romance, managing to be both earthy (as the singer has "breakfast with the blues") and elevated (as autumn tells the swallows "time to fly"). Coates rated the lyrics as among his best and Sinatra phoned back on the day that he received them to say that "No One Ever Tells You" was going on the *Swingin' Affair* album and was coming out as a single – though that took another two years.

Although Coates himself interrupted the recording session when he had the idea of using the word "suddenly" to launch the midpoint of the second stanza, he remembers being concerned that they had attempted 23 takes. But Sinatra's manager, Hank Sanicola, assured him that Frank was "getting to the point where he's cracking his voice so he can get that bluesy feeling".

Get it he did. He delivered one of his most convincing performances in the blues idiom – not normally one of his best – and Riddle, who stayed up all night to score a wailing chart, was, once again, vital.

23. I Wish I Were In Love Again

Written by Richard Rodgers and Lorenz Hart; arranged by Nelson Riddle; recorded November 20, 1956, in Capitol Studio A, Hollywood; available on *A Swingin' Affair!* (Capitol)

The canon

An ingenious list song of all the things one might miss about being in a romantic relationship, "I Wish I Were In Love Again" first appeared in 1938 in Rodgers and Hart's musical *Babes In Arms*, along with "My Funny Valentine". Appearing as the second cut on *A Swingin' Affair!*, it represents the routine brilliance of Sinatra and Riddle in the mid-1950s.

By this stage Riddle's work was that of an auteur: he gives us the two-beat heartbeat feel, the semi-tone key change and gear shift into 4/4 for assertive swing, the witty interjections from Harry "Sweets" Edison's muted trumpet (or, startlingly, the brass section at the end of the second bridge), and the cool, confident decrescendo before the finale.

Working with some of Hart's wordiest, most comical lyrics, Sinatra displays his mastery, by now unsurpassed, in phrasing and timing; sometimes he underlines the gags, sometimes he throws them away, but he's always in control and always swinging. This is the strutting, infectious flipside to the loser-in-love persona of *In The Wee Small Hours*; he still misses the kisses, but this time he's smiling. And so are we.

24. Lonely Town

Written by Leonard Bernstein, Betty Comden and Adolph Green; arranged by Gordon Jenkins; recorded April 29, 1957, in Capitol Studio A, Hollywood; available on *Where Are You?* (Capitol)

Already annoyed at the MGM producer **Arthur Freed** for introducing more commercial material into Leonard Bernstein's score of the 1949 movie of the show *On The Town*, Sinatra was still waiting to sing "Lonely Town", the score's brilliant ballad, when the film wrapped. And he was *still* ranting decades later. "Gene [Kelly] and I worked on a routine for 'Lonely Town' which would have knocked people out," he told the musician and archivist Michael Feinstein. "Can you imagine how wonderful that moment in the film would have been, with Gene dancing and me singing? … But that fucking Arthur Freed got in the way."

He eventually got to sing it eight years later on his first album with **Gordon Jenkins**, *Where Are You?* – and boy, did he sing it. Jenkins sets him up beautifully with hushed string chords and a lone French horn – Sinatra's idea, but Jenkins always loved French horns; and a fanfare and stairway-to-the-stars violins herald the ascending motif in the verse.

Thereafter, captured in compelling detail on his first stereo session, and with the distant harps, flutes and strings leaving the singer acres of lovely, lonely space, Sinatra is at his mature, mournful best.

Both Sinatra and Jenkins were thrilled with the results. "He thought that 'Lonely Town' was the best record he ever made," Jenkins recalled. "And I did too."

25. Witchcraft

Written by Cy Coleman and Carolyn Leigh; arranged by Nelson Riddle; recorded May 20, 1957, in Capitol Studio A, Hollywood; available on *The Complete Capitol Singles Collection* (Capitol)

While Sinatra was in the middle of one his busiest periods, Capitol were desperate for him to record a new single, and when he saw the pile of demos that he was expected to wade through, he told them to "pick *one* song, that's it". The first one played was "Witchcraft", which he liked, and that was the end of the session.

As it turned out, it was by **Carolyn Leigh**, whose "Young At Heart" had turned Sinatra's singles sales around in 1954 and who had taken to writing songs with the pianist **Cy Coleman**. They went on to write the musical *Sweet Charity*, but for now they were pretty pleased with this neat, witty and unconventional piece. "The words belong to the melody," Coleman told Will Friedwald of the song, acknowledging that the union of the two elements is not always effortless. "When it happens right, you can't pull it apart at all. That's when the marriage is good."

The arrangement of the song extended the Sinatra/Riddle honeymoon. Although the singer needed an extended session to get things just right, the results, in the customized *Swingin' Lovers/A Swingin' Affair!* style, sound as effortless and natural as anything that the pair did together.

26. The Lady Is A Tramp

Written by Richard Rodgers and Lorenz Hart; arranged by Nelson Riddle; recorded May 23, 1957, in Capitol Studio A, Hollywood; available on *Frank Sinatra In Hollywood* (Reprise)

Of more than forty tunes by **Richard Rodgers** that Sinatra recorded during his career, perhaps none is more associated with the singer than "The Lady Is A Tramp", first heard in 1938 in *Babes In Arms*. This lampoon of meaningless social behaviour is sung in the show in the first person by a female character to defiantly affirm her realness. When the song comes from a male, and in particular the swaggering Sinatra, it remains a celebration but is also a tease about the lady's stubborn, gauche individuality.

Recorded originally in November 1956 for inclusion on *A Swingin' Affair!*, the song was left off the record because of the imminence of Sinatra's involvement in the screen adaptation of Rodgers and Hart's show *Pal Joey*, and appeared instead on the film's soundtrack album. However, Sinatra rerecorded the song in May 1957 for the scene when he sings it from the stage to Rita Hayworth, and this performance can be seen as the definitive version. The arrangement is essentially the same but Bill Miller gets to stretch out a little more on the piano and Sinatra cranks up the theatricality a notch or two, and the result is replete with jazzy excitement. "He always sang that song with a certain amount of salaciousness," observed Nelson Riddle. "He savoured it. He had some cute tricks with the lyrics which made it especially his."

One of these tricks was his re-written second stanza, in which "Fords" and "frauds" set up the rhyme "broads", Frank's (and the character Joey's) preferred but slightly pejorative term for "girls". This version of the lyric was not used in the film, however, and some of Sinatra's live performances, from the 1980s onwards, also tended to avoid it, even if he set up the rhyme.

27. Come Fly With Me

Written by Sammy Cahn and Jimmy Van Heusen; arranged by Billy May; recorded October 8, 1957, in Capitol Studio A, Hollywood; available on *Come Fly With Me* (Capitol)

Sammy Cahn and Jimmy Van Heusen, who wrote the Oscar-winning song "All The Way" for Sinatra's movie *The Joker Is Wild*, were the nearest that Sinatra had to **house writers**; he recorded dozens of songs with lyrics written by Cahn, and though some were written with Jule Styne, most were from Cahn and Van Heusen. For Sinatra's fun-filled concept album

The Music

COME FLY WITH FRANK: SINATRA IN LONDON IN THE MID-1950S

Come Fly With Me, they were commissioned by Sinatra to compose the opening and closing track. "**It's Nice To Go Trav'ling**" was a lovely tongue-in-cheek finish ("get my slippers … make a pizza") but their title track opener was even better – inspired travelogue tomfoolery about rarefied air, cheering angels and a one-man band tooting his flute, which sings absolutely perfectly. According to Sammy Cahn, the original bar in "far Bombay" contained exotic "views", the word which Sinatra recorded before pointing out that the naughtier "booze" might be more appropriate. Sammy suggested that this might suit Vegas but not a record, but Frank recalled the musicians and recorded it again, his way.

Billy May, Sinatra's new arranger, did a magnificent job, full of character, throughout the album *Come Fly With Me*, and on the title track he excelled himself. The take-off intro – anticipatory off-kilter riffs and giddy, ascending strings – is a masterpiece, all eight seconds of it. For the rest of the piece he stamps his own personality on Sinatra's swinging Capitol style – super-assertive brassy punctuations and the May trademark of slurping saxes – but he also acknowledges Nelson Riddle's approach, through sustaining strings and a surprise aerated ending.

28. **Only The Lonely**

Written by Sammy Cahn and Jimmy Van Heusen; arranged by Nelson Riddle; recorded May 29, 1958, in Capitol Studio A, Hollywood; available on *Frank Sinatra Sings For Only The Lonely* (Capitol)

Though **Sammy Cahn** often wrote lyrics quickly, and glibly, he struggled when Sinatra asked him to come up with a title track for another suicide set, *Only The Lonely*. Van Heusen had composed a long, beautiful, unconventional melody, with dissonant blue appoggiaturas and a cramped, downward direction. Cahn sat for hours without, as Van Heusen recalled, "a glimmer of a line".

Usually one who gave up or suggested musical adjustments if the job seemed too hard, Cahn on this occasion persevered, without accepting his partner's offer to change the music. He eventually produced a sensitive lyric of loneliness that combined tautology ("Some little small café") with sensual poetry ("lips as warm as May"), resulting in one of the best songs that Cahn and Van Heusen ever wrote, and one of the most unusual.

"Only The Lonely" remains relatively unfamiliar and very rarely covered by other singers. It well could be that the already difficult song discourages other artists because of the dauntingly grand Sinatra/Riddle treatment: dark strings, piano that recalls **Chopin**, an achingly slow approach to each out-of-tempo phrase and dynamics that range from anticipatory silence before the vocal to a dazzling swell of remembrance. Its single, bewitching chorus creates a mysterious narrative told through intangible musical shadows.

29. One For My Baby
(And One More For The Road)

Written by Harold Arlen and Johnny Mercer; arranged by Nelson Riddle; recorded June 26, 1958, in Capitol Studio A, Hollywood; available on *Frank Sinatra Sings For Only The Lonely* (Capitol)

"One For My Baby" is the song of the self-pitying bum *par excellence*. First sung (and danced) by **Fred Astaire** in the 1943 movie *The Sky's The Limit*, this classic of saloon solitude is a magical narrative-free character study. The lyrics by **Johnny Mercer** and bluesy cadences from **Harold Arlen** establish a confessional mood; but the rambling, drunken egoist, though mentioning a "torch" that's "gotta be drowned", says nothing about why he's so gloomy. The song packs an emotional punch, perhaps thanks to the melancholy, almost surly side that Mercer, one of the most successful and skilful lyricists who ever lived, apparently developed when he'd been drinking.

Sinatra, not immune to melancholia himself, first tackled the song with Axel Stordahl, as a medium tempo swinger, in 1947, when he wasn't equipped to do more than stroll through it. But his performance of the song in the film *Young At Heart* in 1954 is superb; it's still rhythmically light but has a suitably heavy heart. And on the similarly faultless recording four years later, the performance was even deeper, with Sinatra inhabiting the song like an actor, but seeming to *be* the part rather than be acting it. On this version, part of the ***Only The Lonely*** concept album, Sinatra was accompanied only by the pianist Bill Miller, Riddle's cloudy string arrangements and Gus Bivona's alto saxophone obbligatos. These vivid but discreet adornments underline rather than detract from the singer's isolation – and the effect is heart-stopping.

"I'd always sung that song before in clubs with just my pianist Bill Miller backing me, a single spotlight on my face," Sinatra told Robin Douglas-Home of the final recording on *Only The Lonely*. "At this session, word had somehow got around, and there were about sixty or seventy people there … **Dave Cavanaugh** was the A&R man, and he knew how I sang it in the clubs, and he switched out all the lights – bar the spot on me. The atmosphere in that studio was exactly like a club. Dave said, 'Roll 'em,' and there was one take, and that was that. The only time I've known it to happen like that."

SINATRA THE BEAUTIFUL LOSER

Sinatra used to tell a story about a man in a bar. "Everybody's staring down at the sauce and one of my saloon songs comes on the jukebox. **'One For My Baby'**, or something like that. After a while, a drunk at the end of the bar looks up and says, jerking his thumb toward the jukebox, 'I wonder who *he* listens to'…"

Has anybody loved and lost more than Frank Sinatra? It's certainly true that nobody could bring such poetic elegance to emotional misery; everything about Sinatra's **1950s torch albums** elevates the idea of heartache and pain into a kind of state of grace. The magnificent exaltation of dark, soulful nights turned the character of the broken-down bum into a man who is misunderstood – a downbeat with dignity; and the lonely loser's tokens on the covers – the cigarette, the loosened tie, the rumpled suit, the drink, the lamppost – became iconic symbols of the heartbroken.

30. Day In, Day Out

Written by Rube Bloom and Johnny Mercer; arranged by Billy May; recorded December 22, 1958, in Capitol Studio A, Hollywood; available on *Come Dance With Me* (Capitol)

This unusually sophisticated song from Johnny Mercer and ragtime pianist-cum-composer **Rube Bloom** first appeared in 1939. The singular structure of the 56-bar song can be analysed as A B A C A^1 D (the fifth section differing only slightly from the first and third), which looks convoluted on the page but in the singing has a rolling logic all of its own.

Sinatra sang a rather pompous arrangement of "Day In, Day Out" by Axel Stordahl at his first Capitol session in 1953 that remained unreleased until *The Rare Sinatra* came out in 1978. He had another go in 1954 with Nelson Riddle – who fashioned something similarly dramatic, presumably following Sinatra's instructions – but that too remained in the vaults until it was selected for a limited-release compilation in 1965 by the UK Sinatra Appreciation Society. But in 1958 **Billy May** came up with a no-nonsense arrangement that resulted in perhaps the most successful track on the Sinatra/May tough swing album *Come Dance With Me!*.

The song is transformed, becoming hip, hard and sexy thanks to the propulsion from May and Sinatra's swaggering delivery, which tramples all over the kitschy lines about kisses becoming an ocean's roar and a thousand drums. That the number of drums described would increase to 10,000 or more in concert says much about the piece's over-the-top exuberance – which was typical of late-1950s Sinatra.

31. You Go To My Head

Written by Fred Coots and Haven Gillespie; arranged by Nelson Riddle; recorded March 1, 1960, in Capitol Studio A, Hollywood; available on *Nice 'N' Easy* (Capitol)

When Sinatra reinvented himself and grew in stature in the late 1950s, through his films, records and concert appearances, one area of activity, which had made his name in the first place, went relatively neglected: romantic song. By 1960 he had not made a set of love songs since *Close To You* in 1956, which was received indifferently by critics and by the public, who had wanted the new, swinging Frank. But four years later he needed another idea for an album so that he could fulfil his final contractual obligations and get away from Capitol. How about a set of love songs called ***The Nearness Of You***? The majority of the tunes were recorded with this original, cuddle-up concept in mind – before the album became *Nice 'N' Easy* – and none more so than the remake of "You Go To My Head".

Despite Sinatra's reputation in the mid-1940s as the voice of love, there was something a little chaste about his delivery, and his smooth reading in 1945 of Fred Coots and Haven Gillespie's "You Go To My Head", which featured on his first "album", *The Voice*, was about as good as ballad singing got during that period: it was relaxed, with a hint of Billie Holiday in the title line variation, but quite proper. But by 1960 times had changed, and so had Sinatra – and **the eroticism** was there to hear. He bathes in the song's imagery of love-as-drunkenness, taking a decadent four-and-a-half minutes to list the ways that she turns him on; and after all that, the suggestion that he hasn't a chance becomes a challenge for him to be resisted. "You Go To my Head" is Sinatra at his most sensual.

32. Nice 'N' Easy

Written by Lew Spence, Marilyn Keith and Alan Bergman; arranged by
Nelson Riddle; recorded April 13, 1960, in Capitol Studio A, Hollywood;
available on *Nice 'N' Easy* (Capitol)

Lew Spence was responsible for composing eight Sinatra single releases
on Capitol, which were mostly inessential and unsuccessful, but also
included a disposable hit, "Ol' Macdonald". Spence's "Nice 'N' Easy",
however, which was demonstrated to Sinatra during the shooting of
Ocean's 11, was a gem, but the singer didn't think so; when he first heard
it, he picked up the music and dropped it on the floor to show what he
thought it was worth. But **Hank Sanicola** knew better and made a point
of playing "Nice 'N' Easy" within Frank's earshot whenever he could,
and eventually Sinatra asked him about "that cute little thing". Sanicola
cunningly mentioned that Frank was recording it the following week,
whereupon the singer resolved to "get Nelson and give him a key, I don't
remember giving him a key on that one".

In the recording session, Sinatra apparently struggled to nail this
deceptively casual ditty. "Whaddya expect?" he asks on the outtakes, "I
don't know the song!" He then created the coda himself in the studio,
which probably referred to the famous reprised ending of the **Count
Basie** recording from 1955 of "April In Paris". Sinatra dabbled with adding
"Just put your hand on it, baby, that's all", "Slowly baby", "Yeah, you dirty
mother" and "Isn't that better baby?" before settling on "Like the man
says, one more time."

The finger-snapping feast of **double entendres** turned out so well that it
became the title track of Sinatra's new album. It was the first time that he
had given an album the title track of a successful single (but not the last),
and in terms of business, it certainly did the trick.

"That record may get everyone here arrested."

FS EXPRESSING APPROVAL IN THE STUDIO

33. Let's Fall In Love

Written by Harold Arlen and Ted Koehler; arranged by Johnny Mandel; recorded December 19, 1960, in United-Western Studio A, Los Angeles; available on *Ring-A-Ding Ding!* (Reprise)

After three years of writing songs for revues at Harlem's Cotton Club and for *Earl Carroll's Vanities* on Broadway, in 1933 **Ted Koehler** and **Harold Arlen** went to Hollywood to work on their first movie, *Let's Fall In Love*. The title song of this spoof of Tinseltown's enthusiasm for Greta Garbo was a huge hit; it was an unforgettable ditty whose main strain was so infectious that the delicate ingenuity of the bridge and verse was overwhelmed.

Twenty-seven years later, when Sinatra was planning *Ring-A-Ding Ding!*, the inaugural album on his new label, he was looking for fresh ways to present a song. The verse of "Let's Fall In Love" ("I've got a feeling/It's a feeling…"), was an obvious choice to work on, as it had not been used since the movie, and it was scored with cheeky invention by **Johnny Mandel**, but Sinatra chose to precede it with the bridge from within the chorus ("We might have been meant for each other…"), and to precede *that* with a dizzying multi-key Mandel intro.

This ingenious design results in delicious **delayed recognition**, which is accentuated by Sinatra's insertion of a bar of silence before he eventually delivers the familiar chorus: "Let's fall in love…". Mandel later explained, "[Sinatra] suggested the break, right off the cuff, and he was totally right." And having grabbed the listener's attention, a minute into the track, he and Mandel hold it through exemplary modern swing: it's the precocious child of *Songs For Swingin' Lovers!* and an exhilarating highlight of the only album that Frankie and Johnny made together.

34. When The World Was Young

Written by M. Philippe-Gerard and Johnny Mercer; arranged by Axel Stordahl; recorded September 11, 1961, in Capitol Studio A, Hollywood; available on *Point Of No Return* (Capitol)

Composed by the French songwriter M. Philippe-Gerard and given lyrics by Johnny Mercer in 1950, "When The World Was Young" (also known as

"Ah The Apple Trees") had a feel of **a Parisian chanson**, with its *bon vivant* verses and wistful choruses. The narrator is ebullient on the surface but recalls achingly an intimate summer and is, therefore, a perfect character for Sinatra.

It was chosen to be part of his final LP for Capitol, the themed "farewell" album *Point Of No Return*, about which Sinatra couldn't have cared less. He had his own record company to run and didn't want to be there; he showed up only to honour the contract. Without any run-throughs he did a single take of each tune, or two at most, before moving on. At one point producer **Dave Cavanaugh** tried to get him to sing another take for technical reasons, whereupon Sinatra tore up the lead sheet. "Didn't you hear me?" he said. "Next number."

Amazingly, the album was lovely, and "When The World Was Young" was a highlight. The dancing string figure by **Axel Stordahl** that heralds both the track and the album is so vivid that Sinatra can be imagined springing along the Champs Elysées. Thereafter, Stordahl arranges the whole song with great care and skill, and Sinatra captures the duality of the character – sociable one moment, melancholy the next – with extraordinary sensitivity. "When The World Was Young" is an example of great art entirely transcending the circumstances of its creation.

35. Come Rain Or Come Shine

Written by Harold Arlen and Johnny Mercer; arranged by Don Costa; recorded November 22, 1961, in United-Western Studio A, Los Angeles; available on *Sinatra And Strings* (Reprise)

Ray Charles and the arranger **Ralph Burns** had created an R&B gem in 1959 with "Come Rain Or Come Shine", originally part of the 1946 Harold Arlen/Johnny Mercer show *St Louis Woman*, and their influence on aspects of the version by Sinatra, arranged by **Don Costa**, is clear. But with Costa's dramatic and musical skills and the force of Sinatra's personality, a whole new masterpiece was created; Costa conjures up an intoxicating mixture of barroom blues, concert hall strings and fresh, modern harmonies and Sinatra delivers a forceful vocal, with a hint of R&B holler.

Although it's very persuasive here, Sinatra overdid the Charles-inspired approach a few years later on records that didn't even have the redeeming qualities of a decent song or arrangement, exposing his limited abilities in that style. But on "Come Rain Or Come Shine" the low-down and the lofty are balanced perfectly.

Costa's striking arrangement was a live favourite of Sinatra's throughout his career, and there was something about the material and Costa's stirring treatment that ensured that Frank gave the song a good shaking whatever form he was in elsewhere in the set. "I like this song almost more than any song I've ever sung," he told a Japanese audience in 1985.

36. If I Had You

Written by James Campbell, Reg Connelly and Ted Shapiro; arranged by Robert Farnon; recorded June 12, 1962, in CTS Studios, Bayswater, London; available on *Great Songs From Great Britain* (Reprise)

In legendarily tired voice – the recording sessions in London came in the middle of a punishing European tour – Sinatra brings a fabulous, bluesy lassitude to "If I Had You", which creates a kind of magic when set against the cultured support. Written in 1929 by the British songwriters Ted Shapiro, James Campbell and Reg Connelly, the song had already been recorded by Sinatra as a romantic tune arranged by Axel Stordahl in 1947 and on a swinging Nelson Riddle chart in 1956 when it was mooted for the *Great Songs From Great Britain* album. The arrangement by **Robert Farnon**, with a subdued beat, muted trumpet and shimmering strings, its mood falling between the readings for Columbia and Capitol, is something rather special. And Sinatra makes it even more special.

But it nearly didn't happen. **Alan Freeman**, already as nervous as a producer can be, in a studio in Bayswater that was packed with the press, more than forty of the country's top orchestral players and Sinatra, whose reputation for being impatient with incompetence had preceded him, could hardly believe it when, during the first take of the first tune on the first session, the keyboard action on the piano broke. He held his breath while Sinatra asked, "Have we got another piano?" They hadn't. "Okay, then," shrugged Sinatra, to everyone's relief, "we'll do it on celesta."

37. Please Be Kind

Written by Saul Chaplin and Sammy Cahn; arranged by Neal Hefti; recorded October 2, 1962, in United-Western Studio A, Los Angeles; available on *Sinatra-Basie* (Reprise)

Aside from its distinctive and attractive ascending lick of melody, Sammy Cahn and Saul Chaplin's "Please Be Kind" from the 1930s is a disingenuous piece of nothing. When Sinatra recorded the song for the album with **Count Basie** he wasn't even in good voice: a few days before the session he'd shouted himself hoarse watching his favourite baseball team, the **LA Dodgers**, make it through to the World Series, and though the recordings were preceded by careful rehearsal, he mostly lands only in the rough vicinity of the notes that he has in mind.

But thanks to a smoothness typical of Basie and Neal Hefti's slyly repetitive arrangement – bluesy riffs in the saxophones and stabs in the brass that go against the grain of the original song – Sinatra cruises and delivers. Whether Basie himself was involved in the track is open to question; Bill Miller often played the piano on tunes that Basie didn't know, usually at Basie's suggestion. But those definitely involved in this magic carpet of groove included **Sonny Payne** on drums with steady side-stick snare on two and four, **Buddy Catlett** on bass playing four big beats in the bar, and **Freddie Green**, who during his career with Basie made 4/4 rhythm guitar into a kind of poetry.

"Basie, as we all know," Sinatra said, "epitomizes the greatest kind of tempo for swing in jazz. It was a joy because all I had to do was just stay up on the crest of sound and move along with it. It just carries you through." This happens beautifully in the surprising moment during the second chorus when Sinatra ducks out, and the band just continues. Hefti then builds towards a big finish, unlike the mid-song climax that was favoured by Nelson Riddle. Sinatra slides lasciviously down his final title line and Hefti pokes a provocatively tart flatted ninth into the climactic chord.

"Frank, come on in!" said Hefti from the control booth when the recording finished. "You're gonna cream in your pants when you hear this one."

38. Luck Be A Lady

Written by Frank Loesser; arranged by Billy May; recorded July 25, 1963, in United-Western Studio A, Los Angeles; available on *The Reprise Collection* (Reprise)

If Sinatra was miffed not to have played Terry Malloy in *On The Waterfront*, he was even more upset to miss out on Sky Masterson in the film of *Guys And Dolls*, especially when he heard what **Marlon Brando** did to one of the main songs in the score. When he had his own company, the Reprise Musical Repertory Theatre, record their version, he assigned himself "Luck Be A Lady" as if to say: '*That's* how it goes – Mumbles!'

Billy May scored it close in tempo to the bongo frenzy of the original, but Sinatra suggested easing up on the speed and it turned into a forceful, stately swing epic, more than five minutes in length. The opening riff of the chorus is perhaps the most unforgettable of all the Sinatra fanfares, with the high French horn notes a hunting cry of the swaggering gambler. The tempo lets Sinatra really bite into the text, so he can make his admonishment of the fickle female of the title more threatening, and can underline the suggestive quality of lines such as "blow on some other guy's dice".

Along with "Come Fly With Me", "Luck Be A Lady" was the best of the Sinatra/May partnership, and remained a reliable live highlight until the mid-1990s. It seemed, as did the similarly rigorous and powerful "Come Rain Or Come Shine", to push Sinatra to heightened powers of performance in the latter stage of his career.

39. Fly Me To The Moon

Written by Bart Howard; arranged by Quincy Jones; recorded June 9, 1964, in United-Western Studio A, Los Angeles; available on *It Might As Well Be Swing* (Reprise)

So vivid and exciting is the Sinatra-Basie-Quincy Jones recording of "Fly Me To The Moon", it's sometimes forgotten that the song had another life before it was cast as an archetypal Sinatra swinger.

In the early 1950s a favourite hangout of Sinatra's was **the Blue Angel** in New York, where **Bart Howard** was a cabaret accompanist on piano for figures such as Mabel Mercer. One of the songs that Howard wrote during this period was "In Other Words", a dainty waltz recorded in 1956 by Portia Nelson; and it was given its now familiar name, using the unrepeated first line rather than the recurrent original title, for Peggy Lee's Latinised version in the early 1960s.

Quincy Jones cast it as a 4/4 swinger on Count Basie's 1963 album *This Time By Basie*, but it was the Sinatra-Basie-Jones version that established the song as a swing classic. Jones had worked with Sinatra in 1958 when he was the musical director of a fund-raising concert for Princess Grace of Monaco, and having become established in the early 1960s as one of the brightest young arrangers around and having got his feet under Basie's table, he worked closely with Sinatra on the second Sinatra-Basie album, *It Might As Well Be Swing*. The record wasn't entirely successful, but the best cuts, this marauding chart among them, were some of the finest that Sinatra ever made. The song's excitement is all in the expectation in the strolling groove and the dancing flute, which builds into a fat ensemble statement of the theme, with humorous upward glissandos from the trumpets, and climaxes with shattering brass triplets and a roaring coda.

In the countless live versions that he performed, Sinatra would stretch the song so that it became less and less like the original composition and more and more one of his own creations. Howard might have been put out, but he confessed to Will Friedwald that although such liberties "normally would have irritated the shit out of me", this time they didn't, "because it worked so well".

40. Softly As I Leave You

Written by Hal Shaper, Antonio DeVita and Giorgio Calabrese; arranged by Ernie Freeman; recorded July 17, 1964, in United-Western Studio A, Los Angeles; available on *My Way: The Best Of Frank Sinatra* (Reprise)

In 1964 Sinatra was as popular a draw in Vegas as ever and "the Chairman Of The Board" at his own company, and he had made some terrific albums on Reprise, but he was bugged by his lack of chart action. His best US placing from 22 singles released during the previous four years had been with the novelty "A Pocketful Of Miracles", which in 1961 reached number 34; other efforts – "Everybody's Twistin'" in 1962 and "Call Me Irresponsible" in 1963 – scraped into the Top 100, but most didn't chart at all. And in the summer of 1964 Dean Martin, whom Sinatra had signed to Reprise, was racing up the charts to number one with a contemporary arrangement of "Everybody Loves Somebody", a song that Sinatra had already recorded three times. Frank called the producer responsible, **Jimmy Bowen**, and asked what he would do if he were making music with Sinatra.

On his way to see Sinatra, Bowen grabbed something from what he called his "good song file", and when he played it to him, Sinatra said, "Fine, let's do it." The song was "Softly As I Leave You", a sweet piece that was adapted from an Italian melody and had been a UK hit in 1962 for **Matt Monro**, who many regarded as the British Sinatra. (Monro was actually closer in style to Perry Como, but was a huge Sinatra fan and even impersonated him on Peter Sellers's comedy album *Song For Swingin' Sellers* in 1959.) Arranger **Ernie Freeman** dressed it with a gentle rock beat, some dramatic strings, an even more dramatic choir and flutes piping repetitively twice a beat, which Bowen described as "on the head stuff". Sinatra recorded it and asked Bowen what he thought. Bowen said, as he recounted to Charles Granata: "Well, I think it's about a number thirty record, but it'll get us back on radio." He was right.

Sinatra sings it well, but the song never became established in Sinatra's live shows. However, its modest commercial success ensured that he would look to Bowen for more of the same in the future. "Softly as I Leave You" represents the birth of Sinatra the soft rocker.

41. It Was A Very Good Year

Written by Ervin Drake; arranged by Gordon Jenkins; recorded April 22, 1965, in Hollywood; available on *September Of My Years* (Reprise)

Sinatra selected this song, an unexpected success in the US, as a suitable piece for his reminiscence album *September Of My Years* after hearing the 1961 version by folk group The Kingston Trio on the radio. A series of reflections upon phases of life as if they were vintages, it was written by **Ervin Drake**, whose previous writing credits included the lyrics to

"Perdido", "Good Morning Heartache" and a song of religious affirmation "I Believe", which sold more than 20 million copies.

Drake had composed a musical theme to appear between stanzas and set it to nonsense words that sounded medieval – "Hi-lura-li/Hi-lura-lura-li". It was absent from the Kingston Trio version, and **Gordon Jenkins** turned the insistent figure into a non-vocal heart-tugging motif in the strings that increases in intensity, building up to near-hysterical wailing. When Sinatra heard about the syllables, he told Drake, "You're lucky buddy. If I had sung that, it would have come out "Hi-scooby-do/Hi-scooby-dooby-do".

The elevation of what Sinatra called "an awfully pretty folk song" into high emotional drama creates probably the most memorable arrangement of Jenkins's career, and the string motif was used between each song on a reminiscence medley on the *Man And His Music* TV special in 1965. The song also provided a perfect opportunity for Sinatra the actor to bring a lyric to life, and is a magnificent example of his sensual **enjoyment of words**. He caresses and savours them as if he were imbibing a selection of fine clarets. "It's just like reading poetry," he once said of how he read lyrics. "And that's odd, because poetry bores me."

42. Strangers In The Night

Written by Bert Kaempfert, Charles Singleton and Eddie Snyder; arranged by Ernie Freeman; recorded April 11, 1966, in Hollywood; available on *Strangers In The Night* (Reprise)

Sinatra's biggest hit in years was born when producer **Jimmy Bowen** was listening to Bert Kaempfert's score for a movie called *A Man Could Get Killed* and noticed a memorable melody worthy of a song. Bowen asked several lyricists to come up with words before settling on "Strangers In The Night"; but the publisher soon touted the song around, and when Bowen heard that Jack Jones's recording was three days away from being released he asked **Ernie Freeman** to put together an arrangement at speed – and three days later Sinatra recorded the song in under an hour. Bowen mixed and cut acetates immediately and dispatched them to couriers who, delivering to the radio stations by hand, ensured that Sinatra's version hit the airwaves first.

It's commercial, and Sinatra oversings it, pushing hard in the mid-1960s style that Bowen encouraged. He even messes up the melody of the second "in love forever" after taking a downward chance with his second "lovers at first sight". But Sinatra's scat at the fade ("oobie-doobie-do"), showing faint contempt towards the song, became a catchphrase that he would parody in concert, and millions of copies were sold.

He found himself at the top of the charts with a song he had no real regard for, as he had done in 1950 with "Goodnight Irene" and in 1958 with "Hey Jealous Lover", but he dutifully performed "Strangers In The Night" for years. He attempted to distance himself from the song, however, through jokey substitute lyrics ("a warm embracing dance away" would become "a lonesome pair of pants away") and asides ("I have no idea who any of these guys are," he would say after name-checking the songwriters).

As the writer Gene Lees observed, this demonstrated the singer's "streak of hypocrisy" as regards certain kinds of material. Sinatra may not have needed the money, but he appears to have still needed the acclaim that came with low-grade commercial successes such as "Strangers In The Night". The (presumably accepted) trade off was that his reputation as a musician of exemplary taste and exacting standards was, temporarily, slightly tarnished.

43. Dindi

Written by Ray Gilbert, Antonio Carlos Jobim and Aloysio de Oliveira; arranged by Claus Ogerman; recorded January 30, 1967, in Hollywood; available on *Francis Albert Sinatra & Antonio Carlos Jobim* (Reprise)

One of hundreds of beautiful songs written by the Brazilian master **Antonio Carlos Jobim**, the title of this song came from a small forest named "Dirindi" near where he went on holiday in the state of Rio de Janeiro. Though the song had Portuguese lyrics by the erstwhile Jobim collaborator Aloysio de Oliveira, it was customary after the international bossa nova boom of the early 1960s to find suitable lyrics in English, and "Dindi" became the first collaboration with Jobim for **Ray Gilbert**, an American songwriter whose credits included the Oscar-winning "Zip-A-Dee-Doo-Dah". Gilbert, who went on to write a dozen more lyrics for Jobim, kept the original title and made Dindi a beautiful individual and the object of heightened longing who represents nothing less than a purpose in life.

This collaboration between Sinatra, Jobim and **Claus Ogerman** is stunning. Starting with the out-of-tempo verse featuring only Sinatra and Jobim's guitar chords (later supplanted by a bank of gorgeous strings), the atmosphere is extraordinary. Sinatra murmurs in a way that leaves him vulnerable as never before, the harmonic modulations take a turn that is giddy and unpredictable and the music becomes a dreamland of sensual wonder. Ogerman's arrangement is superbly diffident, the few flecks of sound he chooses only enhancing the serene euphoria.

"I had to write so fast that I didn't have time to put down millions of notes," he told Will Friedwald, "so I left my arrangements extremely transparent, and that made it nice for the singer." Indeed, the arrangement coaxed from Sinatra some of the most sensitive vocalizing of his career.

44. Yellow Days

Written by Alviro Carrillo and Alan Bernstein; arranged by Billy May; recorded December 12, 1967, in Hollywood; available on *Francis A. & Edward K.* (Reprise)

Sinatra was among the first vocalists to record this song, and although it was also covered by **Tony Bennett** and **Freddie Cole**, it remains a neglected and intriguing piece. The song was selected as part of the collaboration between Sinatra and **Duke Ellington**, which was long-awaited but hampered by a lack of preparation by the Ellington orchestra and did not even reach the Top Forty album chart.

The album may not be a classic, but "Yellow Days" sticks in the imagination. The unpredictable, upwardly circuitous melody written by **Alviro Carrillo**, the composer of classical music and Latin pop, is bewitching, and Sinatra negotiates its intricate detail with weary care; and the sense of regret and wounded majesty in the lyrics by **Alan Bernstein** is unforgettable. The singer recalls the sunshine having a special kind of brightness when he was young, and wonders what happened to the "yellow days".

In addition, the Ellington orchestra has a whole chorus, scored by Billy May; there's solo space for **Johnny Hodges** (who the previous day had

SINATRA WITH ELLINGTON WHEN RECORDING TOGETHER IN 1967

provided a stunning sax solo on "Indian Summer"); and an audacious bridge pastiches Ellington's "train whistle" harmonies (present, for example, in "Take The A Train") in the reeds. The song, clocking in at an unhurried five minutes, has a regal tempo, like most of the album.

45. My Way

Written by Paul Anka, Jacques Revaux, Gilles Thilbault and Claude François; arranged by Don Costa; recorded December 30, 1968, in Hollywood; available on *My Way* (Reprise)

"My Way" began life as a French song, **"Comme D'Habitude"**, sung by one of its composers, Claude François, before the publishers cast around for an English lyric, as was sometimes customary with foreign-language hits. One failed attempt came from a young **David Bowie** (who took his revenge by penning "Life On Mars" to a similar chord sequence) but the effort of the former teen idol **Paul Anka** was more successful. With Sinatra in mind, he came up with a peculiar piece of self-congratulatory bombast that anyone with less attitude than the Chairman of the Board would have rejected as completely ludicrous and in appalling taste.

But Sinatra recorded this lumbering Gallic ballad in two takes, probably spliced together, in half an hour; he made light work of Anka's clumsy rhymes ("mention"/"exemption") but something rather powerful and individual of the "bit off more than I could chew" metaphor. The arrangement by **Don Costa** is suitably overblown and, towards the overstated end, compelling beyond any sense of reason.

"My Way" works, of course, because it's Sinatra being unbowed, unrepentant and arrogant; it's not Andy Williams singing "Moon River". "My Way" is popular song as inflated self-construction and Sinatra made it part of his legacy in a way that no one else in the history of entertainment could have done. In performance, the song was more like grand theatre than part of a concert.

Sinatra was cheered for it. Some of the excitement was undoubtedly because of the audiences' feelings for the beloved entertainer, but it may also have been from seeing the possibilities of such unfettered individuality. We too, the audience perhaps felt, could do it our way … if only we could be more like Frank.

But he did not like "My Way". "I loathe it," he said. "A Paul Anka pop song that became a kind of **national anthem**." Given that he belted it out every time he took the stage and basked in a standing ovation, this sounded like protesting too much, but in his mellow years he did appear to regret his association with the sentiment of the song. "He always thought that song was self-serving and self-indulgent," said his daughter Tina. By then, however, he was stuck with it.

46. **Send In The Clowns**

Written by Stephen Sondheim; arranged by Bill Miller; recorded February 5, 1976, in Hollywood; available on *The Reprise Years* (Reprise)

In its day "Send In The Clowns", from Stephen Sondheim's musical adaptation from 1973 of Ingmar Bergman's movie *Smiles Of A Summer Night*, was notoriously different and yet amazingly popular. Every cabaret chanteuse, jazz singer and adult pop artist introduced it into their set – as if tackling an arty Broadway ballad with oblique lyrics somehow conferred upon them instant class. Sung in the show by a faded femme fatale to a previously spurned lover, whom she realises she loves just as she loses him, the piece without context is certainly indirect, but by no means impenetrable.

Sinatra had two shots at recording it. The first, in 1973 on *Ol' Blue Eyes Is Back*, was reasonable, but appears bland next to what he taped after singing it in concert for three years. Aware that some still found the lyrics puzzling, he took it upon himself, in an unprecedented move for a Sinatra studio recording, to give **a spoken word introduction** with his own interpretation ("This is a song about a couple of adult people who have spent, oh, quite a long time together, till one day one of 'em gets restless and decides to leave"). Then, accompanied only by **Bill Miller**, who ebbs and flows on the piano, coming and going right there with the singer, Sinatra delivers one of his most dramatic song readings, full of vivid changes in tempo and intensity, and full of life and loss.

The ragged splendour of the bare Sinatra vocal working with a meaty text is so powerful that most Sinatra followers wish that Frank and Bill had recorded a whole album of similar material.

47. Theme From *New York, New York*

Written by John Kander and Fred Ebb; arranged by Don Costa; recorded September 19, 1979, in Los Angeles; available on *Trilogy* (Reprise)

First powered out by **Liza Minnelli** in Martin Scorsese's 1977 movie musical *New York, New York*, John Kander and Fred Ebb's song of determination in the big city was perfect for Sinatra, and was his biggest song during the latter part of his career. For many it is *the* Sinatra anthem, and he certainly felt a greater personal connection with "New York, New York" than with other show-stopping hits he had to trot out in his live shows, such as "My Way" and "Strangers In The Night". Its attitude – a potent mix of hope and arrogance – embodies the impulse to break out and be somebody; and who better to deliver the **uncannily autobiographical text** than the

Hoboken bum who became "king of the hill" and spent most of his life at the "very heart of it".

It was first flagged up as a possible number for Sinatra by his old right-hand man from the Capitol days, **Frank Military**. With the famous riff in place, Sinatra began performing Don Costa's arrangement as an opening number in the middle of 1978. Realising that it had more impact on an audience than was necessary for an opener, he pushed it further down the programme until eventually it replaced "My Way" as the climax of the set.

Sinatra recorded it in New York in August 1979, but in the following weeks he felt that he had made the number even more vibrant, and he recorded it again in Los Angeles in September. A gentle swinger that quietly gathers momentum and intensity as Sinatra tosses out his promises, it peaks in a dead stop three quarters of the way through, only to wind up again at a slower, deeper swing tempo that takes the music to a new level of exhilaration. The killer punch is all Sinatra: an audacious growling descent on "a-a-a-and" that, even if you've resisted the rest of it, has an astonishing, tingling power almost unmatched in his entire canon.

48. **Something**

Written by George Harrison; arranged by Nelson Riddle; recorded December 3, 1979, in Los Angeles; available on *Trilogy* (Reprise)

Sinatra survived one revolution: in the late 1950s **Elvis Presley** was the king of rock'n'roll, but Sinatra's movie career, shows at Vegas and record sales meant that he had remained near the top of the heap. But in the 1960s came **The Beatles**, and although they may have looked unusual, their songs were good and they were everywhere.

Eventually, in the wake of his success in 1966 with "Strangers In The Night" and "Somethin' Stupid", he became more relaxed about the new guard. Indeed, when **George Harrison** visited a recording session in 1968 Sinatra used it as a photo opportunity, cannily displaying the shot of himself and the Beatle and his wife on the back sleeve of his album of pop covers, *Cycles*. Paul McCartney's adult-friendly "Yesterday" (on the album *My Way*) was, predictably, Sinatra's first musical venture into Beatleland. Less predictably, his second was Harrison's "Something" (and as it turned out, it was his last).

Sinatra first recorded the song, arranged by Lennie Hayton with a rock beat and a swing refrain, just a year after it appeared on the Beatles' album *Abbey Road*. Released as a single at the end of 1970, it didn't chart, and when he sang it that year at the Royal Festival Hall, he announced afterwards, "Gee that's a good song, that 'Something'. If I ever learn it, It'll be a smash." On other occasions he demonstrated his lack of engagement with the younger generation by blithely crediting it to Lennon and McCartney.

By the time of *Trilogy* in 1979, he wanted another crack at what he described as "the best love song of the last 30 years", and asked **Nelson Riddle** to produce the score. Riddle – whose relationship with Sinatra had somewhat soured by this time – had already turned down the offer of arranging the whole of *The Past* album, but for an unknown reason agreed to do "Something". His dramatic colours, especially in the beautiful string segment before the reprise of the bridge and the gorgeous coda, put the song head and shoulders above most of *Trilogy* and made it reminiscent of his exemplary work on *The Concert Sinatra*.

Sinatra continued to perform the song proudly and heartily during the 1990s, with his own variations ("Something in the way she moves … me") and invariably dedicated it to his wife **Barbara**.

49. A Long Night

Written by Alec Wilder and Loonis McGlohon; arranged by Gordon Jenkins; recorded July 20, 1981, in New York; available on *She Shot Me Down* (Reprise)

The criticism that **Gordon Jenkins** received for his *Future* segment of *Trilogy* hurt him and Sinatra, and with the ageing arranger in ill health, Sinatra quickly commissioned an album of torch songs from him as a gesture of loyalty – a project that Sinatra's conductor of the time Vinnie Falcone called "Gordy's last stand". And although Sinatra released further long players (*L.A. Is My Lady* and the *Duets* albums) and continued performing for another twelve years, *She Shot Me Down* was his last stand too; it was certainly the last LP he made that emitted an aura of greatness.

Just as Jenkins was being saluted through *She Shot Me Down*, so was another old friend of Sinatra, **Alec Wilder**, who composed "A Long Night". He had died the year before this recording but would undoubtedly have been proud of Sinatra's reading of the song, a product of Wilder's later period of composing, the tone of which the conductor and composer Gunther Schuller described as "dark and anguished, reflecting a deep loneliness".

It's a tone that Jenkins makes the most of here, dressing the sprawling reflections of a deadbeat with stark strings and bluesy alto flute. Sinatra is grizzled and magnificent, relishing and releasing the grimness, and almost barking with defeat.

50. Mack The Knife

Written by Kurt Weill, Bertolt Brecht and Mark Blitzstein; arranged by Frank Foster; recorded April 16, 1984, in New York, available on *L.A. Is My Lady* on vinyl; and recorded October 30, 1986, in Los Angeles, available on *L.A. Is My Lady* on CD (Qwest) and on *The Reprise Collection* (Reprise)

In John Gay's **The Beggar's Opera** of 1728 Macheath was a swashbuckling gentleman highwayman, and by the time he re-appeared as Mack The Knife in Bertolt Brecht and Kurt Weill's **The Threepenny Opera** in 1928, he was a low-class "eat first-morals later" gangster, who is introduced by a menacing hurdy-gurdy song called "Moritat". Taking its name from "mord" meaning murder and "tat" meaning deed, it's a long series of sixteen-bar verses which describes Mack The Knife's crimes and introduces various other characters, heightening the anticipation of the entrance of Mack himself.

The translation of the original German by John Willett, often used in "authentic" productions of *The Threepenny Opera*, left all the grisly offences, including rape and murder, intact; but when **Mark Blitzstein** translated it for the revival of the show on Broadway in the 1950s, the arson that killed seven children disappeared. After Louis Armstrong realized the jazzy possibilities that the song presented, in 1960 **Bobby Darin** had a massive hit with it, even though he was singing about murder and characters whose names (Sukey Tawdry, Jenny Diver, et al) meant nothing out of theatrical context. The brassy swing arrangement, multiple key changes and cocky Vegas swagger of the Sinatra wannabe were irresistible.

So memorable were the earlier versions, Sinatra hesitated when it was suggested that he should cover the song on *L.A. Is My Lady*, but he was delighted when he heard the huge arrangement by **Frank Foster**, which referred to the previous versions and included an introduction to the musicians. It became a staple in the set and a new crowd-exciter as 70-year-old Sinatra "became" Mack – exuding the dangerous magnetism that film director Billy Wilder had once described as "like Mack the Knife is in town and the action is starting".

In 1986 he was singing the sprawling lyric with more bite and more life than his original recording, and went back into the studio to prove it. The terrific new version was premiered in 1990 on the 4-CD set *The Reprise Collection* and is also on the CD of *L.A. Is My Lady*. Only on dusty old vinyl copies of *L.A. Is My Lady* can the 1984 take be heard.

PART FOUR

Sinatra on Screen

The movies

"If you play yourself, you play something that reveals yourself. You peel off the onion skins and there you are. Frank did that; that's what Frank could do."

RICHARD ATTENBOROUGH

Despite his occasional triumphs as an actor, Sinatra's overall achievement on screen is generally thought to compare unfavourably with his singing career. He even ridiculed some of his films himself. "There have been a lot of movies in the career of Frank Sinatra, actor," he said on the TV special *Sinatra* in 1969. "Some terrible, but some *rotten*."

But a closer look reveals that there is more to Sinatra's screen career than is generally supposed, and a good deal more than anyone has the right to expect of a singer turned actor. For every corny performance, there's another that's true. For every walk-through character, there's another that's interesting. For every lackadaisical movie, there's another that's entertaining or significant. Sometimes he coasted, but other times he took risks, and his choice of roles, when he had the power to choose, is occasionally revealing. And, though he never made a decent Western, few actors have done equally creditable work in **four distinct genres**: musicals, comedies, dramas and thrillers.

But it's clear from the poor quality of some of the films that he allowed himself to make that he was interested only sporadically in film as a serious side to his artistic career. It didn't help that he hated hanging around a film set; the action just wasn't immediate enough for him. Consequently, when he had the power, he often forced the producer to adjust the schedule so that he could be around for as short a time as possible. This inevitably compromised the film; sometimes Sinatra had left the set when close-ups, re-shoots or overdubs were required. And even when he was around, he rarely rehearsed – he sensed that, as an intuitive performer, he needed adrenaline to deliver his best, and became known as **"One-Take Charlie"** for his belief that anything after the first take was going to be sub-standard. When he was good, he was usually very good, but if he was only okay, the scenes still had to go in, because there was no alternative.

Sometimes Sinatra's impatience was appreciated. **Stanley Kramer** had some trouble when directing him, but still described him as "a tremendously talented man, intuitive and fast". **Vincente Minnelli** even suggested that Sinatra's approach could benefit the production. "If you can get the company into Frank's fast tempo and enthusiasm and pace," the director said, "there are fewer shooting days and you spend less money."

But some professionals felt that his potential was unfulfilled. **Shirley MacLaine**, who starred with Sinatra in *Can-Can*, said, "He is about as naturally talented as anybody I've known ... The thing is, I wish he would work harder at what he's doing ... he won't polish. He feels polishing might make him stagnant." Even **Humphrey Bogart**, with whom Sinatra never appeared on screen, noticed that the singer spread himself thinly. "If he could only stay away from the broads and devote some time to developing himself as an actor," he observed, "he'd be one of the best in the business."

Here and there, Sinatra *was* one of the best in the business, and his filmography is a rich and varied one.

The films that have been released on DVD are marked with the symbol ⊙.

THE EARLY CAMEOS

Unbilled, non-acting

Major Bowes Amateur Theater Of The Air

RKO; directed by John H. Auer, released 1935

Sinatra, aged nineteen at the time, appeared twice in this series of shorts filmed at Biograph Studios in The Bronx, as a waiter in *The Nightclub* and as part of a blackface troupe in *The Big Minstrel Act*.

Las Vegas Nights

Paramount; Ralph Murphy, 1941

This minor musical comedy starring Bert Wheeler, known in Britain as *The Gay City*, features a few songs from The Tommy Dorsey Orchestra, but only one with Sinatra ("I'll Never Smile Again"), and even that is interrupted by the dialogue.

Ship Ahoy

MGM; Edward Buzzell, 1942

This time Sinatra has two songs – "The Last Call For Love" and "Poor You" – and a little more screen time. Eleanor Powell and Red Skelton star and the Dorsey orchestra forms part of the plot – they are hired along with Powell's dance group to perform on a floating nightclub in Puerto Rico – but Bert Lahr's eccentric comedy dominates the picture.

Reveille With Beverly

Columbia; Charles Barton, 1943

"Romance on the beam! Rhythm in the groove! Laughs on the loose!" according to the tagline. Future Sinatra co-star Ann Miller plays a record salesgirl who becomes a disc-jockey for soldiers. Sinatra is once more a minor singing attraction. But the word going round that Frankie could be seen crooning "Night And Day", backed by a host of chic female piano players, helped to make the picture a modest hit.

Higher And Higher

RKO; Tim Whelan, 1944

When rich and benevolent Cyrus Drake, played by **Leon Errol**, becomes bankrupt, his loyal servants pose as debutantes in an attempt to ensnare a rich husband – and one prospect is a **Mr Frank Sinatra**, who lives next door. Frankie doesn't do much except show his face, sing four songs uninterrupted this time by dialogue and make the girls in the film (and the cinema) swoon. But enough of his charisma is evident for even a modern audience to get a sense of the crooner's doe-eyed sexual magnetism.

Higher and Higher was originally a Richard Rodgers and Lorenz Hart musical, but their material was replaced by songs by **Jimmy McHugh** and **Harold Adamson**, two of which – "I Couldn't Sleep A Wink Last Night" and "A Lovely Way To Spend An Evening" – would be wartime hits for Sinatra. Another, "I Saw You First", the twinkly duet with **Marcy McGuire**, showed that there was already more to Frankie than being a romantic idol. But it's his performances of the two ballads, and a third, "The Music Stopped", that mesmerize: his soulful, elegant commitment to the romantic material has genuine visual impact. Even the respected writer James Agee wrote of the final moments, when Sinatra is supported only by clouds, as "an effect which can only be described in the … terms of an erotic dream". He also said that Sinatra "has weird fleeting resemblances to Lincoln, which I think may help out in the audience subconscious". *Variety*, on the other hand, was grudging: "At least he gets in no one's way."

Step Lively

RKO; Tim Whelan, 1944

Playing someone other than himself for the first time, Sinatra was slightly better in *Step Lively*, a remake of the Marx Brothers vehicle **Room Service**. As Glen Russell, a playwright who can sing and ends up starring in a musical, he does a reasonable job at reacting blandly to the loud, hammy characters around him, and he has a modest range of emotional states to play; sulky (when he feels cheated), drunk (when slipped a Mickey Finn) and love-struck (whenever the RKO starlet **Gloria De Haven** is around). He even gets the girl, with whom he shares his first screen kiss – and he's certainly more appealing than the future Republican senator **George Murphy**, who as the charmlessly slick producer and dancer Gordon Miller seems never to be off the screen.

The film has a good score by **Jule Styne** and **Sammy Cahn**, much of which was never commercially released. "As Long As There's Music" is as rich a popular song as was written at the time, while "Where Does Love Begin?" and "Some Other Time" (not to be confused with the Bernstein/Comden/Green song from *On The Town*) are not far behind. Their ambition to create art is a little out of place in this old-fashioned backstage romp – the production number "Come Out, Come Out, Wherever You Are" is more in keeping with the tone – but Sinatra performs the songs beautifully.

Anchors Aweigh

MGM; George Sidney, 1945; ⊙US

Anchors Aweigh is considered by most, including Sinatra himself, to be his first proper movie. An **MGM** musical extravaganza in glorious Technicolor, it was a box-office smash, when his previous two films curiously weren't, and was nominated for five Oscars, **George E. Stoll** winning one for his musical direction. In retrospect it's an overlong forerunner of the tighter, hipper *On The Town* – both feature sailors on leave singing songs and winning girls – but there's plenty of frothy fun to enjoy. **Gene Kelly** dances with cartoon mouse Jerry; Kelly and Sinatra deliver three comedy duets; Sinatra sings "What Makes The Sun Set?" to a candle in a restaurant as the Brooklyn-born waitress, played by **Pamela Britton**, falls in love with him; and he then sings the superb "I Fall In Love Too Easily" at the piano in an empty Hollywood Bowl when he realizes he loves her. (The conductor and pianist José Iturbi is fabulously smug but possibly one square star too many.)

While Kelly, who was third-billed, is bright-eyed and super-powered, top-billed Sinatra, on loan from RKO, despite being 28 when filming, portrays the "dope" **Clarence "Brooklyn" Doolittle** as a boy of 18. It's here that he establishes the immature-but-loveable figure that became familiar as his screen persona in several other movies: the character who is painfully bashful and unworldly, except when he sings a love song, of course, when he becomes swoonsome and authoritative. It may have been logical to exploit Sinatra's perceived vulnerability as a singer by casting him as faint-hearted, but today the character comes across as dim-witted.

The Kelly-Sinatra relationship on the screen is a reflection of what was happening on the set. "Sometimes I see you," Sinatra's character tells Kelly's after he has been particularly assertive, "and I wonder what's wrong with me." And the inexperienced Sinatra barely knew what he was doing, but Kelly patiently guided him through the dance routines that he had choreographed, diluting the complexity to make his co-star look good.

Sinatra's status in Hollywood as a relative newcomer did not, however, stop him from throwing his weight around. Offered his choice of composers, he insisted on Jule Styne and Sammy Cahn, despite the objections of the producer, **Joe Pasternak**. He also insisted on seeing the "dailies" at the end of each shoot, much to Pasternak's consternation, particularly when Sinatra turned up with an entourage. Impatient with the schedule, he was overheard complaining that "pictures stink, and the people in them too". It was reported in the media and thus began Sinatra's reputation for truculence.

The House I Live In

RKO; Melvin LeRoy, 1945

A ten-minute short scripted by **Albert Maltz**, who was later blacklisted by the House Un-American Activities Committee, *The House I Live In* features Sinatra as himself, recording "If You Are But A Dream" before going outside the studio for a cigarette and catching a gang of street kids persecuting a Jewish boy. He then lectures them on tolerance, invoking the inter-racial cooperation needed for the war effort. The only person to whom racial or religious differences matter, he tells them, is "a Nazi, or someone as stupid … a first-class fathead". He then sings the title song, a portentous hymn in which details of American living are presented as evidence of the country's democratic ideal: small-town friendliness in a tolerant, multi-racial society. It was one of the most important moments in Sinatra's life.

Made at a time when a liberal message could still be allied comfortably to one that was breast-beating and patriotic, the film firmly established Sinatra as a mouthpiece for modern, democratic views. It was much applauded by those who concurred – though it was taken by others as further proof of Sinatra's subversive "communist" leanings – and all proceeds were distributed to anti-delinquency programmes and charities. It earned **a special Academy Award** at the Oscars in 1946 and Sinatra re-created the whole film in the television studio four years later on *The Frank Sinatra Show*. "That's a fine piece of material," he proudly announced. "I wouldn't mind doing that every week."

Till The Clouds Roll By

MGM; Richard Whorf (with Vincente Minnelli and George Sidney), 1946; ⊙ US, UK

In this icky, all-star biopic of the composer **Jerome Kern**, Sinatra makes a climactic guest appearance singing "Ol' Man River". With the singer in a white suit, on a white pillar, with a white-clad 100-piece orchestra and choir on a ludicrous fairytale set floating in the clouds, justice is hardly done to the bleak toil of Oscar Hammerstein's text; but this grotesquely inappropriate scenario was the most glamorous presentation of Sinatra that would ever be seen.

It Happened In Brooklyn

MGM; Richard Whorf, 1947

By this time a star, on contract to MGM, Sinatra again teams up with Jule Styne and Sammy Cahn, and with **Kathryn Grayson**, who appeared in *Anchors Aweigh*; and again he fails to get her, this time losing out to **Peter Lawford** and ending up once more with a girl who is down-to-earth (on this occasion, Gloria Grahame). The real partnership of the film, however, is between Sinatra and **Jimmy Durante**, who thump their way through "The Song's Gotta Come

From The Heart" and "I Believe" with genuine relish. Sinatra is increasingly convincing as the centrepiece of a movie and also gets to croon "The Brooklyn Bridge" and the big ballad of the picture, **"Time After Time"**. But in a duet with the classically-trained Grayson, "La Ci Darem La Mano" from Mozart's *Don Giovanni*, he limps phonetically through the Italian libretto.

It was during this film that Sinatra went missing while he assisted **Phil Silvers**, who had just lost his regular partner and was struggling to regain his confidence, as a temporary stooge in his act at the Copa in New York. Sinatra's careless approach to schedules at other points during the shoot led to a reprimand from **Louis B. Mayer** and showbiz columnists. Sinatra responded with scorching telegrams that did his image no good at all.

It Happened In Brooklyn was quite well reviewed, but Lee Mortimer wrote that it "bogs down under the miscast Frank (Lucky) Sinatra, smirking and trying to play a leading man". It was for this, and other insults, that Sinatra thumped him in a Hollywood nightclub.

The Miracle Of The Bells

RKO; Irving Pichel, 1948

In almost his first non-singing role – there is only the charming *a cappella* "Ever Homeward" – Sinatra is cast as a priest who endorses a fake "miracle", the turning of the statues of St Michael and the Virgin Mary to face the coffin of a dead actress, played by Alida Valli. This is in order to persuade a reluctant producer, played by **Lee J. Cobb**, to release the actress's last film for the sake of her former sweetheart. The Sinatra camp may have been hoping for the same popular acclaim that **Bing Crosby** received when he played a man of God in the Oscar-winning *Going My Way* and *The Bells Of St Mary's*; or at least to offset some of the disastrous publicity from the breaking story about Sinatra meeting the exiled Mafia boss **"Lucky" Luciano**, which led Sinatra's publicist George Evans to announce that he was donating his $100,000 fee to the Church. But the film was savaged, and so was Sinatra. *Monthly Film Bulletin* described the movie as "an offensive exhibition of vulgar insensitivity" while *Time* called Sinatra's priest "rather flea-bitten ... with the grace and animation of a wooden Indian".

Sinatra blamed RKO, to whom MGM had loaned the star to fulfil his old contract. To punish them for insisting he attend the premiere, he used his expense account to overspend on clothes, gallons of unconsumed alcohol and a piano that was delivered to his suite at four in the morning.

The Kissing Bandit

MGM; László Benedek, 1948

In what is undoubtedly the nadir of Sinatra's film career, he reprises his bumbling Clarence Doolittle act, but in tighter trousers, playing a nineteenth-century business school graduate who reluctantly attempts to follow in his father's footsteps as a Spanish Californian bandit and ladies' man. When daughter Nancy gave birth to Sinatra's first grandchild, in 1974, he said, "All I ask is that Nancy never let the child grow up and see *The Kissing Bandit*."

But as a **so-bad-it's-good** movie, it has its moments. Ann Miller's dance of jealousy has a bit of fizz and two songs by Nacio Herb Brown are lovely: "Siesta", a sleepy comedy number, and "Señorita", a love song which Sinatra sings to **Kathryn Grayson**. In their third film together, he finally gets her – "We've dilly-dallied long enough", he says, unconvincingly – but by then, most viewers won't care.

Take Me Out To The Ball Game

MGM; Busby Berkeley, 1949; ☉ US

Sinatra is back with **Gene Kelly** in a reprise of their *Anchors Aweigh* double act and love triangle, this time with **Esther Williams** at the apex, replacing the original choice, Judy Garland. The musical, composed by Roger Edens, Adolph Green and Betty Comden, is set in the 1890s but combines with real panache late 1940s Hollywood, baseball and the energy and style of vintage variety entertainment. Kelly, as Eddie O'Brien, is at his beefy, bossy best; and **Jules Munshin**, as Nat Goldberg, is brought in for mincing and grimacing – not that the film needed any extra with Kelly in ultravaudeville mode. Sinatra's character, however, is treated almost entirely as a figure of fun; O'Brien is dismissive of him to the point of cruelty, Goldberg is friendly but patronizing, and Betty Garrett's predatory Shirley Delwyn picks him up in her arms like a doll. Sinatra, playing his familiar dumb part with more dramatic poise and comic feeling than he did in *Anchors Aweigh* four years previously, even generates a couple of genuine laughs, with his ineffectual waving to attract the heroine's attention and his earnest question: "Are you sure they're talking about me?"

He certainly works hard. He hoofs with Kelly through the ancient waltz "Take Me Out To The Ball Game" well enough, plays a neat straight-man to Kelly's camp antics through the litany of near-seductions during "Yes, Indeed" and just about keeps up with Kelly and Munshin during the extravagant set-piece **"O'Brien To Ryan To Goldberg"**. But it feels as if neither studio nor singer has as much confidence as in previous films in Sinatra's romantic balladeering. His one love song, "The Right Girl For Me", is pitched in a conspicuously low key, as if Sinatra were scared of exposing himself to the high notes, while another, "Boys And Girls Like You And Me", was cut altogether.

Take Me Out To The Ball Game is solid, entertaining, knowing MGM fare – complete with a winking chorus to the audience during the reprise of **"Strictly USA"** about the formulaic approach ("Kelly gets Williams, Sinatra gets Garrett") – and was quite successful. But how much longer could a ragged-looking 33-year-old who was losing his hair go on playing a gawky ingénu?

On The Town

MGM; Stanley Donen, Gene Kelly, 1949; ⊙ US

On The Town, which finally recognizes **Gene Kelly** in the credits as the leading man and auteur that he was, is not only the peak of the association between Kelly and Sinatra, but also one of the best of MGM's movie musicals.

It was adapted from the 1944 Broadway show written by the lyricists and actors **Adolph Green** and **Betty Comden**, and the brilliant young jazz-influenced composer **Leonard Bernstein**, and was an adaptation of

The movies

Fancy Free, his jazz ballet with the choreographer Jerome Robbins. The screen rights were bought by MGM before the show opened, but when it appeared, Louis B. Mayer was apparently disappointed with the lusty tone and arty music and shelved the project. When **Arthur Freed** was appointed head of production at MGM, however, Kelly – who was dying to dance to Bernstein's music – persuaded him that it was a suitable follow-up to *Take Me Out To The Ball Game* and *Anchors Aweigh*.

Based on three sailors with 24 hours' leave in New York, it was ideal for the Kelly-Sinatra-Munshin trio, a good excuse to get the bell-bottoms back on and a perfect opportunity for Kelly to continue exploring his dance fantasias. But there were still concerns about the score, and most of it was cut and replaced by new songs composed largely by Edens, Comden and Green that were unambitious but accessible. The effervescent opener **"New York, New York"** – a different song from the future Sinatra anthem – stayed put, however, and its combination of fast editing, exciting choreography, dazzling location footage and brash jazzy music from Bernstein creates four movie musical minutes that are exhilarating.

Sinatra and **Betty Garrett** (reprising her Sinatra-eating role in *Take Me Out To The Ball Game*, here as the wonderfully named Brunhilde Esterhazy) get the other Bernstein original, the ingenious "Come Up To My Place". Sinatra, though hanging on to his MGM contract by a thread, by now has his nervous virgin shtick down to a tee which – given his rampant behaviour off-screen – deserves at least some credit. And he does make a sweet job of the throwaway "You're Awful", a jokey love song that is the closest he's allowed to get to his swoonsome best.

But Kelly is the star here, with **Ann Miller** rivalling him for pizzazz, and in this company Sinatra can't help but look like a tired also-ran – which, at the time, he was.

"They Paint The Town With Joy!"

Tagline for On The Town

Double Dynamite

RKO; Irving Cummings, 1951; ⊙ US

The mediocre quickie made in 1948-49 with **Jane Russell** and **Groucho Marx** as *Money Isn't Everything* soon after *The Miracle Of The Bells* was initially shelved by RKO as substandard, and crept out nearly three years later as *Double Dynamite* to little effect. Groucho argued with Frank about his time-keeping and producer **Howard Hughes** argued with him about Ava Gardner, and as a result of the arguments between these two of her ex-suitors Sinatra was demoted to third on the bill.

Playing a straitlaced and uptight bank teller suspected of robbery, Sinatra's reaction when the "guy with the sunglasses" encourages him to bet thousands on a series of horse races is good comic panic, and Groucho gets a couple of zingers in, but there's nothing going on between Sinatra and Russell. That their bedtime duet, the sweetly swinging **"Kisses And Tears"**, is sung from separate rooms just about sums up their lack of chemistry. The other Styne/Cahn song, the witty "It's Only Money", is thrown away; sung with Groucho against an obviously false backdrop, it's symptomatic of the lack of care shown throughout the movie.

Meet Danny Wilson

Universal; Joseph Pevney, 1952

Simply because of where it comes in the trajectory of his life and career, *Meet Danny Wilson* is an underrated piece of Sinatrabilia. Trying to work when his private life was in crisis and his professional life was in turmoil, Sinatra was at his most volatile, ignoring Joseph Pevney's direction and falling out spectacularly with co-star **Shelley Winters**. Following a hurtful slanging match with Sinatra, she returned to the set only when his wife Nancy phoned and begged her to finish the picture. Sinatra was almost destitute and desperately needed his $25,000 fee to stop the bank repossessing the family home.

Despite these circumstances, his performance, as a successful singer who struggles to extricate himself from a punitive earnings deal with a hoodlum club owner, is persuasive. With his darker, troubled loner persona emerging, the Clarence Doolittle act is gone for good. And the songs – no fewer than nine of them – are mostly terrific. Arranger **Joseph Gershenson** puts established Columbia-era standards in sober swing settings in the style of George Siravo, and Sinatra responds with relaxed, jazzy performances that may not be as vocally powerful as his classic Capitol music but foreshadow it stylistically. Standout sequences include **"Lonesome Man Blues"**, written by Sy Oliver – a rare example of Sinatra singing a twelve-bar blues – a lovely version of "I've Got A Crush On You" with the black vocal group The Ebonaires and a ribald duet with Shelley Winters, "A Good Man Is Hard To Find".

Sinatra had high hopes for *Meet Danny Wilson*, booking himself and the picture into his old bobbysox stomping ground **the Paramount** – but the results were humiliatingly luke-warm. Many of the reviews damned Sinatra with faint praise and mentioned that the movie was remarkably similar to his own story. The critic from *Time* magazine wrote: "The story cribs so freely from the career and personality of Frank Sinatra that fans may expect Ava Gardner to pop up in the last reel."

It wasn't the right time or the right vehicle for the big comeback, but with Sinatra better than the script and the overall production, *Meet Danny Wilson* remains a valuable and fascinating item of transition.

From Here To Eternity

Columbia; Fred Zinnemann, 1953; ⊙ US, UK

Based on the James Jones novel set on a Hawaiian army camp just before the Japanese attack on **Pearl Harbour**, this adult melodrama concerning the lives and loves of the soldiers and their women entirely deserves its legendary status, largely because of the quality of acting. **Fred Zinnemann** draws career-best performances from **Montgomery Clift**, **Burt Lancaster** and **Deborah Kerr** that are intense and extraordinarily contained. To be noticed in such company, fifth-billed Sinatra had to be

good, but he's better than good; he's real. As the loveable tearaway Maggio, who likes his drink and his girls and is ready to take on the murderous Fatso (**Ernest Borgnine**), his fluid, funny performance bypasses acting entirely, heading straight into the realm of truth. He simply *is* Maggio.

Although he is celebrated for the spirited death scene that follows his escape from Fatso's prison beatings, Sinatra is equally striking when he bursts in, drunk, on Clift's private and the hooker played by **Donna Reed**. He briefly dominates the action with his surreal babble before leaving the pair with some booze and giving the audience some warmth.

The production team, having taken a risk in casting a singer with no training as an actor, was amazed by his work, which was based on a combination of instinct and obsession. "Sinatra dreamt, slept and ate his part," said the producer, **Buddy Adler**. "He has the most amazing sense of timing and occasionally he'll drop in a word or two that makes the line actually bounce … it was a case of a natural performer up against some great actors. The natural performer was better."

The result, of course, was **the Oscar for Best Supporting Actor** – and a whole new career.

Suddenly

United Artists; Lewis Allen, 1954; ⊙ US, UK

Another low-budget quickie, *Suddenly* is largely notable for Sinatra's role as **an out-and-out villain**. He plays a would-be assassin, John Baron, who holds hostage a retired FBI agent, his widowed daughter-in-law and her young son in a house that overlooks a station where the US President is due to disembark. Sinatra plays the assassin as austere, humourless and with little redeeming complexity – the unhappy war veteran is doing it for the money and to be somebody – and completely dominates the screen. His unpredictable, explosive cruelty is almost entirely responsible for keeping the tension taut in this claustrophobic little film.

While Sinatra undoubtedly welcomed the post-Maggio opportunity to play roles that were dark and layered, and although his reviews were good, the film itself was too bleak and controversial for wide acceptance and was not a success. In 1971 Sinatra heard that Lee Harvey Oswald had watched *Suddenly* a few days before **John F. Kennedy** was assassinated in 1963, and withdrew it from distribution and broadcast, just as after the assassination he withdrew *The Manchurian Candidate*. In the 1990s *Suddenly* became available on several discount labels.

Young At Heart

Warner; Gordon Douglas, 1954; ⊙ US, UK

A musical remake of the small-town drama *Four Daughters* from 1938, this type of down-home soap was old-fashioned even by the mid-1950s, but Sinatra's excellent cynical, weary performance gives *Young At Heart* some grit. Exuding a marvellously fatalistic self-pity, he plays a grouchy, pessimistic piano player, **Barney Sloan**, who is in the shadow of a handsome, successful songwriter, Alex Burke, played by Gig Young. The usual sunny performance from **Doris Day**, one of the biggest movie stars in Hollywood at the time, is pleasingly offset by Sinatra's black clouds, and the unlikely pair created something akin to chemistry – the first time he had managed it with a leading lady. And Sinatra's superb solo pieces – including **"One For My Baby"**, alone at a barroom piano with tilted hat and dangling cigarette – have iconic resonance and were central to establishing his mid-Fifties persona of the romantic, hip loner.

In the light of the endings of *From Here To Eternity* and *Suddenly*, Sinatra decided that the self-destructive Sloan should not perish after attempting suicide – he switches off his car windscreen wipers while driving through a snowstorm – but should instead survive to live and love. Sinatra's use of recently acquired influence resulted in some hasty rewriting and a risible final scene, in which Frank and Doris duet on the silly song he'd been trying to finish in the movie. (This was Jimmy Van Heusen and Mack Gordon's "You My Love": lovely tune, awful words.)

Sinatra's first single hit in years provided the film's title, but aside from glibly implying that a little love and a lighter attitude to life is all that depressives such as Barney Sloan need to survive, it has nothing to do with the film and seems sewn on to the opening and closing titles. This, and its pervading sentimentality, means that the movie is often underrated; Sinatra's scenes are among the best he filmed.

Not As A Stranger

United Artists; Stanley Kramer, 1955

Not As A Stranger, a long, solemn adaptation of the best-selling novel by **Morton Thompson**, was part of the post-*Eternity* rush of work that Sinatra felt compelled to do to capitalize on his burgeoning reputation as an actor. **Robert Mitchum** has most of the fun, playing an unscrupulous, emotionally distant surgeon, Lucas Marsh, who marries a surgical nurse, played by Olivia de Havilland, for her money; has an affair with a horse breeder played by Gloria Grahame; and bungles an operation to save his medical mentor, before returning to his wife, vulnerable and humbled.

Sinatra played Marsh's best friend, which was a gentle role in one of his duller films, but his socializing with Mitchum made up for this. After one particularly drunken evening they demolished Sinatra's dressing room, and **Stanley Kramer**, the film's director, despite recognizing Sinatra's talent, vowed never to work with him again.

The Tender Trap

MGM; Charles Walters, 1955

Sinatra's first comedy as a mature leading man, on his return to MGM, *The Tender Trap* was the film that firmly established the flipside of his Barney Sloan loser-in-love persona: the bachelor who was singing an upbeat tune and adored by a bevy of women. He is roguishly attractive as Charlie Y. Reader, the playboy theatrical agent who sees as a challenge the conquest of Julie Gillis, played by **Debbie Reynolds**. "You know more about how to please a lady than any man on the eastern seaboard," she coos, before asking, "How many girls are there in your life?" If Sloan in *Young At Heart* is the character who might have sung *In The Wee Small Hours*, *The Tender Trap* features the Sinatra of *Swing Easy* and *Songs For Swingin' Lovers!*. As was true of his records, Sinatra's films seemed to reflect other aspects of his life during this period.

Based on the hit play by **Max Shulman** and **Robert Paul Smith**, the film is a little staged and slow, but it has its funny moments – such as Charlie's foiled attempts to canoodle with Julie in front of the TV – before everything is wrapped up neatly in the morality of the time. Sinatra's hedonist Reader is tamed; the straying best friend, played by **David Wayne**, returns to his wife; and the ageing ex-girlfriend (of 27), played by **Celeste Holm**, is conveniently paired off with a distinguished stranger met in the lift. Viewers may wonder, however, why Sinatra's character would prefer Reynolds's perky controller to Holm's witty, sultry sophisticate.

Guys And Dolls

MGM; Joseph L. Mankiewicz, 1955; ⊙ US, UK

With Sinatra starring alongside **Marlon Brando** and **Jean Simmons**, the movie adaptation of the brilliant musical by **Frank Loesser** was keenly awaited. But *Guys And Dolls* is not as good as it could have been.

Based on the stories of **Damon Runyon**, the film presents the author's stylized New York setting well, with theatrical sets and vivid lighting, and much of the characteristically stilted dialogue intact. Sinatra does a reasonable job in the secondary role of the weak-willed, marriage-avoiding, crap-game fixer Nathan Detroit, matching theatre actors **Stubby Kaye** and **Vivian Blaine**, reprising their triumphant Broadway roles, for authentic idiosyncrasy.

However, in the lead role of Sky Masterson, Brando, a non-singing star, had the bulk of the musical material, and while he makes a fair attempt at

"I'll Know" and "Luck Be A Lady", his trickier songs were cut altogether. Conversely, to make better use of Sinatra's musical talents, his character was added to numbers he didn't sing in the original show, and a new Loesser song – the decidedly inferior **"Adelaide"** – was added specially. Brando has his moments – his dialogue with Sinatra in Mindy's restaurant is very funny – but it's hard not to wonder what Sinatra himself would have made of the role.

There was already a personality clash and resentful rivalry between the two stars, and the approach of **"One-Take Charlie"** conflicted with Brando's method acting. Sinatra, who had been beaten by Brando to the role of Terry Malloy in *On The Waterfront*, considered him overrated, and was furious to be left killing time on the set while Brando looked for the motivation of his character. "Don't put me in the game, Coach," he told the director from his trailer, "until Mumbles is through rehearsing." For their scene together in Mindy's that involved Sinatra eating cheesecake, Brando called for take after take, prompting Sinatra to walk off the scene. "These fucking New York actors!" he said. "How much cheesecake do you think I can eat?" Brando speculated that when Sinatra died "the first thing he'll do will be to find God and yell at him for making him bald".

SINATRA WITH KIM NOVAK IN THE MAN WITH THE GOLDEN ARM

The Man With The Golden Arm

United Artists; Otto Preminger, 1955; ⊙ US, UK

One of the most sensational films of its day, for tackling the subject of drug addiction, *The Man With The Golden Arm* is one of Sinatra's most interesting appearances on screen and contains one of his best performances. But the film is not an attempt at realism; the stilted dialogue, the patently studio-bound streets and the frenzied **Elmer Bernstein** big band score make the movie as stylized in its way as *Guys And Dolls*.

Sinatra stars as Frankie Machine, a Chicago poker dealer fresh from rehab who is struggling to give up the game and kick his heroin habit. The performances around him are as big and daft as if in silent melodrama – **Eleanor Parker** as his fake cripple wife Zosh, **Arnold Strang** as puppy-peddling sidekick Sparrow and **Darren McGavin** as drug-peddling villain Louie – but Sinatra holds the centre of the movie with a tormented stillness, and while he was praised for his harrowing cold turkey scenes, his quieter moments are no less impressive. Haunted by guilt for injuring his wife in a car accident and unable to resist the panacea of drugs, Frankie Machine produces a performance from Sinatra that is as focused as any he gave. **Otto Preminger** went for long takes so Sinatra had no choice but to dig deep and stay there, and while he doesn't do much – his eyes do most of the work – he is almost always on the screen and is mesmerizing throughout.

Preminger reportedly said of **Kim Novak**, who plays Molly, Frankie's girlfriend, "I know she can't act, but I want what she's got in my movie." But her sensual motherliness creates a credible foil for Sinatra's anguish, and on set Sinatra was unusually patient with her. "When he was working with beautiful blonde Kim, Sinatra didn't seem to be so eager to get away from the set," Preminger said. "Sometimes he would do twenty-five or thirty takes with Kim." Novak, who at the time was beginning an affair with Sinatra, said of her co-star, "I respect him more than any actor I've met; he's real, he's honest." She added, "That's why he gets into so much trouble."

The fireworks that were expected to be lit between the director and actor working together never were – though Preminger firmly deflected an early attempt by Sinatra to fire a cameraman – for although both were legendarily difficult there was mutual respect and they shared a sense of humour; Sinatra called the director "Herr Doktor" and Preminger called the singer Anatol, after a philandering character in a play by Arthur Schnitzler. And Sinatra worked hard, putting in 12-hour days and preparing rigorously in private; he even went to a clinic to observe a real junkie for research. "It was the most frightening thing I'd ever seen," he said. "I never want to see that again. Never." When it came to the cold turkey scene, Preminger expected to rehearse and do multiple takes, but Sinatra told him to keep the cameras rolling. "You'll get what you want, trust me," he said, before doing the long, distressing scene in a single take.

Finally beating Brando to a coveted role – Brando's agent waited for the entire script while Sinatra accepted having read only forty pages – Sinatra's performance was **nominated for an Oscar** and was widely regarded as his finest moment in acting. Even Sinatra himself considered the film noteworthy; "it says something," he said.

Johnny Concho

United Artists; Don McGuire, 1956

A psychological Western adapted from David Harmon's TV play *The Man Who Owned The Town*, *Johnny Concho* features Sinatra as the cowardly brother of a killed gunslinger who is forced to face up to his responsibilities. Laden with political symbolism, this flop was produced by Sinatra himself and it was the first time (but not, alas, the last) that he would treat film-making as an extension of his social life. He gave a part to his girlfriend at the time, **Gloria Vanderbilt**, but she did not appear – some say she left the movie because of her small part, others because she was hopeless – and she ended the romance. Even daughter Nancy, who can justify most of her father's doings, described it thus: "A bunch of the boys – Sinatra, McGuire, Riddle, Sanicola – got together and made a cowboy movie."

High Society

MGM; Charles Walters, 1956; ⊙ US, UK

In this plush and professional but only occasionally engaging musical adaptation of the 1940 movie *The Philadelphia Story*, Sinatra is billed below **Bing Crosby** and **Grace Kelly**, in the role that James Stewart had played: Mike Connor, the roving reporter with the roving eye. Sinatra gets one too many medium-strength Cole Porter numbers to sing to Kelly's Tracy Lord – "You're Sensational" is tolerable, "Mind If I Make Love To You" is dispensable – but the "Who Wants To be A Millionaire" duet with **Celeste Holm** is marvellous.

The highlight, however – and apparently the reason that Sinatra wanted to do the film, along with his $250,000 fee – is the duet with his old hero Bing on **"Well Did You Evah"**, a delightfully drunken musical joust that cheerily endorses handling encroaching bad news by having another drink. Conspicuously superior to the rest of the score, including the million-selling "True Love", sung by Crosby and Kelly, this number was the only song not written for the movie; it was originally sung in Porter's 1940 musical *Du Barry Was A Lady* by **Betty Grable** and *High Society* director **Charles Walters** in his acting days, and was reworked by Porter for the Sinatra/Crosby team.

Sinatra and Crosby, in their first extended project together, got on well, despite their differing temperaments: Frank's impatience on set led to the nickname "Dexedrine", after the stimulant, and Bing's relaxed approach earned him the sobriquet "Nembutal", after the sleeping pill. Meanwhile Sinatra was fascinated by and friendly with **Grace Kelly**, but there was no affair – perhaps out of respect for her recent engagement to Prince Rainier of Monaco and her alleged fling with Crosby during the filming of *The Country Girl* not long beforehand. Frank and Gracie (as he called her) remained friends until her death in 1982.

THE MID-CAREER CAMEOS

Meet Me In Las Vegas
MGM; Roy Rowland, 1956

In this cameo-laden romantic movie musical, Dan Dailey and Cyd Charisse play gamblers in Las Vegas; after a noisy slot-machine jackpot in the Sands hotel, an astounded player turns around to reveal himself as an unbilled Sinatra.

Around The World In Eighty Days
United Artists; Michael Anderson, 1956; ⊙ US, UK

Producer Mike Todd's star-studded three-hour extravaganza features Sinatra as the bowler-hatted piano player accompanying Marlene Dietrich's San Franciscan saloon singer.

Pepe
Columbia; George Sidney, 1960

The "Mexican Charlie Chaplin", Cantinflas, in a rare English-speaking role – another was Passepartout in *Around The World In Eighty Days* – plays Pepe, a horse-rearer who follows his beloved stallion Don Juan to Hollywood, where he meets an army of movie stars playing themselves; later, in Las Vegas, Sinatra and chums advise him on gambling.

The Road To Hong Kong
United Artists; Norman Panama, 1962; ⊙ US, UK

In the final and limpest Hope and Crosby "Road" movie, Joan Collins fills the glamour role vacated by the retired Dorothy Lamour (who also appeared in

The Pride And The Passion
United Artists; Stanley Kramer, 1957; ⊙ US, UK

A group of Spanish peasants led by Miguel (Sinatra) transports an enormous cannon across land and water in order to besiege a French-occupied fortress after the Napoleonic War. Assisting the effort is Captain

a cameo) and Sinatra appears in the final moments on the planet Plutonius as her spaceman boyfriend.

The List Of Adrian Messenger

Universal; John Huston, 1963

This decent mystery film, featuring George C. Scott and Kirk Douglas, is burdened by the gimmick of featuring heavily disguised stars in bit parts. Though their identities (Messrs Sinatra, Lancaster, Curtis and Mitchum) are "revealed" in the epilogue, it is believed that only here did they work for their $75,000 fee, with doubles being employed for the earlier scenes.

Cast A Giant Shadow

United Artists; Melville Shavelson, 1966; ⊙ US, UK

In this inflated biopic of Colonel "Mickey" Marcus, the American general who assisted the Israeli army in the war of 1948 (played by Kirk Douglas), Sinatra actually acts for a while, as an Israeli fighter pilot. Sinatra, sympathetic to Israel, was apparently hired to try to "unJewish" (according to Shavelson) a film about establishing a Jewish state.

The Oscar

Embassy; Russell Rouse, 1966

The Hollywood actor Frankie Fane, played by Stephen Boyd, steps on everyone to get ahead in his showbiz career and is convinced that he's about to win the best actor Oscar. Sinatra (playing himself) gets it instead.

Anthony Trumball (**Cary Grant**), a British naval officer who falls in love with Juana (**Sophia Loren**), Miguel's girlfriend.

This epic is spectacular and sprawling, over-scored by George Antheil and mostly plain silly. Stanley Kramer handles the action scenes well enough – the scale and physicality of the group's challenge is conveyed vividly – but as in many movies of the genre, the human side is unconvincing. Sinatra

brings a certain wounded-terrier quality to Miguel, but in sporting a fetching forward-comb wig and adopting a vaguely Hispanic accent (and it would not be until *Dirty Dingus Magee* in 1970 that he attempted a change of voice again), he makes himself hard to take seriously. Grant is stiffer than usual, Loren stands around and pouts and the result elicits more chuckles than it intends to.

Kramer had already faced Sinatra's unruly behaviour on *Not As A Stranger*, and found himself with problems again when shooting *The Pride And The Passion*. Sinatra had only taken the part to be with **Ava Gardner**, and when it was clear that there was to be no reconciliation, being stuck on location in Spain for four months was Frank's idea of hell. He made life so miserable for Kramer that the director agreed to film all Sinatra's scenes early in the shoot just to get him off the set.

The Joker Is Wild

Paramount; Charles Vidor, 1957

When Sinatra read Art Cohn's book about the entertainer **Joe E. Lewis**, an old friend with whom Sinatra shared an agent, he was struck by the powerful story and the opportunity to play an edgy role. He bought the rights before it was even published.

Lewis is portrayed accurately as a successful Chicago entertainer who is invited to work for the Mob, but refuses and has his face and throat cut, damaging his vocal cords. He develops an acerbic sense of humour and **Sophie Tucker** (the singer playing herself) gives him a break as a comic; from then on it's stardom, girls, gambling, booze and downfall, until he sees the error of his ways when talking to a ghostly reflection of himself in a series of shop windows.

The Joker Is Wild is popular with some fans, mainly because Sinatra sings and tells caustic jokes, and Lewis told Sinatra, "You had more fun playing my life than I had living it." But this is probably his least convincing role as a self-destructive deadbeat-with-a-heart.

Pal Joey

Columbia; George Sidney, 1957; ⊙ US, UK

If there's a single movie that comes close to conveying the charisma of Sinatra as a person and a performer, it's *Pal Joey*. Adapted from **Richard Rodgers** and **Lorenz Hart**'s musical of 1940, itself based on John O'Hara's seamy short stories, the property in its theatrical form was for many years considered too risqué for Hollywood. There was a plan in 1944 for a sanitized Columbia movie to star the original Broadway lead, **Gene Kelly**, with Rita Hayworth as the young chorus girl he ends up with, but it was shelved when Louis B. Mayer of MGM refused to lend Kelly to a rival studio. But a Broadway revival of the show in 1950, with a gentler tone, was a hit, and when the movie was made later in the decade the plot's racier aspects were implied rather than explicit.

Joey Evans is a singer and emcee who in the opening scene is arrested and thrown on a train for consorting with jailbait. After arriving in San Francisco he muscles his way into a job at a club, beds the chorus girls (with the exception of **Kim Novak**, who resists) and lures stripper-turned-lady Vera Simpson (**Rita Hayworth**) into bankrolling his dream nightclub, Chez Joey.

Sinatra is perfect as Evans, a heel who finds his heart. His borderline-offensive charm, accompanied by a hint of menace, makes its way with disarming ease into the heart of the viewer and of Vera Simpson. His sensual, steel-eyed delivery of **"The Lady Is A Tramp"** to the furred and jewelled Hayworth may be the most electrifying three minutes that Sinatra has ever filmed; afterwards Hayworth simply says, "Come now, beauty," and leads him out the door, and we know exactly what she means.

The score – a selection from various shows – is tremendous, and as arranged by **Nelson Riddle** is untypical in its jazziness for Hollywood musicals of the time. Hayworth's singing is dubbed but it doesn't really matter; she smoulders and smarts beautifully, performing "Zip" and her (implied) post-coital **"Bewitched, Bothered and Bewildered"** to teasing perfection. And the scenes with Sinatra and Hayworth – who was three years younger than Frank but playing a character who was supposed to be older than Joey – have a real mature sizzle about them, reflecting their experience and mutual regard. "To me, Rita Hayworth *is* Columbia," Sinatra said. "They may have made her a star, but she gave them class." Hayworth said, "Working with Frank was electric. He really got into that part." By comparison, Novak as the virginal dumb blonde is outclassed.

In an interview to promote the film, Sinatra recounted a potentially tricky meeting with the studio. "We talked things out," he recalled, "and

SINATRA'S STYLE

When Sinatra sang "you've either got or you haven't got style" in *Robin And The 7 Hoods*, it was with the light-hearted confidence of a man who'd got it. And he'd always had an eye for natty threads. While growing up he earned the nickname "Slacksie", and the charge account he had at **Geismer's department store**, set up by his mother, encouraged him to see certain items of clothing as "spiffy, nifty and swell". Later he would confess to being "a symmetrical man, almost to a fault" and that "my clothing must hang just so". This is a man who would have two men lower him into his trousers before taking the stage so that they would have no creases.

His sense of style changed with the times. In the 1940s Sinatra, standing at around 5ft 10in, wore big double-breasted jackets with shoulder pads, baggy trousers and **floppy bow ties**. These raffish accessories near the top of an unfeasibly slender frame, often sewn by Nancy, became icons in themselves.

In the 1950s his style was visible in **his suits**. More than one hundred and fifty of them were cut for him by Sy Devore, tailor to the stars, or Carroll & Co, both of Beverly Hills, and he had rules about colours: no brown to be worn after dark, but only black or, at a push, dark grey. His favourite suit was the sharp one he wore in *Pal Joey*, and to show it off in the promotional shots he slung his coat over his shoulder. In the 1960s he imported his suits from Savile Row. (In private Sinatra displayed a penchant for pastel colours; his clothing could be pink, lilac or lavender. But his favourite colour was orange; a typical example is the jumper that he wears in his first scenes in *Ocean's 11*.)

And then there were **the hats**. Sinatra had dabbled with them since childhood. But in the 1950s they became a permanent feature – partly as a tribute to the style of Humphrey Bogart, partly as a way of covering his receding hair – and iconic. He wears a snap-brim of some description on fifteen of his twenty Capitol album covers, at a variety of angles, and expressing different moods: the hat perches sprily on *Swing Easy*, is pushed back in open-hearted resignation on *In The Wee Small Hours* but points straight ahead on the winking face of *Come Dance with Me!*, a

then I saw an uneasy look coming into the faces of the Cohn braintrust and Harry [Cohn] himself. I don't like frightened people and I don't like being frightened myself. So I asked, 'What's the trouble?' All were afraid to talk up. 'If it's billing,' I said, 'it's OK to make it Hayworth/Sinatra/Novak. I don't mind being in the middle of that sandwich.' Man were they relieved."

bullish part of Sinatra's confident invitation. "It was like an extension of him," said Nancy.

And then came **the tuxedos**. "There is no better Sinatra," ran the album liner notes of *The Main Event*, "than the Sinatra in a tuxedo." He wore a beautiful white tux for his Hollywood Bowl appearance in 1943, but in the Vegas years he stuck to black. He told the author Bill Zehme that "a tuxedo is a way of life" – and shared some tips. "My basic rules are to have shirt cuffs extend half an inch from the jacket sleeve. Trousers should break just above the shoe. Try not to sit down because it wrinkles the pants. If you have to sit, don't cross your legs." This would elevate his performance into a formal occasion. Sinatra knew that if he walked onto the stage in anything else he would diminish himself and disappoint his audience.

In the late 1960s, when fashions changed, Frank dallied with the prevailing styles: a white polo neck here (on the cover of his 1968 Christmas album), some love beads there (on *Francis Albert Sinatra Does His Thing*) and even a Nehru jacket (also on this 1968 TV special). All were brought off with some dignity. But in the 1970s, after his comeback, there were disappointments: big open collars flapping over shapeless sweatshirts emblazoned with "Ol' Blue Eyes Is Back"; dowdy baseball caps, as far too many photographs demonstrated; and an appalling $3 golf hat on the cover of *Some Nice Things I've Missed*. It was good to see Frank so relaxed, but this inclination towards everyman leisurewear did not suit the Chairman of the Board.

During the concert years from 1974 until 1994, the tuxes stayed – but **the wigs** got worse. They weren't too bad in the 1950s and 1960s: discreet widow's peaks or grown-out crew cuts. He even went without for a time, in the early 1960s, but soon afterwards came the comb-over, which got shorter at the end of the decade and shaggier in the 1970s. By the 1980s his rug had evolved into a brushed-forward silver rake that was extremely distracting.

But even on stage in his latter years, when wielding his microphone and whipping the cord, immaculately tuxedoed, he continued to cut a geriatric dash.

Some Came Running

MGM; Vincente Minnelli, 1958; ⊙ US

In a mannered melodrama based, like *From Here To Eternity*, on a novel by **James Jones**, Sinatra plays Dave Hirsh, an army veteran and lapsed writer, who is returning to his hometown to face his brother Frank (an ebullient and artificial **Arthur Kennedy**), and to drink and gamble with the insouciant Bama Dillert (played perfectly by **Dean Martin**). **Shirley MacLaine** refined her adorable floozy act, first seen in the 1956 Jerry Lewis/Dean Martin film *Artists And Models*; and Sinatra is good when suspicious of his brother and disapproving sister-in-law and when, in an effective reprise of Barney Sloane, slumped in bitter lack of self-belief.

But the self-conscious direction by **Vincente Minnelli** – everything is in medium shot, presumably to indicate the "space" between the characters – in some scenes leaves Sinatra stranded. The occasions when he attempts to seduce **Martha Hyer**'s repressed, conflicted teacher, who adores his writing but is disturbed by his passionate attention, are among the least convincing love scenes he ever made; he moves stiffly from one tableau to the next, struggling to hit his mark. There are some moments of real humanity, especially between Sinatra and MacLaine, and his scenes with Martin have genuine tough-buddy chemistry, but there's an air of pretentiousness that isn't quite warranted by the movie's style or substance.

Sinatra did his friends a favour on this one. He got the part for Martin, who, still looking for a niche after his partnership with Jerry Lewis ended in 1956, buttonholed Frank at a party, bullishly suggesting himself for the role of Dillert: "You're hunting a guy who smokes, drinks, and can talk real Southern? You're looking at him." Sinatra agreed, and though he had known Martin in the 1950s, this first experience of acting together cemented their friendship. Shirley MacLaine also benefited from **Sinatra's power**: he insisted that her character, rather than his, was shot at the end, thereby drawing more attention to her role, and her performance gained an Oscar nomination. Martha Hyer was also nominated, as were Jimmy Van Heusen and Sammy Cahn for the song "To Love And Be Loved".

Kings Go Forth

United Artists; Delmer Daves, 1958; ⊙ US, UK

Sinatra plays an appealingly passive role for much of *Kings Go Forth*, one of the few serious parts after *From Here To Eternity* where he isn't the protagonist. Based on the novel by **Joe David Brown**, the story concerns two American soldiers stationed in southern France during the "champagne campaign" clean-up at the close of World War II and features a sub-plot of inter-racial romance. As Lieutenant Sam Loggins, Sinatra spends the first half of the film quietly fuming, watching as the half-cast girl Monique whom he loves (played by **Natalie**  **Wood**) is swept off her feet by Corporal Britt Harris (an exhilarating **Tony Curtis**).

But while Curtis's Harris creates the film's action, Sinatra's Loggins is its moral centre. The scene where Loggins greets Harris returning late from a night of passion with Monique is typical of their relationship; Harris fidgets and fudges while Loggins's agony is expressed through stony stillness and a hawkish stare. The scene that later shifts the energetic impulse of the story is one that Curtis said was the most difficult of his acting career; Harris is forced to admit to a shattered Monique that he has no intention of marrying her, and tells Loggins that having a black girl was simply "a new kind of kick" for him. Loggins decks Harris and all the energy emanates from him thereafter.

Curtis described the ending as "nicely ambiguous", but it has most viewers howling for an explanation. With Harris having died on a mission, Loggins returns to France after the war to find Monique. He has lost an arm, she is a schoolteacher. Fade to black.

Kings Go Forth has weaknesses – Wood is unconvincing and the "message" of the film remains elusive – but it is an unusual movie with substance and nuance. Although the film was consistent with Sinatra's liberal credentials of the time, he claimed to take the part "as a performer, not as a lecturer on racial problems".

Never So Few

MGM; John Sturges, 1959

Never So Few, a World War II yarn based on the novel by **Tom T. Chamales** about the US soldiers and guerrillas fighting the Japanese in Burma, is richly scripted, but **John Sturges**'s direction is flat; the jungle battle scenes never convince and neither does the acting. It's obvious, however, why Sinatra would have been attracted to the role: he plays Tom Reynolds, a maverick army captain whose rebellious ways reach a controversial peak when he crosses from Burma into China. Discovering that the US is being betrayed by a corrupt arms deal involving the Japanese and the government of Chiang Kai-Shek, he orders the execution of his Chinese prisoners and tells his superiors to "go to hell". But when he is court-martialled, he beats the rap, his nonconformist ways exonerated.

Unfortunately, it's not one of his best performances; Sinatra seems neither tough enough to convince in the army, nor ardent enough when trying to woo **Gina Lollobrigida**. His slow-burn furnace is misplaced here: more flames are needed. As Corporal Bill Ringa, the individualist gin-brewing driver-turned-fighter (a role intended for **Sammy Davis Jr.** – see page 114), a young **Steve McQueen** brings a different kind of cool to the screen – one that in the following decade overshadowed Sinatra's brand – and quietly steals the film.

A Hole In The Head

United Artists; Frank Capra, 1959; ⊙ US, UK

Comedy and sentiment sit together slightly uneasily in *A Hole In The Head*, which is far from vintage **Frank Capra**. His penultimate movie displays some of his customized warm-heartedness and optimism, but a little clumsily when compared with his masterpiece from 1946, *It's A Wonderful Life*.

Sinatra plays the widowed Miami hotelier Tony Manetta, who is charming but romantically and financially reckless. He's answerable to his elder sibling Mario, played by **Edward G. Robinson**, who offers to bail his younger brother out of debt if he gets married to nice Mrs Rogers, played by **Eleanor Parker**. The unlikely denouement has the workaholic Mario announcing his retirement, agreeing with no warning that Tony's free-spirited approach to life may have something to it after all.

Tony's interplay with his smart 11-year-old son (nicely played by **Eddie Hodges**), culminating in a sweet performance of the Oscar-winning song **"High Hopes"**, demonstrates Sinatra's rarely shown affinity with youngsters. The best thing about the movie, however, is Cahn and Van Heusen's theme song **"All My Tomorrows"**, sung by Sinatra over the opening titles.

Can-Can

20th Century Fox; Walter Lang, 1960

Although Cole Porter's stage musical *Can-Can* in 1953 preceded the movie of the similarly Gallic *Gigi* by several years, it was the success of the Lerner/Loewe movie musical that precipitated the filming of *Can-Can*. Set in 1890s Paris and concerning the banning of the notoriously risqué dance, it reunites **Louis Jourdan** and **Maurice Chevalier** from *Gigi* and adds Rat Packers Sinatra and **Shirley MacLaine**, who was given the role after Marilyn Monroe rejected it to star in *Some Like It Hot*. It also features the dancer **Juliet Prowse**, whom Sinatra began dating during filming.

Chic on the surface, the film's dance sequences provide the required sizzle but many of the songs are mundane and the acting – particularly Sinatra's – lacks sparkle. He made the film, for which he received $200,000 and a slice of the profits, as part of his obligation to Fox after walking off the set of *Carousel* in 1955 (see page 353) and it was the kind of apathetic performance from Sinatra that became all too familiar in the coming decade.

The film received some valuable publicity when **Nikita Khrushchev**, the prime minister of the Soviet Union, visited the set, watched the filming of the dance of the title and pronounced it "immoral". If only it were that interesting.

THE RAT PACK MOVIES

"Of course they're not great movies, no one could claim that … but every movie I've made through my own company has made money."
FS, 1962

Ocean's 11
Warner; Lewis Milestone, 1960; ⊙ US, UK

Sergeants 3
United Artists; John Sturges, 1962

4 For Texas
Warner; Robert Aldrich, 1963; ⊙ US

Robin And The 7 Hoods
Warner; Gordon Douglas, 1964; ⊙ US

It was an understatement when Sinatra said that the Rat Pack films were "not great movies"; they are positively poor. As insouciant entertainment gods at **Las Vegas**, these men could amble around on the stage of the Sands and light up the boozy place; but on screen the breeziness comes over as shabby underperformance. The tone is set by Sinatra himself; he instigated and starred in the films but made it clear that he was interested in them only as a bit of fun and easy money. If "the Leader" didn't care how good the movies are, how good can they be? Despite their talented stars, the Rat Pack movies are barely even entertaining; at best they contain a whiff of the cool appeal these men could have, but at worst they are a smug, charmless con.

Ocean's 11, a heist movie in which Sinatra and chums rob several Vegas casinos simultaneously, was released at the height of the Rat Pack's glamorous notoriety and did tremendous business. It has its moments: the touching marriage-on-the-rocks exchange between Sinatra and Angie

Dickinson; Dean Martin singing "Ain't That A Kick In The Head", Sammy Davis Jr. singing "Ee-o Eleven"; and the scene where the besuited gang stroll numbly up the Strip after their ill-gotten gains have been incinerated, which has an iconic hum about it and was clearly recalled in Quentin Tarantino's *Reservoir Dogs*. But Sinatra generally interfered with the production to suit himself, rewriting some scenes while they were being shot and inserting others for pals' cameos, and this inevitably brings an indulgent capriciousness to the movie, killing the pace and making it seem as if it would have been more fun to be in than it is to watch.

Sergeant's 3, featuring Sinatra, Martin, Davis, Peter Lawford and Joey Bishop and directed by John Sturges, is a spoofy transfer of *Gunga Din* from nineteenth-century India to the American West. Although it has its fans among Rat Pack devotees who remember it from when it was released, it remains unseen by most of the rest of the world. Presumably the moguls are too embarrassed to make it available.

4 For Texas features tedious Western larks, and The Three Stooges, as Sinatra and Martin fight for control of nineteenth-century Galveston's gambling and girls (Ursula Andress and Anita Ekberg). With two coasting stars and a director who is sluggish at the best of times, the film is swollen and unfunny.

Robin And The 7 Hoods, a dragging gangster comedy, suffered from Sinatra's interference in the same way that *Ocean's 11* did, to the extent that the original director, Gene Kelly – who wanted more songs in the film than Sinatra could be bothered to rehearse – walked off the picture. It's not without its bright spots – Bing Crosby is a welcome presence and Sammy Davis Jr.'s "Bang Bang" number has a certain excitement to it – but few of them have anything to do with Sinatra. The film is seen by some as a winking tribute to **Sam Giancana** and by others as a symbolic turn away from him – the final message is "Don't Be A Do-Badder".

The Devil At 4 O'Clock

Columbia; Mervyn LeRoy, 1961; ⊙ US

A disaster movie with elevated themes – faith, bigotry, moral relativism – *The Devil At 4 O'Clock* is a peculiar film that manages to engage and even move the viewer despite a clunky script, an indifferent performance by Sinatra and poor special effects. He plays a convict stuck on an erupting volcanic island who chooses not to take the boat to safety but instead to accompany the local priest on a rescue mission to a cut-off leper hospital. He gets to do things that should be memorable (attempting to seduce a blind girl, losing his life so others can have theirs) but his character is underdeveloped; there is little sense of who he is or what he's up to. Sinatra, keen as ever to finish his scenes as quickly as possible, must take some of the blame.

Luckily, **Spencer Tracy**, as the maverick man of the cloth Father Doonan, is an astounding presence and acts everyone else off the screen. It's his conviction – he nearly became a Catholic priest – that holds the audience and ignites the story. Sinatra was in awe of him as an actor – and Tracy was suitably impressed by the singer's supremacy in the film business. "Nobody at Metro," Tracy told reporters at the time, "ever had the financial power Sinatra has today." It's a shame he didn't use that power more wisely.

The Manchurian Candidate

United Artists; John Frankenheimer, 1962; ⊙ US, UK

The Manchurian Candidate, the brilliant Cold War thriller and political satire based on the novel by **Richard Condon**, demonstrates what Sinatra could do with his power. And in contrast to his efforts on the Rat Pack movies, Sinatra – trusting the professionals around him and sensing the importance of the piece – did his job obediently and brilliantly, and the result was his finest movie.

It nearly didn't get made. **John Frankenheimer** and the scriptwriter **George Axelrod** had got Sinatra interested, but **Arthur Krim**, the head of United Artists (with whom Sinatra had a distribution deal) thought the themes of communism, Cold War spies and presidential assassination were too contentious for the time. As the Democratic party's chairman of finance, Krim was wary of creating political ripples and refused to give the film the go-ahead. Sinatra asked **John F. Kennedy** if he would object; the President said he had enjoyed the book and thought it would make a great movie, and phoned Krim to tell him so.

Surrounded by forceful acting, notably by **Laurence Harvey** and **Angela Lansbury**, Sinatra rises to the occasion once more and gives a taut, ego-free performance as the troubled Major Bennett Marco, who struggles to unlock the secret of a brainwashing plot to assassinate a presidential candidate. Sinatra later described Harvey as "a consummate, powerful actor [with] a great inner strength"; Harvey later said of Sinatra, "I think I learned more from Sinatra about acting than from anyone with whom I ever worked."

Just as Sinatra had the power to get the film made, he had the power to withdraw it for 25 years; following Kennedy's assassination, he insisted that the film was neither distributed nor broadcast, and it remained rarely seen until its reissue on video in 1987. During a promotional interview with Axelrod and Frankenheimer about the movie's re-release, Sinatra reflected on the professionalism of the entire production and said that the project was "a wonderful, wonderful experience of my life". He continued: "It only happens once in a performer's life. Once."

Come Blow Your Horn

Paramount; Bud Yorkin, 1963

In *Come Blow Your Horn*, a sex comedy based on the play by **Neil Simon**, men are either husbands or swinging bachelors, and women either have sex and get passed around (**Jill St John**) or don't have sex and end up with the guy (**Barbara Rush**). On that level, it's like a racier version of the similar *The Tender Trap*, and offensive trash. But as a period piece it has its virtues: the bachelor pad decor, the party scene full of "intellectual degenerates", as Sinatra's character calls them, and the title track by **Sammy Cahn** and **Jimmy Van Heusen** sung on location on Madison Avenue.

Sinatra is about ten years too old for his role as the swinging bum Alan Baker, and his acceptance of maturity and conversion to marriage in the latter part of the film is not convincing. But his comic material in the first quarter of the film is sharply delivered and winningly cheeky, there is affectionate chemistry with **Tony Bill** (playing his kid brother Buddy and looking spookily like Frank Jr.) and Frank's presence is enough for the film to dim when he's not on screen. **Lee J. Cobb** is memorably explosive as the impotent and amusingly confused father, but elsewhere the characters are little more than types; **Molly Picon**'s Jewish mother shtick grates, Tony Bill, as he becomes a swinger himself, irritates, and Jill St John's dumb redhead is just appalling.

Sinatra's promo team wanted to tag the movie "Art It Ain't, Fun It Is!" before Frank disapproved, sensing that mild disparagement might be gleaned. They settled for a near quote from the title song, "I tell you chum … laughs it is!" Forty years on, *Come Blow Your Horn* has a few laughs but more reasons to kick your TV in.

None But The Brave

Warner; Frank Sinatra, 1965

Sinatra's one attempt at **directing** is a laudable effort with obvious deficiencies but with its heart in the right place. The story concerns a group of GIs in World War II who crash-land on an island and find it already inhabited by a stranded Japanese platoon. Neither side has radio contact with the outside world and an uneasy truce ensues which involves the American medic operating on a gangrenous Japanese soldier, fish caught by the Japanese being traded for US cigarettes, and a united effort to save the water supply during a storm. As US communications are restored, the truce breaks down, with inevitably bloody results.

After the film takes much care in its extensive subtitled scenes to establish the Japanese soldiers as human beings (in sharp contrast to their portrayal as treacherous killing machines in, among other films, *Never So Few*) the shocking decimation of their squad is quite sufficient to make the film's heavy-hearted point. That it was felt necessary to blazon the caption "No one wins" over the final carnage shows a lack of confidence on the film-makers' part; and this is a shame, for above the hammy performances (that of Sinatra's son-in-law **Tommy Sands** has to be seen to be believed) and the over-written dialogue (every soldier is a poet and philosopher), there is a subtle, unusual film of deep conscience and quiet power.

Sinatra steals a few scenes as the wise but cynical, whisky-guzzling doctor with all the best lines ("Dirty Jap? They invented the bathtub!"), but his direction, assisted by an uncredited **Gordon Douglas**, is discreet and unaffected. Although the US soldiers' exchanges are sometimes awkwardly staged, he displays a sensitivity towards character that is unseen in many war and action movies, and it's clear that, as a director of small-scale films, he had something to offer. It's a shame that he didn't take this path, given some of his subsequent roles as an actor.

Von Ryan's Express

20th Century Fox; Mark Robson, 1965; ⊙ US, UK

In this ripping World War II yarn Sinatra plays Colonel Joseph L. Ryan, and gives a more convincing portrayal than his Captain Tom Reynolds in *Never So Few*. The troubled US officer, known as "Von Ryan" to his troops for his harsh man-management, assumes control of British prisoners of war in Italy and leads them through a series of nail-biting situations – including their hijack of a German train while they escape to Switzerland. He scythes through the blustery British wartime pride (as represented by Major Eric Fincham, played brilliantly by **Trevor Howard**) with no-nonsense American pragmatism; and when he shows humility, he pays a heavy price. He spares the Italian commander when the POW camp is overthrown but the Fascist later recaptures Ryan's men and massacres the wounded. Later, Ryan refuses to kill two prisoners they are holding on the train – including Gabriella, an enticing Italian girl whose charms he has gallantly resisted – only for them to escape and kill several of his men.

Following the lead of *The Great Escape* earlier in the decade – it even has a perky flute theme set over a military snare drum – the film inspires excitement rather than involvement with the characters. The customary tension between British and American officers is played by Sinatra and Howard nicely if perfunctorily, but their moment of understanding, after Sinatra has been forced to shoot Gabriella when she runs away, is almost lost in the maelstrom of the action.

The original script called for Ryan to escape over the Swiss border with the other surviving men, but Sinatra felt that after his gunning down of Gabriella – whose treachery doesn't stop the scene from being shocking – he shouldn't be allowed to survive. Despite the studio making noises about a sequel, Sinatra had his way and Ryan is shot while chasing the train, reaching for Fincham's hand. After the gripping whiz-bang of the movie, the moral balance feels about right.

Marriage On The Rocks

Warner; Jack Donohue, 1965

A shocker. Sinatra is a boring husband and **Deborah Kerr** is his bored wife; they divorce. **Dean Martin** is an unmarried swinger who, following tedious contrivances, accidentally marries Kerr, and Sinatra's character starts dating his daughter's friends. This dreary movie says less about romance, responsibility and the generation gap than is probably intended, and might have worked better with a better script, snappier direction and Rock Hudson and Doris Day. Sinatra is slow and dry, Kerr is shrill, Martin is a vacuum, and **Cesar Romero** (as a Mexican lawyer) and **Hermione Baddeley** (as Kerr's Scottish mother) compete for the abysmally phoney cameo award. With little of interest, let alone wit, the movie grinds from one unfunny set-up to the next.

The project demonstrates Sinatra's periodic lack of interest in working hard at films – in choosing a good script, appointing appropriate talent and putting in a decent performance himself – and the movie was reviewed accordingly. The *New York Herald Tribune* called it "flat, insipid and watery" while the *New York Post* critic described is as "well below the best Sinatra-Martin movie levels and out of sight of Deborah Kerr's best". Kerr was persuaded out of movie retirement by Sinatra's promise of a fun-filled shoot, and was reportedly amused by his habit of tearing out pages of the script if they didn't suit him.

Assault On A Queen

Paramount; Jack Donohue, 1966

This is the last Sinatra film that should be seen. An uninteresting movie resulting from uninspired movie-making, it's another unpolished heist saga, the target this time being the Queen Mary ocean liner. Sinatra, who played a former submarine officer turned mercenary, hired the former TV director **Jack Donohue**, who had done a poor job with *Marriage On The Rocks* but was unlikely to ask Sinatra for another take. Sinatra delivers another non-performance and the *Monthly Film Bulletin*'s verdict was: "Just about as enthralling as plastic boats in the bath."

The Naked Runner

Warner; Sidney Furie, 1967

Sidney Furie's tense espionage thriller has the mannered style of his previous hit, **The Ipcress File**: freakish close-ups are juxtaposed with panoramic vistas, and claustrophobia and agoraphobia combine to emphasise the pervasiveness of paranoia and discomfort. Sinatra plays a London-based American businessman who is pressured into carrying out a Cold War assassination, and his acting consists of wandering around London, Copenhagen and East Germany looking blank and nervous.

He was restless, distracted by thoughts of marrying **Mia Farrow**; and after an incident when a helicopter pilot lost his way and Sinatra lost his cool, he left the London production base prematurely. The producer, **Brad Dexter**, had to cobble a film together from footage that Sinatra had already shot, and so the already eccentric story was made harder to appreciate by awkward pacing and compromised editing. It's more than watchable, but overall the movie is fudged and the audience is cheated.

Tony Rome

20th Century Fox; Gordon Douglas, 1967; ⊙ US

In an effort to emulate the movie success that **Dean Martin** had in the mid-1960s through being identified with a particular kind of role – the spoof spy Matt Helm – Sinatra played hard-nosed detectives with complex moral codes in his next three films.

The first, *Tony Rome*, based on Marvin H. Albert's novel *Miami Mayhem*, was in the spirit of the tortuous tales of dames, murder and corruption by **Raymond Chandler**. Sinatra starred as the title character, a 1960s approximation of Humphrey Bogart's wisecracking private investigator Philip Marlowe, but with smuttier vocabulary. Rome is his own man, emotionally guarded and tough as nails, so all Frank had to do to make it work was show up, which is just as well. With the film shooting in Miami during the day and Sinatra performing at the city's Fontainebleau Hotel in the evening, it's unlikely that One-Take Charlie would have been in any mood to stretch himself.

With its gay villains, double entendres and self-conscious "sexy" tone, the film is now beyond dated trash and makes for an agreeable kitschy night in.

The Detective

20th Century Fox; Gordon Douglas, 1968; ⊙ US

The wisecracks stopped for this grimy thriller: one of Sinatra's first lines, as he matter-of-factly examines a corpse, is "Penis cut off, lying on floor." He puts in one of his grimmest, most intense performances, as Joe Leland, a New York policeman who has principles but also gets results his way. The scene where Sinatra lulls the innocent homosexual murder suspect (played with brilliant hysteria by **Tony Musante**) into "confessing" by talking gently and caressing his hand is perhaps the most insidious and disturbing he filmed, especially as the suspect is later executed.

The script by **Abby Mann** has the virtue of complexity but is often doggedly seedy and, like *Tony Rome*, the film is full of unsympathetic homosexuals and lusty women; even Sinatra's estranged wife Karen, played by **Lee Remick**, is portrayed as an incurable nymphomaniac. Considered daring at the time, it seems transparently modish and sensationalist today. But it can be seen as a thoughtful, serious film with adult themes – injustice, loyalty, corruption and incompatibility – and Sinatra's performance is a part of this.

SINATRA AS JOE LELAND IN THE DETECTIVE, WITH LEE REMICK AS HIS WIFE KAREN

Lady In Cement

20th Century Fox; Gordon Douglas, 1968; ⊙ US, UK

Tony Rome had fared reasonably well at the box office, so in 1968 the Miami private dick returned and Sinatra was booked at the Fontainebleau again. Smarting from the break-up of his marriage to **Mia Farrow**, Sinatra was apparently less patient than usual on set and quickly lost interest, so despite the presence of **Raquel Welch** and an even ruder, more knowing tone than the original, *Lady In Cement* inevitably has a warmed-over feeling. However, anyone who got anything from *Tony Rome* will like the labyrinthine plot, the strip joint/artist studio vignettes and the enjoyably hammy cameos. Sinatra is his customary, casual self and gets to deliver an **Ava Gardner** in-joke: "I used to know a broad who collected bullfighters."

Critics were divided: Vincent Canby hated the "vulgarity and sloppiness" but John Mahoney liked the "fresher script" and "sharp direction". But box office sales were respectable.

Dirty Dingus Magee

MGM; Burt Kennedy, 1970

That director Burt Kennedy had just had a moderate hit with another comedy western, *Support Your Local Sheriff*, explains *Dirty Dingus Magee*'s existence but doesn't justify it: witless and bawdy, it's so pathetic, it's almost endearing.

Sinatra plays the title role, a low-grade outlaw frolicking in the desert, stealing money and sleeping with squaws and schoolteachers. Sporting a Beatles-style wig and grubby orange long-johns for much of the movie, and unfeasibly white teeth, Sinatra gurgles and giggles his way through a range of puerile gags and a series of encounters with the sheriff, played by George Kennedy, who's out to "git" him. Like **Blazing Saddles** without the laughs, or **Carry On Cowboy** without the mincing, this nonsense was slammed – the critic in the *LA Times* described it as "merely disgusting" – and it killed off Sinatra's acting career for seven years.

LATE CAMEOS

That's Entertainment!

MGM; Jack Haley Jr., 1974; ⊙ US

An excellent celebration of the golden age of MGM and a surprise box-office hit. Sinatra was one of the narrators for the first part, along with Gene Kelly, Fred Astaire and Bing Crosby, and a fair sprinkling of his MGM movies are represented here and in *That's Entertainment II*, which was released in 1976.

Cannonball Run II

Warner; Hal Needham, 1984; ⊙ US

A misguided attempt to reunite the Rat Pack in this shambolic cameo-fest, an atrocious Burt Reynolds attempt at comedy adventure.

Listen Up: The Lives Of Quincy Jones

Warner; Ellen Weissbrod, 1990

Sinatra lines up with Barbra Streisand, Michael Jackson and many others in a documentary movie paying tribute to the esteemed arranger and producer.

Young At Heart

CBS; Allan Arkush, 1995

Produced by daughter Tina, this TV movie looks at how music – particularly Sinatra's – helps people to cope with life. It features Frank in a fleeting cameo, alongside Olympia Dukakis, in his final screen appearance.

Contract On Cherry Street

Artanis; William A. Graham, 1977

Instigated by Sinatra and produced by his company Artanis, the three-hour TV movie *Contract On Cherry Street* was based on the **Philip Rosenberg** novel that was the favourite book of **Frank's mother**, and was filmed a few months after she died. In his first acting gig for seven years,

Sinatra committed to two months' location work and is good as an anti-Mafia police inspector who turns vigilante when his partner is gunned down by the Mob. Sinatra's small-screen drama debut was trumpeted in the media at the time as an event, and was quite well received, though some reviewers compared it unfavourably with contemporary cop shows like *Kojak* and asked why Frank was starring in what critic Judith Crist called a "mealy-mouthed morality tale".

THE FAKE FRANKS

Sinatra

Warner; James Steven Sadwith, 1992

This moderately entertaining four-hour TV mini series, produced by Sinatra's daughter **Tina**, was expected to be a whitewash. Indeed, while it doesn't avoid some of the unsavoury aspects of Sinatra's life, it's bland, in the tradition of TV movies. The early scenes generate some period atmosphere and the production certainly benefits from its use of Sinatra's recordings; but some of the sequences, such as Frank's first rehearsal with the Dorsey orchestra, will have Sinatraphiles howling at the inaccuracies of detail and the corny staging, all the horn players taking turns to look impressed at the young singer.

   As with all biopics, the impersonations of the famous make it hard not to cringe. But the characterizations here are largely tolerable, with Olympia Dukakis's Dolly and Bob Gunton's Tommy Dorsey especially engaging and believable. **Philip Casnoff** is not bad as Frank, but he's too handsome, beefy and smooth, and there's not enough magic; Casnoff's Sinatra is inevitably not charismatic enough to seem worthy of the indulgences that were given to him for being such a heel. But how could it be?

The Rat Pack

HBO; Rob Cohen, 1998; ☉ US, UK

Much better than the family-approved *Sinatra* mini-series, *The Rat Pack* is a gritty, stylish two-hour romp through the events of the late 1950s and early 1960s that surrounded Frank and his pals in entertainment, politics and the underworld. Cramming in as much as it can of the messy story of **John F. Kennedy**, **Sam Giancana**, **Marilyn Monroe** and **Judith Campbell**, the movie balances near-truthful manufactured conversations

The First Deadly Sin

Filmways; Brian G. Hutton, 1980

Sinatra is once more a New York cop, this time on the verge of retirement, who divides his time between hunting an ice-pick killer and visiting his sick wife, played by **Faye Dunaway**, in hospital. Faced with a ticking

with reasonable stabs at accuracy, and as an entertaining Sinatra extra, it's good fun.

Don Cheadle and **Joe Mantegna** perform particularly impressively, the former as a dignified Sammy Davis Jr. and the latter as a remote Dean Martin; and **Ray Liotta** is nothing like Sinatra but brings to the portrayal a sense of menace that was beyond Philip Casnoff. And the film contains an exchange that comes as close to defining Sinatra's magnetism as any. "What is it about that man?" asks Pat Kennedy, played by Phyllis Lyons, at a party. The hostess, Rocky Cooper, played by Veronica Cartwright, replies, "You want to fuck him. You want to mother him. You ... don't want to piss him off. Oh God, is it a combination."

The Rat Pack – Live From Las Vegas

Lace; Steve Kemsley, 2004; ⊙ UK

This reasonable DVD souvenir of the UK touring show that became a London's West End staple in 2003 and 2004 stars **Stephen Triffitt**, a good singer who makes a living impersonating Sinatra. Though a little stone-faced, he captures many of Frank's musical mannerisms, and Dean Martin's boozy croon and comic timing are well conveyed by Mark Adams. Both, however, are topped by **Gilz Terera**, who virtually merges into Sammy Davis Jr.'s complex persona. The show doesn't pretend to be anything other than a feel-good evening of nostalgic impersonations, though Sammy's poignant "What Kind Of Fool Am I" creates an emotional centre to the piece.

Sinatra on Screen

clock and an uninterested police chief, he quietly takes the law into his own hands. Like the movie equivalent of the album from the following year, **She Shot Me Down**, *The First Deadly Sin* has a stately tempo and is infused with gloom.

Far from playing another no-nonsense maverick cop, Sinatra brings detailed shading to the character of Edward Delaney. He banters tenderly with his bed-ridden wife and indulges a lonely museum curator by allowing him to be involved in the investigation. Impassive and still for most of the film, Sinatra's worried eyes and stony face convey how his character hurts.

The critic from *The Sunday Times* called Sinatra's performance "a sullen endorsement of redneck authority", the film was panned widely for its dreariness, and audiences stayed away. Disheartened, Sinatra never found another role to tempt him back to the movies, but his final leading role is subtle enough to reward a patient viewer.

The small screen

"You've got to be relaxed and you've got to be straightforward and believable, or it's murder, as Sinatra is now experiencing."

VARIETY, 1957

ON TELEVISION: 1950–60

Frank Sinatra never conquered the small screen in the same way that he conquered music and movies, but it didn't stop him trying.

During the post-war years, a boom in **sales of televisions** in America saw a medium that had previously been accessible only to the privileged become a means of marketing to the masses; and it was particularly appealing to film and radio stars who were still famous but not the box-office attractions that they once had been. In 1950 one such star was **Bob Hope**, and it was on his variety show *Star Spangled Review* in May of that year that Sinatra made his first appearance on the small, flickering, black and white screen. He sang **"Come Rain Or Come Shine"** and, in a comedy sketch with Hope, impersonated Bing Crosby. Although Sinatra had little regard for the medium, during a career low he accepted an offer from CBS to appear in his own weekly variety series, and his hit-and-miss TV career began.

The Frank Sinatra Show

Broadcast 1950-52

Of the fifty hour-long variety shows on CBS sponsored first by **Bulova Watches** and then by **Ecko Housewares**, a few of which have crept out on video, those that survive show a Sinatra who looks ill and ill-at-ease; broadcast live between 9pm and 10pm on Saturday nights (and later moved to Tuesdays), the programmes demonstrate his lack of rehearsal and commitment. His nervous eyes show a lack of confidence in his cue cards and he stumbles only semi-interested through the usual variety show fare of 1950s US television: musical numbers, lame sketches with comedy guests (Jackie Gleason, Jack Benny) and wobbly sets. The ratings were never more than moderate and the reviews were poor; according to *The New York Times*, "Sinatra walked off the TV high end but unfortunately fell in the shallow end of the pool."

When the show was cancelled after limping through two seasons, Sinatra blasted the whole medium. "Television stinks, except of course if you can do a filmed show," he said, reflecting how much he hated the rehearsal required by **live broadcasts**. "That way you avoid a lot of the panic and no-talent executives who get in it from merely writing an essay on fire prevention … my blood boils when I see the mediocrities sitting on top of the TV networks."

Our Town

1955

In the only one-off TV drama to feature the singer during this period, a currently unavailable adaptation of the play by Thornton Wilder, Sinatra played the stage manager, alongside **Paul Newman** and **Eva Marie Saint**. He sings one of Cahn/Van Heusen's first and best songs, "Our Town", and one of their most popular, the Emmy-winning smash hit **"Love And Marriage"**. The production was well received but Sinatra complained again about the lengthy rehearsals necessary for the complicated live broadcast on NBC. "And for what? It had a lot of merit, I'll admit, but after all that work you have nothing to show for it but a bad black-and-white kinescope," he said, revealing much about his attitude to TV work. "I could make a good movie in that time."

The Frank Sinatra Show

1957-58

In one of his busiest periods as an actor and singer, Sinatra took on his second TV series, an ambitious set for ABC of twenty-one hour-long musical variety shows and ten half-hour dramas, which were filmed rather than live and designed to show off his range of talents. He was paid a reported **$3 million** along with profits and was granted unprecedented artistic control. "One Friday I'll be a singer, another I'll be an actor," he told the press. "If any bad mistakes are made, I want to be responsible for them."

The first mistake he made was to try to knock out eleven shows in fifteen days with little or no rehearsing; the under-cooked results were savaged in the press. *The New Yorker* called the programme "underorganized and a little desperate", *The New York World Telegram* accused Sinatra of "simply making a fast buck" and the *Chicago Sun-Times* thought it detected an attitude of "let's give the peasants out there a few songs and jokes and get this nuisance over with". Even though the guest list included some of the biggest stars of the day – **Peggy Lee**, **Bob Hope**, **Dean Martin**, **Robert Mitchum**, **Ethel Merman**, **Ella Fitzgerald**, **Bing Crosby** – the series was still described in one weekly TV guide as "one of the biggest and most expensive disappointments of the current season". It was Sinatra's final attempt at a TV series. "I'll do a special now and then," he said, " but no more of this series crap."

The Frank Sinatra Timex Show

1959

The first of these four one-hour variety specials for ABC, which unlike its three successors had no title of its own, was broadcast in October 1959 and helped ABC to recoup its investment. It featured **Dean Martin, Bing Crosby** and **Mitzi Gaynor** in a slickly delivered set, and a fabulous mini-set of small-group performances from Sinatra that represented his live act at the time; there's more polish and more belief than in his previous shows and Sinatra's eyes shine with spirit. The show is available on budget videos with various titles, such as *The Frank Sinatra Show No. 3*, released by VTS in 1995.

The Frank Sinatra Timex Show: An Afternoon With Frank Sinatra

1959; ⊙ US, UK

An Afternoon With Frank Sinatra was meant to be taped in the Palm Springs desert, but a rare downpour forced the production onto a bare studio sound stage and meant that the script had to be hastily rewritten. Guests included **Ella Fitzgerald** (singing a beautiful "There's A Lull In My Life"), the vocal group **The Hi-Lo's** (with whom Sinatra re-creates "I'll Never Smile Again") and **Hermione Gingold**; and Sinatra and Juliet Prowse, his girlfriend at the time, sexily reprise their "It's All Right With Me" number from *Can-Can*. But there is way too much of Peter Lawford.

The Frank Sinatra Timex Show: Here's To The Ladies

1960

Here's To The Ladies, a Valentine's Day special broadcast in February 1960 and currently unavailable, featured an unusual appearance by **Eleanor**

SINATRA WITH ELEANOR ROOSEVELT BEFORE HER RECITAL ON HIS SHOW IN 1960

Roosevelt, who recited the lyrics to "High Hopes" accompanied by a special Nelson Riddle arrangement; Lena Horne, who sang a Harold Arlen medley with Sinatra; Juliet Prowse again; and Mary Costa and Barbara Heller.

The Frank Sinatra Timex Show: Welcome Home Elvis

1960; ☉ US, UK

The fourth show was called *It's Nice To Go Traveling* but is more commonly known as *Welcome Home Elvis*. It was, at last, the TV hit that Sinatra had been waiting for, even though it was on the back of the king of rock'n'roll's return from the army. Sinatra had once thought that Elvis's kind of music was "deplorable, a rancid-smelling aphrodisiac"; but not any more. **Peter Lawford**, **Sammy Davis Jr.**, **Joey Bishop** and **Nancy Sinatra** are on the show too, but it was Elvis's presence that gave the show its huge ratings. The Frank–Elvis duet, a

collision of entirely different entertainment worlds, is quite charming; Sinatra sings "Love Me Tender", Elvis sings "Witchcraft", and they harmonize on the former for the climax. "Gee, that's pretty," Frank grins.

ON TELEVISION: 1962–85

During a hectic period in the early 1960s, Sinatra found time to appear as a guest on TV shows hosted by Dean Martin, Dick Powell, Judy Garland, Bob Hope, Bing Crosby, Ed Sullivan and Joey Bishop. There was also the occasional filmed concert, including an unfortunately unavailable ninety-minute command performance recorded at the Royal Festival Hall in London in June 1962.

A **second stage in Sinatra's TV career** began in 1965 with a series of initially annual TV music specials, which were recorded in only a few hours. Largely dispensing with gimmicky settings, the programmes concentrated on presenting Frank singing a dozen songs or so, often with musicians in view and sometimes with singing guests. Although the viewing figures varied at the time, the first six annual shows, between 1965 and 1970, culminating in a concert at the Royal Festival Hall, provide the best official, unadulterated glimpse of Sinatra the singing performer very near the top of his game. In the two decades after his comeback from retirement, sporadic TV specials were interspersed with recordings of concerts. The thirteen shows described are all available on DVD in the UK from Warner Music Vision.

A Man And His Music

1965; ⊙ US, UK

This is the first in Sinatra's series of mid-Sixties colour TV specials, and one of the best. There are no modish guests or old pals – just **Nelson Riddle** and **Gordon Jenkins**, a bunch of classics, some studio sets that now look fetching and some patronizing patter to the camera. Sinatra – natty in a yellow waistcoat, then a black one, and then a tux – is perhaps only in medium voice, but he has probably never been more twinkly and intimate with the TV camera. He has a fresh way of exiting from "I Get A Kick Out Of You" and delivers a lovely ballad medley – a format used for the next four shows – interspersed with the string motif from "It Was A Very Good Year". Timeless Sinatra.

A Man And His Music Part II

1966; ⊙ US, UK

There's more of the same here, but it's not quite as timeless, with its electronic organ and icky guest spot from daughter **Nancy**. Frank's spots, however, are possibly even better than those in Part I: standing bang in the middle of the orchestra, he sings "Moonlight In Vermont" flawlessly and makes thrilling work of the excitable frenzy that is "The Most Beautiful Girl In The World". Later there's another lovely Jenkins medley of ballads, this time combined with stanzas from "Just One Of Those Things". Sinatra messes up the ending to "My Kind Of Town", but as his company was producing the show, who was going to ask him to do it again?

A Man And His Music + Ella + Jobim

1967; ⊙ US, UK

A driving "Day In Day Out", a momentous "Ol' Man River" and a couple of terrific numbers from **Ella Fitzgerald** are followed by a little bit of slippage.

Ella: "Frank, how do you feel about the music the kids are playing today?" Frank: "Groovy, groovy, I love it."

Cue an awkward medley of mid-1960s "pops"; and Ella's discomfort with Sinatra's slick TV style is painful to behold. But the **Antonio Carlos Jobim** section is exquisite, the two sophisticates face-to-face on wicker furniture conjuring musical magic together. And Frank and Ella redeem themselves later with a fun-filled, swinging set, as sizzling and infectious as the earlier one was uneasy.

Francis Albert Sinatra Does His Thing

1968; ⊙ US, UK

The opener, "Hello Young Lovers", sets the tone. A go-go groove, electric pick bass, doo-wah backing vocals. Frank is getting down with, as he has it, the "youth of today". "Simple tunes, simple words … profound thoughts", he reasons, before singing Gayle Caldwell's folky waltz "Cycles" in a tuxedo while smoking a cigarette, blending the old Frank with the new. A medley of tunes with guest **Diahann Carroll** "to reflect the spirit" of black America's forefathers re-establishes Sinatra's stance on civil rights, which was much more common in 1968 than when he first adopted it. He seems genuinely taken with the psychedelic sunshine pop of the vocal group **The Fifth Dimension**, hamming it up with them as "the sixth dimension" before singing "Nice 'N' Easy" in a Nehru jacket and love beads. And because he's on excellent form – endearingly self-deprecating and singing superbly – he pulls it off.

Sinatra

1969; ⊙ US, UK

Sinatra, without guests, is mostly on blue-chip form here. "For Once In My Life", "Please Be Kind", "The Tender Trap" and "Street Of Dreams" are exciting performances to treasure. The ballad medley for once comprises modern songs (Rod McKuen's "A Man Alone", Jimmy Webb's "Didn't We" and "Forget To Remember") and works beautifully. But the highlight may be a genuinely funny ten-minute segment, scripted by **Sheldon Keller**, where Frank introduces some lowlights of his movie career. "Now you've got to admit, that's past method acting," he laughs, following a clip of a particularly wooden performance from *Johnny Concho*. "That's in the Twilight Zone."

In Concert At The Royal Festival Hall

1970; ⊙ US, UK

This baffling blend of the cavalier and the spine-tingling – typical of Sinatra performances during this period – is the beginning of the bad-wig, unreliable pipes era. There are comedy voices (lisping in "You Make Me Feel So Young") and botched lines ("What the hell's the next line…" in "Pennies From Heaven"), and the orchestra of London session players don't reach the required roar on "I've Got You Under My Skin" and "My Kind Of Town". But there's also a deep "Didn't We", the best version on film of **"One For My Baby"** (a four-minute movie of its own), and, as the centrepiece, Paul Ryan's attempt at an egocentric Sinatra anthem to follow "My Way", the fiercely anti-hippy **"I Will Drink The Wine"**.

Ol' Blue Eyes Is Back

1973; ⊙ US, UK

The comeback special is heralded by an awkward setting of "You Will Be My Music" and Sinatra emerging from the dark, tuxedoed, to greet a gaggle of young ladies in evening dress, who remain standing while he croaks through a pompous long-note adult pop song that seems designed to expose the flaws in his instrument. There follows a fine four-song swing set, a high-quality ballad medley and a nostalgic romp with Gene Kelly. But the highlight is **"Send In The Clowns"**, filmed with a single close-up shot of Sinatra's face and immeasurably more vivid than the album version. In this reading of the Sondheim theatre song the question of whether he still has it is answered emphatically.

The Main Event

1974; ⊙ US, UK

This concert, recorded at **Madison Square Garden** in front of 20,000 people, has the odd musical moment to savour but is mainly about the charisma and the spectacle of Sinatra. "I've never felt so much love in one room," Frank tells the rowdily appreciative thousands, beside themselves with excitement, happily clapping on the beat. He silences them with a compelling "Angel Eyes", and "My Way" does its job, but elsewhere there's something disagreeable in the air. His arrogance is neither supported by his music-making – he's in especially unconvincing voice – nor alleviated by his customary light humour, and physically he's lost all his snap. It was on *The Main Event* that this inappropriate, self-congratulatory tone reached its nadir.

Sinatra And Friends

1977; ⊙ UK

Sinatra is in much better vocal shape and having old-fashioned variety fun with an odd assortment of "friends" on this more amiable show. Unfortunately, however, this kind of TV had become complacent and everyone's eyes are fixated on the life raft that is the autocue. The duettists include **Natalie Cole**, on a charming "I Get A Kick Out Of You"; **Dean Martin** and opera baritone **Robert Merrill**, on a shambolic "The Oldest Established (Permanent Floating Crap Game In New York)"; country singer **Loretta Lynn**, on a hilariously poor "All Or Nothing At All", Loretta losing the plot entirely on this "disco" arrangement; actress and singer **Leslie Uggams**, at ease with "The Lady Is A Tramp"; and **John Denver**, on a surprisingly touching "September Song". And everyone comes on during Paul Anka's **"Everybody Ought To Be In Love"** and gives Frank a little kiss.

The First 40 Years

1980; ⊙ UK

Filmed at Caesar's Palace, Las Vegas, this bloated all-star tribute is so obsequious that it becomes clear why Kitty Kelley sharpened her pencil and burst the bubble of awed reverence that surrounded Sinatra by then. And when Frank eventually gets to sing after the interminable sycophancy, it's not worth the wait.

The Man And His Music

1981; ⊙ US, UK

No variety show, no guests, no canned applause, no disco arrangements, no over-familiar chestnuts – just Sinatra, **Count Basie** and some good music. *The Man And His Music*, 1981 vintage, is a bold attempt by Sinatra to engage with the songs and the camera as he had done in the best TV specials of the 1960s. At 65 Frank is a little grey around the edges, but several of the well-selected numbers generate magic – notably Neal Hefti's arrangements of **"Pennies From Heaven"** and **"At Long Last Love"**, Nelson Riddle's majestic setting of **"Something"** and Quincy Jones's explosive **"The Best Is Yet To Come"**.

Concert For The Americas

1982; ⊙ UK

Ninety minutes of Sinatra in concert, edited from two performances from August 1982 in the Dominican Republic with **the Buddy Rich Orchestra** – and a classic. Sinatra is in good musical shape and amiable mood and his set list combines old tunes with new. There is a superb recasting for big band of Don Costa's "Come Rain Or Come Shine" from *Sinatra And Strings* and a powerful **"The House I Live In"**, which is all the more stirring because it is preceded by a little speech in which Sinatra restates his belief in the brotherhood of man and his pride in the Americas. There's a rare performance of the Jule Styne and Sammy Cahn song "Searching" and though Buddy Rich doesn't play throughout Sinatra's set, he arrives mid-show to play a stupendous drum feature with his own orchestra on an instrumental *West Side Story* medley. Sinatra's voice is by no means crack-free, but when he's in this kind of form, it doesn't matter. He splits a crucial note at the climax of "New York, New York", but makes a joke of it and still delivers the tingles.

Sinatra In Japan

1985; ⊙ UK

Less fun than other TV specials, *In Japan* is more predictable in its repertoire and less involving: the camera shots are from further away than those for *Concert For The Americas* and the polite Japanese audience is the opposite of the frenzied rabble at *The Main Event*. But this concert is a valuable example of a tight, professional show by a 69-year-old still loving to perform and still seeking to do a good job. However, his teasing of the applause as the intro to "Strangers In The Night" strikes up – "Oh, you know this one?" – and his questionable decision to sing the title line of "Luck Be A Lady" as "Ruck Be A Rady" means that there's still a little danger in the air.

Further broadcasts

Less readily available later TV appearances included *Portrait Of An Album* (1984), a documentary of the *L.A. Is My Lady* sessions; *The Voice, The Event* (1986), a concert in Milan; *The Ultimate Event* (1988), concert and documentary footage of the Frank, Sammy and Liza tour; various 1991 concerts filmed and broadcast in Australia, Japan, Italy, Norway and Ireland; *The Making Of Duets* (1994), a documentary about the album; and a concert in Japan in 1994 with Natalie Cole.

Frank Facts

Sinatra country

"Most people believe that politics is a game of quid pro quo. But I want to assure you that following Frank's endorsement of me, it is only sheerest coincidence that there is going to be a freeway run right through Caesar's Palace."

RONALD REAGAN, AFTER SINATRA HAD HIS CREDIT REFUSED AND A GUN PULLED
ON HIM BY THE CAESAR'S PALACE MANAGER SANFORD WATERMAN, 1970

Hoboken

As visitors approach Frank's old home town in **New Jersey** a sign on the Observer Highway at the junction with Jackson Street welcomes visitors to "Hoboken: Birthplace of Baseball and Frank Sinatra"; the baseball allusion refers to the first record of the game being played, on June 19, 1846, on Hoboken's **Elysian Fields**. The iconic eatery on the waterfront, the now-demolished **Clam Broth House**, once had a sign in the shape of a large white hand that read, "Hoboken: Birthplace of Frank Sinatra and Baseball"; whichever way round they are billed, the humble waterfront town is clearly proud to have been the cradle of the national game and the voice of the century.

The island of **Hoboken**, covering one square mile, was bought in 1784 by Colonel John Stevens for $90,000; he then developed the area into a resort for the wealthy people of New York, just across the Hudson River. After the land passed to his family in the middle of the nineteenth century, it was further developed as an industrial and residential area. By the early part of the twentieth century it was mainly a working-class district populated by immigrants, largely from Europe. It was into this mixed-race neighbourhood that Francis Albert Sinatra was born on December 15, 1915, at **415 Monroe Street**, a four-story tenement that housed eight families. The house burnt down in 1967, and only a brick arch remained on the site. In 1996 local Sinatra fan Ed Shirak Jr. had a commemorative star placed in the pavement opposite the address and two years later he opened a one-room tribute museum next door at 417 Monroe Street called **From Here To Eternity: The Museum**. Opposed by the Sinatra family and short on substantial memorabilia (though there were lots of photos, a few letters, a handkerchief given to a fan during a show and a menu from the Rustic Cabin in Englewood), it lasted only a few years before closing.

Sinatra was baptized in 1916 at **St Francis Church** on Third Street. After he died in 1998, a local memorial service was held there.

Dolly Sinatra was unable to have any more children after Frank's difficult birth, and so the Sinatras found themselves better off financially by the mid-1920s than many large families nearby. With Marty a fireman and Dolly an influential neighbourhood midwife, the Sinatras went up in the world in 1927, when they moved ten blocks to **703 Park Avenue**. Frankie had found Monroe Street tough, but he found the Park Avenue hoodlums to be "brighter, more insidious; well mannered, with good clothes, and deadly". During prohibition, Dolly and Marty opened a speakeasy called **Marty O'Brien's** on the corner of Fourth Street and Jefferson Street.

In 1931 Frank briefly attended **A.J. Demarest High School,** still functioning at **Fourth and Garden**. In 1932 the Sinatras moved to **841 Garden Street**, a showplace with three storeys, four bedrooms, a French telephone, a baby grand piano and a golden birdbath outside the front door. Dolly allegedly performed abortions in the basement. Sinatra lived there with his parents until he married in 1939.

The final semester of Sinatra's formal education came at **Drake Business School**, though he wanted to attend the well-regarded **Stevens Institute**, an engineering school named after the founder of Hoboken and whose track Sinatra used when building up his lungpower. It's still there today, and Sinatra visited to receive an honorary degree in 1985 on the same day that he received the Medal of Freedom at the White House. "My Way" was played on Flemish bells and Sinatra was clearly moved as he addressed "the school I dreamed of attending when I was a kid". He went on to say: "This is more enjoyable than being at the White House."

One of Sinatra's first engagements as a singer, the result of hustling by his mother, was in 1935 at **the Union Club** at 600 Hudson Street. It was a two-month engagement, for which he was paid $40 for a five-night week. An imposing building built in 1864, it is now a block of 39 exclusive rental apartments called the New Union Club.

MARTY SINATRA, HOBOKEN FIRE CAPTAIN, PUTS HIS HAT ON HIS SON'S HEAD AS THEY RIDE THROUGH TOWN DURING "FRANK SINATRA DAY" IN OCTOBER 1947

After Sinatra left Hoboken, he never talked about the town with much warmth. He returned in October 1947 for a "Sinatra Day" parade and although his reception was largely positive, a handful of hecklers threw rubbish at him in City Hall and derisory pennies as he sang "Put Your Dreams Away" at the Union Club. His bitterness surfaced when he reportedly referred to his old stomping ground as "a sewer", and for a while Hoboken's relationship with its favourite son was strained. But restaurants such as **Piccolo's** on First Street, **Leo's** at Second and Grand and **Fiori's House of Quality Deli** on Adams Street, and **Lepore's** chocolate shop on Garden Street, could be relied upon for music, photographic tributes and affectionate anecdotes.

After Sinatra's death Hoboken was not slow to honour the singer. In 1998 the **Frank Sinatra Memorial Park** was completed, on **Sinatra Drive** between Fourth and Fifth Street, and quickly became known as **Sinatra Park**. A sunken, paved amphitheatre with a café and glorious views of the New York skyline, it is used for outdoor musical and theatrical performances, often by the Hoboken Shakespeare Company.

Although there is not yet an official Sinatra Museum, **Hoboken Historical Museum** at **1301 Hudson Street** runs a two-hour walking tour that takes in various locations, including the Hoboken Public Library, which features a painting of Sinatra with his mother, and the Hoboken firehouse where Marty worked.

In 2003 the Post Office at 89 River Street was renamed the **Frank Sinatra Post Office Building**, at the instigation of councillor Bob Menendez. "While naming a post office after New Jersey's proudest to some may seem unusual," wrote Menendez, "the symbolism is unmistakable; like Sinatra's voice and music, the postal service brings people – family and friends – together."

Jersey City

Marty Sinatra and Dolly Garavente eloped to Jersey City when her family refused to acknowledge the couple's intentions. They were married on February 14, 1913, at **City Hall** on Grove Street.

A generation later, in the summer of 1935, it was at **Loews Theatre** on Journal Square that Frank and his date Nancy, who lived in Jersey City, saw Bing Crosby perform. "After seeing him that night," Sinatra recalled, "I knew I had to be a singer." The theatre remains open for business.

Frank and Nancy married at **Our Lady of Sorrows Church** on Clerk Street on February 4, 1939. Later their first two children were born at **Margaret Hague Maternity Hospital** on Clifton Place at Fairmount Avenue; Nancy on June 8, 1940, and Frank Jr. on January 10, 1944.

The couple honeymooned and then resided for a while in a three room flat on **Garfield Avenue** for $42 a week. Later they relocated to an apartment at **137 Bergen Avenue**, but by 1943 the newly affluent Sinatras had moved to a brick house with seven rooms at **220 Lawrence Avenue** in the smart New Jersey suburb of Hasbrouck Heights. It was this home that was besieged by bobbysoxers; Nancy would send out doughnuts to the fans sitting on the lawn who refused to go home.

New York

Most of the famous venues from Sinatra's early career have disappeared. The **Capitol Theatre** on Broadway is no more, the **Riobamba** is long gone and the **Paramount Theatre** was demolished in 1964. (The modern salsa club the **Copacabana** should not be confused with the club that Sinatra played in the 1940s and sang about on "Meet Me At The Copa".)

The **Waldorf-Astoria** still exists in its Art-Deco glory at 301 Park Avenue, though the famed Wedgwood Room where Sinatra played for eight weeks in 1943 is now named The Hilton Room. Sinatra kept a suite at the hotel and in 1974 shared it with Ava Gardner. He performed at the hotel in 1988 when his wife Barbara was honoured by a "Friars tribute", a light-hearted show business testimonial dinner; and in 1992 at a political fundraiser with Liza Minnelli and Shirley MacLaine.

Madison Square Garden on Seventh Avenue, where Sinatra appeared in 1943 for a Greek Civil War relief benefit and in November 1991 as part of his Diamond Jubilee World Tour, is still one of the world's premier concert halls, as is **Carnegie Hall** on 57th Street and Seventh Avenue, which hosted Sinatra appearances from the 1940s until the 1980s.

Many of Sinatra's favourite New York watering holes have gone, including the two name-checked in "Me And My Shadow": **Jilly's**, which was at 52nd

Street and Seventh Avenue (seen briefly in *The Manchurian Candidate*), and **Toots Shor's** restaurant at 51 West 51st Street. A few remain, however, including the **"21" Club** at 21 West 52nd Street. Ninety years old and still going strong, it lived through prohibition – and through the gossip journalist Walter Winchell hinting that it had been serving alcohol, after he had been banned. Sinatra dined here often and brawled outside with a photographer in 1966 when with Mia Farrow but behaved himself, more or less, with Jackie Onassis in 1975.

P. J. Clarke's, the legendarily unspoiled saloon at 55th Street and Third Avenue where Frank used to shoot the breeze with his cronies in the 1960s and 1970s, was finally modernized in 2002, but not appallingly so; Sinatra's music is still on the jukebox and the new owners have tried to retain some of the 120-year-old pub's original charm. Sinatra was apparently so fond of the pizzas from **Patsy's** that he had them flown out to Vegas; the original restaurant can be found at 2287 First Avenue, between 117th and 118th streets, in East Harlem.

Las Vegas

Two weeks after Sinatra died, his friend Gregory Peck addressed the assembled participants and guests of the Frank Sinatra Las Vegas Golf Tournament. "He brought unmatched excitement to the Strip and defined the word 'swinger' for all times," the actor said. "With his little gang of merry men he established forever a sense of free-floating fun and frolic that captured the imagination of the world."

But Sinatra's Las Vegas is all but gone. **The Desert Inn** at 3145 Las Vegas Boulevard lasted the longest; the venue on "The Strip" (as this street is generally known) hosted his first appearance as a performer in 1951 and, much expanded, had him back in the 1990s, but finally shut in 2000. Also on Las Vegas Boulevard was **the Sands**, Sinatra's Vegas venue from 1953 until his contretemps with Carl Cohen in 1967, which was eventually demolished in 1996 after various expansions and refurbishments, to make way for modern developments.

Still thriving, at 3570 Las Vegas Boulevard, is **Caesar's Palace**, where Sinatra's Vegas appearances took place exclusively from 1968 until his disagreement with Sanford Waterman in 1970. After his return from retirement this was his Vegas venue again between 1974 and 1984 and the fountain outside the hotel was named the **Frank Sinatra Fountain** in 1979.

He performed between 1984 and 1987 at the **Golden Nugget** at 129 E. Fremont Street, between 1987 and 1990 at **Bally's** at 3645 Las Vegas Boulevard, and between 1990 and 1992 at **The Riviera** at 2901 Las Vegas Boulevard. After a 77th birthday season in 1992 back at the Desert Inn, his final fling with the city was at the **MGM Grand,** the new but quintessential Vegas venue, at 3799 Las Vegas Boulevard in 1993-94. But by then he hardly knew where he was.

When Sinatra died, the lights of Las Vegas Boulevard were meant to dim in their customary show of respect, but technical difficulties meant that the gesture was not as powerful as it might have been. And although there was some lobbying to have Las Vegas Boulevard renamed The Sinatra Strip, fans have to be content with the completion in 1998 of a road for local traffic to relieve congestion on the Strip called **Frank Sinatra Drive**.

California

When the Sinatra family moved to California in the spring of 1944, they took up residence in a house that had once belonged to the actress Mary Astor at **10051 Valley Spring Lane**, in **Toluca Lake**, a suburb of Los Angeles. One advantage of the property was the high security wall that kept fans off the property. Sinatra's third child, Tina, was born at the **Cedars Of Lebanon Hospital** in **Hollywood** on June 20, 1948, after Frank sped through every red light to get Nancy there.

In the summer of 1949 Sinatra moved his family to an expansive, hacienda-style property at **320 Carolwood Drive, Holmby Hills**, in West Los Angeles. Within months he moved out to be with Ava Gardner, but it was at the Holmby Hills address that the Sinatra children grew up with their mother, and where Frank returned when he could to play Dad. In the mid-1950s, however, he was just as often nearby at **232 South Mapleton Drive**, the home of Humphrey Bogart and Lauren Bacall and the Holmby Hills "Rat Pack".

1148 E. Alejo Road, Palm Springs, also known as "Twin Palms" because of the trees at the front of the property, was originally conceived for Frank and Nancy to their specifications, but after the breakdown of the Sinatras' marriage, in the early 1950s it was Frank and the second Mrs Sinatra who moved into the house. Designed in a style that was known as "desert modern", it had a piano-shaped swimming pool, a projection room and seven bathrooms. It was the venue for many a party and many an emotional scene, including one infamous evening when Sinatra threw Gardner's belongings onto the drive. When Ava left him, it was this property that onlookers described as a shrine to her. For $15,000 a week, the place can be hired, all decked out in 1950s glory and with Sinatra's original hi-fi in place; the details are available at www.timeandplacehomes.com.

After Ava and Frank divorced in 1957, Sinatra bought an extra house, at **2666 Bowmont Drive**, **Beverly Hills**, overlooking Coldwater Canyon – the bachelor pad described by Sinatra's valet George Jacobs as a "sprawling, Japanese-style estate", where much of the Sinatra-Bacall romance took place. When between houses Sinatra sometimes stayed at another of his properties, **882 North Doheny Drive, West Hollywood**; on other occasions he would house girlfriends such as Marilyn Monroe and Jean Carmen there. People who knew about this called the building "The Sinatra Arms".

In the late 1950s Sinatra also purchased the legendary two-and-a-half acre site known as **the Compound**, designed by William Cody, which would be his California base for many years. Located on Wonder Palms Road, Palm Springs – now known as 70588 Frank Sinatra Drive, Rancho Mirage – near the Tamarisk Country Club, it played host to guests as diverse as the Kennedys and Sam Giancana. When JFK became president, Sinatra put up a plaque in the bedroom Kennedy had used that read "JOHN F. KENNEDY SLEPT HERE NOVEMBER 6TH AND 7TH 1960" – but he was a year out; JFK had stayed there in 1959. In anticipation of the JFK visit in 1962 that never happened, Sinatra expanded the three-bedroom property to include guest bungalows and a heliport. Mia Farrow was shown around in 1965 and was overwhelmed, recalling later the vast glass side to the living room; she moved in during 1966, and out again in 1967. Further guest bungalows were added – named "My Way" and "The Tender Trap" – each with "his and hers" bathroom facilities, and a bungalow for mother Dolly was completed in the early 1970s; she lived at the compound until her death in 1977. There was a projection room, sauna, barbershop, tennis court and painting studio, two pools and, according to one count, thirteen bathrooms.

In 1995 the Compound was sold for around $5 million to the Canadian tycoon Jim Pattison, who used it for business entertaining. Sinatra left behind his huge train set – he developed the hobby in the 1960s – and Pattison, a model railway enthusiast, released a video of Frank's set-up, *Celebrity Train Layouts Part 1, Frank Sinatra* (available on McComas/Stachler Video).

Frank and Barbara Marx lived at the Compound in the early years of their marriage, but from 1986 also spent an increasing amount of time at a new 14-room house at **915 Foothill Road, Beverly Hills**, which they bought for more than $6 million. They also bought a beach-house in 1990, at **30966 Broad Beach Road, Malibu**.

For four decades Sinatra was a regular at many bars and restaurants around California, which kept many saloonkeepers and restaurateurs on their toes. He was a regular at **Chasen's** at 9039 Beverly Boulevard, where he abused the author Mario Puzo in the early 1970s; a renowned celebrity restaurant for 59 years, Chasen's closed in 1995. **Ciro's**, where Sinatra punched Lee Mortimer in 1947, was located at 8433 Sunset Boulevard, where the Comedy Store now stands. **The Chi Chi Club** on North Palm Canyon Drive, Palm Springs – where Sinatra took both Lana Turner and Ava Gardner – is now the site of the Desert Fashion Plaza. Other favourite Sinatra hangouts that no longer exist are **Puccini's**, the restaurant at 224 South Beverly Drive, Beverly Hills, that Frank opened with Peter Lawford in 1959, **Romanoff's** on Rodeo Drive, Beverly Hills, and a latter-day favourite, **Dominick's**, at 70030 Highway 111, Rancho Mirage, where the speciality was "Chicken Sinatra".

Several of Sinatra's favourite places to eat are still around. A 1950s favourite, **The Doll House**, became **Sorrentino's** in 1966, and still trades at 1032 North Palm Canyon Drive, Palm Springs, boasting "Steak Sinatra" – onions, bell peppers, mushrooms simmered in a red wine sauce – for only $19.95. Frank and Barbara threw a pre-wedding party in 1976 at **Melvyn's At The Ingleside Inn** at 200 West Ramon Road, Palm Springs, an establishment that continues to pride itself on its traditional service. The Old English theme pub and restaurant **Lord Fletcher's** at 70385 Highway 111, Rancho Mirage, was a longtime hangout. Frank had a favourite table (in the corner), liked the pot roast and in 1985 celebrated his 70th birthday there.

Frank Facts

Sometimes cited as his favourite restaurant, **Matteo's** is at 2323 Westwood Boulevard, **Westwood**. Opened in 1963, it was run by another native of Hoboken, Matty Jordan, who was delivered at birth by Sinatra's mother Dolly and grew up across the street from Frank. Sinatra liked its red-checked tablecloths and homely atmosphere and had a favourite corner booth that he occupied on many Sundays. The restaurant is still open and an abstract painting by Sinatra hangs near where he used to dine.

Other landmarks in California include the tribute to Sinatra on the "**Walk of Stars**" on the west side of North Palm Canyon Drive, Palm Springs, between Tahquitz Canyon Way and Amado Road, and his handprint outside **Grauman's Chinese Theatre** at 6925 Hollywood Boulevard; the ceremony took place in July 1965. There are the two recording venues where he created his 1950s masterpieces: Welton Beckett's distinctive stack-of-records tower, the **Capitol Records Building**, at 1750 Vine Street, Hollywood – still a working studio – and **Capitol Studios** at 5515 Melrose Avenue, Hollywood, now used for TV. Next door is **Paramount Studios**, where Sinatra made *The Joker Is Wild* in 1957. **The Cal-Neva Resort,** which caused Sinatra so much bother in 1963, is still open on Lake Tahoe as a spa and casino, but is much changed.

The picturesque, peaceful **Wolfson Park**, on the corner of DaVall Drive and Frank Sinatra Drive, Rancho Mirage, has a welcoming message spoken by Frank himself, which is triggered by pressing a red button on a stand near the entrance. **Sinatra's grave** is at Desert Memorial Park, 69920 Ramon Road, **Cathedral City**. The headstone gives his name, his dates and the title of the Cy Coleman/Carolyn Leigh song that he first recorded in 1964 and last sang at his final gig in February 1995: "The Best Is Yet To Come."

The lost Sinatra

**The projects that never were –
and those that should never have happened**

The lost music

Finian's Rainbow

An animated feature of the Burton Lane and Yip Harburg musical was planned in 1955 and the soundtrack was to feature Sinatra, **Ella Fitzgerald** and **Louis Armstrong**, among others. Parts of the score were recorded, including Sinatra singing "That Great Come-And-Get-It Day" and "If This Isn't Love", improvising on a blues with Louis and duetting on "Necessity" with Ella. The financing of the movie foundered, however, and the surviving soundtrack was unheard for many years. It was eventually released in 2002 on *Sinatra In Hollywood*.

Lush Life

This sophisticated, artsy paean to saloon living by **Billy Strayhorn** – written when he was only seventeen – was an ideal song for Sinatra's album of hymns of solitude, *Only The Lonely*. But the melody is notoriously tricky, and when it came to recording it – on a session in May 1958 at which he recorded another seven songs – Sinatra lost interest after three attempts. Arranger Nelson Riddle suggested, "Frank would have been momentarily put off by all the changes that had to go on ... he might have gotten a little tired." Pianist Bill Miller remembered that Frank "didn't take the trouble to learn it". On the outtakes, when someone suggests putting it aside for a minute, Sinatra is heard to say, "Put it aside for about a year!" He never went back to it. (When Strayhorn's close musical associate Duke Ellington was recording the tribute album *And His Mother Called Him Bill*, he also passed on "Lush

Life", but for more cryptic reasons. "It's not him," Duke was heard to say, "And it's not me.")

The Italian Songbook

The Italian Songbook would have been a follow-up to *Sinatra And Strings*. **Don Costa** prepared an album's worth of arrangements of Italian favourites, including "La Strada", "Arrivederci Roma" and "Non Dimenticar" – with the help of his mother, who sang the melodies into a tape recorder. The project was on and off for much of the 1960s, and the album never came into being.

Frank and Ella

Sinatra was a long-standing admirer of **Ella Fitzgerald** and spoke often in the mid-1960s about making an album with her. In 1967 a few tunes were selected ("Love And Marriage", "A Taste Of Honey", a revival of their *Finian's Rainbow* duet "Necessity"), Nelson Riddle was appointed arranger and there was an initial run-through. Sinatra, who had an antipathy towards Ella's manager **Norman Granz**, was disappointed at the way the material was working, and the project fizzled out. Ella was Frank's only suggestion for a singing partner on *Duets* in 1993, but was too ill to participate, and although they appeared together in concert and on television, they never managed to make a record together.

Lonely At The Top

In the late 1960s Sinatra followed keenly the efforts of some of the new generation of songwriters. Randy Newman, whose debut *Randy Newman Creates Something New Under The Sun* had appeared in 1967 on Reprise, was one of the brightest, and wrote "Lonely At The Top" specifically for Sinatra. The song portrays the isolation of an idol in Newman's customary economical, edgy style. "I've been around the world/Had my pick of any girl/You'd think I'd be happy but I'm not," it opens, concluding, "Listen all you fools out there/Go on and love me, I don't care." Unfortunately, Sinatra didn't find this kind of irony appealing and passed on the idea. The song later appeared on Newman's album *Sail Away*.

Here's To The Ladies

After several years of estrangement, Sinatra and **Nelson Riddle** began to work together again in 1977 on the *Sinatra And Friends* TV special and on this album of songs with female names in the title. In March Sinatra sang five of the ten or so charts Riddle had prepared: tender, swinging remakes of "Nancy" and "Sweet Lorraine", a sumptuous "Emily"; a first recording of the 1945 Jack Lawrence/Ann Ronell song "Linda"; and the Sammy Cahn/Jimmy Van Heusen commission "Barbara" for his new wife. Although the results are quite charming and certainly no worse than most of *Trilogy*, the project was abandoned after two sessions and Riddle and Sinatra never worked together again. Three of the tracks appeared on *The Reprise Collection* in 1990 and all five appeared on *The Complete Reprise Studio Recordings* in 1995.

Frank and Lena

The pairing of Sinatra with singer **Lena Horne** was the brainchild of producer and arranger **Quincy Jones**, who envisaged a triple album featuring an all-star line-up of jazz musicians, including Dizzy Gillespie, Herbie Hancock and Gerry Mulligan. He got as far as choosing 36 standards, setting the keys and planning a week of recording sessions in February 1983; but after a series of disruptive events – Don Costa died, Lena Horne developed a vocal nodule and Frank was snarled up in previous engagements – the momentum was lost and the album was cancelled. Jones described the lost Sinatra/Horne project as "one of the biggest disappointments in my life".

The lost films

Knock On Any Door

Hearing that Columbia were making a picture of this Willard Motley novel, centred on Nick "Pretty Boy" Romano, a street kid from the slums who is arrested and tried for murder, Frank approached David Selznick's assistant, **Anita Colby**, and told her how much he identified with the character. "That's my life," he apparently told her. "Everybody in my class either went to the electric chair or was hung. If I hadn't had a voice, I'd have been right along with them." Selznick decided that at 33 years old, Sinatra was too old, and the part went to John Derek. Humphrey Bogart starred as his defence lawyer, Nicholas Ray directed and Romano's mantra – "Live fast, die young and leave a good-looking corpse" – entered the lexicon of rebellious youth.

Pink Tights

A film from 20th Century Fox in Cinemascope mooted to star Sinatra and **Marilyn Monroe**, *Pink Tights* (aka *The Girl In Pink Tights*) would have been a remake of Betty Grable's picture from 1943, *Coney Island*, a variant of the Pygmalion story of refining a rough diamond, with new songs by Jule Styne and Sammy Cahn; and one number was "The Best Shoulder To Cry On", which Frank would have sung while attempting to woo the character played by Marilyn. During an assertive phase of her career, she declared the dumb blonde material unsuitable and decided to boycott the movie. Failing to show on the first day of shooting in January 1954, she married Joe DiMaggio a few days later and Fox suspended her. The film was never made.

On The Waterfront

Sinatra desperately wanted the role of Terry Malloy – the spunky stevedore who defies union corruption on the New York docks – in the production of Budd Schulberg's novel *On The Waterfront*, which was to be shot in Hoboken. He felt as close to the character as he had done to Maggio in *From Here To Eternity*, and the role would have been perfect for allowing him to develop his fresh credibility as an actor. He even got the impression from producer **Sam Spiegel** that the role was his ("For Chrissakes, you are Hoboken!"); but when he cast Marlon Brando (who had changed his mind about working with "whistle-blower" director Elia Kazan) Spiegel claimed that he had always wanted Sinatra to play the priest. The furious and hurt Sinatra sued for $500,000, claiming breach of contract. The dispute was settled out of court, but Sinatra forgave neither Spiegel nor Brando.

Carousel

Well cast as the feckless fairground barker Billy Bigelow in the Rodgers and Hammerstein musical *Carousel*, Sinatra even recorded part of the soundtrack ("Soliloquy" and "If I Loved You"). However, when he arrived on the set and discovered that he was expected to shoot each scene twice – once for a regular 35mm print and once for CinemaScope, Fox's patented widescreen system – he walked off the picture. "You're not getting two Sinatras for the price of one" is one of his legendary parting shots.

Paris By Night

When it was rumoured that Sinatra was to make a film called *Paris By Night* with **Brigitte Bardot**, the press – *Playboy* in particular – were very excited. "What happens when these two volatile substances mingle in the same crucible, when the Voice meets the Broad of Broads?" the magazine posited. "The concept is enough to make Olympus tremble, the skies darken, the oceans churn, and to knock the whole world on its collective clyde." (See p.361).

It was the singer (according to *Playboy* "a hip brand of love god") who played hard to get. After meeting him several times on several continents, Bardot's manager Raoul Levy finally got Sinatra to state his terms: $250,000 and 40 percent of the profits as co-producer, as well as 6 percent of the profits as co-star. And the film wouldn't be made on location in Paris; "I've had that location bit," said Frank. "There are too many idiots around watching." Stunned by Sinatra's demands, Levy eventually admitted defeat and the Sinatra/Bardot partnership never made the screen.

Some Like It Hot

With Tony Curtis and Marilyn Monroe already lined up to star in Billy Wilder's classic comedy, Sinatra got as far as reading the script before he passed on it to shoot *A Hole In The Head* instead. The role was filled by **Jack Lemmon**, whose performance won him an Oscar nomination, and the rest is history.

Frank Facts

Born Yesterday

In the early 1960s Sinatra was concerned about the fragile state of his friend and erstwhile lover **Marilyn Monroe** and was looking for projects that would give her some direction. One of these, which went as far as Frank offering $500,000 for the rights, was a musical remake of the 1951 Judy Holliday movie *Born Yesterday* – yet another variation on the *Pygmalion* theme. Monroe would have been in Holliday's Oscar-winning role Billie Dawn, the chorus girl who gets given lessons in "class" from Paul Verrall, with whom she falls in love. Sinatra would have taken that role, which William Holden had in the original, but Monroe died before the plans went further.

A Clockwork Orange

Brad Dexter had the idea of developing Anthony Burgess's cult novel into a film; Sinatra read the book, claimed not to understand it and deemed it unsuitable for a movie. Stanley Kubrick thought differently.

The Only Game In Town

Both Sinatra and **Elizabeth Taylor** were committed to George Stevens's film about an ageing showgirl who falls for a piano player in Las Vegas. The production was delayed while Taylor had an emergency hysterectomy, and Sinatra had to bow out to fulfil other engagements. His part was taken by **Warren Beatty**.

Dirty Harry

John Wayne had passed on the role of vigilante cop Harry Callahan when the Harry Fink and Rita Fink screenplay was called *Dead Right*, and Sinatra was lined up to do the film and to be directed by Irvin Kershner. However, a hand problem that had been aggravating Sinatra for some time – muscle contraction causing his fingers to set in a claw – needed surgery and he was forced to withdraw from the project. Paul Newman turned down the role before **Clint Eastwood** was cast as Harry; Don Siegel was made director.

The lost Sinatra

The Godfather

Amazing but true: **Otto Preminger**, the director who had coaxed a thrilling performance from Frank in *The Man With The Golden Arm* and the original choice of director on the Paramount movie of the book by Mario Puzo, wanted Sinatra as Don Corleone. Frank's antipathy towards the book and its suggestion that the singer Johnny Fontane's Mafia-assisted career was based on his own was well known (see page 88), so Preminger offered to cut the Fontane character from the screenplay. Sinatra couldn't be persuaded so Preminger, denied his favoured leading man, left the movie. It was eventually made by Francis Ford Coppola with Sinatra's old nemesis **Marlon Brando** in the title role. (When it came to *The Godfather: Part III* Sinatra was lined up by Coppola for the supporting role of Don Altobello, but he turned down the opportunity because of the three-month shoot – and the part eventually went to Eli Wallach, who Sinatra had beaten to the role of Maggio in *From Here To Eternity* more than thirty years earlier.)

Sinatra's worst recordings

The Dum Dot Song

1946; available on *The Complete Columbia Recordings 1943-1952* (Columbia/Legacy)

Sinatra is reunited with The Pied Pipers on an appalling novelty about getting chewing gum from a machine by putting a penny in the "gum slot", or "dum dot" in toddler talk.

One Finger Melody (Yum-Dee-Da-Dee-Da)

1950; available on *The Complete Columbia Recordings 1943-1952* (Columbia/Legacy)

A witless sentimental waltz. Frank misses his girl so much, he picks out with one finger a saccharine tune on a piano while humming like a moron.

Frank Facts

Mama Will Bark

1951; available on *The Complete Columbia Recordings 1943-1952* (Columbia/Legacy)

In his novel little rumba about romancing dogs, featuring the multi-talented Dagmar, Sinatra hams it up for all he's worth but at least refuses to perform the canine howls himself; that privilege went to Donald Baine. Execrable, but weirdly cute.

Tennessee Newsboy

1952; available on *The Complete Columbia Recordings 1943-1952* (Columbia/Legacy)

A clattering washboard, a steel guitar and another tawdry piece of rhythmic slop, about a tap-dancing paperboy. Composed by Percy Faith and Dick "Mama Will Bark" Manning.

Two Hearts, Two Kisses

1955; available on *The Complete Capitol Singles* (Capitol)

Sinatra had already tried rocking the blues on "Castle Rock" and "Bim Bam Baby" (both 1951), with dire results. This doo-wop horror with the vocal group The Nuggets, on which Sinatra is enthusiastic but clueless, sinks even lower.

There's A Flaw In My Flue

1956; available on *The Rare Sinatra* (Capitol)

This faultlessly performed Jimmy Van Heusen ballad in the style of *Close To You* concerns the faulty fireplace in the title. Johnny Burke's ludicrous lyric was deliberately inapt ("From every beautiful ember a memory arose/Now I try to remember and smoke gets in my nose") and the song was recorded as a joke to test Capitol's discernment. The executives didn't notice and Sinatra had to own up. The straight-faced send-up eventually appeared in 1978.

The lost Sinatra

Everybody's Twistin'

1952; available on *The Complete Reprise Studio Recordings* (Reprise)

"Everybody's Twistin' " was updated from Ted Koehler and Rube Bloom's sophisticated mid-1930s song about an ancient dance craze, "Truckin'", in the hope that it would earn the down-on-his-luck writer Bloom some dough. The attempt at commentating wryly on a contemporary trend while simultaneously trying to cash in on it was bound to fail on all fronts.

Downtown

1966; available on *Strangers In The Night* (Reprise)

Tony Hatch's hit for Petula Clark is performed by Sinatra with discernible distaste in a go-go style; he makes a peculiar noise in the back of his throat before each title line as if he's about to throw up. He sings it even more campily on the 1966 TV special *A Man And His Music Part II*, with daughter Nancy.

Some Enchanted Evening

1967; available on *The World We Knew* (Reprise)

Arranged by the mysterious H. B. Barnum, this grotesque attempt to swing Rodgers and Hammerstein is so farcically misguided, it may be the funniest thing Sinatra ever did.

Noah

1973; available on *Ol' Blue Eyes Is Back* (Reprise)

Patronizing, overwrought Joe Raposo babble about the world being an ark, all of us being Noah and our obligation to sing with the nightingale and live in peace with all the animals. Solemn and righteous enough to have the average vegetarian signing up for an elephant shoot.

Night And Day

1977; available on *The Complete Reprise Studio Recordings* (Reprise)

A cop-show trombone lick and a funky bass line herald the fabulous news that on one of his all-time classic songs, Sinatra has gone disco. The work of Joe Beck, the jazz guitarist turned fusion arranger, this inappropriate arrangement was performed a few times (including on the 1977 TV special *Sinatra And Friends*) and was released as a single, which flopped, but eventually was dropped.

That's What God Looks Like To Me

1980; available on *Trilogy* (Reprise)

Frank's fictional young son wants to know what God looks like. Sinatra explains: rainbows, flowers, moonlight, but more than anything, you, my son. Nauseous.

Frankspeak

Sinatrification

Sinatra had a penchant for manipulating lyrics, in particular during live performances. Here are some of his more curious efforts.

The Lady Is A Tramp (Richard Rodgers/Lorenz Hart)

Original: "She loves the free, fresh wind in her hair"
Sinatra: "She loves the cool, free, fine wind in her hair"
Sinatra: "She loves the fine, cool, wild, wild, kookoo wind in her hair"
Sinatra: "She loves the free, fine, wild, knocked-out, kookoo, groovy wind in her hair"

Original: "She's broke, it's oke"
Sinatra: "She's broke, ha ha"
Sinatra: "She's broke, what the hell"
Sinatra: "She's broke [shrugs silently]"

It Was A Very Good Year (Ervin Drake)

Original: "It was a very good year…"
Sinatra: "It was a mess of good year…"

Stars Fell On Alabama (Frank Perkins/ Mitchell Parish)

Original: "Stars fell on Alabama last night"
Sinatra: "Stars fractured 'Bama last night"

Frank Facts

I Get A Kick Out You (Cole Porter)

Original: "I get a kick…"
Sinatra: "You give me a boot…"

It's All Right With Me (Cole Porter)

Original: "They're not her lips, but such tempting lips"
Sinatra: "They're not her chops, but they're such tempting chops"

Just One Of Those Things (Cole Porter)

Original: "So goodbye, dear, and amen"
Sinatra: "So goodbye, goodbye, bye bye, goodbye baby, and amen"

Come Fly With Me (Sammy Cahn/Jimmy Van Heusen)

Original: "We'll just glide starry-eyed"
Sinatra: "We'll just glide clyde to clyde"
Sinatra: "We'll just glide absolutely petrified"

Something (George Harrison)

Original: "You stick around and it might show"
Sinatra: "You hang around Jack, it might show"

Mrs Robinson (Paul Simon)

Original: "Jesus loves you more than you will know"
Sinatra: "Jilly loves you more than you will know"

Sinatra's slang

Part of the allure of Frank and the Rat Pack in the 1960s was their particular use of slang and established hipster terms, blended with certain phrases and words that they had coined themselves. Sinatra gave an interview in the early 1960s to Art Buchwald, a Paris-based columnist for the now defunct *New York Herald Tribune*, and offered the following interpretations.

Broad an affectionate word for "woman". Less uncouth, allegedly, than "dame".

Bunter "The opposite of a gasser ... a nowhere. He can never get to first base."

Clyde a catch-all noun. "If I want someone to pass the salt I would say, 'Pass the clyde.' 'I don't like her clyde' might mean 'I don't like her voice.' 'I have to go to the clyde' could mean 'I have to go to the party.' "

Fink "A fink is a loser. Fink comes from a strike-breaker named Fink who killed his friend during a strike. So to me a fink is a guy who would kill his own friends."

Gasser "Applies to a person. He's a big-leaguer, the best. He can hit the ball right out of the park."

Harvey "A square. Harvey, or Harv, is the typical tourist who goes into a French restaurant and says, 'What's ready?' "

Other elements of Sinatraspeak, mostly identified by Arnold Shaw in his book from 1968, include:

Bag an area of interest, as in "What's your bag?"

Big casino dead, as in "bought the big casino in the sky"

Big-leaguer a capable, reliable fellow who will handle all manner of things correctly

Bird a catch-all noun, often referring to the male member

Bombsville or *Endsville* disappointment, breakdown, failure

Bum or *creep* or *crumb* a disliked person

Charley or *Sam*: a general form of address, as in Charley Greenface or Suntan Charley for the pale-faced Bill Miller

Charlies a lady's chest

Chick a girl who is youthful and attractive

Cool or *crazy* an adjective of approval

Dame a mildly derogatory term for a woman, possibly older and possibly unattractive

Dig to approve, as in "I dig you, baby"

End a noun that shows extreme approval, as in "That chick is the end, man"

Gasoline alcohol in general, and in particular Jack Daniel's

Hey-hey: fun, often physical, as in " a little hey-hey"

Mothery adjective of approval, often for a party

Mouse a demure female

Player a significant fellow

Punk a disagreeable, lower-class fellow

Rain a noun used in phrases such as "I think it's going to rain" to indicate displeasure with social proceedings

Ring-a-ding an adjective showing approval

Scramsville a hasty departure

Square a Harvey

Tomato a female who is a "ripe tomato" may be ready for seducing or marrying

Twirl a female who likes to dance

Sinatra jokes

"I was sitting with a girl in the lounge of the Sands. I knew she was somebody I could score with if things went right. So I went up to him at his table and said, 'Listen Frank, I'm with this girl, and if you came over and said hello to me and her, it would help a lot.' He said no problem. So after a while he walked over and said, 'Hey Don, it's nice to see you and the beautiful lady.' I looked up and said, very loud, 'Frank, not now! Can't you see I'm with somebody!' "

DON RICKLES, 1960S

"Come in, Frank, make yourself at home. Hit somebody."

DON RICKLES, 1960S

Frankspeak

"I have no idea who it was tried to shoot me. After the shots were fired, all I heard was someone singing, 'Doobie doobie do'. "

JACKIE MASON, ON BEING ATTACKED AFTER TELLING FRANK AND MIA JOKES, 1967

"Hear about the trouble at Frank Sinatra's house? Mia Farrow dropped her Silly Putty in Frank's Poligrip."

JOHNNY CARSON, 1968

"They finally let Frank out of the country, right after the head of the union down there woke up one morning and saw a kangaroo's head on the next pillow."

BOB HOPE, AFTER THE DEBACLE IN AUSTRALIA IN 1974

"He was special kind of guy and very generous. If you admired his tie, he'd send you over a tie just like it. If you said, 'I like your suit', Frank would send you a suit. If you said, 'I like your girl', he'd send over two guys named Carmine and Nunzio."

GENE KELLY, 1977

"This is a great crowd. But half of Frank's pals couldn't be here. Half didn't find the time and the other half are doing time."

MILTON BERLE, AT SINATRA'S "ROAST", A LIGHT-HEARTED TRIBUTE DINNER, AT THE MGM, LAS VEGAS, 1978

"I'm glad you came out of retirement, Frank. Too bad your voice didn't join you."

MILTON BERLE, 1978

Kant: "To be is to do."
Nietzsche: "To do is to be."
Sinatra: "Do be do be do."

SINATRA AT THE ROYAL ALBERT HALL IN 1980

Books and websites

Books about Sinatra

Just as Sinatra generated miles of column inches in the press when he made news, his life and career have also inspired dozens of books. Some are hostile and some are hagiographic, but few provide assiduous critiques of his work and grapple with Sinatra's entirety. Here is a selection of the more diverting works, presented in chronological order, with their publication dates and their original publishers in the US and/or UK.

Robin Douglas-Home: **Sinatra**

Grosset & Dunlap/Michael Joseph; 1962

In 1961 the British journalist Robin Douglas-Home wrote an informed, intelligent article on Nelson Riddle for *The Queen* magazine and got a copy to Sinatra via the singer's friends the Romanoffs, whom the journalist had met by chance. Sinatra was impressed by the article and granted the writer several weeks of **unprecedented access** to his world in 1961 and 1962 – which included the early Reprise years, the *Point Of No Return* sessions, the *Great Songs From Great Britain* sessions and the premiere of *The Manchurian Candidate*. Douglas-Home was treated to generous reminiscences, which he quotes at great length and which have since been requoted in countless Sinatra books and articles. His reportage is observant and involving and his portrayal of Sinatra is deferential but vivid. He was dazzled, and as a result the reader is too. For Sinatra fans who want an uncritical whiff of the man's presence, this is the book.

Arnold Shaw: **Sinatra**

Holt, Rinehart and Winston/W. H. Allen; 1968

This is an elegant, substantial trawl through the events of Sinatra's life and career until the late Sixties, which Arnold Shaw identifies as a period when the singer became "more deeply immersed in the quest for money and status". Shaw, a composer and musicologist, does better than Douglas-Home at portraying Sinatra as "a figure of tension, turbulence and most of all, provocative contradictions", and although parts of his chronological account have been superseded by further rigorous research, his comments about Sinatra's music show an intelligent receptivity towards it.

Earl Wilson: **Sinatra**

Macmillan/W. H. Allen; 1976

Earl Wilson was a show business columnist who followed Sinatra's career closely throughout his years of fame, and at times he was even a confidant. He dined with the Sinatras in the 1940s and was close to Frank and Ava Gardner, and it was to Wilson that Sinatra turned when he used the press in an attempt to woo Ava back after a row in 1952. Wilson obliged with the headline: "Frankie Ready To Surrender; Wants Ava Back, Any Terms". But in the mid-Sixties, after a quarter-century of supporting Sinatra in the press – sometimes being in the conspicuous minority – Wilson found himself barred from Sinatra's presence and his shows. He never found out why.

Wilson was in a reasonable position to attempt a biography, and understandably his account of Sinatra's life is told from a media angle, the tale being spun out in a whirl of dialogue, reviews, headlines and interviews. Although he is cheerfully gossipy and reports the warts, Wilson is admirably free of rancour and remains to the end of the book – the dawn of the Barbara Marx years – an admirer. He has little to say about Sinatra's art, but few show business reporters of his generation did. Written in the heat of Sinatra's mid-Seventies comeback, it's all about the legend and the power.

Kitty Kelley: **His Way**

Bantam; 1986

Kitty Kelley's comprehensive **demolition** of Sinatra the man, written with the help of more than 800 interviews, can't be ignored, for *His Way* did for Sinatra's reputation what Albert Goldman's books did for Elvis's and John Lennon's. But what shocks the most is the author's delivery of a hatchet job that paints the blackest portrait possible. Hardly anyone quoted has a good word for Sinatra – many of his friends were not interviewed – and the book provides a character assassination.

The scandal amounts to this. Among other things, his mother was an abortionist; Sinatra knew underworld figures, some well, but always lied about it when questioned; he lost his temper sometimes and let fly, mostly with reporters and photographers; between wife number two and number three, he swung as no one has swung before, and introduced **JFK** to such pleasures; he panicked about his place in the world as the Sixties progressed and married a 21-year-old, and when that failed he bought himself respectability by fund-raising for the Republicans; he held grudges and sometimes he could be rude to people; and his bodyguards could occasionally be a little over-zealous.

The reader is left with the numb feeling that Sinatra was not so much an entertainer with character flaws and contradictions, but among the most unpleasant men in history, who did nothing but bad deeds. So be warned: read this book and you'll feel a little guilty about still loving Sinatra.

Frank Facts

There's no doubt that the pompous mythology that had been cultivated around Sinatra by the mid-1980s needed a little gainsaying. And whatever Kelley's motivation, method and style, here and there she illuminates some truth. But many of Kelley's revelations, which made headlines when published, have been accepted in diluted form as the darkish aspect of a more complex story.

Nancy Sinatra: Frank Sinatra: An American Legend

General Publishing Group/Virgin; 1995

The **almost official biography** – the Sinatra estate's version – is full of rare photographs, personal reminiscences and extensive documentation of every charitable act performed and tribute received. Daughter Nancy goes some way in this glossy hagiography towards producing a rebuttal of Kelley; the upside is emphasized, the accolades fulsome and the illustrations handsome. As a case for the defence, it has conviction, but it's still not entirely candid. In some sticky instances (when referring, for example, to Sinatra and Sam Giancana) Nancy has to resort to pointing out that her father has never been indicted for anything. Other contentious issues (Marilyn Monroe, beatings by his bodyguards) are not even mentioned.

Structured like a chronicle, it is best used as fascinating source material. For it contains long sections on incidents such as the kidnapping of Frank Sinatra Jr., "the worst nightmare of our lives", and details of family life; he was a "penny-candy kind of guy" who chuckled when she gave him a tie with sweets on for his 75th birthday. The website www.sinatrafamily .com has an updated version of the text, including Sinatra's final words: "I'm losing."

Will Friedwald: **Sinatra! The Song Is You: A Singer's Art**

Scribner; 1995

Will Friedwald is the discerning man's Sinatraphile. His passion for Sinatra goes way beyond the collection and cataloguing of V-Discs and rare TV appearances: he's got something to say and he says it. For his energy for writing about Sinatra's artistry at great length, in persistent detail and with intelligence, he truly is **the Chairman of the Bores**, and that's a compliment.

For anyone who has loved Sinatra's music and wants to know what fuels a fan's enthusiasm, *Sinatra! The Song Is You* is a revelation. His extraordinary book *Jazz Singing* had revealed in 1990 a remarkably young writer – he was in his late twenties – who had something worthwhile to express about years of swing and vintage adult pop, and the fizzy chapter that he devoted to Sinatra left Frank enthusiasts hungry for more. Five years on we got more than we bargained for.

Sinatra! The Song Is You is a remarkable achievement. Friedwald sought out as many of the surviving songwriters and musicians as he could, including people that no author on Sinatra had bothered to speak to or had access to, and gained fascinating insights into Frank's musical world. He's impatient with Sinatra's forays into what he insists on referring to unpleasantly as "kiddie pop" and despises the *Duets* albums. But, like a true Sinatraphile, he's fiercely loyal to Frank and there's barely a word of vulgar non-musical biography (no Mafia, little Ava), let alone negativity.

The 500-plus pages of exhaustive, exhausting discussion of all the music (from "Our Love" to *Duets II*) may eventually have the most ardent Frank fan shouting "enough already!", but the book is not for a single sitting. Like the music itself, it's to be savoured and returned to, often.

J. Randall Taraborrelli: **Sinatra: The Man Behind The Myth**

Carol Publishing Group/Mainstream; 1997

This is just one more showbiz saga for the tireless J. Randall Taraborrelli, who has written blockbuster biographies of Madonna, Michael Jackson, the Kennedy women and Grace Kelly, among others. Essentially building on the Shaw, Wilson and Kelley books with his own research and salacious style, his 700 pages and five years of writing yield some **fresh, wild material**. We learn that as an adolescent lover Sinatra used to call his penis "Big Frankie" and that Mia Farrow cured his mid-life impotence. Taraborrelli gets the first interview with one of Frank Sinatra Jr.'s kidnappers, Barry Keenan, and speculates that Sinatra was seriously considering marrying Marilyn Monroe when she died. Some of his research is sound, but Taraborrelli is not one to let sources who requested anonymity get in the way of telling a good yarn. Fifty-year-old conversations between Sinatra and George Evans – one of which has Sinatra suggesting blackmailing Lee Mortimer for being a homosexual – are reported as verbatim dialogue. It's spicy, but it's hard to trust.

For all his feeling for the detail and sweep of Sinatra's story, like others who have taken on the minutiae of a life, Taraborrelli displays only a partial sense of what is interesting about Sinatra as an artist. But, because of set agendas, limited viewpoints and plain prejudice, few books on Sinatra are expansive enough to capture all the essences of the man.

Fred Dellar and Mal Peachey:
Sinatra Night And Day: The Man And His Music

Chameleon; 1997

Fred Dellar and Mal Peachey make the unusual move of combining an account of the Sinatra story from **inside Frank's head** with musical critiques of his key records. So in the space of two paragraphs the reader goes from Frank thinking to himself, "that'll teach me to be a hero", when he contemplates nearly drowning on the shoot of *None But The Brave*, to him bringing "I Wish You Love" to a "full-flowering, spectacular end" on *It Might As Well Be Swing*. Or Frank is portrayed as thinking, after filming *Dirty Dingus Magee*, that "maybe he should go to Britain soon, that always made him feel better".

Once the eccentric narrative becomes familiar, the book is easy to enjoy; through its atmosphere and zip it conveys the energy of Sinatra's life, and covers a lot of ground and detail, stylishly and succinctly. And the photographs are beautifully chosen, too.

Bill Zehme: **The Way You Wear Your Hat: Frank Sinatra And The Lost Art Of Livin'**

Harper Collins; 1997

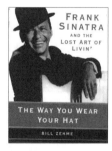

An irresistible, shamelessly fetishistic work of idolatry, *The Way You Wear Your Hat* focuses on Sinatra as **an icon of cool** and leader of men; in the author's own words, it is "part biography of sensibility, part handbook for dreamers of large dreams". It began life as an *Esquire* piece based on Sinatra's answers in 1996 to life's eternal questions, asked by Bill Zehme. How does one live large? ("You just keep moving.") What's the most important thing a father can tell his children? ("Be true to yourself and stay away from dark thoughts.") What should a man never do in the presence of a woman? ("Yawn.") What is the secret to doing good work? ("Never to accept anything without question. Never ignore that inner voice that tells you something could be better, even when other people tell you it's okay.")

Zehme then hangs a neat summary and elucidation of the Sinatra mystique on the topics broached, in old-style hip magazinese. Like an article-length extension of Stan Cornyn's sleeve notes for Reprise – in which every tie-knot and twitch was reported in portentous, staccato detail – this is a fabulous, over-the-top celebration that does much to revive the non-musical magic of Sinatra and is therefore the true counter to Kelley. On Frank's sleeplessness: "He would break more dawns than most mortals." On Frank's drinking: "Hangovers feared him." On Frank's hat: "The favoured slant: His back brim always curled aloft and the front snap was tugged down a couple of inches above his right brow. The move required two hands – aft hiking up, fore pulling down." He goes on like that brilliantly all the way through the book.

Zehme describes the way Sinatra mixes his martini, the kind of glasses he likes his JD in, how he tipped and why he was irresistible to women. He discusses his style, his swagger, his friendships and his loves. The account itself feels as if it's been dressed up in a tuxedo and topped off with the smell of Yardley English Lavender. Zehme doesn't, however, try to explain Sinatra. "The shadings of his psyche belong only to him," he wisely observes. "The life he has lived is as uncontainable as he is."

As a respite from the routine demolition of Frank in print, this is a heart-warmer.

Pete Hamill: **Why Sinatra Matters**

Little, Brown; 1998

A terrific 180-pager from the tough-graceful New York journalist and novelist who had been one of Frank's drinking pals. It's pungent with **first-hand reminiscences** of boozy late nights in P.J. Clarke's when the jukebox begins to play Billie Holiday singing "I'm A Fool To Want You" and a quietly pensive Sinatra announces that it's time to go. In the wee small hours Frank buttonholes Hamill with his confessions. "Women – I don't know what the hell to make of them. Do you? Maybe that's what it's all about. Maybe all that happens is you get older and know less."

Hamill also brings great heart and atmosphere to his description of Sinatra's background and gives one of the few generous descriptions of Sinatra's mother. "There was nothing mediocre or reserved about Dolly Garavente," he writes, before painting a colourful, compelling portrait of a powerful, gregarious, essentially good person. He also takes the trouble to reach into Sinatra's artistry, writing that "Sinatra had only one basic subject: loneliness" before going on to explain why, movingly and eloquently.

Shawn Levy: **Rat Pack Confidential**

Doubleday/Fourth Estate; 1998

A hip, snide, compelling portrait of the boys, the broads and the booze, Shawn Levy's book is a distillation of previously published material on the pertinent issues that led to the gathering of the clan, and on the surrounding underworld and overworld events, and an account of the disparate ripples that followed its unravelling. Levy's beady eye and economical, punchy writing manner reaches the heart of things with infectious style. Frank, Dean, Sam, Peter and Joey leap off the page at the reader and while it's not always nice, it's always compulsive.

Charles L. Granata: **Sessions With Sinatra: Frank Sinatra And The Art Of Recording**

A Cappella; 1999

Charles Granata is an established Sinatraphile. He was the chief researcher for Friedwald's *Sinatra! The Song Is You* and has had a hand in some important CD releases, including the *Complete Columbia Recordings* and *Sinatra In Hollywood*. His *Sessions With Sinatra* reworks many of the interviews done for these projects and fashions a fascinating history of Sinatra in the studio. His interest in the technical details of recording technique – acoustics, microphones, tape recorders – may have some readers glazing over, but it's an important part of Granata's recreation of the world of record-making. Add in his transcriptions of the session out-takes and the reminiscences of the musicians, engineers and producers who were there and the result is a uniquely vivid portrait of Sinatra the recording artist.

There's detail here to satisfy the fan – eight pages on *Close To You* – but much to dip into for the general reader too.

Tina Sinatra: **My Father's Daughter**

Simon & Schuster; 2000

In this intensely personal **memoir** of her father by the youngest of Frank's daughters, Tina doesn't flinch from detailing her powerful, often conflicting emotions towards her father at different times of their lives: the emotional deprivation during her childhood when Frank was largely absent and her attraction to his aura; the pride she took in his professional work and his refusal to fade away; but also her embarrassment at his final, befuddled performing years. Most vivid of all is her portrayal of her father as she experienced him during his fourth and final marriage to Barbara: regretful, passive and depressed, feeling unworthy of happiness, "the loneliest, most guileless man in the world".

She describes the marriage itself as a bickering union of convenience, its public face different from its private reality. Barbara – "a relentless strategist, a professional survivor" whose every utterance is offered as evidence of what Tina interprets as her shallow ambition – is presented in an almost entirely unforgiving light as a cold, manoeuvring woman who alienated Frank's friends and family and doggedly diverted his wealth in her direction. With the latter part of the book vacillating wildly between, on the one hand, clenched-teeth accounts of "joint tenancies" and the couple's rescission of the pre-nuptial agreement and, on the other, sorry descriptions of Frank's failing health, Tina's side of the story is an amazing blend of the bilious and the broken-hearted.

Michael Munn: **Sinatra: The Untold Story**

Robson; 2001

In 1969 Michael Munn was a teenage runner for a London film company, and after delivering a package to Ava Gardner he was for several years the movie queen's lover and confidant. (Munn was so naïve at the time, he was impressed that Gardner had even known Sinatra.) During the period of their friendship, Gardner, according to Munn, spilled the beans on the story of Sinatra, Marilyn Monroe, the Kennedys and the Mob. She persuaded a drunken Peter Lawford to tell Munn the truth about his role in the whole affair and also got Sammy Davis Jr. to corroborate the tale. Why? "Because this is the generation who has to know," she explained to Lawford. "We'll all be dead and gone one day, and they'll bury the fucking truth with us all." Munn even got to talk to Frank himself when he was in Ava's flat and Sinatra was on the phone. "Never, ever tell anyone else what you know," Frank told the unnerved kid, "in my lifetime."

In 2002, four years after Sinatra's death, Munn was finally able to reveal to the world what he was told, which is this. The dangerously unstable Marilyn Monroe – threatening to "blow the lid off" her affair with erstwhile boyfriend Robert Kennedy and thereby jeopardize all kinds of chicanery, including the relationship between the Mafia and the CIA – was killed by Sam Giancana's henchmen in an operation timed to implicate Bobby, or at least expose him. Lawford, mysteriously in and out of the death scene on Bobby's behalf, cleaned the place up to ensure that no connection could be made. Sinatra, genuinely fond and protective of the vulnerable Marilyn, first suspected Bobby of murder but then learnt of Giancana's involvement. Carefully extricating himself from the mobster's orbit, Munn's story continues, Sinatra turned secret informer and quietly pursued a vendetta against his old gangster buddy that culminated in Giancana's downfall and Frank's (at least partial) salvation.

Munn tells the story with some gusto, and the idea of Frank reaching for redemption is undeniably appealing.

George Jacobs and William Stadiem: Mr S: The Last Word On Frank Sinatra

Harper/Sidgwick & Jackson; 2003

Juicy, insightful and vibrant. George Jacobs's position as Sinatra's valet from 1953 to 1968 put him in situations of unparalleled intimacy with Frank and his circle; he was there when Lawford rang about Kennedy staying at Crosby's, when Sam Giancana got into a fight at Cal-Neva and when Frank Jr. was kidnapped. He waited on the politicians, the gangsters and the girls; he watched, helpless, as Frank trashed rooms (because of Ava, the Kennedys, and Ava again); and he was the erstwhile confidant of JFK (who loved to chat with Jacobs about the Hollywood sex scene) and Marilyn Monroe. He seems to have been hit on by most (including Marilyn) and claims to have remained aloof, but he admits to spying on Garbo and Dietrich making love to each other by Sinatra's pool and to admiring his employer's "Big Frankie".

When Jacobs was spotted dancing innocently, he claims, with the estranged Mia Farrow, he found himself locked out of Frank's house and life forever, after 15 years of faithful service. Having previously been warned off by Sinatra's lawyers when word leaked that he was considering **candid memoirs**, Jacobs waited until Sinatra was dead before he went ahead. He had taken a little revenge by talking to Kitty Kelley in the mid-1980s, but his own exposition provides much more detail, while still demonstrating how much he liked Sinatra. Stadiem's professional sensationalism is evident throughout the prose and gives a sly wisdom to Jacobs's servility that probably wasn't warranted; nevertheless, it's a rattling, eye-opening read.

Chris Rojek: Frank Sinatra

Polity; 2004

A professor of sociology and culture at Nottingham Trent University, Rojek is a scholar of celebrity. Commissioned to write the book by the head of his department, he was initially unenthused by the subject; he suggests that he and others of the rock music generation found Sinatra's style "mannered and objectionably fatherly". But he emerged from his research thinking that Sinatra's achievements were "diverse and impressive".

The weight of his book concerns what he calls Sinatra's "Caesarism, his audacity, immorality, self-righteousness and deep-seated menace". He recognizes that "more people revered him as a legend than cursed him as a tyrant and dissembler", before arguing clinically that Sinatra should, perhaps, be more cursed. The Mafia links, episodes with women, impulsive violence, political promiscuity and casual cruelty all add up and are observed by Rojek loftily. He also has much of fascination to say about **the cultural significance of Sinatra** as an artist and an icon, and the psychology and politics of "achieved celebrity", a concept of his own.

The book feels a little arbitrary, but Rojek's energetic, bright mind ensures that pithy, searing analyses explode unexpectedly over the page, like little land mines of wisdom. Some Sinatra lovers may lose patience with his rather cool, overtly academic approach – phrases such as "urban-industrial legato" are almost parody – but there is much here to stimulate the thoughtful Sinatra fan.

Richard Havers: **Sinatra**

DK; 2004

This heavy, glossy hardback by Richard Havers, a devoted fan who had previously worked in the airline industry, combines detailed context with stunning photographs in a way that is characteristic of Dorling Kindersley. There are hundreds of images, ranging from classics by Bob Willoughby to rare pictures including Sinatra as a baby, as well as maps, interiors, programmes and posters. The arrangement of the text is also pleasing to the eye: the chronological account of Sinatra's life is accompanied by colour-coded boxes on the albums, films and contemporaries. Indeed, this detailed coverage of the world in which Sinatra grew up and developed – the first Columbia album features a third of the way through – is where the book distinguishes itself. Similarly, Havers writes that "too many biographies of Frank ignore his contemporaries", and through focusing on the musicians more than the Mafia, this tome redresses the imbalance. It's an attractive book that strikes a good balance between visual appeal, information and analysis.

Charles Pignone: **Sinatra Treasures**

Bulfinch/Virgin; 2004

A handsome, extravagant, picture book endorsed by the Sinatra Estate, *Sinatra Treasures* is full of anecdotes from Sammy Cahn, Bill Miller, guitarist Al Viola and Frank himself, and also contains a CD of rare radio broadcasts, interviews and performances. But what makes it the ultimate book for **Sinatra fetishists** is the collection of thirty facsimiles of radio scripts, letters, telegrams, tickets, magazines, memos, business cards, invitations and scrapped album covers. Carefully removing them from the semi-opaque envelopes, examining them and replacing them has a faint but ludicrous ritualism to it, and the adoring fan worship is captured in Jerry Lewis's letter to the singer from 1976: "I love you, and it feels marvellous." While *Sinatra Treasures* may be a guilty pleasure, it is, nonetheless, a pleasure.

Come Surf With Me: Sinatra on the web

www.blue-eyes.com

A shop for CDs, DVDs and memorabilia related to Sinatra, the Rat Pack, jazz singers and Vegas. Cheaper than Amazon.

www.franksinatra.com

The official site, run by Sheffield Enterprises (owned by the Sinatra children), and offline for a revamp at the time of writing.

www.graphicinsight.co.za/sinatra.htm

A curiously accurate analysis of Frank's handwriting.

www.mrtraffic.com/sinatra.htm

A memoir of working with Frank on the film *Contract On Cherry Street* in 1977 by Kenny Morse, the host of *Ask Mr Traffic*, a Southern California call-in show on motoring issues. Read it while listening to a tasteful midi file of "My Way".

www.sinatraarchive.com

The amalgamation of several early Sinatra sites and now probably the largest Sinatra database on the web. There's a complete online "sessionography" and discography, and all known concerts, radio and TV appearances are logged. The site also offers a research service for the media.

www.sinatrafamily.com

The slightly tacky official family site with the professional schedules of Nancy, Frank Jr. and Tina, along with links to their agents, family snapshots, and news of current Sinatra products; these could be anything from the latest Rat Pack CD to whatever memorabilia the Sinatra kids see fit to endorse, such as the Frank Sinatra Christmas ornament, a plastic figure that lights up and plays "Fly Me To The Moon". The best reason to visit is that the whole of Nancy's *An American Legend* is now online.

www.sinatra-main-event.de

A substantial German tribute to Sinatra the singer and actor, online since 1999 and gradually being translated into English. There are lists galore, quizzes and a quote of the day.

www.songsbysinatra.com

A terrific database of every song that Sinatra recorded (searchable by title and composer) and his radio appearances. It also contains vintage magazine articles, sheet music, record labels and scans of rare memorabilia.

Sinatra on Screen:
illustration acknowledgements

(283) Metro-Goldwyn-Mayer/Warner Studios (287) Metro-Goldwyn-Mayer/Warner Home Video (289) Metro-Goldwyn-Mayer/ Warner Studios (291) Columbia Pictures Corporation/Columbia Tri-Star (292) Libra Productions Inc/United Artists/Sanctuary Digital Entertainment (293) Warner Bros/Arwin Productions/Universal Pictures Video (295) Samuel Goldwyn Company/Metro-Goldwyn-Mayer/ Samuel Goldwyn Corporation, Inc/MGM/UA Studios (297) Carlyle Productions/United Artists/Delta Expedition (299) Bing Crosby Productions/Metro-Goldwyn-Mayer/Sol C. Siegel Productions/Warner Home Video (302) Stanley Kramer Productions/United Artists/Metro-Goldwyn-Mayer (307) Frank Ross-Eton Productions/United Artists/MGM/UA Video (308) SinCap Productions/United Artists/MGM/UA Studios (311) Dorchester/Warner Bros/Javelin Films Ltd/Warner Studios (312) Columbia Pictures Corporation/Columbia Tri-Star Horn (313) M.C. Productions/United Artists/Twentieth Century Fox (315) 20th Century Fox/P-R Productions Picture (323) Lace International Ltd (324) Artanis Productions, Inc/Cinema VII/Filmways/Warner Studios (329) American Broadcasting Company/Quantum Leap Group Limited

Index

Index

Index

Index

Index

Index

Index

Index

Index

Index

Index

Index

Index